John Brown

Southern Classics Series

M. E. Bradford, Editor

Southern Classics Series
M. E. Bradford, Series Editor

John Brown

The Making of a Martyr

ROBERT PENN WARREN

with an introduction by C. Vann Woodward

J. S. Sanders & Company

NASHVILLE

Library of Congress Catalog Card Number:
92-062890

ISBN 1-879941-19-8

Published in the United States by
J. S. Sanders & Company
P. O. Box 50331
Nashville, Tennessee 37205

J. S. Sanders 1993 Edition
Manufactured in the United States of America

To

R. F. W. and A. R. P. W.

Contents

Illustrations

Introduction

*J*ohn Brown: The Making of a Martyr was written before its author reached the age of twenty-four, while he was still a student at Oxford. Published in 1929, it was Robert Penn Warren's first book. One discerning critic has called it—in a descriptive rather than in a derogatory phrase—"very much a young man's book." Warren was indeed remarkably youthful to have written such an ambitious and challenging work. Brown still remained for many the symbol of a noble cause and in the penalty he paid with his life a sainted martyr—his faults ignored, denied, or excused.

With very few exceptions the twenty or more books about John Brown published before Warren's work were devoted in some degree to the making or the perpetuation of his name as a hero and a martyr. And the same could be said of the great majority of seven times that number Warren included in his list of books "related" to Brown. The early biographies passed over in silence many of the shady and all the criminal episodes of Brown's career, including his personal role in the butchery on Pottawatomie Creek, where five men were murdered and their bodies horribly mutilated. After James Townsley, one of the participants, confessed the truth about the massacre, the faithful resorted to sundry evasions or justifications of his deeds as means to a noble end.

The first and for a time the only work professing objective and scholarly standards was that of Oswald Garrison Villard, *John Brown: A Biography Fifty Years After*, published in 1910. Villard brought forth new evidence, settled numerous debated points, and discredited many myths, for which Warren acknowledges indebtedness. In his preface, however, Villard wrote that he was "particularly indebted" to five named members of John Brown's family for much of his information, including "the exact facts as to the happenings on the Pottawatomie," which support claims of personal innocence of any bloodshed by Brown himself. Warren was surely justified in pointing out "the self-interest, contradictions, and proven dishonesty involved" in statements by such witnesses. In some instances, indeed, "the *murderers themselves* are on the stand." Brown's theft of the murdered men's horses and his cattle rustling in various parts of Kansas are not approved by Villard but are explained as acts of war, with motives "wholly unselfish." The instances of fraud and embezzlement in Brown's business career before his Kansas adventures are attributed to mistakes occasioned by a poor head for business. The assault on Harper's Ferry is described as a poorly planned demonstration intended to inspire a few slave stampedes for freedom. Despite the Provisional Constitution he brought along for his revolutionary government and the federal arsenal he seized Brown is said to have had no insurrectionary or treasonous intentions.

Villard's book was followed in 1913 by an all-out assault on its findings and its hero by Hill Peebles Wilson in *John Brown: Soldier of Fortune*. An ardent admirer at one time, Wilson felt himself betrayed by his erstwhile hero, whom he now portrayed as an unscrupulous brigand who used abolitionism as a cover for his thievery. "If Mr. Villard is by far the ablest and most scrupulous spokesman of the defense," wrote Warren, "Mr. Wilson is the most acrimonious, the most downright, and the soundest prosecutor."

Speaking neither for the defense nor for the prosecution, the youthful biographer in the next decade took the stand professing himself determined to avoid the oversights and simplistic solutions of the adversarial approach. In their polemics Warren believed that both Villard and Wilson had neglected an important key to John Brown's character: "his elaborate psychological mechanism for justification which appeared regularly in terms of the thing which friends called Puritanism and enemies called

fanaticism." Warren believed that the contradictions and paradoxes of John Brown's story could only be understood in terms of
this mechanism for self-justification and the vicissitudes behind it.
"Such an understanding is the final aim of this book," he wrote.

It is only fair to ask how successful the future novelist and poet
was in achieving his aim as historian and in avoiding the partisan-
ship and special pleading that he deplored in other writers. There
was no denying, for example, his Southern origins and identifica-
tions. Within a year after publication of his *John Brown* appeared
his contribution to the Nashville Agrarians' symposium, *I'll Take
My Stand*. Was Robert Penn Warren any more successful in
controlling biases of his region and forebears than was Oswald
Garrison Villard, grandson of the famous abolitionist William
Lloyd Garrison?

In canvassing the evidence one should take care not to judge
usages and conventions of one era by standards common in
another. What at present are regarded as offensive racial slurs
were in the previous generation not so considered. John Brown
himself wrote a pamphlet entitled *Sambo's Mistakes*, and Villard
no more thought of capitalizing "negro" than did Warren. The
latter went further in referring to Yankee slave traders as "Guinea
nigger stealers," but more as a slur on the traders than the slaves.
He once quoted his father (in a letter to the writer) as declaring
"that word is never to be spoken in this house." Further removed
from his later convictions were some things in his essay on race
relations for the Agrarian book. There he referred to hopes for
desegregation as "millennial," whereas he was later to place
himself in the lead of those demanding prompt removal of seg-
regation barriers.

Warren wrote his book on John Brown before some of the most
important scholarship on the subject had appeared. One example
is Professor James C. Malin, *John Brown and the Legend of Fifty-
six*, published in 1942. This work tore through myth and legend
about Brown in Kansas and before to "leave no doubt of flagrant
dishonesty on his part in both business and family relations."
Malin's rigorous scholarship, his findings and conclusions, tended
to support rather than to discredit Warren's interpretations of

such evidence as was available to him when he was writing. More and fuller biographies were to appear in later years. But Allan Nevins, the leading historian of this field of history in the 1950s, cited and used Warren's *Brown*, and so have other reputable historians.

But young Warren's book is not history written primarily for historians—a limitation shared by many products of those who now pursue the ancient profession. It is history for the reader, a biography to be read with pleasure by anyone of sufficient intelligence and curiosity about the past, whatever his profession. This is history as an art as well as a discipline, a combination honored by long and worthy tradition. The art lies in the writer's power to seize the reader's imagination with the sequence of events and carry him along with the impelling force of the narrative. Another aspect of narrative history as art is the use of imagination in the reconstruction of past events. Evoking or recreating any event in which the writer was not a participant or a personal witness requires the use of imagination, particularly if it goes beyond *what* happened to include the *how* and the *why*.

This is not to suggest that Warren confused history with fiction. "The rules are different ... in this sense," he said: "the historian must prove points, document points, that the novelist does not have to document." And again: "Now the big difference between history and fiction is that the historian does not know his imagined world; he knows *about* it, and he must know all he can about it. . . . But the fiction writer must claim to *know* the *inside* of his world for better or for worse. . . . This is a fundamental difference it seems to me." Yet he was equally interested in the similarities, in what history and fiction had in common. In spite of the novelist's license to invent, he was conditioned by the "historically possible," and "tied to the facts of life." And in Warren's fiction, according to Cleanth Brooks, "as with Yeats, there is a tough-minded insistence upon the facts, including the realistic and ugly facts—a fierce refusal to shield one's eyes from what is there." He was not one to create heroes, or to celebrate causes that were lost or pasts that were golden.

To anyone acquainted with the corpus of Warren's fiction and poetry it should hardly seem a cause for wonder that his first book belongs on the history shelves. He read avidly and deeply in history, Southern history especially, but by no means exclusively. He read Tacitus and he read Gibbon as well. Pressed to explain why the historical work on John Brown and that period should have been his first and how it related to his career as novelist and poet, Warren said this youthful venture in history "led to fiction," that in an unpremeditated and "instinctive way" it proved to be "a step toward fiction."

He undoubtedly had several things in mind when making this connection between history and fiction with regard to the shaping of his own career. One thing was the frequency with which historical events inspired or provided the setting and background for his novels and poems. Historical figures either entered or suggested characters in his fictional cast. One thinks of *Brother To Dragons* and events in Kentucky of 1811 in which Thomas Jefferson and his relatives figure, or events of Kentucky in the next decade that parallel the plot of *World Enough and Time*. And, similarly, on to the Civil War in *Wilderness*, Reconstruction in *Band of Angels*, *Chief Joseph* in 1877, and into the early twentieth century with *Night Rider*. Perhaps the best known of Warren's novels, *All the King's Men* most provoked its author's exasperation with being called a "historical novelist" and having his fictional characters identified or confused with historical figures. In spite of parallels and similarities between Huey Long and Willie Stark, he once declared that he had "no idea what Long was really like" and could not have put him in a novel if he did.

John Brown: The Making of a Martyr was the first but not the last venture into history that Warren made, though the later ones were more in the nature of reflections on history. One was *The Legacy of the Civil War: Meditations on the Centennial*, that appeared in 1961, the other *Jefferson Davis Gets His Citizenship Back* in 1980 to commemorate an act of Congress to restore it ninety years after his death. In these meditations as in his creative writing is woven in and out an awareness of the past in the present, which he said, "somehow intertwined constantly." This theme is especially prominent in what he writes about the "land

of the fiddle and whiskey, sweat and prayer, pride and depravity"—his native region.

Warren's mastery of the ironic and the oxymoronic, as well as
his taste for the paradoxical and the tragic are prefigured in his
John Brown. And in Brown himself can be found the prototype of
many of Warren's fictional characters. Brown acted out in real
life the contrast between intent and result in human motives,
between expectation and outcome, between noble ends and foul
means used in attempts to achieve them. Thus evil can result from
good and sometimes vice versa. Misanthropy can become philanthropy, and philanthropy self-love. Heroes can be seen as villains
and the other way around.

In the process innocent idealists of society's elites can be recruited for support as fellow conspirators, donors, and defenders.
Thus Brown's co-conspirators, the so-called Secret Six, came
from the cream of New England society: philosopher, surgeon,
minister, professor, philanthropist, and capitalist. And the eulo-
gists of Concord, who pronounced John Brown a saint and martyr who had made "the gallows as glorious as the cross," were
leading transcendentalists and spiritual models of their time.

Ironies and paradoxes of Warren's fiction and poetry during
the sixty years that followed the publication of this biography
often bring to mind themes characteristic of that youthful experiment. One thinks, for example, of Percy Munn, protagonist of his
first novel, *Night Rider*, the perfect Southern gentleman, whose
struggles for justice lead him to acts of betrayal, brutality, atrocity and murder. And there is Jack Burden, high-minded intellec-
tual of a sort, who becomes a servant of Willie Stark in a quest for
social justice by devious means in *All the King's Men*. Or *Band of
Angels*, which pictures emancipation culminating in enslave-
ment. And there are numerous other examples. In Warren's verse
one thinks of Thomas Jefferson in *Brother to Dragons* contemplating the horror of brutality with which his own nephews
desecrated the soil of the West that he had acquired for the
realization of hopes and ideals of the nation he had framed at
its birth.

So it is that the reader of *John Brown: The Making of a Martyr*, if so minded, can find in this biography more than an account of a famous figure in antebellum history. Embedded in its pages, between the lines, are suggestions of themes and preoccupations characteristic of the work of a major figure in the history of American literature. Chilling as some of them are, they are not to be construed as cynicism about human nature, determinism in interpreting history, or despair of mankind's efforts to achieve justice and humane ideals. They do mean, however, that the biography reveals much about the biographer as well as about his subject.

This very attribute of the book, remarkable and valuable as it is, says something about its character and purpose as history. While Warren's biography serves well as a replacement of myths, pro and con, contrived by previous biographers, and is the more interesting for that reason, it is something more and something less than objective history in the usual sense. James Justus is reminded of the tone and style of such Tory rebels of the 1920s as Lytton Strachey and Aldous Huxley in their biographical works on famous Victorians, of which he considers Warren's *Brown* "a kind of countrified version." Like the English rebels, their American counterpart was in revolt against the pieties and certitudes of previous generations and the heroes they chose to embody them. At the same time he was setting forth unawares themes of human complexity and ambivalence, paradoxes of good and evil, philanthropy and misanthropy, nobility and depravity, themes that were to appear and reappear in Warren's prose and verse throughout his long and productive career. Read with awareness of these dimensions and portents, *John Brown: The Making of a Martyr* takes on meanings and insights well beyond those promised by the title.

New Haven, Connecticut C. VANN WOODWARD

MILITARY MAP
SHOWING THE
TOPOGRAPHICAL FEATURES OF THE COUNTRY
ADJACENT TO
HARPER'S FERRY, VA.
INCLUDING
Maryland, Loudoun and Bolivar Heights, and
portions of South and Short Mountains,
WITH THE POSITIONS OF THE
DEFENSIVE WORKS,
ALSO THE
Junction of the Potomac and Shenandoah Rivers and their
Passage through the Blue Ridge
Surveyed from August 3ᵈ to Sept.30ᵗʰ 1863
UNDER THE DIRECTION OF
CAPT. N. MICHLER, CORPS OF ENG.ᴿˢ U.S.ARMY
BY
MAJOR JOHN E. WEYSS, PRINCIPAL ASSISTANT
ENGINEER DEPARTMENT
ARMY OF THE POTOMAC.

Scale
1000 500 0   1000   2000   3000   4000   5000   6000   7000   8000 feet

—— Union

Note
...se indicates the heights in feet of the several points above the level of the canal at the pontoon bridge
The horizontal curves indicate distances of 20 feet perpendicular height

Magnetic Meridian

POTOMAC RIVER

Road to Charlestown

B ALTIMORE & OHIO R.R.

Lemen's Mill

FORT DUNCAN

GEN. BARNARD

Proposed Work

BOLIVAR

Graveyard
174

Charlestown Pike

Toll-Gate

SHENANDOAH RIVER

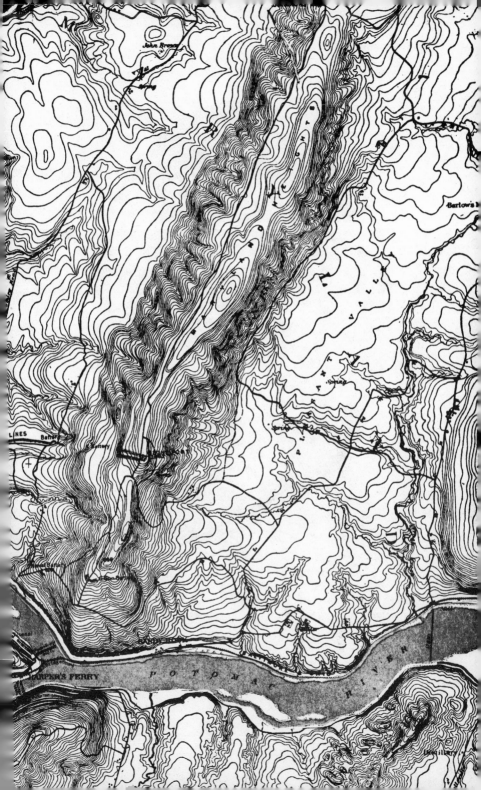

John Brown

(Courtesy of Houghton Mifflin Co.)

(This picture is reproduced from " John Brown A Biography Fifty Years After " by Oswald Garrison Villard by courtesy of Mr. Villard.)

John Brown

1

BUT NOT IN A RENTED HOUSE

IT happened on an early spring day of the year 1511. In the general barge bound to Gravesend over on the south bank of the Thames, two men, a sturdy common fellow and a priest, sat side by side. Because of the considerable press of people or because of some natural insolence toward the holy cloth the fellow crowded and elbowed his companion from that space which the priest took to be the temporal prerogative of his buttocks.

" Dost thou know," he finally demanded in great stomach against the pushing bench-mate, " who I am? Thou sittest too near me and sittest on my clothes."

" No, sir," said the other, " I know not what you are."

" I tell thee, I am a priest! "

" What, sir," the common fellow exclaimed in mock astonishment, " are you a parson, or vicar, or some lady's chaplain? "

" No, I am a soul priest; I sing for a soul."

" Do you so, sir? That is well done." And then he proceeded to add dialectics to sarcasm, as he had added sarcasm to a simple shove. " I pray you, sir, where find you the soul when you go to mass? "

" I cannot tell thee," the priest replied.

9

"I pray you, where do you leave it, sir, when the mass is done?"

"I cannot tell thee."

"Neither can you tell where you find it when you go to mass, nor where you leave it when mass is done; how can you then save the soul?"

"Go thy way! I perceive thou art an heretic, and I will be even with thee."

The priest had found his answer at last — the only answer which his stubborn companion could have understood.

Some few days afterwards, the bailiff and the bishop's men burst into the heretic's house at Ashford as he was in the hospitable act of carrying a mess of porridge to his guests. They laid hands upon him, put him on his own horse, bound his feet beneath the animal's belly, and conducted him away to Canterbury, where sat Archbishop William Warham. The guests and the wife of the heretic were left with their cold porridge but with no idea where he had been taken or why.

Forty days passed, and there was no word of the prisoner's offense or of his fate. At the end of that period, on the Friday before Whitsunday, a maid of his household came upon her master held in the public stocks of Ashford. She ran home and told her mistress, who went to him and sat with him all night, listening to the story of tortures administered by order of the Archbishop and of Dr. Fisher, Bishop of Rochester, and learning at length that on the morrow he was to be burned for his faith. So on the next day, it being Whitsun Eve, they took the heretic, as it was commanded, stood him at a stake, and lighted the fire about him. Standing at the stake, in the midst of the flames, he lifted up his hands and prayed.

U. S. MARINES STORMING ENGINE HOUSE AT HARPER'S FERRY

(From *Frank Leslie's Weekly*, October 29, 1859)

But Not in a Rented House

O Lord I yelde me to thy grace,
Graunt me mercy for my trespace,
Let neuer the fiend my soule chace.
Lord I wyll bow and thou shalt beat;
Let neuer my soule come in hell heat.
Into thy handes I commend my spirite; thou
* hast redemed me O Lorde of truth.*

In such fashion this blessed martyr, John Brown of Kent, ended his life on Whitsun Eve, *anno* 1511, because he sat on a priest's robe, and would not deny his God.

If another John Brown, more than three hundred years later, ever picked up Foxe's *Acts and Monuments* from its honored place on a shelf or parlor table, he may have wondered if that fellow who bore his name had any connection with himself. After a blow of the sheriff's hatchet had sprung the gallows trap and made this John Brown a martyr, some of his friends half-mystically reflected on the similarity of name and fate. But three hundred years is a long while, and when the accession of the Protestant Queen Elizabeth relieved Richard Brown, son of the martyred Brown of Ashford, from his own sentence of death, he stepped out of prison into that happier obscurity from which the incident on the Gravesend barge had raised his family.

Those friends were no more wrong in their speculations than they were in a certain genealogical conviction which John Brown shared with them. In the good company of the Mayflower was numbered a Puritan carpenter by the name of Peter Brown. John Brown firmly believed this man to be the father of his line in New England. He did not know that when Peter Brown, the carpenter, was put away in one of the graves of the colony, no son survived to bear

11

his name. At Windsor, Connecticut, in 1632, another Peter Brown was born, and sixty-two years later this man became the father of a son whom he christened John. When the Revolution began a third John Brown marched off from his home at West Simsbury, Connecticut, to strike a blow for freedom and no taxation without representation. Under his command went Train Band 9 of the Eighteenth Regiment of the colony, but these patriots saw no great service with his captaincy, for a few weeks later John Brown died of the dysentery in a barn in New York.

Many years later, four other epitaphs were chiselled on the old gravestone which had commemorated the Revolutionary Captain John Brown.

In
Memory of
CAPT. JOHN BROWN
who Died at
New York, Sept. yᵉ
3, 1775, in the 48
year of his age.

In memory of
FREDERICK,
Son of John and Dianthe
BROWN,
Born Dec. 31, 1830, and
Murdered at Osawatomie,
Kansas, Aug. 30, 1856,
For his adherence to
the cause of freedom.

WATSON BROWN
Born Oct. 7, 1835, was wounded
at Harper's Ferry,
Oct. 17, and Died
Oct. 19, 1859.

JOHN BROWN
Born May 9, 1800
Was executed at Charlestown
Va., Dec. 2, 1859.

OLIVER BROWN
Born May 9, 1839, was
Killed at Harper's Ferry
Oct. 17, 1859.

BUT NOT IN A RENTED HOUSE

The patriot who died in the barn in New York left a widow and ten children back home in West Simsbury. During the years of the war life was exceedingly hard for that family. Most of the laboring men were away in the army which was putting up a losing fight against the king's redcoats. The crops spoiled in the fields, the cattle strayed and died, and the Browns, who had once been comfortably situated in the world, became poorer and ˌpoorer. But at last the war ended, and the children were old enough to shift for themselves. Among them was a boy named Owen. He grew up with the memory of hunger in the terribly hard winter of 1778–79, of fighting, of revival meetings and singing conferences, and of his trips as a cobbler to neighboring towns. In his old age Owen Brown looked back with a sort of amiable complacency on that early poverty, for it had kept him and his brothers and sisters from the society of loose, vain young gentlemen and ladies who wore gay clothes and had plenty of money to spend and good horses to ride. He remembered, also with complacency, that two or three of those West Simsbury blades had filled the graves of suicides, and he could remark that God knows what is best.

With his coming of age two great events occurred in the life of Owen; he felt some vague but powerful conviction of sin and he fell in love. He was never in his life sure that God pardoned him that sin. After two years, however, he did marry the daughter of the Reverend Gideon Mills, and so his conscience by that time must have been reasonably at peace. With more good counsel than property Owen and Ruth Brown began to keep house in March, 1793. But their labors turned to good account, they were at peace with all their neighbors, and had cause for thanksgiving. One son

13

was born to them — a thrifty forward child named Salmon.
All was well in the new family of West Simsbury except that
they lived in a rented house.

The thought of that rented house irked Owen Brown's
independence. With the encouragement of the people of
Norfolk, he bought a small farm in their community, sank
tanning vats, and planted the year's crop. There he rose
a little in the world and employed a foreman for the tanning
business, but with this success came a family sorrow; Salmon,
the thrifty forward child, died before reaching the age of
two. Owen Brown was always restless and quick on the
move. When a chance came to sell the place at Norfolk, he
went hastily to Torrington, Connecticut, without consulting
his neighbors, who felt they had some claim on his further
services. The country here was less hospitable than that
around Norfolk. The plowshare more often rasped and hung
on the grey rock which the soil thinly mantled, and great
boulders, too heavy to be piled for fences, dotted the fields.
But the tanning business and difficult farming sufficed to
give a living, and so they stayed.

In a bare boarded house, unprotected in winter and without shade in summer — but not in a rented house — Ruth
Brown bore her husband a son. They named him John Brown.
The child was born on May 9, in the year 1800, one hundred
years after the birth of its great-grandfather John. Nothing
else about the son's birth was very uncommon.

Four years passed in the bare boarded house. The old
restlessness, the hope for something better in the next township, in the next state, in the country beyond the mountains,
was again on Owen Brown. There were other children besides
John, and the prosperity at Torrington had not kept pace
with the growing family. By this time rumors of opportunities

in the Western Reserve were drifting back to Connecticut. The Reserve had been divided among the proprieters, and David Hudson and Birdsey Norton had received the townships of Hudson and Chester in the Ohio country. In 1779 David Hudson pushed into the wilderness, slept under an oak tree in the rain with only the comfort of ownership, and surveyed his property. When Owen Brown reached Hudson township exactly twenty-five years later he found a transplanted Connecticut village whose people were very harmonious, fairly prosperous, and mostly united in religious sentiments. In this little community, so like the ones he had left three hundred miles behind him, Owen Brown bought some land and determined to settle for good and all. By the end of the next summer his family was established in Hudson. They were received with all the kindness which greeted any new able-bodied resident in a struggling settlement; and furthermore, they were from Connecticut, were Congregationalists, and had come with the determination to help build up civil and religious order. Owen Brown displayed in his craft and farming that industry which his neighbors so much admired, and after the famine summer of the second year there, when no corn got ripe, he prospered as much as he had reason to expect. But the Browns, somehow, were never the best of business men.

This Ohio country in which John Brown spent his boyhood was in those years a real frontier, even though it had been admitted as a State in 1803. The Indians still outnumbered the settlers, but they were a broken-spirited lot, harmless enough except for a few sporadic liquor-inspired depredations. Of course there were still about the settlement some of the indomitable Indian-killers, such as old Jonathan Williams, who carried on the tradition of the days when British

15

rum and bounties had paid for scalps. But many of the settlers dealt with the Indians and looked upon them as more of a help than a hindrance, even if their kindliness was colored by a mild contempt. Owen Brown was one of the sort who had gratitude, for the Indians taught him to dress deerskin. John also profited, for at the age of six he was installed in a fine buckskin outfit. Indeed, the Indians were greatly interesting to the boy from Connecticut, and when fascination overcame his fear of their long rifles, he hung about their camps as much as was consistent with good manners and even learned a little of their talk.

But a child had to justify his existence in that society, and there was no great opportunity for leisurely association with the lazy red-skinned hunters and drudging squaws. There was little chance for going to school, a fact not much regretted by the boy, for the occasion to run, jump, and wrestle, and knock off old seedy wool caps was the only pleasure to be balanced against the dull hours of sitting indoors. He would rather stay at home and do the hardest sort of work than to go to school at all. But better still he liked to drive a herd of cattle through the wilderness, alone, barefooted and bareheaded, with the buckskin breeches his father had made him suspended now with one leather strap over the shoulder, but sometimes with two. All together, there was more cattle-driving than schooling.

John Brown said that he went early to the school of adversity. He did not refer to the hungry winter of 1806 or the hard work that was required of him through his boyhood in Hudson. An Indian boy once gave him a yellow marble, which he prized much but finally lost beyond recovery, and a little bob-tailed squirrel which he captured and tamed at the expense of being bitten escaped into the

woods and never turned up again. An ewe lamb which his
father gave him almost reached its growth and then sick-
ened and died. When John Brown was fifty-seven years old
and had discovered that he possessed no head for getting
along in the world and had passed through many lawsuits
and bankruptcy, he wrote of those early griefs as the beginning of a much needed course of discipline, which had ended
by teaching him that the Heavenly Father saw best to take
out of his hands whatever little thing he might place in them.
At that time he was living on the generosity of some New
England gentleman who had comfortable businesses or
owned factories, believed in a high protective tariff, and
felt that the Southern States would be a better market if
there the people did not hold slaves. By that time also, John
Brown had in mind the project that was to end at Harper's Ferry.

Beyond those other losses was the death of John Brown's
mother. On December 9, 1808 she gave birth to a child, a
daughter, who died a few hours after. " She had a short passage through time," said Ruth Mills Brown; she herself
was dead a little later. When these two first graves had been
made in the cemetery at the center of Hudson, Owen Brown
was left with five children besides John, as well as an
adopted son named Levi Blakesly. Less than a year later,
Owen Brown married Sally Root, a competent estimable
woman on many accounts, but John never adopted her in
his feeling and was thus left without any tempering influence on his diffident but haughty and self-reliant nature.

Trouble was brewing along the frontier. Tecumseh, chief
of the Shawnees, was growing in influence and power. From
Fort Malden the British were distributing flintlocks, rifles,
rum, and blankets among the Indians. Echoes of their ma-

17

rauding came back to the security of Hudson. In New England the remnant of the old Federalist Party wanted to ignore these aggressions in the Ohio country and along the Mississippi. Furthermore, for a different reason, they were content enough if the British pushed a line of forts down the river.

In New England there were similar negative views on this subject, but Louisiana was applying for admission as a state. On January 14, 1811, Josiah Quincy, Representative from Massachusetts, spoke on this matter in the House. " I am compelled to declare it as my deliberate opinion that, if this bill passes, the bonds of this Union are virtually dissolved; that the States which compose it are free from their moral obligations; and that as it will be the right of all so it will be the duty of some, to prepare definitely for a separation amicably, if they can, violently, if they must." Talk of this sort was to become more common in the chambers of Congress as the years passed. But the reason why so many people from one section opposed the making of a new State at the mouth of the Mississippi meant nothing to John Brown at this time.

The war came on, and Owen Brown made a good thing of it. He did a fair business in furnishing the troops with beef cattle, and to his sons fell the duty of rounding them up and driving them through the wilderness to the posts where they were needed. Meanwhile General Hull surrendered his army at Detroit and there seemed little to prevent the British from moving into the Ohio country. There was real apprehension in Hudson. Some of Hull's men who had been paroled by their captors wandered back on foot to their homes; troops marching west left their sick at the town and the people were infected. There was much sickness in the Brown family but no deaths. The whole spectacle seems to have disgusted John with all military matters, for when he came of age he paid fines like a Quaker to escape the required drilling.

It seems that John acquired another conviction as well as that one concerning military affairs. He had travelled alone more than a hundred miles from home, driving a herd of the cattle destined for soldiers' rations. A certain land-holding gentleman who was impressed by the twelve-year-old boy's independence took him in and treated him with the greatest kindness, bringing him to the table with the older, more prosperous guests and applauding every smart thing John said or did. The gentleman also held a slave about John's own age, who was poorly clothed and fed, lodged badly in cold weather, and beaten before the guests with iron fire-shovels or whatever came to the master's hand. This pitiful spectacle brought the more fortunate youth to reflect on " the wretched, hopeless condition of fatherless and motherless slave children, for such children have neither fathers or mothers to protect and provide for them." And he sometimes would raise in his mind the question, " Is God their father? " Wiser heads before that time had indulged in the same speculation. That incident led him " to declare or swear eternal war with slavery." In any case these are the details that John Brown related after he had become the relentless Kansas Captain John Brown. In the nondescript reading which pieced out his four ground rules of arithmetic and the little grammar, had he come across the story of Hannibal's infant oath on the altar of Baal? Or in the book he knew best the story of the voice calling at night to the child Samuel?

That nondescript reading began in the books of history owned by a friend when John was about ten years old. There were probably not many of these books nor much time for reading, but from them it seems he took the habit of dramatizing himself a little; he learned the meaning of ambition. There was a social advantage as well, for older people listened to him with a shade more attention despite his extreme bashfulness. With that bashfulness went a certain hauteur, and he got a dislike for vain and frivolous conversation and persons. "I hate vain thoughts but thy law do I love." But the tanning trade was a more profitable and necessary matter than reading, and by the time he was fifteen he was working regularly in his father's establishment, sometimes as a sort of foreman. However, despite a rather skeptical turn of mind, John had experienced religion and become to some extent a convert to Christianity. He got the idea of being a minister.

A tall, sedate, and dignified young man presented himself at the door of the Reverend Moses Hallock in Plainfield, Massachusetts. The school of the Reverend Moses Hallock had trained a number of well-known missionaries and ministers, as well as a young poet — William Cullen Bryant by name. The new student seemed well fitted to make another fruitful branch in Reverend Hallock's vineyard. His schooling may have been fitful, but he was earnest and serious-minded, did not know one card of the pack from another, had never danced a step in his life, possessed an imperious eye and an unshakeable conviction that he was right in all matters. He was tasty in his dress, and about washing, bathing, and brushing — at least, people in Hudson had thought so; and when he washed himself he pushed his hair back from the straight brow of his unusually small head. Among the effects of John Brown was a fine piece of leather, about a foot square, which he himself had tanned for seven years. He brought this along to resole his boots.

But Not in a Rented House

Whatever were the endowments of the tall, sedate, and dignified young man, these gifts were not to grace the pulpit. A severe inflammation of the eyes set in, and John Brown had to give up any ambition in Amherst or the ministry. He went back to Ohio and worked as foreman for his father's tannery. Levi Blakesly, his adopted brother, lived with him and the two young men kept bachelor's hall. In the division of labor John Brown served as cook, fulfilling that office with considerable satisfaction. In any case, tradition has it that he kept a neat, clean kitchen. He conducted the tannery with a youthful severity and sense of authority, kept the pots and pans meticulously scrubbed, and again took up the study of common arithmetic. Surveying appealed to him as a means of supplementing his farming and tanning, and so he studied the business from a copy of the old *Flint's Survey.*

One night the quiet routine of the cabin occupied by the two young men was broken into by a run-away slave, who appealed to them for aid in his flight toward the ' North Star.' They took him in, as almost any Northern citizen would have done if the pursuit were not too hot or no scrupulous sheriff near. Levi Blakesly went into the settlement for provisions, leaving the renegade in the keeping of his friend. Suddenly, the pair in the cabin heard the noise of horses' hoofs; John Brown helped the negro through a window and told him to hide in the underbrush near the house, while he himself prepared to defend his charge. But the noise was only caused by some neighbors riding past on their way home, and John Brown went outside to find the frightened black fellow. He found him lying behind a log. " I heard his heart thumping before I reached him," said John Brown. Incidentally, he seized on the opportunity to again swear eternal enmity against slavery.

JOHN BROWN

Later John Brown had a son named John Brown Jr.
Strangely enough, this son once related this same story with
a few circumstantial embellishments, making himself an eye-
witness as well. Again John Brown concealed the fugitives
in the dark woods at the noise of approaching horses; and
again he was able to find and fetch them in by the guiding
sound of startled heartbeats. Again John Brown swore eternal enmity to slavery. Some people have professed surprise
at the coincidence; others have professed surprise only at
the acoustics of Hudson township, Ohio.

There was a widow by the name of Mrs. Amos Lusk who
lived near the cabin of Blakesly and John Brown. At first she
only baked bread for the two men, and then, when affairs
at the tanyard became more prosperous and there were new
workmen and new apprentices to occupy John Brown's attention at the expense of his kitchen, she moved to the cabin
to become housekeeper. With the widow came her daughter,
Dianthe, who was less than a year younger than John Brown.
Dianthe Lusk was no beauty, to be sure; even her brother,
Milton, admitted that much, and he seems to have had an
unusual affection for her. Milton Lusk worked on the place
belonging to old Squire Hudson, the founder of the town;
his duties kept him occupied most of the week and he could
only get out to the Brown cabin to see his mother and sister
on Sunday. "Milton," said the head of that house one day,
"I wish you wouldn't make your visits here on the Sabbath."
"John," replied Milton Lusk, "I won't come Sunday, nor
any other day." He stayed away for a long time; when John
Brown married Dianthe on June 21, 1820, he did not even
go to the wedding. His brother-in-law doted too much on being the head of the heap to suit Milton Lusk's mind.

Dianthe Lusk was admirably devised to make a good wife

for John Brown. In the first place, she had no sense of humor; she never said anything but what she meant. Her disposition was amiable and quiet and she sang sacred hymns beautifully. John Brown liked especially " Blow ye the trumpet, blow " and " Oh, lovely appearance of death." She was very religious and had a hidden place in the woods where she was accustomed to go to pray; once or twice she took Milton there with her but never her husband. Furthermore, she was economical. July 25, 1821, she bore her husband a son, whom they christened John Brown Jr.

For several years the family lived in the log house where Mrs. Amos Lusk had managed things before her daughter had succeeded her. Another son, Jason, was born there. The log cabin became too small for the family, and, besides, business was looking up with John Brown. In 1824 he built himself a new place — not a log house, but a boarded house, as suited his solidity and his new position in the social scale as a prosperous tanner and a father of sons. He laid out a garden and an orchard which were to remain for many years. Behind the house was a wood on a little knoll sloping down to the brook which watered the tanpits. In this house Dianthe and John Brown had another son, whom they named for his grandfather, Owen Brown.

John Brown had the instincts of the patriarchal despot. Not only his wife and children but the journeymen and apprentices under him felt the rigidity of his rule. Even Sunday meant no escape for the workmen; if they were to receive wages and training from John Brown they had to go to church every Sunday, as well as gather with the family for worship every morning before their work in the tanyard began. Every morning the Bibles were distributed and all had to read a set number of verses. When the reading was finished, John Brown stood up, grasped the top of his chair-back, leaned a little forward over it, and prayed.

John Brown once recorded that in his own youth he had been somewhat addicted to lying, and now that habit in his sons, even their childish imaginings, met with especial severity. But John Brown had other and more terrible methods of punishment than a beating. During the summer of the year when he built his new house, a journeyman stole a fine calfskin from the tanyard. The employer found it out, called the man aside and extorted a full confession from him. As long as the fellow stayed with John Brown and did his work he was not to be handed over to the law, but while he was there no person on the place was to speak to him not even to answer a practical question. The man stayed about two months and endured his punishment. It is said that he later became a useful and conscientious citizen. Perhaps, John Brown's discipline did work a change of heart and habits after all.

2

THE MERCHANT PRINCE

JOHN BROWN inherited Owen Brown's instinct to wandering. The new house, the young orchard just laid out, and the prosperous tanyard were not enough to hold him in Hudson. Owen Brown had come west to Ohio when it was an almost unviolated wilderness, and now his son was lured away from the more solid and established life of Hudson to the new region of western Pennsylvania. John Brown owned a successful tannery and lived in a large new house in Hudson township, but old Squire Hudson, who had come first and slept under an oak tree in the rain, was the head of the heap there. Perhaps things would be different in Pennsylvania.

Business matters in Ohio were arranged, the wagons were loaded, and everything set to rights for the departure with all the scrupulous order which characterized John Brown when preparing for a decisive action. In the spring of 1825 the Browns settled in Crawford County at Richmond, where Dianthe Brown had relatives in the Delamater family. By the fall they were already established, with twenty-five acres of land cleared, a good tanyard built, and leather in the vats.

JOHN BROWN

John Brown was energetic enough in opening up this new country, and his family were thrifty. He quickly became well-known in the section, and for a time he prospered. A guarantee of his importance came when, in the year 1828, he was appointed as an official of the United States Government. John Brown was the first postmaster at the Randolph office. At this time John Quincy Adams was President and the new postmaster was a strong Adams man. Besides fulfilling his official duties John Brown carried on his surveying and tanning, brought the first blooded cattle into that district of Pennsylvania, had religious services carried on in his fine barn every Sunday morning, and organized a school. This school was conducted in winter at the Brown house and in summer at the Delamater's. The children of the two related families were the pupils. In the cold early winter mornings John Brown prayed with his workmen and the children, as he had in Hudson, standing behind his chair with his hands tightly gripping the top, and leaning a little forward over it. There was only one thing to disrupt the even order of life here: Dianthe Brown had a mental sickness which became more pronounced as time went on.

Despite his many years in frontier country, John Brown had an aversion to hunting, gunning, and fishing; he believed that such sports taught men and boys to idle away their time, neglect the more exacting farm work, and to fall into lazy habits of living. He didn't even like to trust a man with a piece of leather if the customer came with a gun on his shoulder. John Brown himself didn't own a gun until he was twenty-six years old. For a time John Brown was a Mason, but for some reason he withdrew from the order. A short while after the Browns moved to Pennsylvania, the country was greatly excited over the secrets of Masonry which William Morgan had revealed. Morgan suddenly disappeared, and John Brown, the ex-Mason, was rather free in his talk about the murder. One day when he was in Meadville on business, an agitated crowd gathered around the hotel where he stayed. Rumors of his anti-Masonic opinions had been passed from mouth to mouth, and there was every prospect that he would share the fate of William Morgan at the hands of the mob. But the keeper of the hotel let his guest out through a back entrance. John Brown then bought himself a huge long-barrelled pistol, only to discover that there was a certain satisfaction in its use, for on several occasions he managed to kill deer with the weapon, and in later years he could give good advice on such things. " In a fight," said John Brown, " shoot low and keep your eye on the hind sight."

Early in 1829 Dianthe had another child, a girl whom they named Ruth. The next year another son was born. One Sunday John and Dianthe Brown carried the babies across the fields and through the woods to a meeting at a neighbor's house. After a short while the parents stood and held the children up to the minister; he blessed them and poured a little water on the face of each. When the father sat down again he took from his pocket a beautiful brown silk handkerchief with diamond-shaped yellow spots on it and gravely wiped the baptismal water from the face of his baby daughter.

JOHN BROWN

The next two or three years saw several deaths in the Brown household. The four-year-old son, Frederick, died in 1831; and another son, born the year before, received that name. Dianthe Brown's illness became more severe and prolonged; John Brown, who was an efficient, careful nurse, watched her during the periods of her sickness with what was for him considerable tenderness. She bore a son in the August of 1832. The child did not live long enough to receive a name, and the mother died insane only a little while after. Dianthe Brown and her son were buried near the tanyard, where the stern widower carried on his trade and ruled the five children who remained to him. But this was not all. News came that the more successful brother, Salmon Brown, whom John had beaten at school, was dead in New Orleans. Salmon had gone on with his education, studied law at Pittsburg, travelled extensively over the country, engaged in politics as a henchman of Henry Clay against Jackson, and ended as editor of the *New Orleans Bee*. When he died at the age of twenty-seven with some note as a gentleman, this did not provide much comfort to old Owen Brown, who never knew whether or not his most brilliant son had given evidence of being a Christian.

Dianthe Lusk was the daughter of John Brown's housekeeper when he married her. After her death there was no one to manage the home, and so the Browns boarded with the family of a certain Mr. Foreman, a one-time journeyman for John Brown. This arrangement did not prove finally satisfactory, and John Brown, perhaps with a consciousness of the repeated circumstance, hired a second housekeeper. After a while the new housekeeper brought her sister to the Brown place to help with the spinning.

THE MERCHANT PRINCE

Mary Anne Day was the sixteen-year-old daughter of Charles Day, a ruined blacksmith who had come originally from Whitehall in New York State. Charles Day was a good craftsman, but he had been too trusting, had gone security for too many friends, and the result was a hard, meager living in the Pennsylvania backwoods. Anything that the daughters now might earn came gratefully enough.

John Brown soon got used to the big-boned, reticent girl who did chores about the house or sat at the spinning wheel, manipulating the yarn with heavy, competent hands. One evening he gave her a letter. This restless, severe man, more than twice her age and looking even older, must have terrified her a little. In any case it was the next morning before she dared to read the letter, nor did she dare, when she saw John Brown, to answer the question he had written for her. Instead, she took the bucket and went about the customary work of bringing the morning water from the spring. He followed her to the spring and got his answer there. Mary Anne Day married John Brown in July, only a little less than a year after Dianthe and her unnamed son had been buried by the tanyard.

But the new wife had in her more of the stuff that made for survival; beneath a certain awkwardness was a great physical vigor, and the embarrassed silences covered a profound, unquestioning devotion to the hard responsibilities of her life. She was ignorant, but possessed a primitive stoicism which meant an efficient if sometimes uncomprehending adaptability to fact. It is doubtful if the grave by the tanyard lay much in her thoughts.

The family soon settled into its old routine. The stepmother managed things well, and John Brown had more time to devote to his various projects. These were not turn-

ing out as profitably as he had hoped when he loaded the
wagons and left Hudson almost ten years before. He would
come in late at night, tired out, with brows more tightly
drawn and lips more rigidly compressed. Sometimes he held
the smaller children and sang to them: " Blow ye the trumpet, blow," or " With songs and honors sounding loud." Not
infrequently he read *Rollins Ancient History* or Josephus,
but even better he liked *Napoleon and his Marshals*, Plutarch, and a *Life of Oliver Cromwell*. Always, both night and
morning, there was a chapter of the Bible. The Old Testament appealed to him most, especially the *Psalms of David*
and the last chapter of *Ecclesiastes*. A verse from *Psalms*
127 was often on his lips: " Except the Lord build the house,
they labor in vain that build it; except the Lord keep (eth)
the city, the watchman waketh but in vain." Like many
others, John Brown became convinced that he knew where the
Lord built and kept the watch. The Bible was to give him another text that he found satisfying: " Without the shedding
of blood there is no remission of sins."

Despite all efforts things went suddenly from bad to worse
with the worldly concerns of John Brown. He got a new
project in his head that might do something to retrieve his
affairs. On November 21, 1834, he wrote his brother Frederick a letter. It was franked by his own hand as postmaster
of Randolph.

Dear Brother, —
As I have had only one letter from Hudson since you left here
and that some weeks since, I begin to get uneasy and apprehensive that all is not well. I had satisfied my mind about it for
some time, in expectation of seeing father here, but I begin to
give up that for the present. Since you left me I have been try-

ing to devise some means whereby I might do something in a practical way for my poor fellowmen who are in bondage, and having fully consulted the feelings of my wife and my three boys, we have agreed to get at least one negro boy or youth, and bring him up as we do our own, — viz., give him a good English education, learn him what we can about the history of the world, about business, about general subjects, and, above all, try to teach him the fear of God. We think of three ways to obtain one: First, to try to get some Christian slave-holder to release one to us. Second, to get a free one if no one will let us have one that is a slave. Third, if that does not succeed, we have all agreed to submit to considerable privation in order to buy one. This we are now using means in order to effect, in the confident expectation that God is about to bring them all out of the house of bondage.

I will just mention that when this subject was first introduced, Jason had gone to bed; but no sooner did he hear the thing hinted, than his warm heart kindled, and he turned out to have a part in the discussion of a subject of such exceeding interest. I have for years been trying to devise some way to get a school a-going here for blacks, and I think that on many accounts it would be a most favorable location. Children here would have no intercourse with vicious people of their own kind, nor with openly vicious persons of any kind. There would be no powerful opposition influence against such a thing; and should there be any I believe the settlement might be so effected in future as to have almost the whole influence of the place in favor of such a school. Write me how you would like to join me, and try to get on from Hudson and thereabouts some first-rate abolitionist families with you. I do honestly believe that our united exertions alone might soon, with the good hand of our God upon us, effect it all.

This has been with me a favorite theme of reflection for years. I think that a place which might be in some measure settled with a view to such an object would be much more favorable to such an undertaking than would any such place as Hudson, with all its conflicting interests and feelings; and I do think such advantages ought to be afforded the young blacks, whether they are all to be immediately set free or not. Perhaps we might, under God, in that way do more towards breaking their yoke effectually than in any other. If the young blacks of our country could once become enlightened it would most assuredly operate on slavery like firing powder confined in rock, and all slave-holders know it well. Witness their heaven-daring laws against teaching blacks. If once the Christians in the free States would set to work in earnest in teaching the blacks, the people of the slave-holding States would find themselves constitutionally driven to set about the work of emancipation immediately. The laws of this state are now such that the inhabitants of any township may raise by a tax in aid of the State school-fund any amount of money they may choose by a vote, for the purpose of common schools, which any child may have access to by application. If you will join me in this undertaking, I will make with you any arrangement of our temporal concerns that shall be fair. Our health is good, and our prospects about business rather brightening.

Affectionately yours,

JOHN BROWN.

This is the first time John Brown ever recorded any anti-slavery sentiment, and the conviction here is not any stronger than that cherished by thousands of people in the North, especially in the rural districts. The means to the end proposed seem mild enough and legal enough to have contented even the non-resistant Abolitionists, such as Garrison, Child, and Thompson, who were beginning to talk themselves into trouble at the hands of Boston mobs. Those " heaven-daring laws against teaching blacks " were not confined to the slave-holding States. The State of John Brown's birth had passed a law the year before to the effect that no school should be conducted in any town of Connecticut for the education of colored people from other towns " without the consent in writing, first obtained of a majority of the civil authority, and the selectmen of the town." Miss Prudence Crandall, who ran a school in Canterbury, went to jail under this law; furthermore, some of her fellow-citizens supplemented justice by setting fire to her house. And Connecticut had passed laws against slave-holding many years before.

John Brown was using good judgment in choosing Crawford County, Pennsylvania, as the niche in the rocks where he could fire off his powder blast. In Boston at this time most people saw that the issue of Abolition might split the Union, and even those who were gifted with no such divination felt that too many meetings and too much talk of this sort would hurt the Southern market for their goods. Twenty-five or thirty years later they might think differently in regard to the Southern market: " that nation is the best customer that is freest," said Henry Ward Beecher to his audience in Liverpool. " Pounds and pence," added Henry Ward Beecher with easy piety, " join with conscience and honor in this design."

Meanwhile in Boston posters might appear on the public streets:

THOMPSON
THE ABOLITIONIST!!!

That infamous foreign scoundrel THOMPSON, will hold forth *this afternoon*, at the Liberator Office, No. 48 Washington Street. The present is a fair opportunity for the friends of the Union to *snake Thompson* out! It will be a contest between the Abolitionists and the friends of the Union. A purse of $100 has been raised by a number of patriotic citizens to reward the individual who shall first lay violent hands on Thompson, so that he may be brought to the tar-kettle before dark. Friends of the Union, be vigilant!

Boston, Wednesday, 12 o'clock.

People of Crawford County, however, had no manufactured goods to offer in Southern markets and they had no slaves. The prejudices characteristic of the North and South were not so well-defined here. The region was still close to the pioneering stage and its social structure had not hardened; there were not those conflicting interests and feelings which were already existing in the thirty-five-year old town of Hudson. All in all, the situation seemed rather favorable for John Brown's new project. He was willing to do what was right by Frederick in regard to their temporal interests in the school; and, furthermore, the local tax arrangement was in order for the school fund. There is a chance that he might have concurred in this matter with the sentiment so ably put by his eminent contemporary: " pounds and pence may join with conscience and honor in this design."

The school did not materialize, and when the opportunity came to join in partnership with the wealthy Zenas Kent of Franklin Mills, John Brown was ready to return to Ohio. No more successful expedient than the school had presented itself; he was in debt, could not collect such money as people owed him, and was forced in the end to borrow enough to make the move. When he reached Ohio, ten years after he had left for Richmond, he was back at the beginning again, with a large family on his hands and debts to be paid. A tanyard was built at Franklin Mills under his supervision, but the new firm never actually did any business, for Marvin Kent, the son of John Brown's partner, rented the establishment and proceeded with the affair on his own account.

About this time the new Ohio and Pennsylvania canal was being built through Portage and Summit Counties of Ohio. Speculation ran ahead of the digging crews; prosperity was certainly to follow. At first John Brown merely found the canal a substitute for the partnership with Zenas Kent, which had ended so abruptly, for he managed to get a contract of construction from Franklin Mills to Akron. But here was an opportunity for real success; the canal would bring factories and business to the quiet agricultural village of Franklin. The temptation was too great, and John Brown, with the last lean years at Richmond barely passed, formed a partnership with Seth Thompson, borrowed more money, and bought the Haymaker farm on the edge of the town. They paid $7000 for a little more than one hundred acres; the land stood security to Heman Oviatt and Frederick Wadsworth who had put up most of the money. The partners immediately divided up their property as " Brown and Thompson's addition to Franklin Village," and waited for the canal.

But Brown and Thompson's addition was only the beginning. The Franklin Land Company was organized by twenty-two gentlemen of Ravenna, Franklin, and Akron, who bought up all the water-power and land between the upper and lower villages of Franklin. John Brown was one of the twenty-two gentlemen. The project here was even more ambitious; an entire new town was staked out between the villages and the Canal Company was to coöperate with the Franklin Land gentlemen for the good of all. But John Brown was not content and added to his holdings three more rather large adjoining farms at Hudson. People began to look upon him as a person of great business sagacity and importance. The value of the land he had purchased in Franklin had now leaped to almost $20,000. Then John Brown became a bank director.

Besides the ventures in real estate John Brown tried

breeding race horses. At this time the only race track in the Western Reserve was at Warren, Ohio, where many Kentuckians came to bet their money and enter their own fast horses. Dr. Harmon had two good racers, " Count Piper " and " John McDonald," and John Brown bred his colts from them. There were no scruples in his mind at this time about the business, for if he didn't breed them someone else would. John Brown Jr. reminded him that such was the argument of gamblers and slave-holders but this did not trouble him then. He broke the young horses himself and gave them their training. He was not a graceful rider but a hard, efficient one; the wildest, most untamed colt found it impossible to throw him. But John Brown's main hope for financial success was in his land ventures. His Franklin property continued to go up in value, and the Hudson farms were a good investment.

The Canal Company suddenly refused to stand to its agreement. They drew off water from the Cuyahoga River, and Akron instead of Franklin Mills got the benefit. The investments of John Brown and Seth Thompson and those of the Franklin Land Company dropped to their old level, interest accumulated on the heavy loans, and as sure as death the pay-day came around. The year of 1837 was a bad time in other ways, and John Brown's excellent reputation for sagacity and his speculative bubble exploded together.

With this decline in fortune came a certain social and religious disrepute. John Brown's wife and three of his sons had joined the Congregational Church in Franklin. The Reverend Mr. Avery of Cleveland came to the Mills and organized a protracted meeting of all the churches — the Methodists, the Episcopalians, and the Congregationalists.

The Congregationalists had the biggest meeting house, and so there Mr. Avery preached his four famous sermons from the one text, " Cast ye up, cast ye up! Prepare ye the way of the Lord; make his paths straight." Church folks from nearby towns came in to the help of the Lord against the mighty, and with them came some of the free negroes of the neighborhood and a few fugitive slaves. The negroes got seats near the door where the stove stood in winter. One night John Brown escorted some of the negroes to the family's slip. The next day the Deacons in a body called on the horse-breeder, the speculator, the tanner, to admonish and labor with him. John Brown had once talked a Methodist preacher down; that night the negroes were back in John Brown's pew.

John Brown returned to Hudson, which now was no longer a frontier settlement but a thrifty Connecticut town transplanted to Ohio. He gave up breeding race horses; probably young John Brown's argument had its effect at last. He became a drover and took a herd of cattle back to Connecticut. In New York he tried to secure the agency of a Steel Scythes house, and when he reached West Hartford, Connecticut, he spent one hundred and thirty dollars for ten pure-bred Saxony sheep. The sheep were loaded on a boat to Albany, and then driven across the country to Ohio. John Brown liked best to hear the *Psalms of David* read; David once kept sheep in obscurity, and the life of a shepherd was a calling for which in early life he had a kind of enthusiastic longing.

One day John Brown's family got a letter from the good Deacon Williams of Franklin: it was to inform them that " any member being absent a year without reporting him or herself to that church should be cut off." The rule had been passed after John Brown seated negroes in his pew, ceased to be the sagacious business man and bank director, and migrated to Hudson. John Brown did not take the rebuke with Christian meekness, and his sons later believed that this letter was the reason they had not remained church-going people.

The brother-in-law, Milton Lusk, also got into trouble. The colonization societies that wanted to dispose of the negroes by shipping them off to Africa, were in full flower at this time. The free negroes were generally unpopular in Ohio; there were stringent " black laws," and a negro had few rights of citizenship. When Mr. Randolph of Virginia died he set all his slaves free on condition that they should be settled in Ohio; the free negroes got their land only to be mobbed by white farmers, who didn't like those new neighbors. The colonization idea was popular; it gave an opportunity to do a benevolent deed and remedy a social nuisance at the same time. Furthermore, it appealed to the few radicals, for some of the promoters claimed that it was a blow to slavery itself. The church took up the crusade and raised money to deport black brethren. Ladies' Colonization Societies and Children's Colonization Societies flourished side by side with missionary societies, sewing circles, and revival meetings. Only the negroes seemed to object to the project; they would hold conferences, pass violent resolutions, and condemned colonization as unchristian. Black laws or no black laws, Ohio was a better home to them than the jungle.

One day Milton Lusk saw a statement by Chief-Justice Marshall to the effect that colonization would help the slave-holders of Virginia by disposing of the trouble-making free negroes. A paradox began to dawn in Milton Lusk's mind;

in Ohio the ministers said that colonization was a step toward Abolition and in Virginia they got money by saying it would bolster up their peculiar institution. He threw the paper down and stamped on it. " What ails you, Milton," asked his sister. " I'm through raising money for colonizing the negroes," was his answer. That night the pastor called on Brother Lusk to pass the plate for the colonizing collection, and Brother Lusk flatly refused. " If our money goes into the same fund with the Virginia money, I'll never help raise another dollar," he explained.

Brother Lusk may have had logic on his side, but then other heretics have sometimes possessed the same bolster to their opinions. But logic never quenched fire and not long afterwards Milton Lusk was excommunicated for various errors of opinion. Being naturally heretical and a little too much given to speculation did not make for a comfortable life in Hudson. Among other fallacies Milton Lusk took stock in visitations from the invisible world, table-rapping, and such rat-hole revelations. Even John Brown himself was to claim that in times of trouble Dianthe returned to guide his erring feet. There is, unhappily, no record as to Mary Day Brown's feeling on this point.

Whether that repudiation by Deacon Williams and the Franklin Congregationalist Society had anything to do with it or not, the Lord seemed to have withdrawn his hand and blessing from the administration of John Brown's temporal concerns. But Tertius Wadsworth and Joseph Wells came to his assistance by going into partnership with him to again buy cattle to be driven back to Connecticut. John Brown herded these back east, and disposed of them for a fair profit, but his part was far from enough to raise the distress which hung over his affairs. On the twelfth of June,

1839, he wrote his wife a letter from New Hartford, Connecticut.

My Dear Wife and Children, —

I write to let you know that I am in comfortable health & that I expect to be on my way home in the course of a week should nothing befall me. If I am longer detained I will write you again. The cattle business has succeeded about as I expected, but I am now somewhat in fear that I shall fail of getting the money I expected on the loan. Should that be the will of Providence I know of no other way but we must consider ourselves verry poor for our debts must be paid, if paid at a sacrifise. Should that happen (though it may not) I hope God who is rich in mercy will grant us all grace to conform to our circumstances with cheerfulness & true resignation. I want to see each of my dear family verry much but must wait Gods time. Try all of you to do the best you can, and do not one of you be discouraged, tomorrow may a much brighter day. Cease not to ask Gods blessing on yourselves and me. Keep this letter wholly to yourselves, excepting that I expect to start for home soon, and that I did not write confidently about my success should anyone enquire. Edward is well, & Owen Mills. You may show this to my Father, but to no one else.

I am not without great hopes of getting relief I would not have you understand, but things have looked much more unfavourable for a few days. I think I shall write you again before I start. Earnestly commending you every one to God, and his mercy, which endureth forever, I remain your affectionate husband and father

JOHN BROWN

The friends here I believe are all well.

J. B.

"Tomorrow may be a much brighter day," wrote John Brown. The brighter day did not come tomorrow; it was three days later when the blessing of Providence which John Brown had invoked appeared in the person of George Kellogg, agent for the New England Woolen Company at Rockville, Connecticut. He handed over twenty-eight hundred dollars to be used in buying wool for the concern. Need was immediate and pressing, and the twenty-eight hundred dollars did not go to buy Ohio wool; instead of that it went into John Brown's empty pockets. The New England Woolen Company was not too importunate and could be stalled off a little while.

All that John Brown had made by the return to the Ohio towns was the twenty-eight hundred dollars and he began to look about for some new undeveloped region where he might recoup his fallen fortunes. Oberlin College owned a considerable amount of land in Virginia. On the first of April, 1840, a committee of the Oberlin Trustees listened to an offer by John Brown to survey and purchase some of their Southern holdings. If things went well he was to receive one thousand acres of the new land in a body with a living spring of water sufficient to supply a tannery.

The Virginia country pleased him as much as he had expected and the people rather more. But he had a few criticisms of their way of life; strangely enough the criticisms were practical and not ethical. He wrote them to his wife from Ripley:

Were the inhabitants as resolute and industrious as the Northern people, and did they understand how to manage as well, they would become rich; but they are not generally so. They seem to have no idea of improvement in their cattle, sheep, or hogs, nor to know the use of enclosed pasture-fields for their stock, but spend a large portion of their time in hunting for their cattle, sheep, and horses; and the same habit continues from father to son.

JOHN BROWN

In his mind the Browns, were they so disposed, could be very useful on many accounts to the people of Virginia. Superior industry and superior resolution should receive their just reward in that country where most men seemed so unambitious and so easy-going. A plantation of a thousand acres and springs of living water — a worthy dream indeed.

The problem of adapting himself to the social customs and pro-slavery prejudices of the Virginians seems not to have crossed his mind. He would need their good-will in general and their money for his leather in particular if the venture was to succeed; and the situation would be a precarious one indeed for a forthright Abolitionist — even for a non-resistant Abolitionist. It is a little queer that the letters home in which John Brown discussed so ably the people and customs of Virginia did not even casually refer to slavery, that peculiar institution whose evils lay so close to his heart. After John Brown's final Virginia project had ended on the Charlestown scaffold some persons decided that the Oberlin lands were to have been an outpost of liberty, " an eagle's nest among the rocks." It is barely thinkable that for a moment the dream of that thousand acres, with fine cattle on nicely fenced pastures, crops ripening in the fields, and leather in the vats, obscured other possible dreams.

It was not to be. After returning from his surveying trip, John Brown had considerable difficulty in making up his mind for the move; meanwhile, the Oberlin Trustees changed theirs very definitely. John Brown waited too long and they closed the issue. The surveyor got thirty dollars for his pains and the pleasure of pointing out in a letter to Mr. Levi Burnell of the Board the injustice they had done him. The thousand-acre plantation vanished; John Brown began to herd sheep for Captain Oviatt of Richfield, Ohio.

Herding another man's sheep might give a living, but it was not calculated to pay up the debts which had accumulated for years. Mr. George Kellogg, who turned over the twenty-eight hundred dollars to John Brown, had been put off by promises for a time, but the cat was out of the bag before this. The New England Woolen Company was more anxious to salvage what they could from Mr. Kellogg's poor judgment than to indulge the pleasure of vindictiveness; they permitted Brown to go through bankruptcy rather than criminal prosecution, under the assurance that he would pay the amount with interest thereon from time to time as the Divine Providence enabled him to do so. Divine Providence did not decree it thus, despite a few prosperous years to follow; John Brown left a last will and testament in the Charlestown jail, bequeathing fifty dollars to the New England Woolen Company. After the twenty years that had lapsed, they put the fifty dollars in a business-like fashion to the account of John Brown. However matters may have stood with others, at least the New England Woolen Company got a little profit out of Harper's Ferry.

After the bankrupt had been discharged Mr. Kellogg did not get any money, but he did receive a manly letter.

Richfield, Summit County, Ohio, Oct. 17, 1842.

GEORGE KELLOGG, ESQ.

Dear Sir, —

I have just received information of my final discharge as a bankrupt in the District Court, and I ought to be grateful that no one of my creditors has made any opposition to such discharge being given. I shall now, if my life is continued, have an opportunity of proving the sincerity of my past professions, when legally free to act as I choose. I am sorry to say that in consequence of the unforseen expense of getting the discharge,

the loss of an ox, and the destitute condition in which a new
surrender of my effects has placed me, with my numerous family, I fear this year must pass without my effecting in the way
of payment what I have encouraged you to expect (notwithstanding I have been generally prosperous in my business for
the season).

> Respectfully your unworthy friend,
>
> JOHN BROWN.

Perhaps Mr. Kellogg had really hoped for nothing; he
had certain grounds to be a little cynical about what John
Brown might encourage him to expect.

Mr. Kellogg was not alone. Tertius Wadsworth and
Joseph Wells, the friends who had come to John Brown's
aid in buying cattle with him to be sold in Connecticut, were
not satisfied by the accounting he had given them and after
a lapse of three years they sued him. This was the summer
of his bankruptcy; there is no evidence that he bequeathed
them fifty dollars. The Bank of Wooster had an action
against John Brown for a check, which he had drawn on the
Leather Manufacturers Bank of New York and which had
been rejected by them on the grounds that Brown had no
account there. They were content in the end with a judgment for $917.65. About a dozen other concerns who sued
John Brown at various times had at least the same moral
satisfaction of victory, which, however, did little to balance
their ledgers.

Strangely enough John Brown himself won a few suits in
his career; one of these was brought by a horse-thief on the
grounds of assault and false arrest when John Brown and
some other citizens asserted their civic duty in helping the
constable take the fellow to jail.

Only once in these confused years of business did John

Brown see, as many more honest men have seen, the very
unattractive inside of a jail. The matter was a backwash of
the land speculations of 1836, when John Brown persuaded
Heman Oviatt and several other friends to stand security for
$6000 on a note to the Western Reserve Bank. When the
land bubble exploded the following year and most of the
Brown property was lost by assignment to creditors the bank
had no choice but to sue Mr. Oviatt and his fellow endorsers.
The bank got a judgment bond payable in sixty days, and
when this was not cancelled at the end of the required time,
another suit was brought. This time Mr. Oviatt was forced
to pay in full, and to get justice for himself had to sue John
Brown and his other endorsers. The principal of the whole
transaction secured himself, temporarily at least, by hand-
ing over as collateral to the aggrieved Mr. Oviatt a penal
bond of conveyance which he held on the " Westlands."
Shortly afterwards, John Brown secured the proper deed to
the " Westlands," recorded it at the court-house, and, without informing his innocent friend Oviatt, got more money
by mortgaging the farm to two other gentlemen of the
neighborhood. Meanwhile, Daniel C. Gaylord won a suit
against John Brown, and to fulfill his judgment was compelled to appeal to the sheriff. The sheriff promptly put up
the " Westlands " for sale. The buyer was Amos Chamberlain, a friend of John Brown, who perhaps bid the land in
with the intention of permitting John Brown to take it
off his hands when better days came. But Mr. Chamberlain's
problematically kind intentions were blasted when Mr.
Oviatt produced his penal bond and sued to have the sale
put aside as illegal. Mr. Chamberlain won the contest.

However much Mr. Oviatt may have desired it, he could
not touch John Brown. That gentleman was safe enough

from the legal point of view. Meanwhile his cattle were eating the grass which the court had decided was Mr. Chamberlain's rightful property. When Mr. Chamberlain appeared to take possession of the " Westlands " he found the Brown boys camping in a tumble-down cabin on the farm and fortified with a few old-fashioned muskets which had not outlived their days of usefulness. He first resorted to a new law-suit and then sent the constable and a posse to the farm. The constable and his party looked at the muskets and appealed to the sheriff of Portage County. John Brown, and his sons, Owen and John, went to the Akron jail. " Of course we could not resist the sheriff," Jason Brown once philosophically remarked. That was a method the Browns learned later.

Mr. Chamberlain received a letter from the chief prisoner in the April of 1841.

. . . I have looked with sincere gratification uppon your steady growing prosperity, and flattering prospects of your young family. I have made your happiness and prosperity my own instead of feeling envious at your success. When I antisipated a return to Hudson with my family I expected great satisfaction from again having you for a neighbor. This is true whatever you may think of me, or whatever representation you may make of me to others. And now I ask you why will you trample on the rights of your friend and of his numerous family? Is it because he is poor? Why will you kneedlessly make yourself the means of depriveing all my honest creditors of their Just due? Ought not my property if it must be sacrifised to fall into the hands of honest and some of them poor and suffering Creditors? Will God smile on the gains which you may acquire at the expence of suffering families deprived of their honest dues? And let me here ask Have you since you bid off that farm felt the same inward peace and consciousness of right you had before felt? I do not believe you have, and for this plain reason that you have been industrious in circulating evil reports of me (as I believe) in order to prevent the community from enquiring into your motives and conduct. This is perfectly natural, and nothing new under the sun. If it could be made to appear that Naboth the Jezreelite had blasphemed God and the King, then it would be perfectly right for Ahab to possess his vinyard. So reasoned wicked men thousands of years ago. I ask my old friend again is your path a path of peace? does it promise peace? I have two definite things to offer you once and for all. One is that you take ample security of Seth Thompson for all you have paid and for what you may have to pay (which D. C. Gaylord has ever wickedly refused) and release my farm and there fore provide for yourself an honorable and secure retreat out of this strife and perplexity and restore you to peace with your friends and yourself. The other is that if you do not like that offer that you submit the matter to disinterested, discreet, and good men to say what is just and honest between us.

Mr. Chamberlain, however, did not pursue the proffered suggestion to get for himself such an honorable and secure retreat. The new Ahab occupied the coveted vineyard and demolished the troublesome cabin in order to provide for himself a path of peace. But his heart may have been touched by the Biblical parallel after all, for he did not press the case and the prisoners were released to go about their business.

The business was shortly that of getting John Brown's bankruptcy plea through the District Court. The discharge came in October of 1842. The court had decided that certain properties were absolutely essential to the existence of the Brown family; they kept possession of eleven Bibles, a copy of *Beauties of the Bible*, one *Church Member's Guide*, two hogs, two cows, two mares, seven sheep, three lambs, nineteen hens, and three pocket knives. The gentlemen of the court took into consideration the needs of both the material and the spiritual life, and it is praiseworthy that they seem to have exercised a certain partiality in regard to the family's equipment for the latter. With this capital John Brown continued the labor of herding Captain Oviatt's flock.

The family lived in Richfield, Captain Oviatt's home, where John Brown also tried his craft of tanning with moderate success. There was further reason for a certain amount of self-congratulation in winning a few prizes for sheep and cattle at the Summit County fair, but these brightening prospects of the life at Richfield were accompanied by fresh and more grievous disasters. Four of the younger children died before the end of the first year there. In September they carried three coffins out of the house at one time and covered them in the same grave. Perhaps this tribulation softened John Brown's rigid rule of his family's life, for the next year he could write to his wife:

If the large boys do wrong, call them alone into your room, and expostulate with them kindly, and see if you cannot reach them by a kind but powerful appeal to their honor. I do not claim that such a theory accords very well with my practice; I frankly confess it does not; but I want your face to shine even if my own should be dark and cloudy.

The Divine Providence which John Brown had invoked so many times on such a variety of undertakings smiled on his affairs in the next year. The tannery had more calls for work than it could fulfill, and, even better, Simon Perkins Jr., a wealthy man of Akron, went into partnership with the bankrupt to carry on the sheep raising industry on a large scale. The Browns were to take complete charge of Mr. Perkins' fine flock of fifteen hundred sheep, and he was to furnish all the feed and winter shelter. Furthermore, the herdsman's family was to go into a very good house which stood a half-mile or so out of town; the house also belonged to Mr. Perkins. John Brown rightly considered the partnership the most favorable arrangement of his worldly concerns that he ever had. But he expressed the hope " that God has enabled us to make it in mercy to us, and not that he should send leanness to our souls." It was indeed no mean alliance, and John Brown looked upon it as completely vindicating a reputation which had become slightly tarnished by two or three days in the Akron jail and the conduct of a few other matters.

When John Brown took charge of the large flock he had not profited much by his earlier experience with his own sheep and cattle, for he was a rough herdsman and too much given to the use of dogs, which Mr. Perkins thought did more harm than good. There was considerable loss in the flock at first from grub in the head and other causes, but Mr. Perkins seems to have borne with his partner's methods and hoped for the best. However, the business answered that early enthusiastic longing which John Brown had written of; it may have satisfied a certain desire in his nature for mastery, for he took great pride in a professed power over animals. Once in a Concord parlor he boasted that he could make a cat or dog so uncomfortable merely by fixing his eyes upon it that the beast would leave the room. All in all, John Brown never seems to have taken much stock in the old saw that a cat may look at a king. People in Akron supplemented the boast in the Concord parlor by telling how Mr. Perkins' partner killed a good sheep-dog merely because it was too fond of someone else.

In the beginning of 1846 things were going so well with the firm of Perkins and Brown that the junior member could write to his son John: "I think we have quite as much worldly prosperity as will be likely to be a real blessing to us." Meanwhile, the New England Woolen Mills were waiting for a share of that prosperity to bless their ledgers, which still carried the account of twenty-eight hundred dollars for John Brown. His own conduct was not thoroughly consistent with the sentiment here expressed, for he had in mind the idea of a wider and more profitable business than shepherding.

There was an opening for a project which would give the wool growers a chance to combat the New England manufacturers. It was the custom of the mills to buy unsorted wool at the low-grade wool prices which they practically dictated, and then to have it sorted for their purposes. If the sheep owners could dispose of their wool by grade the mills would have to take it at a price near the true value of the goods received. Growers began to receive circulars which promised some such adjustment:

THE UNDERSIGNED, commission wool-merchants, wool-graders, and exporters, have completed arrangements for receiving wool of growers and holders, and for grading the same for cash at its real value, when quality and condition are considered. Terms for storing, grading, and selling will be two cents per pound, and about one mil per pound additional for postage and insurance against loss by fire.

The undersigned wool merchants were Perkins & Brown, whose headquarters were in Springfield, Massachusetts. They added to their circular an imposing list of references in the persons of many solid citizens from New York, Pennsylvania, Ohio, and Virginia.

The office in Springfield was under the charge of John Brown. He managed things much according to his own impulses, accepting few suggestions from his partner or others. Mr. Perkins was back in Ohio, and probably by this time he had ceased to give advice: " I had no controversy with John Brown," the partner remarked, adding his simple reason, " for it would have done no good."

One of the first devices of John Brown's management was an honest and canny letter to Marvin Kent, asking him for his wool with the promise that commissions from its sale would be applied on the debt which John Brown still owed him and his father. Meanwhile, the circular announcing the new firm was having its effect. Large quantities of wool came in from widely separated regions and the amount increased through the summer; by August, fifty to eighty bales a day were unloaded at the Perkins & Brown warehouse. The wool was graded and stored, but the real problem was untouched, for the manufacturers had no intention in the world of letting such an organization upset their old profitable methods of doing business with the growers. Other things besides the determined stand of the mill owners worked against the new firm; the Walker Tariff came into effect, war was brewing with Mexico, and farmers who needed money hated to wait for returns until the slower process of the warehouse sales was finished. Perkins & Brown barely saved their first year's business from disaster by selling their own Saxony clip early in the summer for the fair price of sixty-nine cents and by turning over a good amount of their higher grades to an English buyer four days before Christmas.

During the fall, when prospects looked darkest, John Brown had even contemplated a trip to England with a large shipment in order to fight the American buyers. But a family misfortune had prevented such a step and had added to his troubles. The carelessness of his daughter Ruth had caused the death by scalding of one of the younger children. Business prevented a return to Ohio, and the comfort of his wife was a letter which philosophically pointed out the moral that amazing unforeseen consequences may follow from the right or wrong doing of apparently trifling things. The next year the diminished family came east to join him.

The second season's business saw the firm in John L. King's old warehouse by the railroad. It was a substantial brick building and gave every appearance of commercial success. Frederick Douglass, once a fugitive slave and later a prominent agitator and a United States marshal at Washington, called on John Brown there and was greatly impressed with the seeming prosperity of the establishment. When he went to the merchant's home the expectations which had been fed by the appearance of the warehouse were somewhat disappointed. He found a small wooden house on a back street where workmen and mechanics lived. The interior was even plainer than the outside, and the plainness seemed to more nearly suggest destitution than simplicity. His first entertainment in the bleak unfurnished room passed under the misnomer of tea; Frederick Douglass ate beef soup, cabbage, and potatoes, while his erect, hawk-faced host, dressed in a good brown suit and cowhide boots, appraised the visitor and did most of the talking. The negro ventured a little opposition to some points in John Brown's argument; the family had long since learned better.

" No political action will ever abolish the system of slavery. It will have to go out in blood. Those men who hold slaves have even forfeited their right to live."

This talk rang a little strange to Frederick Douglass, for, despite the hardships of his childhood and youth in slavery, he felt that freedom could come for all the negroes through peaceful means. He said as much. Then John Brown rose and took down a map of the United States. He placed the tip of a bony, nervous finger on the borders of New York State and ran it along the shadings of the Alleghanies. It rested on the mountains of Virginia.

"These mountains," said John Brown, "are the basis. God has given the strength of the hills to freedom; they were placed here for the emancipation of the negro race; they are full of natural forts, where one man for defense will be worth a hundred for attack; they are full of good hiding places where large numbers of brave men could be concealed, and elude and baffle pursuit for a very long time. I know these mountains well; I could take a body of men into them and keep them there despite of all the efforts of Virginia to dislodge them. The true object to be sought is first of all to destroy the money value of slave property and that can only be done by rendering such property insecure. My plan, then, is to take at first about twenty-five picked men, and begin on a small scale; supply them arms and ammunition, post them in squads of fives on a line of twenty-five miles. I would send the most persuasive and judicious of them down to the fields from time to time as opportunity offers, and induce the slaves to join them, seeking and selecting the most restless and daring."

"How would you support even twenty-five men?" Frederick Douglass was practical; he was also unconvinced.

"From the enemy. Slavery is a state of war. The slave has a right to anything he needs for freedom."

"But suppose you succeed in running off a few slaves, and impress the Virginia slave-holders with a sense of insecurity in their slaves, the effect will only be to make them sell their slaves further south." Frederick Douglass knew this method of old; he himself had once barely escaped ' going down ' to a new master in Alabama when he planned his first runaway and was caught.

" Sell them south," retorted John Brown. " That will be first what I want done; then I would follow them up even to Georgia."

" Mr. Brown, I tell you they would take bloodhounds and hunt you out of the mountains before a month was up."

" They might try that but the chances are we would whip them, and when we had whipped one squad they would be careful how they pursued afterwards."

" Perhaps once or twice it would be so, but in the end they would surround you and starve you under."

" They could never do it, so that I could not cut my way out!" John Brown was more earnest now and leaned forward in the chair. His blue-grey impersonal eyes darkened with excitement and glittered a little as when he was stirred by somebody's opposition. " They could never do it, I tell you." This last he added abstractedly, almost to himself. For the instant his doubting guest seemed forgotten.

Frederick Douglass had not given up the idea of peaceful Abolition even in the face of such confidence; he repeated his hope that the slave-holders might see their economic advantage of the one hand and justice on the other.

" That can never be at all," replied John Brown with an intensity that startled Douglass a little. " I know their **proud hearts and that they will never give up a single slave** until they feel a big stick about their heels."

So it ended with the run-away slave unconvinced but impressed. Time passed and he came to address an anti-slavery convention in Salem, Ohio. For the first time he expressed a fear that slavery might only end by bloodshed. His good old friend Sojourner Truth interrupted sharply; " Frederick, is God dead? "

" No," answered Douglass, " and because God is not dead slavery can only end in blood."

He had not forgotten the tip of the bony, nervous finger that ran down the map — New York, Pennsylvania, Maryland — and paused over the mountains of Virginia.

John Brown had told his mulatto guest that all his severe economy was to save money for his plan. But there were other good reasons. Business matters were no better, and this year no convenient English buyer appeared. There was more trouble with Mexico, and the tariff situation became even more unsettled. But the chief difficulty was with John Brown's business methods. He was no trader; he waited until all the wools were sorted and then fixed a price to the mills. The mills bought if they liked but more frequently they could find wool elsewhere and Perkins & Brown had to sell in the end for what they could get. The growers also had other grievances. Those who shipped their wool early and in time for the high market of the opening season had their profits discounted by the later falling prices. The clips that came in fine and clean likewise suffered in the returns by the inferior quality and treatment of other wool. John Brown had a democratic idea of justice; he simply averaged out the profits at the end of the season, with no reference to individual merits. There was other negligence in the conduct of the business; shipments were not acknowledged, inaccurate accounts were rendered, and at times the clerk, John Brown Jr., had his hands full in writing letters of apology for his father's methods. To salve the irritated customers John Brown would make large advances on the season's prospect; he had a naturally sanguine disposition and infinite trust in himself, and by consequence the payments on hypothetical profits at the beginning of each year were too large for the firm's good if not large enough to keep the farmers content.

By the next year John Brown was looking around for some place where he might establish his family permanently. He may have foreseen disaster in the commission business — simple arithmetic of the four ground rules could predict that end unless matters changed — and it seems to have been his custom after each failure in business to hunt out some undeveloped region and begin again with his axe and plow. What appeared to be a fine opening soon presented itself.

In Peterboro, in New York State, lived Gerrit Smith. Mr. Smith was a man of liberal ideas and considerable wealth. He was against tariff as an infringement of personal liberty, against the sale and manufacture of liquor, against a national debt as robbing one generation to pay the debts of another, against land monopoly, and against slavery. He believed in woman suffrage, the " Free Religion " movement, and was opposed to government owned schools. Furthermore, he held that all law was from the bosom of God; and used the term of " Bible Civil Government " on all occasions. Mr. Smith said that Christians did not thank him for such a definition; the cry of " infidel," " Sabbath breaker," and " preacher of politics " had made him a little cynical. But Mr. Smith was a man of wealth and could afford the luxury of his convictions.

Mr. Smith's wealth also permitted him to carry some of his convictions into practice. On August 1, 1846, the anniversary of West India emancipation, he threw open one hundred and twenty thousand acres of his enormous patrimony in northern New York to settlement by deserving negroes. Two years later, on April 8, he received a visit. " Mr. Smith," said the visitor, " I am something of a pioneer; I grew up among the woods and wild Indians of Ohio, and am used to the climate and ways of life that your negro colony find so trying. I will take one of your farms myself, clear it up and plant it, and show my colored neighbors how such work should be done; will give them work as I have occasion, look after them in all needful ways, and be a kind of father to them." Mr. Smith was hunting a person of that sort, for his negroes were having a hard time of it in the face of the six-month winter and the hostility of the few white settlers in that Adirondac region. Moreover, his visitor looked the part. He stood a little less than five feet eleven, and weighed about one hundred and fifty pounds. He was not actually a tall man, but he looked so, for hard work in the Ohio woods and on the Pennsylvania farm had cut away any roundness of middle age and given a deep chest and narrow flanks whose robustness the loose, deacon-like suit could not conceal. There was a great difference between his appearance of nervous vigor, endurance and taciturnity, and the figure of his large, almost affable host, as they sat in the wide room of the square old house that stood back from the Peterboro street. Gerrit Smith was impressed, and John Brown got a couple of farms on easy terms and the option on others. This was not his last profit from Mr. Smith's generosity.

John Brown did not waste time before becoming a father to the negroes at North Elba. The original settlers there did not relish the idea of so many colored people and their treatment had been anything but friendly, for the new arrivals could only buy provisions at ruinous prices. John Brown did what he could to help by forwarding five barrels of pork and five of flour to Mr. Hodges, to be doled out among the negroes. He also forwarded them by Mr. Hodges some excellent advice during the winter. " Say to my colored friends with you that they will be no losers by keeping their patience a little about building lots. They can busy themselves in cutting plenty of hard wood and in getting any work they can find until spring, and they need not fear getting too much wood provided. Do not let any one forget the vast importance of sustaining the very best character for honesty, truth, industry and faithfulness. I hope every one will be determined to not merely conduct as well as the whites, but to set them an example in all things."

The advice was sound, for the new settlers had several faults to live down. Even the naïve, perennial faith in human nature, which sustained Gerrit Smith when his purse suffered at the hands of the unworthy, had received a sort of shock when indisputable evidence forced him to admit that many of the free negroes and run-away slaves had adopted their Southern masters' habit of drinking too much. Mr. Smith felt very strongly on the subject of drinking, in any amount, and when he spent his one stormy term in Congress in 1852 and kept open house at Washington, even the Southern politicians, whose company he enjoyed but whose principles he abhorred, had to go without their wineglass at his table. But they came back again, for the table was otherwise excellent, Mr. Smith's social presence was superb, and they were somewhat accustomed to having their principles abhorred by all right-thinking men. Mr. Smith also felt very strongly on the subject of thrift. He had to admit that the negroes were lazy, for he was an honest man; but it was his theory that their second bad habit resulted from never having done any work except under the stimulus of the lash. Like many others he regarded laziness as almost a sin and not as an amenity of the civilized man and a privilege of the savage. In any case it is too bad that John Brown's fine letter did not fall into the hands of his benefactor; Mr. Smith would probably have felt gratified in the choice of a guardian for his blacks.

All the good advice in the world, however, could not shorten the long winter or get work for the negroes. They shivered in the terrible, unaccustomed cold and went hungry. John Brown had suggested that they hire out, but the few farmers there were not enthusiastic employers. Aside from prejudice, something may be said on their side; in such a country there was little need for coachmen, barbers, and waiters, and many of the negroes had no training for anything else.

In the spring John Brown brought his family up to the Adirondac region. The property which he had gotten from Mr. Smith on such agreeable terms did not include a house, and he rented from a Mr. Flanders another farm where a small, one-story cabin already stood.

On a dreary day, in the face of a spring rain, the family left the village of Keene and started over the mountains to their new home. Their spirits were low, and, indeed, it seemed anything but an auspicious time for making a new beginning. The rain drifted over the ridges and hung like a heavy mist above the tops of spruce and hemlock in the valleys. John Brown tried to encourage his people by pointing out the magnificence of the scenery. " It is awfully grand," said Ruth, the oldest daughter. They stopped the wagon once or twice to get a cup of water from streams they crossed. The water was always clear and very cold, and the bottom could be seen covered with clean sand and beautiful white pebbles. The spring odor of the balsam and spruce occasionally came to them as their wagon lurched slowly along the precarious mountain road. John Brown commented on this.

The second house they reached after coming over the mountain from Keene was the one they had rented from Mr. Flanders. It was a small affair for nine people. One good-sized room answered pretty well for kitchen, dining-room and parlor. There was a pantry, and two bedrooms, and another room gave space for four beds, so that no stranger or way-faring man need be turned away from their gate — or, more specifically, from their bars. With a little crowding the place would do; " the main thing," said John Brown," is all keep good natured."

Next morning the rain was over; drops of water still clung to the leaves, glittering in the sunlight, and the logs of the house were black with moisture. Old White Face, its sides scarred by landslides to a white and pale grey against the general greens and browns, stood plain in view at the head of Lake Placid to the north. The nearer ridges slipped sharply down to the twisted road over which they had driven in the rain the day before. That ride was behind them now. It was a fine country after all.

A little before noon a pleasant-faced colored boy came down the road, hesitated before the bars, and then called to the booted man who was standing in the yard and looking abstractedly off to the north where Old White Face could be seen in the sunlight. " Is this where John Brown lives," asked the boy. " Here is where he stays," the man replied.

His eyes had lost the impersonality of that gaze to the mountains; they were questioning, almost kindly. The boy had been a slave in Virginia, probably not a very submissive one, for he had been sold into Florida — that limbo of refractory negroes. But unlike most slaves sent into the deep South, the boy contrived to run away from his master at St. Augustine. Eventually he had reached Springfield and managed to get work there. A bad slave had made a good free nigger, for he had been neither shiftless nor drunken, and had gotten hold of a little property by way of reward. John Brown hired him to help put the farm in order, and the new negro, Cyrus, made ten in the small house. There is evidence that Cyrus, at least, kept John Brown's admonition and remained good-natured; it was a failing of his race.

John Brown had noticed other and more serious failings in the negro race than chronic good nature. About this time he began the writing of a pamphlet which he called *Sambo's Mistakes*. The author, supposedly a negro, looks back on a long life and sets about the business of pointing out its mistakes. He learned to read but had devoted this talent to silly novels and other miserable trash. Smoking and chewing tobacco had taken money which might better have paid for a farm, a library, or benefited the suffering members of his own race; but the smoking and chewing had made a man of him but little inferior to some of the whites. He had also wasted his time with Free Masons, Odd Fellows, Sons of Temperance, and a score of other secret societies instead of seeking the company of intelligent, wise, and good men. John Brown's Masonic difficulties of almost thirty years before were obviously still in his mind. Sambo, furthermore, had been too proud of his spouting talents to ever get any business accomplished when some crisis called a meeting of colored people together. He had other things to regret in his misspent life: self-indulgence, failure to coöperate with fellow Abolitionists because of religious differences, prejudice against people who would help him. But the writer is most bitter when he comes to the climax of his paper:

Another trifling error of my life has been, that I have always expected to secure the favor of the whites by tamely submitting to every species of indignity instead of nobly resisting their brutal aggressions from principle, and taking my place as a man, and assuming the responsibilities of a man, a citizen, a husband, a father, a brother, a neighbor, a friend, — as God requires of everyone (if his neighbor will allow him to do it); but I find that I get, for all my submission, about the same reward that the Southern slavocrats render to the dough-faced statesmen of the North, for being bribed and browbeat and fooled and cheated, as the Whigs and Democrats love to be, and think themselves highly honored if they may be allowed to lick up the spittle of a Southerner. I say I get the same reward. But I am uncommon quick-sighted; I can see in a minute where I missed it.

Sambo's Mistakes began to be published in an obscure Abolitionist paper of New York. The *Ramshorn* carried John Brown's one attempt at journalism and the walls of Jericho did not even tremble at the blast; the trumpet might be blown in the name of the Lord, but John Brown was never to learn that all the archangels fought on the side of the big battalion. There were several events in his life of fifty-nine years which should have carried that doctrine to his heart. He was alone, and always acted alone, for his egotism would permit nothing else. But always he executed the will of God and always he saw the hand of God working in the affairs of men. In the December of 1851, when the Hungarian patriot

Kossuth had just come to America and was soon to disappoint the Abolitionists by his policy of neutrality in regard to slavery, John Brown wrote to his wife:

There is an unusual amount of very interesting things happening in this and other countries at present, and no one can foresee what is yet to follow. The great excitement produced by the coming of Kossuth, and the last news of a new revolution in France, with the prospect that all Europe will soon again be in a blaze, seems to have taken all by surprise. I have only to say in regard to those things, I rejoice in them, from the full belief that God is carrying out his eternal purpose in them all.

So he felt in 1851. He had faith in the will of God, and that faith was so great, perhaps, that he began to know what thing God willed. And to foreknow was to will also; at last his own will and the divine will were one. " I acknowledge no master in human form," he said to Mr. Vallandigham. He was lying wounded on his pallet, waiting for justice of the Commonwealth of Virginia. God had been on the side of the big battalion, on the side of Colonel Bob Lee's Marines.

But such things were far away now. It was only the will of God now that he build a house at North Elba. As many hands as could be had would be needed to establish the family in this country. It was real pioneer work, such as the Browns had seen before in Ohio and Pennsylvania, but the land here was more intractable and the climate more harsh. When the hillsides had been ' slashed ' over and burned there were only difficult fields where the crop had to be planted and reaped between the half-charred stumps and where the plow for years would catch on old roots and stone. But worse, the winter hung over the region for six months of the year, and snow still clung in deep patches of drift at a time when crops were already green in the country the Browns had left. In ordinary times neither corn nor wheat could mature on those hillsides. Rye, oats, potatoes, and vegetables were all that the land would produce, and that only at painful expense of labor and anxiety. But the rough fields that came out of the slashing and burning had one advantage; a handful or so of grass seed would turn them into a good pasture. So the people raised some cattle and sheep, and their wealth was calculated in those terms. When Oliver Brown was killed at the Ferry in 1859, the young wife he left on the North Elba farm was not considered absolutely penniless, for she inherited five sheep.

John Brown did not lose much time before he brought his favorite breed of cattle into this backwoods. The native farmers envied him the fine animals of his herd, for the common kind that grazed among their stumps had little to distinguish them. John Brown was very proud of his cattle; they were not Devons, but a cross on the Devon stock with some Connecticut cattle. He also got public praise for his handiwork when he entered the best specimens from his herd in the Essex County cattle show. The report for the year 1850 of the local agricultural society had this much to say about John Brown:

The appearance upon the grounds of a number of very choice and beautiful Devons, from the herd of Mr. John Brown, residing in one of our most remote and secluded towns, attracted great attention, and added much to the interest of the fair.

But in the summer of 1849 John Brown did not stay longer at North Elba than was absolutely necessary to his family's interest. He hired a negro woman to do the cooking for his ailing wife, exhorted the colored settlers, gave his children and Cyrus a few pointed instructions, and returned to

Springfield where the commission wool business was falling
on evil days. For some time he had been nursing an idea that
might break the tacit conspiracy of the New England mills;
the idea was to sell in England and force the American buyers to do justice to 'Perkins & Brown' and the native farmers.
Many people had told him that the English were suspicious
of American wools, but John Brown rarely got an idea out
of his head except by putting it in action. On the fifteenth of
August he stepped on board the *Cambria*, a steamer, and
was off to England. In the hold of the *Cambria* were many
bags bearing the label of 'Perkins & Brown, Springfield,
Massachusetts.'

He landed at Liverpool on Sunday, August 26, and left
almost immediately for London. In that city he found that
there was little chance of selling any wool before the middle
of September, and so he decided to set out at once for the
continent. He left for Paris the evening of the 29th, but before his departure he got a letter ready for the next return
boat. In it he retailed some of his opinions to his son John.

England is a fine country, so far as I have seen; but nothing so
very wonderful has yet appeared to me. Their farming and
stone-masonry are very good; cattle, generally more than middling good. Horses, as seen at Liverpool and London, and
through the fine country betwixt these places, will bear no comparison with those of our Northern states, as they average. I
am here told that I must go to the park to see the fine horses of
England, and I suppose I must; for the streets of London and
Liverpool do not exhibit half the display of fine horses as do
those of our cities. But what I judge from more than anything
is the numerous breeding mares and colts among the growers.
Their hogs are generally good, and mutton-sheep are almost
everywhere as fat as pork. Tell my friend Middleton and wife
that England affords me plenty of roast beef and mutton of the
first water, and done up in a style not to be exceeded.

John Brown

During a hurried trip across Germany, France, and Flanders he very decidedly made up his mind on a number of other items. He concluded that the Germans had a bad agricultural system because the farmers lived in villages and the natural manures did not get back to the soil. He admired English farming very much and, in fact, he thought England was the best cultivated country he had ever seen. At Waterloo he surveyed the battlefield, and made up his mind that the common theory of a strong military position was not sound. " A ravine, a wooded ravine," he said, " is the easiest place in the world to defend." At least he was confident enough to scorn considerable authorities, and when the time came he was consistent enough to act on his own ideas. John Brown saw the Austrian troops drill on several occasions and could say after his inspection that the Austrians would always be defeated by soldiers who had been trained to manœuvre more rapidly. The judgment was accurate enough but scarcely profound. The French troops were very well drilled, he thought, but he refused to believe that they had much individual courage. That was an American attribute.

The tour did not take long. John Brown was back in London before the 17th of September, when a disastrous auction of his wool occurred. He withdrew all the unsold wool from public market and tried to patch up the loss by private sales. But four days after the auction, his sanguine temper had again asserted itself when he wrote his son John: " the agent of Thirion, Mailard & Co. has been looking at them today, and seemed highly pleased; said he had never seen superior wools, and that he would see me again." And there was the tell-tale comment added: " we have not yet talked about price."

Whether John Brown could drive a Connecticut bargain or not, he did know how to grade wools. One evening when he was telling some of his ideas on the subject to a group of English merchants, one of them put his hand in his pocket and took out a sample. He gravely passed it over to the Yankee.

"What would you do with such wool as that," the Englishman questioned.

John Brown rolled the wool between his fingers for a moment and then handed it back to the owner.

"Gentlemen," he said with equal gravity, "if you have any machinery in England that will work up dog's hair, I advise you to put this into it." John Brown did have a sort of humor when the situation was enough in his own favor. Somewhere in the city of London that night Providence was tempering the wind to a shorn poodle.

John Brown's efforts to retrieve the ill luck of the auction were not happy. He bore considerable resentment against "stupid obstinate prejudice," conflicting interests, and certain echoes of the struggle with American mills which had influenced the British market. By the latter part of October the unsold wool and John Brown were on board ship for New York. He had walked down the streets of London, Liverpool, Calais, Hamburg, Paris — a tallish man, dressed with a sort of rural neatness, striding with long springing steps, and deeply absorbed in his own reflections. Now and then he would seem suddenly to realize himself, the air of abstraction would vanish, and he would regard the strange prospect of the city or countryside with sharp, appraising eyes. He was on his way back home now to confront a partner whose judgments might be uncharitable, but he still felt that the idea behind the venture was right. Fortune had merely been against him. Perkins & Brown had lost forty thousand dollars or thereabouts, and John Brown had only the solace of his new opinions on agricultural or military matters in foreign parts and of the joke on the British wool-merchant. Perhaps Simon Perkins would be neither interested in the former nor amused by the latter.

John Brown Jr. had been managing the business in Springfield and the season's developments there were not too gratifying. Indeed, the fate of the firm had been already sealed by the trip to England. There only remained the winding up of affairs through a series of tedious law-suits and the conduct of a steadily dwindling business. Mr. Perkins took the matter better than his partner had anticipated, or at least by the time of their meeting in April of the next year, he had been able to possess his soul in patience. John Brown was so elated at the escape from recriminations that he wrote a letter to his family as soon as Mr. Perkins left town.

Burgettstown, Penn., April 12, 1850.

DEAR SON JOHN AND WIFE, —

When at New York, on my way here, I called at Messrs. Fowler & Wells's office, but you were absent. Mr. Perkins has made me a visit here, and left for home yesterday. All well at Essex when I left; all well at Akron when he left, one week since. Our meeting together was one of the most cordial and pleasant I ever experienced. He met a full history of our difficulties and probable losses without a frown on his countenance, or one syllable of reflection; but, on the contrary, with words of comfort and encouragement. He is wholly averse to any separation of our business or interest, and gave me the fullest assurance of his undiminished confidence and personal regard. He expresses strong desire to have our flock of sheep remain undivided, to become the joint possession of our families when we have gone off the stage. Such a meeting I had not dared to expect, and I most

heartily wish each of my family could have shared in the comfort of it. Mr. Perkins has in the whole business, from first to
last, set an example worthy of a philosopher or of a Christian.
I am meeting with a good deal of trouble from those to whom we
have over-advanced, but feel nerved to face any difficulty while
God continues me such a partner. Expect to be in New York
within three or four weeks.

Your affectionate father,

JOHN BROWN.

The claims against the partners in 1850 were some forty
thousand dollars. A letter from his father to John Brown Jr.
admitted that if these claims were lost he would be left " nice
and flat." A characteristic canny comment followed: " This
is in confidence." But Mr. Perkins was still bearing up under
the trouble a good deal better than his partner had feared. A
month later, in December, John Brown was again apprehensive about that sufferer's state of mind and thought that he
might be getting out of patience and distrustful at the delay
in winding up the firm's affairs. But he found space to pass
a few well-earned encomiums. " He is a most noble-spirited
man," said John Brown, " to whom I feel most deeply indebted; and no amount of money would atone to my feelings
for the loss of confidence and cordiality on his part." Then
he gave his sons some good counsel: " a world of pleasure and
of success is the sure and constant attendant upon early rising." He also felt that the fine-wool business was improving.

The clip from the Perkins & Brown flock was unusually
beautiful that year; the little compact Saxony fleeces were
as clean and as nice as possible. Mr. Musgrave of the North-
ampton Woolen Mills looked the clip over and offered sixty
cents a pound. " No," said John Brown, " I am going to send
this to London." Mr. Musgrave was himself a Yorkshire man
and he knew the English market, even though his knowledge

may not have been paid for to the tune of forty thousand dollars. He tried to buy it again for his shawls and broadcloths. " American wulls won't sell in London, no matter what kind they are; the London men don't think them good. You ought to know that yourself." It was no use. John Brown graded it himself, bought new sacking, and had it packed under his own eye. The bags came out round, firm, hard, and almost as true as if they had been turned on a lathe. Away it went to London. A little afterwards news came back that it had been sold, but the price was not named. One afternoon Mr. Musgrave dropped into the counting-room of Mr. Leonard who occupied the store under the Perkins & Brown wool lofts. Mr. Musgrave was all aglow over some private joke. " Come with me," he invited Mr. Leonard, " I'm going to have some fun." Then he stepped to the stairs and called to the merchant above. " Uncle John, I want you to go over to the Hartford depot and see a lot of wull I've bought." John Brown put on his coat, came downstairs, and went off to the depot. Just as they were going into the freight house, Mr. Musgrave turned and said, " I want you to tell me what you think of this lot of wull that stands me in just fifty-two cents a pund." John Brown took one glance at the pile of wool bags. Mr. Leonard and Mr. Musgrave, still aglow, watched their friend as he disappeared down the street with the brown coattails floating behind him and his nervous long strides fairly devouring the way. On the floor of the freight house was the pile of full bags — round, firm, hard, and almost as true as if they had been turned on a lathe — and on each was a worn label with its letters nearly effaced. " Perkins & Brown, Springfield, Massachusetts, U. S. A." the labels read.

Despite the failure of this last English wool venture the

year's end found John Brown still hopeful and but a little
chastened. " I do not believe the losses of our firm will in the
end prove so very severe, if Mr. Perkins can only be kept
resolute and patient in regard to matters," he wrote back to
young John. " I have often made mistakes by being too
hasty, and mean hereafter to ' ponder well the path of my
feet.' "

Messrs. Cleveland and Titus of New York had charge of
the suit with Pickersgill as well as other business of the
wool firm. The lawyers wanted a shepherd puppy for a pet;
John Brown pondered well the path of his feet, and the son
in Ohio got an order for a " real prompt, fine-looking, black
shepherd puppy, whose ears stand erect." John Brown was
satisfied that if he gave the barristers such an excellent animal by way of friendship that it would do more to secure
their best services in the suit with Pickersgill than would a
hundred dollars in fees. John Brown had moments of astonishing candor.

The puppy may have spurred on Messrs. Cleveland and
Titus to greater energy and greater subtlety in the cause
of their client, but it was all to no considerable purpose. The
suits dragged disastrously on. There were trials at Pittsburg, Troy, Utica, New York, and Boston. The Burlington
Mills of Vermont had sued for sixty thousand dollars for
breach of contract in supplying wools of a certain grade.
Rufus Choate and Francis B. Hayes had the case against
John Brown, whose senior counsel was the eminent Joshua V.
Spencer from New York. In Boston the case finally came to
trial after many delays and postponements; it looked dark
for the defense, and Mr. Spencer brought the business to a
compromise out of court, in February, 1853. In New York,
a little after, John Brown won a similar suit for breach of

contract; he always felt somewhat defrauded because the Boston court had not been permitted to give its certain decision against the Burlington Mills.

But John Brown's especial resentment was reserved for the Mr. Warren who lost a suit to him at Troy in 1852. That case was appealed and the whole tedious business was on foot again — depositions to be taken, witnesses to be called, dwindling means to be stretched to the last penny. And all such anxiety made greater by the bitter consciousness of being perfectly in the right.

All of his increasing distresses may well have kept John Brown's mind off of affairs that did not bear on the commission wool business. " I am extremely ignorant of miscellaneous subjects," he said a little before this time. But in that year when the prize clip of Perkins & Brown went off to England and returned as the machinery of Mr. Musgrave's joke, great things were happening in Washington, and many people throughout the country could sense their greatness. General Taylor was President, a slaveholding President, and he could write to his son-in-law, Jefferson Davis, that if any effort was made to deprive the slave States of their constitutional rights, he was willing that the South " act promptly, boldly, and decisively, with arms in their hands if necessary, as the Union in that case will be blown to atoms or will be no longer worth preserving." California was applying for admission as a State and its constitution would forbid slavery within the border. Its entry would upset the balance of power, for there was no new slave State to be paired off. Back in 1811 Josiah Quincy from Massachusetts had talked about secession if Louisiana was admitted; now many gentlemen from the South were talking about secession and worse. General Taylor sympathized with his class, but he was simple enough to see other issues and other obligations; if California wanted to enter the Union without slavery he did not believe that slavery could be forced on her, Missouri Compromise or no Missouri Compromise, and he did not believe that she should be compelled to wait. Despite the letter to Jefferson Davis in the year 1847, the old general who was President threatened to take command of the army himself and put down any rebellion. But there were other " Union-splitters " besides the hotspurs from the South; up North some few scattered people felt that their section should go its way rather than acquiesce in the institution of slavery. And in the South there were many men who felt that the Union was a thing worth preserving; among these men was Henry Clay from Kentucky. John Brown was probably not much interested in the Union one way or another.

Such was the situation when John Brown returned from London in the fall of 1849 and when the aged Henry Clay came up to the Senate, seeking to be but " a calm and quiet looker-on, rarely speaking, and . . . endeavoring to throw oil upon the troubled waters." It was the last meeting of the giants. Clay, Calhoun, and Webster sat in their honored places. Around them were younger men, representing a new way, a more bitter way, of treating the old question of slavery — Jefferson Davis, Benton, Cass, King of Alabama, Henry Foote, Butler of South Carolina, Stephen Douglas, Mason, William Seward of New York, and Salmon P. Chase of Ohio. Rancor, vehemence, savagery. Southern interest against Northern sentiment; Northern interest and Southern honor. The waters soon were troubled.

Henry Clay was to endeavor to pour oil on the waters, but his hopes of being a calm spectator were blasted. On January 29, 1850, the Senator from Kentucky laid down his " comprehensive scheme of adjustment." " Will you lend me your arm," the old Senator asked of a friend as they climbed the long steps to the Capitol. " I feel myself quite weak and exhausted this morning." Then he added, " I consider our country in danger, and if I can be the means in any measure of averting that danger, my life and health is of little consequence." It was February 5, the day of his great speech. Here was a final appeal to the floor, the packed galleries, the nation. An appeal to the North for concession, to his own State and section for peace. " War and dissolution of the Union are the same," he said. " It would be a war in which we should have no sympathy, no good wishes, and in which all mankind would be against us, and in which our own history would be against us ! " He was worn out with the two-day effort. Crowds of men and women rushed about him to shake his hand and kiss him; the great speech was over.

On March 4 they brought Calhoun into the chamber. He sat in his chair, a dying man sustained only by the terrible energy which for years had fought out the cause of Southern justice. Mason of Virginia read the sick man's speech. Its grim accurate logic outlined the quarrel: the anti-slavery Ordinance of 1787, the Missouri Compromise, tariffs against the planters, the necessity to maintain the equilibrium of the States. The admission of California was a test as to whether or not the South could ever expect justice; and if this justice did not come the Union was doomed. The old man from South Carolina, whom Andrew Jackson regretted having neglected to hang, sat in his chair, the dark eyes watching the effect of the remorseless argument on the assembly. Crowds did not rush about Calhoun to shake his hand or kiss him when it was finished; he had not expected such a thing. Four weeks later he was dead. Webster and Clay said fine things about their lost colleague, and turned back to the business in hand.

Three days after Mason of Virginia had read Calhoun's speech, Webster addressed the Senate in favor of the Compromise. The man to whom the anti-slavery people looked for support now sold out — or so they said of him. He declared that the Abolitionists had done nothing but aggravate the evils of slavery, that he was willing to support an effective fugitive slave law, and that he opposed the application of the Wilmot Proviso to the cases of Utah and New Mexico. He had sold out for a mess of pottage; his bargain might be the presidency of a divided nation. At least that charge could not have been brought against Henry Clay as he ascended slowly the long steps of the Capitol or against Calhoun sitting in his last Senate. Perhaps it was not true of Webster; he may have felt a duty to Union above other considerations in this argument which Mr. Garrison termed " an indescribably base and wicked speech." In Boston, in the Revere House, Webster was soon to say that the Abolition spirit had its basis in " unreal, ghostly abstractions." There is a chance that Mr. Garrison and the Senator from Massachusetts were equally mistaken.

The contest dragged on. Seward and Chase were bitterly against it, and made their " higher law " speeches. But by the end of August all of Clay's measures except the interdiction of slave trade in the District of Columbia had passed: California was admitted, the Texas boundary dispute adjusted, New Mexico was to have a territorial government with the problem of slavery to be settled by its constitution when it should apply for admission, and the Fugitive Slave Law went into force. General Taylor had died in office and Fillmore, his successor, signed the bills. Things were patched up for a while and business men in the North and planters in the South settled down to enjoy the new tranquillity. Calhoun, who had seen the issue of slavery more clearly than either of his two great contemporaries, was in his grave.

On November 28 of that fateful year, John Brown wrote from Springfield to his family concerning the new legislation. " It now seems that the Fugitive Slave Law was to be the means of making more Abolitionists than all the lectures we have had for years. It really looks as if God had his hand on this wickedness also. I of course keep encouraging my colored friends to ' trust in God and keep their powder dry.' I did so to-day, at Thanksgiving meeting, publicly."

The injunction to keep their powder dry was no metaphor. The idea of an organization among the negroes to resist the Fugitive Slave Law took active form early in the following year, when John Brown organized the Springfield branch of the " United States League of Gileadites." By his own hand the " Words of Advice " were written out.

WORDS OF ADVICE

Branch of the United States League of Gileadites. Adopted Jan. 15, 1851, as written and recommended by John Brown

Union is Strength

Nothing so charms the American people as personal bravery. Witness the case of Cinques, of everlasting memory, on board the *Amisted*. The trial for life of one bold and to some extent successful man, for defending his rights in good earnest, would arouse more sympathy throughout the nation than the accumulated wrongs and sufferings of more than three millions of our submissive colored population. We need not mention the Greeks struggling against the oppressive Turks, the Poles against Russia, nor the Hungarians against Austria and Russia combined, to prove this. *No jury can be found in the Northern States that would convict a man for defending his rights to the last extremity. This is well understood by Southern Congressmen, who insisted that the right of trial by jury should not be granted to the fugitive.* Colored people have ten times the number of fast friends among the whites than they suppose, and would have ten times the number they now have were they but half as much in earnest to secure their dearest rights as they are to ape the follies and extravagances of their white neighbors, and to indulge in idle show, in ease, and in luxury. Just think of the money expended by individuals in your behalf in the last twenty years! Think of the number who have been mobbed and imprisoned on your account! Have any of you seen the Branded Hand? Do you remember the names of Lovejoy and Torrey?

Should one of your number be arrested, you must collect together as quickly as possible, so as to outnumber your adversaries who are taking an active part against you. Let no able bodied man appear on the ground unequipped, or with his weapons exposed to view: let that be understood beforehand. Your plans must be known only to yourself, and with the understanding that all traitors must die, wherever caught and proven to be guilty. " Whosoever is fearful or afraid, let him return and part early from Mount Gilead." (Judges, 7, 3: Deut. 20, 8) Give all cowards an opportunity to show it on condition of holding their peace. *Do not delay one moment after you are ready; you will lose all your resolution if you do. Let the first blow be the signal for all to engage; and when engaged do not do your work by halves, but make clean work of your enemies, — and be sure you meddle not with any others.* By going about your business quietly, you will get the job disposed of before the number that an uproar would bring together can collect; and you will have the advantage of those who come out against you, for they will be wholly unprepared with either equipments or matured plans; all with them will be confusion and terror. Your enemies will be slow to attack you after you have done up the work nicely; and if they should, they will have to encounter your white friends as well as you; for you may safely calculate on a division of the whites, and may by that means get an honorable parley.

Be firm, determined, and cool; but let it be understood that you are not to be driven to desperation without making it an awful dear job to others as well as to you. Give them to know distinctly that those who live in wooden houses should not throw fire, and that you are just as able to suffer as your white neighbors. *After effecting a rescue, if you are assailed, go into the houses of your most prominent and influential white friends with your wives; and that will effectually fasten upon them the suspicion of being connected with you, and will compell them to make a common cause with you, whether they would otherwise live up to their professions or not. This would leave them no choice in the matter.* Some would doubtless prove themselves true to their own choice; others would flinch. That would be taking them at their own words. You may make a tumult in the courtroom where a trial is going on, by burning gunpowder freely in paper packages, if you cannot think of any better way to create a momentary alarm, and might possibly give one or more of your enemies a hoist. But in such case the prisoner will need to take the hint at once, and bestir himself; and so should his friends improve the opportunity for a general rush.

A lasso might possibly be applied to a slave-catcher for once with good effect. Hold on to your weapons, and never be persuaded to leave them, part with them, or have them far away from you. *Stand by one another and by your friends, while a drop of blood remains; and be hanged, if you must, but tell no tales out of school. Make no confession.*

Union is strength. Without some well-digested arrangement nothing to any purpose is likely to be done, let the demand be never so great. Witness the case of Hamlet and Long in New York, when there was no well-defined plan of operations or suitable preparation beforehand.

The desired end may be effectually secured by the means proposed; namely the enjoyment of our inalienable rights.

AGREEMENT

As citizens of the United States of America, trusting in a just and merciful God, whose spirit and all-powerful aid we humbly implore, *we will ever be true to the flag of our beloved country, always acting under it.* We, whose names are hereunto affixed, do constitute ourselves a branch of the United States League of Gileadites. That we will provide ourselves at once with suitable implements, and will aid those who do not possess the means, if any such are disposed to join us. We invite every colored person whose heart is engaged in the performance of our business, whether male or female, old or young. The duty of the aged, infirm, and young members of the League shall be to give instant notice to all members in case of an attack upon any of our people. We agree to have no officers except a treasurer and a secretary *pro tem*, until after some trial of courage and talent of able-bodied members shall enable us to elect officers from those whose shall have rendered the most important services. Nothing but wisdom and undaunted courage, efficiency, and general good conduct shall in any way influence us in electing our officers.

After the " Agreement " came nine resolutions concerning the best methods of putting that good counsel into practice. The last read: " Resolved, That as citizens of the United States of America we will ever be found true to the flag of our beloved country, always acting under it." John Brown seems to have insisted on this point. Forty-four negroes put their names down as members of the first and only branch of the League of Gileadites. It is not certain whether all forty-four parted early out of Mount Gilead or whether no opportunity for action ever presented itself; in any case, the project was born and died on the paper that John Brown laboriously scribbled out in his best style.

But the " Words of Advice " showed a pretty sound estimate of the negro's character, just as *Sambo's Mistakes* had done. The strategy for the mob is good: " Do not delay one moment after you are ready: you will lose all your resolution if you do." And there is considerable cunning in the method of embroiling the white sympathizers; John Brown later said of the organized Abolitionists that they did nothing but talk and he was even now trying to trick them into action. If eight years after this his opinion of the negro character remained the same, it must have taken considerable

optimism to make him depend on slave support when the
eighteen men composing the Provisional Government of the
United States straggled down the road that Sunday night
into Harper's Ferry. And then he was still acting under the
beloved flag of his country and government; he *was* the government.

But elsewhere than Springfield the Fugitive Slave Law
was creating disturbance and to some extent fulfilling John
Brown's judgment that it would make more Abolitionists
than years of lecturing. In Syracuse, New York, the American Anti-Slavery Society held its anniversary, with a re-
newed enthusiasm and increased numbers. John Brown was
not there when the meeting began on May 7, 1851. But his
benefactor, Gerrit Smith, was on hand to grace the platform
with his large genial presence and cry, " Joy, then, to
you, William Lloyd Garrison; to you, George Thompson! "
It was the same George Thompson, M. P. and foreign scoundrel, whom the Bostonians once hoped to tar and feather.
The Fugitive Slave Law would now have made the English
agitator a little more welcome there.

Daniel Webster turned up in Syracuse about three weeks
after the meeting opened. He was ready to stand by his guns,
even in a hostile town. " Depend upon it," he declared, " the
law will be executed in its spirit and to its letter. It will be
executed in all the great cities — here in Syracuse — in the
midst of the next Anti-Slavery Convention, if the occasion
shall arise. Then we shall see what becomes of their lives and
their sacred honor."

The test came in October when the Liberty Party held a
convention at Syracuse. About dinner time the alarm bell
rang and the gentlemen of the Vigilance Committee knew
that a fugitive slave had been taken. Gerrit Smith was in the

mob that finally worked itself to the pitch of battering the door of the prison down, putting the fugitive, Jerry McHenry, in a light carriage drawn by a span of the fastest horses in Syracuse, and seeing him safely on his way to the North Star. The next morning Gerrit Smith put a congratulatory resolution before the convention. He referred to Daniel Webster as " that base and infamous enemy of the human race." " We rejoice," he concluded, " that the city of Syracuse — this anti-slavery city, our beloved and glorious city of Syracuse — still remains undisgraced by the fulfillment of the satanic Daniel Webster." The people of the city were very proud of themselves and for some years they held an excellent dinner on the anniversary of Jerry's deliverance and made speeches. In the end Gerrit Smith was a little disgusted and ceased to attend.

When John Brown read the news of that affair in Syracuse on October 1, he might have been a little envious, for it would have been a chance to see if his Gileadites really could make clean work of it. Almost three years later, John Brown was to have similar regrets at missing a show, though by this time the forty-odd Gileadites were scattered. The Mr. Warren who lost the suit to John Brown in 1852 had appealed the decision. Now the winner was frequently at Vernon, near Utica where the case was to be tried, helping his lawyer.

News came of the Anthony Burns affair at Boston — how the fugitive slave was locked up in the Court House, as others had been before his time — how Mr. Wendell Phillips and Mr. Theodore Parker had spent their most impassioned eloquence in old Faneuil Hall — how people, the same sort of people who had hooted the Abolitionist Thompson twenty years before, had poured into town from the suburbs with some vague idea of getting the negro off — how they had made an assault on the Court House, killed one deputy marshal, and been scattered in the end with no good at all done to Burns.

John Brown read the news, while Mr. Jenkins, his lawyer, worked over the papers of the case. Suddenly the client got up and began to pace back and forth in the room, his hands clasped under the snuff-colored coattails of his Quakerish suit. He stopped in front of the lawyer. " I'm going to Boston." Mr. Jenkins laid down his pen. " Going to Boston! What do you want in Boston? " John Brown took another long stride or two, with his head bent forward and chin thrust out. " Sir, Anthony Burns must be released, or I will die in the attempt! " he announces to the dumbfounded Mr. Jenkins. Mr. Jenkins was a conscientious lawyer and had the interests of his client rather than of Anthony Burns at heart; this sort of thing would do no good. He reminded John Brown that there was an appeal to be answered in just so many days, that if it wasn't answered the whole case would go to pot, that no one except John Brown had the information, the memory, and the acuteness to win.

In Boston the troops sent by President Pierce patrolled the streets. Commissioner Loring executed the verdict of the court. Down State Street Anthony Burns walked between files of soldiers on the way back to his Virginia master. There was much indignation and muttering among the people, but President Pierce's men and the other military fulfilled their duty. John Brown was not in Boston; Mr. Jenkins had made another legal triumph.

But John Brown might just as well have gone to Boston to watch the sad procession down State Street or to get mixed up with marshals and soldiers; the detested Warren won the law-suit. The enmity of the loser never died, for when he was buying a farm for his family in North Elba with money contributed by various philanthropists, he had fears that Warren might try to make good some of his old claims. In April, 1858, he wrote to his family:

Since I wrote you, I have thought it possible; though not probable; that some persons might be disposed to hunt for any property I may be supposed to possess, on account of liabilities I incurred while concerned with Mr. Perkins. Such claims I ought not to pay if I had *ever so much given me;* for my service in Kansas. Most of you know that I gave up all I then had to Mr. Perkins while with him . . . *all the family* had better decline saying anything about their land matters. Should any disturbance *ever be made* it will most likely come *directly or indirectly* through a scoundrel by the name of Warren who defrauded Mr. Perkins and I out of several thousand dollars.

The demands of the many law-suits and other exacting details of winding up the commission business had caused John Brown to give up North Elba and return to Ohio. The family had moved back to Akron in the March of 1851 and the sons had driven the prize-winning Devon cattle over the mountains to the western pastures. Only Ruth had stayed behind; she was now the wife of a young North Elba farmer, Henry Thompson, who was a good match in her father's judgment. With his passion for early rising, he could record with some satisfaction that Henry Thompson got Ruth out of bed in time to have breakfast before light. John Brown Jr. was also married, but he and the other brothers were still occupied with the Perkins & Brown sheepraising venture in Ohio, and with farming on their own account. Frederick was beginning to be a great cause of anxiety; fits of mental disease were becoming more frequent despite treatment by various doctors.

Mr. Perkins had remained a philosopher and a Christian, for in 1853 a farming and stock raising partnership was still in effect. " He seems so pleasant," said John Brown, " and anxious to have me continue, that I cannot tear away from him." But by the next year Mr. Perkins' mind had changed somewhat and he was magnanimous enough to let the partner tear himself away. Some people thought that political differences had not a little to do with the change. Mr. Perkins held very decided opinions about his partner's doings of later years and he expressed himself rather directly: " I consider him and the men that helped him the biggest set of fools in the world." Mr. Perkins may not have been so outspoken at the talk which terminated their business relations; in any case John Brown defined that conference as " good-natured." At first he was a trifle worried about the settlement Mr. Perkins intended, but in the end the sum was generous enough to make John Brown admit that his partner was every inch a gentleman. And so it was determined that John Brown would go back to North Elba and leave Mr. Perkins — that philosopher, gentleman, and Christian — to his own devices. But the severe life of North Elba did not appeal to the sons; they wanted a country of more opportunity. Jason, John, and Owen were talking of going west across the Mississippi, of going to Kansas.

The start for the Adirondack country was delayed by lack of funds. The best John Brown could do was to hire three farms and work them during the summer of 1854 when a terrible drought withered the crops of the region. But his hired farms got off better than most, and by the sale of some of the Devon cattle John Brown had enough for moving back to New York. That was the country, he said, where he wanted to rest his bones in peace.

Peace would be the only thing salvaged from the past fifty-five years of strenuous, restless life — tanneries, farms, the Randolph post office, speculations, Devon cattle and Saxony sheep, the wool warehouse in Springfield, the London auction room and the merchant with the hank of poodle hair, law-suits, domestic wine in carefully cleaned junk-bottles. Peace and a little experience. But he had been able to give John some good advise on wool-buying when that son intended to take up the business for himself: " Wool-buyers *generally* accuse each other of being unscrupulous liars; and in that *one* thing *perhaps* they are not so. Again, there are but very few persons who need money, that can wholly resist the temptation of feeling too rich, while handling any considerable amount of other people's money. They are also liable to devote God's blessed Sabbath to conversation or contrivances for furthering their schemes, if not to the examination and purchase of wool. Now, I would not have you barter away your conscience or good name for a commission." The New England Woolen Mills might have endorsed some of these sentiments, whatever their views may have been on the subject of Sunday buying.

As another fruit of experience John Brown could analyze the source of his own failure. To his mind it had one root — doing business on credit. He had believed that a poor man must borrow, and borrow still more, to offset his handicaps of poverty, forgetting the pay-day that came as sure as death. An ambition beyond its means, a mind too restless and too fixed on its end to ever scrutinize or be overly scrupulous about its means — perhaps that was the trouble. But he said it was the false doctrine of credit that kept him like a toad under a harrow and in the end drove him off to North Elba, where he wanted to rest his bones in peace. In the next few years it was charity money and not credit that financed his undoing.

But for the moment a backwoods farm with a few of his children settled near seemed good enough. The fine herd of fifteen hundred Saxony sheep, the impressive store in Springfield, the deference of the Gileadites, had all vanished. Emerson said this about those years of playing the shepherd and selling other men's wool: " If he kept sheep, it was with a royal mind; and if he traded in wool, he was a merchant-prince, not in the amount of wealth, but in the protection of the interests confided to him." An indiscreet gentleman once asked Colonel Simon Perkins of Akron about those dealings of wool growing and wool selling. " The less you say about them the better," responded Colonel Perkins, who, obviously, had not read the works of the sage of Concord.

3

A SOUND REASON

IT was a day in April of 1855. The Brown boys were
puttering about their new claim which they had
reached only a few days before. One of them glanced
up to see a group of horsemen cantering in their direction.
The horsemen rode up and drew rein. The new settlers curiously looked over their visitors. They were hardy fellows,
wearing broad-brimmed hats, dirty flannel shirts, broad
belts, and heavy boots into which their breeches were tucked.
They were well armed, and from the boot-tops protruded
the hilt of the bowie-knife. They sat their saddles with care-
less expertness. A good-day was passed, and the visitors regarded their hosts with the frank appraisal of the frontier.
"Have you seen any stray cattle over this way," one of
them asked by way of opening conversation. "No, we
haven't," came the emphatic answer. The visitors continued
their scrutiny; the accent of the answer told them that these
new fellows were Yankees. "Well," a horseman asked with
a certain meaningful inflection, "how are you all on the
goose?" "We are Free State, and more than that, we are
Abolitionists." That was enough; without another word the
strangers gave the horses their heels and were off. At their

head rode a minister of the gospel, the Reverend Martin White. The Browns watched him out of view.

By the spring, five of Brown's sons were ready to try their luck in the Kansas Territory — Jason, John, Owen, Frederick, and Salmon. They liked the country and thought that nowhere else could a poor man, endowed with a share of common sense and health, get a start so easily. But incidents such as the Reverend Martin White's visit made them feel that they needed something beyond their common sense and good health. Toward the end of the month John Brown Jr. wrote to his father for help.

We have among us 5, 1 Revolver, 1 Bowie Knife, 1 middling good Rifle, 1 poor Rifle, 1 small pocket pistol and 2 slung shot. What we need in order to be thoroughly armed for each man, is 1 Colts large size Revolver, 1 *Allan & Thurbers'* large sized Revolver manufactured at Worcester, Mass, 1 *Minnie Rifle* — they are manufactured somewhere in Mass or Connecticut (Mr. Paine of Springfield would probably know) and 1 heavy Bowie Knife — I think the Minnie Rifles are made so that a sword bayonet may be attached. With these we could compete with men who even possessed Cannon. The real Minnie Rifle has a killing range almost equal to Cannon and of course is more easily handled, perhaps enough to make up the difference. Now we want you to get for us these arms. We need them more than we do bread. Would not Gerrit Smith or someone, furnish the money and loan it to us for one, two or three years, for the purpose, until we can raise enough to refund it from the *Free* soil of Kansas?

The Brown boys were obviously taking their private crusade to Kansas very seriously, and taking even more seriously the little crusades which Missourians now and then made across the line to talk big or vote. John Brown Jr. and his brothers lost no time before they mixed themselves in the political affairs of the Territory, and they also seem to

have done enough talking to make themselves unpopular
with people such as the Reverend Martin White. But before
their arrival much history of the Kansas Territory had already been enacted.

The Kansas-Nebraska Bill was signed on May 30, 1854.
It marked the end of the Missouri Compromise and the opening of the territories to " Squatter Sovereignty." The voters
of a new region were to decide whether it would be slave
or free; the contest was transferred from the chambers of
Washington to the prairies, ravines, and river-bottoms of
the country across the Mississippi. More than the question
of Kansas was involved; it was the peculiar institution
brought to a life and death issue. In Charleston, South
Carolina, the *Mercury* put the matter:

First. By consent of parties, the present contest in Kansas is
made the turning-point in the destinies of slavery and abolition. If the South triumphs, abolitionism will be defeated and
shorn of its power for all time. If she is defeated, abolition will
grow more insolent and aggressive, until the utter ruin of the
South is consummated.

Most people looked upon the Bill as a distinct victory for
the South. Wendell Phillips wrote to a strong-minded lady:
" So far as *national* politics are concerned, we are beaten
— there's no hope. We shall have Cuba in a year or two,
Mexico in five; and I should not wonder if efforts were made
to revive the slave trade, though perhaps unsuccessfully, as
the Northern slave States, which live by the export of slaves,
would help us in opposing that." Cuba would have made
several States; the Southern politicians wanted the island
very much, and had they gotten it considerable trouble might
have been saved that new Union which rose after '65. On the
Fourth of July Mr. Garrison got considerable satisfaction

for himself before his meeting at Framingham, Massachusetts, by burning a copy of the Fugitive Slave Law, the decision against Anthony Burns, and the charge of Judge Curtis to the United States Grand Jury in regard to the attempt to release Burns. " And let all the people say, *Amen*," invoked Mr. Garrison when the offending papers had been consumed. Then the gentleman took the Constitution out of his pocket. " A covenant with death and an agreement with hell," said Mr. Garrison. The Constitution also went up in smoke. " So perish all compromises with tyranny! And let all the people say, *Amen!* " Obviously Mr. Garrison had done his worst.

Mr. Garrison's people would burn paper and waste words, but somebody else had to settle Kansas. If the entire American Anti-Slavery Society had settled there it would not have made a great deal of difference, for they didn't believe in voting and they didn't believe in resistance. It was up to others to do the job. Before the Kansas-Nebraska Bill was signed the Massachusetts Emigrant Aid Society had been incorporated to help Free State settlers to Kansas. The next year the organization received another charter as the New England Emigrant Aid Company, with John Carter Brown as president, and Eli Thayer as vice-president. The whole affair was Mr. Thayer's idea. It was to make money and was to save Kansas for God and freedom. " When a man does a benevolent deed and makes money at the same time, it merely shows that all of his faculties are working in harmony." Mr. Thayer was not a cynic.

In Missouri the rumor was that the Emigrant Aid Company had five million dollars to invest in freedom. The rumor was considerably in error, but the effect was the same. There was great indignation on the border. The Missourians were an individualistic lot; they didn't like too much organization

for themselves and they certainly didn't approve of it among
the Yankees for such a purpose. But fire was to be fought
with fire, and so " Blue Lodges " and secret societies for the
control of Kansas sprang up. The Missourians did not have
a capital of five millions dollars, but they had voters. There
was a rush into the new Territory to stake out claims ahead
of the Emigrant Aid parties. They had their own claim
office back in Westport, Missouri, for many of the owners
never considered for a moment the possibility of living in
Kansas. Before the first party arrived from the East the
" Platte County Self-Defensive Association " was organized
at Weston, Missouri, with the open purpose of making Kansas an inhospitable stopping place for all emigrants who
came under the auspices of the aid societies of the North.
The general feeling along the border was that the Kansas-
Nebraska Bill represented a tacit bargain; Kansas for slave-
holders, and Nebraska for Free State men. The aid societies
represented a breach of the bargain. The Missourians were
extraordinarily naïve.

As early as the autumn of 1854, the Missourians crossed
their line to vote for J. W. Whitfield, the pro-slavery candidate for Territorial Delegate. Whitfield was elected and
went up to Washington where his seat was at first not questioned; but the joke was on the Missourians, for there was
already a pro-slavery majority in the Territory without
their aid. But the election for the Territorial Legislature
on March 13 was a more important matter. The " Blue
Lodges," " Sons of the South," " Social Bands," and
" Friends' Societies " loaded their wagons and saddled their
horses. There was no secrecy about their business; they hung
out banners, a band or two provided music to cheer them on,
and inverted whisky bottles on sticks rattled as the wagons

lurched along. " We air gwine across the line ter vote."
Some had claims in Kansas and intended to settle there;
others, only a little less conscientious, regretted that they
would have to lose their Missouri vote for a year; and some
changed a hat or coat and walked confidently up to the
polls several times to sign their names or make their marks.
Over six thousand votes were cast, and about three-fourths
were from Missouri. It was a sweeping victory.

Governor Reeder had a problem on his hands. He called
for a bodyguard before he declared the returns, and Dr.
Charles Robinson, an Emigrant Aid representative, responded with thirteen other anti-slavery men. The Governor
demanded protests, but these only appeared from six or
seven of the eighteen districts. When the time came for decision the thirty-nine newly elected members, armed to the
teeth, stood before Governor Reeder and waited for his decision. At Reeder's back were Dr. Robinson and his friends.
They fully expected the election to be thrown out; they also
knew that it would mean trouble. Beside the papers relat-
ing to the case lay the gubernatorial pistols, cocked and
ready on the table. Mr. Reeder had lived near the Missouri
line, and on that morning in the preceding March he could
have looked out of his window and seen the so-called Border
Ruffian wagons as they drove into Kansas. Now the Governor had his pistols cocked, but he had profited by his legal
education. He was not obligated to set aside the returns if
these were not protested. Seven of the twelve men whose
election depended on the disputed districts were denied their
certificates but the election stood. Dr. Robinson and his men
were disgusted with what they considered the Governor's
cowardice. Perhaps he, too, was a little disillusioned; if the
anti-slavery men in all their righteous ardor had not pos-

sessed the courage to enter the regular protests from their districts in the face of Missouri threats, it was not his place to gratuitously make himself the mark for some sharp-shooter by annulling the entire election. Governor Reeder was a fine orator, a Democrat of strong Union sentiments, and an upright, genial and honest man; he was also a good lawyer.

A new election was held to replace the gentlemen who had been denied their certificates. Pro-slavery men who considered the matter settled did not take the trouble to vote and all the members elected were Free State men. The legislature convened early in July, its first work being to promptly refuse seats to these members. Only one anti-slavery man kept his seat, but after a few weeks he decided that his period of usefulness was over and resigned. The legislature remained at Pawnee only four days before it adjourned itself to Shawnee Mission, which was located somewhat nearer to the Missouri border. The Governor vetoed the adjournment on the basis of a clause in the Act organizing the Territory. The removal was passed over his veto, and he broke off all official connection with the legislature. But S. D. Lecompte, the Chief Justice of Kansas Territory, Rush Elmore, the Associate Justice, and A. J. Isacks, the United States District Attorney, refused to support Governor Reeder's claim that the legislature was now an illegal body. One of the first things the legislature did was to petition President Pierce for the dismissal of the offending executive, but before their message reached Washington Reeder had been removed on the charge of speculating in Indian lands. Mr. Reeder was still a good lawyer; a better way than the use of the cocked pistols had presented itself. But he had played his cards and was beaten.

The Free State men set about two methods of combating

the legislature; they procured Sharpe's rifles and they held conventions. Dr. Robinson despatched G. W. Deitzler with a letter to Eli Thayer for arms. One hundred Sharpe's rifles were forwarded to Kansas in boxes marked " books," arriving there just before the special election for the seven vacancies in the legislature. This was merely the beginning, for " Beecher's Bibles" came in greater and greater numbers. A mountain howitzer, procured by the zeal of Horace Greeley, accompanied one consignment. The gentlemen of the Aid Society practiced a little sophistry in regard to the matter; the official right hand penned denials of the Southern accusation that an armed emigration was being organized, and the private left hand dug into the pocket to foot the bills for those boxes marked "books." About the time the first box arrived, John Brown Jr. wrote to his father for a family arsenal; the new rifles over at Lawrence had probably suggested the idea that Eastern philanthropy would be interested in buying guns for Kansas.

The problem for the various Free State conventions which for months were called on each other's heels was to decide their action toward such laws as the Territorial Legislature might pass. That body, despite its technical validity, was ' bogus ' and no Free State man doubted that for a minute. John Brown Jr. who figured as the leader of the Brown settlement, was elected vice-president of a rebellious convention held at Lawrence during late June. The chief work of this body, aside from the taste of politics which it gave its vice-president, was to draft the defiant sentiment, " that in reply to the threats of war so frequently made in our neighbor state, our answer is, We Are Ready." The Sharpe's rifles were making the Free State settlers feel more like men, and on the first Fourth of July celebration their confidence was to go even further. Dr. Robinson made a speech in which he urged the repudiation of the legislature and resistance to its acts, adding the declaration that if slavery in Missouri was not possible with Kansas a Free State, then slavery in Missouri must go by the board. In theory, at least, there was now to be meddling on both sides of the line.

While Dr. Robinson was exhorting the people of Lawrence, the legislature was going the limit with the powers vested in it. The seduction of a slave from its master in the Territory was grand larceny punishable by death. The decoying of a slave into Kansas from another place carried the same penalty. The denial, by word of mouth or in writing, of the right to hold slaves in Kansas was made a felony to be punished by imprisonment at hard labor for not less than two years. That was far from all, but it summed up the worst the gentlemen at Shawnee Mission could do; the rest of the laws were lifted by the scissors and pastepot from the Missouri Statutes. In September J. H. Stringfellow wrote to the *Montgomery Advertiser;* " We have now laws more efficient to protect slave-property than any State in the Union. These laws have just taken effect, and have already silenced Abolitionists; for in spite of their heretofore boasting, these know they will be enforced to the very letter with the utmost rigor." It was a sad day for the Southern cause. When some of John Brown's men at Harper's Ferry got Lewis Washington out of bed and informed him that he was a prisoner, one of them asked; " I presume you have heard of Ossawatomie Brown? " " No, I have not," replied the nephew of General Washington. " Then you have paid very little attention to Kansas matters." " You are right," answered the eminent prisoner; " I have long since become so disgusted with Kansas and everything connected with it, that whenever I see a paper with ' Kansas ' I throw the thing aside without reading it." He was like many others in the South across the Mississippi; what they chiefly wanted was to be let alone.

Other conventions were organized and the machinery of the Free State resistance began to take form. At Lawrence on the fourteenth and fifteenth of August there were two meetings at the same time, one with the intention of giving solidarity to the Free State men despite certain political differences among them, and the other to discuss plans for establishing a Free State government. James H. Lane, a political adventurer, had already attempted to organize a Democratic Party in the Territory, but most of the Free State men realized that one issue and only one needed settlement at the time. Another convention was called to meet at Big Spring on September 5 to perfect the Free State Party organization; delegates were to be appointed for this convention at a meeting on August 25. The efforts of the second of the simultaneous Lawrence conventions was to culminate in the ratification of the Topeka constitution and application for admission to the Union. John Brown Jr. was occupying himself at Lawrence as a member of the steering committee of the second, more radical, gathering which was concerned with forming a Free State government. Meanwhile his claim was not being greatly improved nor the make-shift dwelling prepared for a hard winter. It was a generous trait of the Browns to take more interest in the public business than in their own. Once or twice what they considered to be public business turned out to be somebody else's affair . . . or property.

Governor Reeder had come to Kansas as an ardent believer in the idea of popular sovereignty. After his removal, the pro-slavery party lost a man who was willing to see fair play done on the grounds they themselves had defined, for Reeder went over to the Free State Party and drafted their resolutions at the Big Springs convention. The new Governor was Wilson Shannon, who entered upon his duties of office in early September. Governor Shannon had been educated to believe that executive and judicial functions should be exercised with absolute regard to the laws, *de facto* — and the laws that stood on the statute books were those of the Shawnee Mission legislature. He had no part in the elections which put them there; it was his duty to see them executed until the people altered them by the regular channels. The pro-slavery men were not enthusiastic about his appointment, but they welcomed him with great pomp and show when he arrived in the Territory, and made haste to allay any doubt he may have cherished concerning the legality of the Shawnee Mission Legislature and the work they had done.

Coming with these ideas Governor Shannon must have been somewhat puzzled by the earnestness of Free State men, who continued their conventions, and speech making, and resolutions. He couldn't help regarding their actions as treasonable, though there was no overt evidence that would convict them: treason was levying war against the United States or any of the States, or adhering to those who are doing so by giving them comfort or aid. The malcontents might go ahead to frame a constitution, elect officers, and voluntarily obey their laws, but until force was used in executing those laws no charge of treason could be brought. On the other hand it was the problem of the Free State leaders to dodge any situation which would embroil them with the National Government. It was a case of tight-rope walking and they did it well; otherwise that first execution, for treason in Charlestown, might have been anticipated by two or three years, with a different set of gentlemen in the limelight.

In the month of October, the month of John Brown's arrival in Kansas, the delegates met at Topeka to frame a constitution. James Lane, who had given up his idea of a Democratic Party on the bait of a Free State senatorship, Dr. Charles Robinson, M. F. Conway, J. K. Goodin, and S. D. Houston were prominent in the affair. John Brown Jr. was also there as a member of the Free State Territorial Executive Committee. More radical members such as Dr. Robinson voted for universal suffrage with no line of color or sex admitted. More conservative and " wobbly " members were held by the pressure of the pro-slavery violence or by desire for office under a new regime. The constitution which finally emerged reflected the mixed sentiments behind the movement. Kansas was to be a Free State according to the new document, but love of the negro seems not to have prompted the action, for all free colored settlers were to be excluded from the Territory. In fact, James Lane had made the remark that so far as the rights of property were concerned he knew no difference between the negro and a mule. Mr. Lane later became a militant Abolition hero; Mr. Lane usually recognized an opportunity, and in the end was among the respectables. One of the conventions leading up to the constitution had completely repudiated the Abolitionists, and Charles Stearns, a Garrisonian, retorted concerning the Free State platform: " All sterling anti-slavery men, here and elsewhere, cannot keep from spitting upon it; and all pro-slavery people must, in their hearts, perfectly despise the base sycophants who originated and adopted it." The

Garrisonians were regularly against most things. They burned constitutions and spit on resolutions. Some of them were even against having Sunday in the week and held conventions about it. On the whole they must have been very unhappy people; one sometimes suspects that such unhappy people must also have been just a little wicked.

This constitution with the negro exclusion clause was passed in December, and the date for election of State officers and a legislature under it was set for January 15, 1856. But the dual government of the State had already begun. In early October ex-Governor Reeder was elected a delegate to Congress. The pro-slavery men on a different date repeated their former performance and reëlected Whitfield to the same office; many votes again came from Missouri. When both gentlemen presented themselves at Washington Whitfield temporarily won the seat, only to be ejected in disgrace after a committee had investigated Kansas elections; but Reeder never got the contested place.

Despite the turbulent spirits which poured into the Territory on election days with rifles under their arms, whisky jugs in the wagons, and bowie knife handles protruding from boot-tops, there had actually been very little shedding of blood. True, the Free State men were threatened with tar, feathers, ducking in the river, and death, but these empty compliments, especially after the " Beecher's Bibles " arrived, were returned with interest. The Missourians came over at intervals, voted, and talked big, but such was about the sum of the matter until the fall of '55. Up to that time Kansas had a record for violence no worse than any frontier community. A large number of settlers, whether they might vote slave or free, were the usual restless people who had been defeated in the more tightly organized society of their origin and had drifted into the new country, impatient of restraint and anxious to try out the suddenly discovered freedom. Some from the North came as crusaders with the words of the eminent divine, Henry Ward Beecher, ringing in their ears; " give each man a Bible in one hand and a Sharpe's rifle in the other and send him to Kansas." Some came to get a living after failure at home. Some came merely because of a taste for lawlessness and excitement. The old South was also to send its crusaders when Jefferson Buford of Alabama led a large party of men to Kansas. The Southerners, too, started out with Bibles in their hands, but before they reached Kansas most of those parting gifts had found their way into the trash cans of the steamboats. Mr. Buford should have been more honest; he was no match for the Reverend Beecher in the art of casuistry.

John Brown had not at first intended to go to Kansas. In the August of 1854 he had written to John who was then contemplating the move westward: " If you or any of my family are disposed to go to Kansas or Nebraska, with a view to help defeat *Satan* and his legions in that direction I have not a word to say; *but I feel committed to operate in another part of the field.* If I were not so committed, I would be on my way this fall. Mr. Adair is fixing to go, and wants to find ' good men and true ' to go along." And so John Brown returned to North Elba to contend with Satan and his legions in those parts, and spend his age in peace. Then he received the enthusiastic accounts from his sons in Kansas; perhaps life there seemed to offer more opportunity and perhaps his restless, ambitious nature would not let him be content to rest his bones in peace at North Elba after all. A sentence in one of his son John's letters did not deter him:

" owing to the rapid settlement of the country by squatters, it does not open a good field to speculators."

The letter asking for arms came to John Brown's hand and he took the proposition to Gerrit Smith, a gentleman who teetered on the verge of a nonresistance doctrine but who had a reputation for liberality. Gerrit Smith did not furnish the money for the guns and bowie knives, but he did John Brown a better turn than lending him money — indeed, a better turn than giving him money outright. He introduced him to the Abolitionist convention at Syracuse. Then the Peterboro philanthropist read in his fine melifluous voice two letters from John Brown Jr. to such good effect that many eyes in the large assembly were wet with tears at the tale of how the South might " fasten slavery upon this glorious land, by means no matter how foul." After that there came a collection. Some nonresistance people present — honest peace friends, John Brown called them — opposed the idea of contributing arms, but in the end a little over sixty dollars was turned in for the cause of Kansas freedom, twenty dollars of which came from Gerrit Smith himself. " The convention has been one of the most interesting meetings I ever attended in my life," wrote John Brown.

John Brown made up his mind to go with the consignment of arms to Kansas. By August he was among old acquaintances in Akron, but not as a race horse breeder, land speculator, or shepherd. Instead, he got the use of a public hall and held Kansas meetings. People in Akron were generous in their contributions of guns and clothing, and committees were appointed to work the shops in town for further funds and supplies. The State of Ohio unwittingly provided some of the arms from the Akron and Tallmadge militia, and Lucius V. Bierce made a handsome gift of artillery sabres. These sabres already had a history. Mr. Bierce had received the title of " General " as well as the weapons from the " Grand Eagles," a secret society of northern Ohio which once had cherished filibustering designs on the Canadian Government. Now the old swords still bore the device of an eagle on the hilt or blade. Their history was not finished.

At Cleveland, also, there was a rich harvest. In fact, Brown was so successful in his appeals that he determined to remain a day or two longer than his original plan to complete the garnering, and at the end of that time he and his son-in-law, Henry Thompson, proceeded on their way with contributions amounting to two hundred dollars. John Brown Jr. had been right; Eastern people *were* interested in guns for Kansas. When a letter would bring tears it would bring money. Harriet Beecher Stowe knew the trick, for her *Uncle Tom's Cabin* had provided a tidy fortune.

John Brown Jr. advised his father to make the trip with a covered lumber buggy and one horse or mule, for reasons of economy as well as for the service this outfit would later be in surveying. Besides that, the Brown boys were thoroughly disgusted with navigation on the Missouri River, which, they said, was a horrid business with pro-slavery captains and low water.

At Chicago John Brown bought a nice young horse for one hundred and twenty dollars, but their baggage was so heavy and cumbersome that the party looked forward to walking most of the distance to Kansas. They soon left the straggling but already bustling city and struck out across country. Oliver had joined them at Chicago with the idea of trying his own luck in the West with his father and brothers.

Travelling was a slow business. The stout young horse that had promised so well took the distemper, and they had grave fears that he would fail them completely. The three dusty men, with hat brims pulled down over their eyes against the sun, plodded along day after day beside the heavily loaded wagon. Now and then a prairie chicken flew up from the tall brown grass and one of the men would fire. Much water had flowed under the bridges since those early days before the Masonic excitement when John Brown disapproved of guns; he was now a good enough marksman. The heat of summer still lay over the dry prairies during the day, but toward evening when they picketed the horse and made a crude camp there was a chill in the air. They sat close about the small fire and ate the crackers, boiled eggs, fresh prairie chicken, and tea. Sometimes John Brown fumbled in the mass of bundles on the wagon and got out his paper for a letter home. He told the lonely family at North Elba of the trip, the horse's distemper, how Oliver was a good shot at bringing down prairie chickens, and of the dearth of running water in the Iowa country. He commended all of the family to the mercy and infinite grace of God. Then the three travellers slept, wrapped in their blankets against the new cold which presaged the winter. The small fire died down quickly and the coals burned out.

At Waverley, Missouri, the company stopped long enough to take up the body of Jason's little son, Austin, who had died of cholera when the brothers passed through on the way to Kansas. The earlier party had buried the child at night during a thunderstorm, — hurriedly, for an epidemic was in the town and people were terrified. Before they had finished the crude funeral, the steamboat *New Lucy*, on which they were travelling, pulled in its plank and was gone, leaving them to complete the remainder of the journey by land. The bereaved mother was in no state of mind to meet the necessities of pioneering, and Jason talked a little of taking her back to Ohio. But now when John Brown arrived with the body it was a comfort to her, and she stayed.

The arduous trip ended the first week of October. Practically all of the money was spent, and they had only sixty cents in cash among them at the time of arrival. Late on a Saturday night Henry Thompson and Oliver Brown pushed on into the settlement of their relatives, but John Brown was so worn out that he stayed alone in the tent a mile or two back to rest until the next day. They found all the settlement sick or feeble from " fever and ague and chill-fever " except Wealthy and Johnny, John Brown Jr.'s wife and son. The people with Mr. Adair, who had married John Brown's half-sister, were all ailing, for the sickness seemed general. But the Adairs were better housed than the others, who shivered in tents about their miserable little fires, exposed to the dreadful cutting winds at morning and evening and on stormy days. They had postponed the time of putting up their cabins, had lived on low ground in tents all summer, and now they were paying the sure price for their lack of foresight. The only compensation was a good vegetable crop for the summer and the satisfaction of duty well done at the conventions. To add to the trials there was a prairie fire or two which kept the whole settlement up all night to save their slender possessions and made their eyes smart almost to blindness the next day. The Emigrant Aid circulars and Northern newspapers and the clergymen who preached the crusade had omitted some items of Kansas life.

The first Tuesday that John Brown spent at Osawatomie saw the election of Mr. Reeder as the Free State Delegate to Congress. Some trouble was anticipated from the Missourians, and so the Brown family, with the exception of

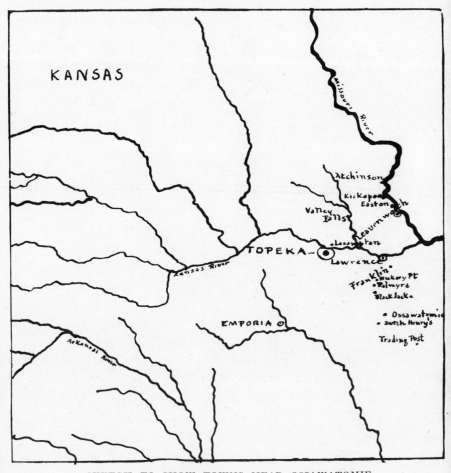

KANSAS

Missouri River

Atchinson

Kickapoo

Easton...th

Valley Falls

Leavenworth

Kansas River

○Lecompton

TOPEKA— ◉

Lawrence ⊕

Franklin○
○Hickory Pt
○Palmyra

Black Jacks

EMPORIA ○

• Ossawatomie
• Dutch Henry's

Trading Post

Arkansas River

SKETCH TO SHOW TOWNS NEAR OSSAWATOMIE

Jason who was too feeble from his ague, turned out thoroughly armed, along with most of the Free State voters. The pro-slavery men of both Kansas and Missouri simply ignored what they considered to be an illegal election, and no chance presented itself to try out the brand new arsenal which had jolted into the Territory in John Brown's wagon. He wrote an optimistic letter to North Elba on the subject: "Indeed, I believe Missouri is fast becoming discouraged about making Kansas a slave state, and I think the prospect of its becoming free is brightening every day. Try to be cheerful, and always 'hope in God,' who will not leave nor forsake them that trust him." The whole comment was merely a sort of footnote to an elaborate account of affairs at "Brownsville." It was not a piece of burning news.

If John Brown had come to Kansas to fight and not to settle, the peaceful end of election day must have found him a little disappointed. Before the end of the month the street of a neighboring town was as bloody as if hogs had been slaughtered there, as the result of a political quarrel, but when John Brown wrote home a week afterwards the concerns he related were those of the settlement. Everybody was still sickly except Wealthy and Johnny, none of the crops had been taken care of, the unfenced corn had been wasted by cattle, no meal was to be gotten except from a little handmill, and Jason's folks had no sugar. They had raised a shanty three logs high, chinked it with mud, and roofed it with the tent. A rough chimney was far enough along to permit a fire for the ailing Jason. Again the letter concluded on a cheerful note for the political future of Kansas: "I feel more and more confident that slavery will soon die out here, . . . and to God be the praise!"

Furthermore, it seems that at some time during his stay

in the Territory, John Brown took out a claim there with the intention of settling. As late as 1857 his friend William A. Phillips wrote him about the matter: "Your old claim has, I believe, been jumped. If you do not desire to contest it, let me suggest that you make a new settlement at some good point, of which you will be the head. Lay off a town and take claims around it." In the old days of the Franklin Land Company such a proposition would have appealed mightily to John Brown. As it was, he still wanted to be head of the heap, but now, in 1857, he had a bigger speculation on his hands than dealing in town lots.

After all, one cannot afford to read the motives that took John Brown to Kansas as being pure and simple. He merely went there with his eyes open. One of his daughters once made a candid remark on the subject: "Father said his object in going to Kansas was to see if something would not turn up to his advantage." A sound reason.

4

THE TIGHT-ROPE ACT

UP near the town of Atchison lived an Irishman by the
name of Patrick Laughlin, who for a while had been
active in one of the secret societies with which the
region abounded. He had been elected as delegate to the
Big Springs Free State convention, and had attended along
with Samuel Collins, the vociferous proprietor of a sawmill at Doniphan. After the convention had finished its business Laughlin returned by way of Lawrence, where G. W.
Brown, editor of the *Herald of Freedom*, exhibited to him
Sharpe's rifles, blue jackets, white trousers, drums, and all
the paraphernalia of freedom. Mr. Brown gave him four
sealed books containing the constitution and ritual of the
grand encampment of the " Kansas Legion," which Laughlin was to administer to Free State sympathizers at his home
of Doniphan and in the country north of that town. Laughlin was also to take statements from Free State men concerning the conduct of elections and Missouri interference;
later he maintained that the men who gave him this information admitted it to be exaggerated. Laughlin did not organize the projected encampments of the " Legion," and
after he suffered this change of heart, his sense of honor

somehow did not impel him to keep the secrets of the brotherhood to which he had belonged.

On the night of October 24 Pat Laughlin went to the office of Dr. Oscar Brown — the Territory seemed full of Browns — to get medicine. Samuel Collins, who had heard of Laughlin's disclosures, dropped in. Collins remarked that a certain James Foreman had given Laughlin a cow to change his politics, and the accused made an appropriate retort. The lie was passed several times. A friend of Collins, James Lynch, tried to smooth matters out and got a threat for his pains. "God damn you, I will kick every rib in you out of you!" Lynch was a sensitive chap and once said that this embarrassed him very much coming from the mouth of a friend. Collins left the office with a promise to Laughlin: "You or I will land in hell before breakfast tomorrow morning." Mr. Lynch overcame his embarrassment and rushed out to get a peace warrant on the fire-eating Collins; he told the constable that the specified time was before breakfast.

The night was cold, with the hardest fall freeze John Brown had ever seen south of Elba, but Laughlin was in the street before breakfast with a bucket of flour on his arm. Collins rushed out from his sawmill, brandishing a double-barrelled shot-gun, and demanded that Laughlin take back a variety of his previously expressed sentiments. "I haven't got anything to take back," said Laughlin, and his adversary aimed at the point-blank range of six yards. The gun clicked. There was a little one-sided knife play, with Laughlin dodging around, dangling his bucket, until Collins stabbed him in the left side. Collins again raised the gun with the idea of finishing his job. This time the gun went off, but Foreman, the alleged donor of the political cow, had knocked down the barrel so that the charge entered the ground at Laughlin's feet. Then Lynch, who had been aroused by the shout that Collins was going to kill everybody in town, fired from a doorway. The shot spattered on a board wall, Collins laid his sensitive friend out with the butt of his shot-gun and charged Laughlin. The victim of Collins' bowie knife now ran no chances. He got his pistol out, took cool aim, and fired. Collins dropped his upraised gun-barrel, and clasped his arms about his chest, crying, " O Lord." He wavered in his tracks for a moment and then sank dying to the ground. Mr. Collins' son clubbed Laughlin. His nephew threw a half-brick at the prostrate Irishman. Laughlin's brother got hold of the pistol, fired at the nephew, and deliberately presented it at the son. Young Collins threw up his hands. " Don't shoot me. He's killed my father! " Laughlin's brother lowered his gun. " The ground was covered with blood," said a witness, " like one had been butchering a hog."

The excitement did not die down quickly. No one took out a warrant for Laughlin, but there were threats of summary justice for both him and Lynch from Free State sympathizers. The house where he lay was guarded, and as soon as possible he was moved over the Missouri line to St. Joseph. The news of the bloody matter must have reached Brownsville before John Brown wrote his letter home on November 2: " I feel more and more confident that slavery will soon die out here, . . . and to God be the praise! " It is interesting to speculate what John Brown's sentiments were in the light of his own Masonic adventure and the murder of William Morgan; it is not at all unlikely that those sentiments were, logically, somewhat inconsistent. In any case the incident became grist for the Free State mill.

The Free State men, however, soon had more pressing business on their hands than talk about the rights of the

Laughlin-Collins affair. As the result of a claim dispute which originated in the cutting of some timber, Franklin M. Coleman, a settler from Virginia, shot Charles Dow. Again the victim was a Free State man. Therein lay the strength of their cause; for a time, at least, they could claim the majority of victims. Coleman, immediately after the shooting near Hickory Point, gave himself up to the Territorial officials with the claim of self-defense, and said that he was willing to bear a judicial investigation and trial. Dow was left to die in the frozen road and his body lay there all day untouched by the neighbors who feared being mixed in the feud. Slavery seems not to have been involved in the trouble, for the region before this incident had not given much attention to the issue.

But the murder became a political quarrel. There was a meeting at the roadside where Dow's body had lain, and the day after his burial another one was held at the house of a Mr. Branson with whom Dow had lived. Coleman's house was burned down as were those of one or two pro-slavery men in the neighborhood. Mrs. Coleman saved what she could and fled to Missouri. Meanwhile, Coleman had seen the officials at Shawnee Mission and was being returned by Sheriff Jones to the place of the crime, but an express met the party and informed them that Coleman, despite the Sheriff's protection and the prospect of a trial, would have short shrift if he came back home. Branson, who once or twice before had threatened Coleman's life, now had a considerable party who shared the idea. For Branson's side of the case it may be said that he later made stout claims of being a very peaceful man.

The night after the indignation meeting at Branson's house there was a hammering at his door. " Who's there? "

called Branson from his bed. "Friends," came the answer and the door was burst open by a party of men. Sheriff Jones cocked his pistol and presented it at the breast of the man who sat on the bed's edge clad only in his shirt. "You are my prisoner, and if you move I'll blow you through." They let him put on his pants, and then mounted him on a mule which had belonged to Coleman. After a while the prisoner asked Jones what great crime he had committed that it required such a large posse to bring an old man in. "Nothing much," answered Jones, "only I've got a peace warrant or two against you. These men that came along with me expected to have a little fun; we heard that there were around a hundred men at your house today, and we hoped to find them there tonight. We wanted a little sport out of them." The party rode on through the clear moonlight night. Once or twice they stopped to take whisky against the raw cold.

When they came within a half-mile of Blanton's bridge, which crossed the Wakarusa, some men ran out from behind a house and blocked the road. When they were within speaking distance Jones called: "What's up?" "What's up! That's what we want to know. What's up?" News had travelled fast; it was a body of Free State men who blocked the road. Branson recognized them and said, "They've got me here a prisoner." "Come on over here if you want to be among your friends," was the invitation from the rescuers. Branson rode over, dismounted from his mule, and asked what he should do with the beast; he had scruples about some one else's property. "Let it go to hell," some Free State man advised and booted it back to Jones. Guns were up on both sides, but one of the posse spoiled the fight. "I ain't going to shoot," the fellow remarked tentatively and uncocked his weapon. Sheriff Jones retired upon his dignity and introduced himself as the chief officer of Douglas County, Kansas. " We don't know any Sheriff Jones. There's a postmaster Jones over at Westport, Missouri, but he ain't a sheriff. We haven't got any Douglas County in Kansas, and what's more, we don't intend to have." There was nothing Jones could do about it, and Branson got away. Indeed, Sheriff Jones of Douglas County was also Postmaster Jones of Westport, Missouri. He filled both offices with bluster, vindictiveness, enthusiasm, and courage.

Branson was conducted to Lawrence where the pleasure at his release was somewhat tempered by belief that the incident was not closed. A public meeting was called and committees were appointed to direct the defense of the town if such should be necessary. Resolutions applauding the rescue were wisely rejected. The people of Lawrence might just as well have not strained at the gnat of putting their sentiments on paper, for the self-control did them no great good. As soon as Sheriff Jones could find pen and ink after leaving Blanton's bridge he wrote two letters; the first of these was to Missouri and the second to Governor Shannon. He had been resisted in the performance of his duty and he demanded men enough to serve his warrants. The people of Lawrence were correct in their fear, for the sheriff's idea of his duty was now a march on the town.

When Governor Shannon received the letter from Jones he ordered General Strickler and Major General Richardson to supply the sheriff with the force he required. Jones had been modest about his personal resources; he said that he needed three thousand backers. The day after issuing these orders, the Governor wrote to President Pierce.

The Tight-Rope Act

Executive Office, Shawnee Mission,
Kansas Territory, November 28th, 1855.

Sir:

Affairs in this Territory are daily assuming a shape of great danger to the peace and good order of society. I am well satisfied that there exists in this Territory a secret military organization, which has for its object, among other things, resistance to the laws by force. Until within a few days past I have looked upon the threats of leading men and public papers, who have placed themselves in an attitude of resistance to the laws, as not intended by those who made them to be carried into execution. I am now satisfied of the existence of this secret military organization, and that those engaged in it have been secretly supplied with arms and munitions of war, and that it is the object and purpose of this organization to resist the laws by force. The strength of the organization is variously estimated at from one to two thousand, but I have no satisfactory data from which to estimate its real strength, and I do not believe they can command for any given purpose more than one thousand men. They are said to be well supplied with Sharp's rifles and revolvers, and that they are bound with an oath to assist each other in the resistance of the laws when called upon to do so.

Then the Governor outlined the incident of Dow's murder and the Branson rescue. To him it was nothing short of anarchy, for Jones' report was taken as the gospel. He proceeded with a description of matters along the border.

This military organization is looked upon as hostile to all Southern men, or rather to the law-and-order party of the Territory, many of whom have relations and friends, and all have sympathizers, in Missouri; and the moment it is believed the laws will not furnish adequate protection to this class of citizens against the lawless acts of this armed association, a force will be precipitated across the line to redress real and supposed wrongs, inflicted on friends, that cannot be controlled, or, for the moment, resisted. It is vain to conceal the fact; we are standing on a volcano; the upheavings and agitations beneath, we feel, and no one can tell the hour when an eruption may take place.

Such was Governor Shannon's side of the story. To him the Southern men were the sufferers and those who needed defense. They had proclaimed themselves the law-and-order party and the officials accepted the definition. Coleman's surrender to the authorities turned out to be a tactical triumph and the rescue of Branson a tactical disaster. The public repudiation of the rescue did Lawrence no great good, for the Missourians were being mobilized and Jones had his army at his back.

In wagons decorated with their whisky bottles on sticks and the insignia of their lodges, on horseback and on foot, the enormous posse began to gather at Franklin and along the Wakarusa. They were a hardy lot: lean, slouching, athletic, drawling in speech, and quick on the draw. At night they unlaced their boots, took the eternal bowie knife from the boot-top, and sat around their camp-fires, passing the brown Missouri jug full of corn whisky. When the jug was empty they unbuttoned the tops of the dirty red or grey flannel shirts, loosened the buckles of their broad leather belts, and, with a casual curse or two at the Abolitionists or the sharp fall night, dropped off to sleep. Altogether these were jubilant and rather savage camps; there was little pretense of discipline or military regulations. Sometimes a company drew up in ragged parade to execute a few formations, and the roads were patrolled by guards both day and night, but the gathering was little better than a great mob, unruly, truculent, and barely under the control of its leaders. Some desultory pillaging occurred, chiefly for provender for the horses and mules, and a few travellers, who couldn't give the right answer as to how they were on the goose, got scared out of their wits and rushed into Lawrence to spur the inhabitants on with the drilling and preparations for defense.

A Committee of Safety had been appointed in the town and the able-bodied inhabitants were organized in a regular regiment. They were not left to themselves, for men from outlying villages and the country came in with their Sharpe's rifles and shotguns. A hundred citizens of Topeka, where the constitution had been drawn up, marched to Lawrence and were received with great applause. Leavenworth sent a conservative contingent, who at first felt that the action of Lawrence was jeopardizing the entire Free State cause, but who in the end decided to stay and see the show through. One of the Leavenworth men, who had been to Lecompton, brought the news that Shannon was going to demand the surrender of all the " Beecher's Bibles " as illegal weapons. It seems that he was informed by Dr. Robinson that, in such a case, another " Missouri Compromise " would be in order; namely, to keep the rifles and surrender the contents. After the military organization was completed the Committee was replaced by a council of officers, with Lane at the head to act under the supreme command of Dr. Robinson. Lane still had his eye to the main chance, with little scruple as to what it might be. Breastworks were thrown up here and there and scouts kept out to watch the movements of the posse. " They have some ridiculous earthworks at Lawrence which I could ride my horse over," was the way an army officer of the Territory once judged the means of defense. No horses, however, were ridden over them.

The chief dependence of the Free State men was not in their earthworks or regiment. They felt that their moral position was unassailable, for when Jones or the Governor would make the demand to serve warrants, those gentlemen would be received in the town only to find that no culprits were present. It was the supreme test of their ability to continue the tight-rope walking over a dilemma; neither Jones nor Shannon would have any reason to employ the United States troops, and that fatal collision, with its treasonable consequences, would be avoided. The joke would then be on the Sheriff and Governor, who had called out a thousand men to execute a few warrants only to meet with no resistance when the army arrived. However, the Free State men had no idea of giving up their right as individuals to bear arms, especially with the Missourians in the neighborhood. They were convinced that there was double-dealing in the gubernatorial office when news of such things as the following letter from Shannon's assistant fell into their hands.

Hon. E. A. McClarey, Jefferson City:
Governor Shannon has ordered out the militia against Lawrence. They are now in open rebellion against the laws. Jones is in danger.
(Private.) Dear General: The Governor has called out the militia, and you will hereby organize your division, and proceed forthwith to Lecompton. As the Governor has no power, you may call out the Platte Rifle Company. They are always ready to help us. Whatever you do, do not implicate the Governor.
DANIEL WOODSON.

Mr. Woodson later maintained that the letter was a forgery. All in all the men of Lawrence were willing to abide an appeal to the nation at large if the issue should be forced, and their trust was in God and their technical moral position. This was taking a somewhat unfair advantage of the poor Missourians, who didn't pretend to know much about God or moral positions. But Lawrence also had its Sharpe's rifles.

During those days Sheriff Jones passed through the town on several occasions without any molestation from the citizens except a question as to his intentions. " I'll let you know when I get ready," was his reply. Finally two young men were sent as ambassadors to Governor Shannon, to righteously demand an explanation of the excitement along the Wakarusa. Furthermore, they stated that Lawrence had no official part in the Branson rescue, that the reports of house burning and persecution of pro-slavery men were exaggerated, and that if the Missourians got loose the innocent and guilty would have their throats cut together. They denied that the issue of the legality of the Territorial Legislature had anything to do with the present Lawrence situation, and in the end suggested that if Shannon had any idea of asking for a surrender of the Sharpe's rifles as terms for a settlement he had best stay out of Lawrence. " They are unlawful and dangerous weapons," insisted the Governor. One of the ambassadors agreed: " Yes sir, they are dangerous weapons."

The Governor had his eyes opened to some facts; the chief of these was that the Free State men were adepts at their tight-rope walking stunt. He immediately repaired to the posse headquarters where another problem greeted him. The Missourians were restive and anxious to see the action for which they had come. Shannon wrote to Colonel Sumner and asked for United States troops to get matters arranged in a peaceable way, for he now saw that if an agreement was made with Lawrence the Missourians would probably take things into their own hands. " It is peace, not war, that we want," he wrote to the Colonel, " and you have the power to secure peace." Sumner declined that gracious office on the grounds that he had received no orders from Washington, and the Governor was left to his own devices. Shannon now desperately wanted to patch matters up.

JOHN BROWN

On December 6, when the Wakarusa region had already been in a hubbub for more than ten days, John Brown and his sons received a call to join the defenders at Lawrence. They immediately set about providing themselves for the campaign by baking some cornbread and meat, getting blankets and pots together, running bullets, and loading all the rifles and pistols. John's camp was broken up and Wealthy and her son were taken over to Jason's place some two miles off. Henry, Jason, and Oliver were too feeble to go along and these were left to manage affairs at Brownsville. The remaining five men set out in the afternoon, marched most of the night with only a little rest, and reached Lawrence before dinner time the next morning.

At the time of their arrival peace negotiations with Governor Shannon were under way, but the people of Lawrence were taking no chances and still busied themselves by fortifying the town with more embankments and circular earthworks. Even if an agreement could be reached with Shannon, it was far from improbable that the black flag would be hoisted in one of the Wakarusa camps and the assault on the town executed. Further excitement was created by the news that Thomas Barber, a Free State man, had been shot down on the road from Lawrence by the beseigers. Two gentlemen claimed the honor of firing the fatal shot — a Major Clark and a Mr. Burns. " Another damned Abolitionist to his winter quarters."

John Brown's arrival at Lawrence with his contingent got mentioned in the Lawrence *Herald of Freedom*; its item was to the effect that on December 7, " Mr. John Brown, an aged gentleman from Essex County, N. Y." had come to town. Furthermore, the aged gentleman from Essex County acquired the title of Captain and his company got the name

of the " Liberty Guards." It was a highly organized body;
there were three lieutenants, four sergeants, four corporals,
and eight privates. And John Brown was the belted Captain
over them all. Something had turned up to his advantage
in Kansas.

After unsatisfactory communications back and forth Governor Shannon signified willingness to descend from his dignity and come himself to Lawrence if a fitting escort could be
provided. The Governor was conducted to the unfinished
Free State Hotel, a large stone building, which the pro-
slavery men referred to as a fort. It was one of their pre-
texts for legalizing the attack on the town. The council
rooms were on an upper floor, and the eminent visitor was
invited to ascend. At the top, stretched on a rough wooden
bench, lay the body of Barber, dressed as when he fell from
his horse with the disputed slugs in his thigh. The Governor
heard the cries of the widow from a room nearby. The man's
open eyes seemed to gaze down the crowded stairway with
that deliberate questioning expression of the dead. John
Brown was also to meet those eyes as he climbed the stair.
" One of the sure results of civil war," was the moral he drew
from the sight; Shannon did not state his.

The Governor was willing to take the Free State protestations at their face value. His only solicitude now, with
the fresh remembrance of the dead eyes staring into his own,
was to disperse the posse without more shedding of blood.
He did not maintain that it was his right to disarm the
people of Lawrence, but he was sure that this was the least demand the Missourians would make before a peaceable retreat. Dr. Robinson's revised idea of the " Missouri Compromise " was carefully explained to him; they would keep the
Sharpe's rifles and surrender the contents upon demand. The

poor fellow was indeed at a loss, but he still hoped to hear from Colonel Sumner that United States troops would arrive to insure peace. The conference was adjourned until the next day, and each party was to prepare a statement of the case which might reconcile the restive invaders to return across their line with all their vows unfulfilled.

The cold autumn morning brought no Colonel Sumner. That officer had not received orders from the government to interfere in the Lawrence affair, and Shannon's appeal for a Roman peace-maker did not move him. It was a long way to Washington. Jefferson Davis was head of the War Department, and some have suggested that he desired nothing more than an open fight and the destruction of Lawrence; this explanation, perhaps, is a little unkind to the very able Secretary. In any case the solution was left to the diplomatic powers of Shannon and the gentlemen of Lawrence.

Shannon wanted to save his face and to get peace; the Free State men were willing to indulge the former desire if it would secure the latter. The treaty which Shannon, Robinson, and Lane signed was a fine piece of casuistry to serve both ends. The Wakarusa war was politely referred to as a " misunderstanding between the people of Kansas and the Governor thereof." The men at Lawrence agreed to give their help in serving any legal writs in the vicinity, and the Governor was to use his influence in getting damage money for any depredations the Jones people might have committed. There was one issue on which Dr. Robinson and his party wanted no casuistry. The last sentence of the agreement read: " That we wish it understood that we do not herein express any opinion as to the validity of the enactments of the Territorial Legislature."

It was all very fine on paper, with the three impressive signatures at the bottom of the sheet. Only the Missourians and perhaps the people of Lawrence remained to be satisfied. The three diplomats saddled their horses and rode to the pro-slavery stronghold at Franklin, where they were met by the militia captains from across the line. Governor Shannon made his speech in the cause of justice, justice to Lawrence, and was received with some apathetic grumbling, but when Colonel Lane rose and began, the grumbling became disorder. The thirteen captains of militia were on their feet; they hadn't come to be insulted. All of the anxious Governor's solicitude for peace and Dr. Robinson's tact were needed to put them back in their seats. Dr. Robinson explained the impregnable moral position of Lawrence; no officer of any kind had ever attempted to execute a writ in the town. " Jones," one of the council called out," is that fellow telling the truth? " " Yes, he's telling the truth," answered Jones. " Then we have been damnably deceived! " And so they had.

In Lawrence there was speech making. Colonel Lane assured the defenders that there was no concession of honor. There was a considerable amount of relief and hard drinking, and Governor Shannon was probably as much relieved and as tipsy as anyone else. After nightfall the news was brought to him that the militia which he had formally disbanded were hoisting the feared black flag and marching on Lawrence. A paper was put before him and he signed it.

To Charles Robinson and J. H. Lane:
You are hereby authorized and directed to take such measures, and use the enrolled forces under your command in such manner, for the preservation of the peace and the protection of

121

the persons and property of the people of Lawrence and vicinity, as in your judgment shall best secure that end.

Lawrence, December 9, 1855.   WILSON SHANNON

The Doctor and the Colonel picked up the paper with pardonable satisfaction; their position was now legally as well as morally impregnable. When the excitment, fumes of whisky, and the tobacco smoke had cleared away, the amiable Governor felt that his trusting nature had been imposed upon rather ungratefully, for the news of the attack turned out to be quite false. Charles Robinson and J. H. Lane, he intimated, were not gentlemen.

There were more speeches the next day. Reflecting on the pleasant document obtained the evening before, Dr. Robinson could again say: " the moral strength of our position is such that even the ' gates of hell ' could not prevail against us, much less a foreign mob and we gained a bloodless victory." He got six cheers in approval of those sentiments. But there were some in no mood for cheering. The aged gentleman from Essex County, New York, climbed the shaky platform and began speaking before the cheers had died down. " Lawrence is betrayed," he insisted. " I am an abolitionist — dyed in the wool. I'll be one of ten men to go out and attack that Border Ruffian camp at night." The ten men were to take lanterns, place themselves around the invader's camp, and, just before the hour of dawn, shout with all their might and fire on the sleeping tyrants. Gideon would have blushed for shame. It is really too bad from the standpoint of melodrama that John Brown did not climb the shaky platform and did not call for his ten heroes to go with him into the night with their Sharpe's rifles and smoky lanterns, but the whole story simply shows how the

Old Testament can give rise to vulgar errors in modern history. But the fact that John Brown did not so distinguish himself is evidence of his good sense. What he probably did was to grumble about the camp before he knew the terms of the treaty, and in any case no one of prominence heard or heeded his blood-thirsty advice.

What the family at North Elba learned about John Brown's feeling on the subject of the treaty and the bloodless victory is clear enough, and if he grumbled in camp he changed his mind very soon. The first Sunday evening back at Brownsville he sat down in the unfinished cabin to write to his " dear wife and children, every one."

So ended this last Kansas invasion — the Missourians returning with *flying colors*, after incurring heavy expenses, suffering great exposure, hardships, and privations, not having fought any battles, burned or destroyed any infant towns or Abolition presses; leaving the Free State men organized and armed, and in full possession of the Territory; not having fulfilled any of all their dreadful threatenings, except to murder one *unarmed* man, and to commit some robberies and waste of property upon defenseless families, unfortunately within their power. We learn by their papers that they boast of a great victory over the Abolitionists; and well they may. Free-State men have only hereafter to retain the footing they have gained, and *Kansas is free*.

So the aged gentleman from Essex County put himself on record as being very well pleased with the treaty after all.

The autumn had been mild, as if to let the men who played at war along the Wakarusa tire themselves out. The delayed winter burst suddenly. Stinging cold came down on the Missourians as they retreated into their own country. The muddy streets of Lawrence froze over. Wind swept the open prairies and stripped the cottonwoods by the ravines

and along the creeks. At Brownsville near the Pottawatomie
the people huddled in their unfinished cabins around their
slow fires, while the snow drifted about the walls. Miles away
at Lawrence the snow drifted over the grave of Thomas
Barber, where his body had been buried with fine words by
Dr. Robinson, and salutes of the militia, in a sort of awkward
rural pomp.

5

JONES GETS SLAPPED

JOHN BROWN had come to Kansas to bring arms to his sons and to help use them if there happened to be need. He had also come to see if something would not turn up to his advantage. He hated slavery and he had to live. What was it the rich Mr. Thayer, member of the Massachusetts Legislature, had said? When a man does a benevolent deed and makes money at the same time it only shows that his faculties are working in harmony. The faculties of old man Brown of Osawatomie were not working in harmony. He had marched off to benevolently strike a blow for Lawrence and freedom, and had marched back after the bloodless victory with boot soles a little thinner and only the fine title — Captain of the Liberty Guards — by way of reward. The dignity of those words — Captain of the Liberty Guards — didn't chink the cabins, or get corn, or pay for leather to mend boots, when there was ice in the river, in the timber, and under the snow eighteen inches thick, or when the level blizzard wind off the prairies drove the snow like dry sand and whipped the smoke back down the unfinished chimney to scatter sparks and burning ash over the rude hearth. The only aid came from the sale of the stout young horse and the wagon that had lumbered into Kansas bringing the guns and camp pots and blankets and parcels during the preceding autumn.

The hopes of some advantage that might turn up at the end of that long march across the prairies now seemed buried and lost under the dry blizzard-driven snow of Kansas. John Brown could endure hard times. Only once or twice had he been prosperous: in the days of the Franklin Land Company and later when the rich Simon Perkins was his partner. Those speculations had gone to pot, leaving debts and lawsuits and threats of prosecution. He and his family had tried each time to regain their fortune by pioneering in some new region — in Ohio, at Richmond, at North Elba — and each time he had come out just a little poorer, and a little older, from that hard speculation with crops, drouths, storm, and disease. Nature had been as perfidious as the Canal Company, or Mr. Chamberlain, or the New England Woolen Mills. A little older. Pride at seeing his name in print, when the Lawrence *Herald of Freedom* mentioned the arrival of his party, must have been tempered by another feeling. " An aged gentleman from Essex County," that paper had called him. And the neighbors spoke of him as Old Brown. The former erectness was gone. His hair was greying, and the lines about the compressed mouth and small knitted brow seemed to suggest something besides power of will. At night when he sat in silent abstraction close to the fire, those lines suggested more than a little the marks of age. He was fifty-five years old and those years had been strenuous ones. When the winter was over and spring came it would bring another birthday. In May, in the May of 1856, he would be fifty-six years old.

It was not only the hard winter, the running out of the corn, and disease among his sons that confronted John

Brown. Off at North Elba his wife was having a bad time of it, trying to keep body and soul together and provide for the children there with her. The raw-boned, silent girl, who had left the spinning in John Brown's house to take up the more arduous business of being his helpmate, was now a woman, worn by the hard experiences of her life, still awkward, still ignorant, but competent and stoic. She didn't write for help to the husband, who was having " middling tough times " in Kansas; after all, he had nothing to send her. He could try to strike a five-dollar bargain with Henry Thompson who had come to Kansas, for his wife's use of the " line-backed cow " at North Elba, and he could write letters to Mr. Hurlbut in Connecticut about the cattle business, or give advice to Watson about boarding the house for winter, but that was all. It was not quite all: he could end the letters to North Elba with the words: " May God abundantly bless you all, and make you faithful," or: " I hope you will all be led to seek God ' with your whole heart '; and I pray him, in his mercy, to be found of you."

The future for him was shrouded in doubt and uncertainty. The Free State men might have only to hold what they had gained, as John Brown said after the retreat from Lawrence, but the free soil of Kansas during those months did not seem so ready to repay the effort and expense of making it so. In February John Brown had no plans. A letter to Mary Day Brown mentioned a return to North Elba as only the possibility of some remote future. " The idea of again visiting those of my dear family at North Elba is so calculated to unman me, that I seldom allow my thoughts to dwell upon it, and I do not think best to write much about it; suffice it to say, that God is *abundantly* able to keep both us and you, and in him let us trust." So it seemed that he was to stay in Kansas, trust in God, and keep an eye open for the main chance. He trusted in a very simple God who had some great and perfect plan, who finally smote those who did not fear Him and scourged those whom he loved, but who might yet give very material blessings to the man with faith and a sense of opportunity. It was a question of patience, a question of fearing God and waiting and at the same time remembering the Yankee saw that God helps those who help themselves. And John Brown had passed through experiences which would teach patience; he had almost learned the lesson well. He could wait for a long time and possess his soul, but when the game was just in his hand that tremendous energy, that immediate restless will would assert themselves, and he would overreach the end. He could endure hardness and waiting in the lean times, even if every failure and slight of circumstance ate deep into his pride, and emerge more resolute and more secretive, with a greater faith in God and in himself. The man, John Brown, once wrote of the boy, " John ": " He followed up with *tenacity* whatever he set about so long as it answered his general purpose: & hence he rarely failed in some good degree to effect the things he undertook. This was so much the case that he *habitually expected to succeed* in his undertakings. With this feeling *should be coupled;* the consciousness that our plans are right in themselves." When he wrote this he had left Kansas and was on the crest of his fortune; he was received with honor in rich men's houses, his words were listened to with great respect, and affairs were ripening to the one big *coup* which would obscure the shabby past. He could afford to forget that past; he was about to be vindicated. Tenacity, self-confidence, right: it was another way of saying that his faculties were in harmony at last.

It was always the one big *coup* that he wanted — a stake that would wipe out all the miserable score of the past at a single sweep. But that was very far away during this winter in the Kansas cabin. He was no longer a young man with great possibilities before him; those possibilities were narrowing down, one by one, with every day that passed. Old Brown, the people in the section called him; it was half a term of respect for greater experience and courage and sagacity, but it also carried a little of that tolerant contempt with which the world greets the old. The people with him were the children, now full-grown men, whom, in the new house at Hudson or in the poorer dwelling at Richmond, he had held in his lap while he sang the big hymns such as "With songs and honors sounding loud," which seemed to foreshadow the day when he would win his own throw and be head of the heap. The case was now desperate, and the opening of spring would bring the necessity for decision.

Spring might also bring the Missourians again as soon as high water from the melting snow had gone down. John Brown didn't regard that as calamity; it would at least be action and would give him scope for doing something he thought he knew better than most how to do. "Aim low and keep your eye on the hind sight." Shooting a Sharpe's rifle in behalf of human liberty was efficient benevolence and gave one the consciousness of being in the right; it might also bring its collateral rewards in more tangible terms. And John Brown wrote home about the possibility of political disturbance in place of spring plowing with something near complacency.

We have just learned of some new and shocking outrages at Leavenworth, and that the Free-State people there have fled to Lawrence, which place is again threatened with an attack.

Should that take place, we may soon again be called upon to
" buckle on our armor," which by the help of God we will do, —
when I suppose Henry and Oliver will have a chance. My judgment is, that we shall have no general disturbance until warmer
weather.

The severe weather that prevailed during the winter sufficed to keep off the Missourians, but it did not put an end
to trouble in the Territory itself. The Topeka Free State
constitution had been adopted in December, and in January
its election machinery began to work. On the seventeenth
of the month an election was held at Easton. There was some
rumor that the Kickapoo Rangers, a volunteer company of
pro-slavery temper, intended to break up the proceedings,
and R. P. Brown of Leavenworth brought in a wagonload
of Free State champions, armed to the teeth. The voting
took place in the big room of Mr. Minard's house, which
stood some little way up the frozen, snow-covered road from
Dawson's grocery, where a few pro-slavery men of the neighborhood were spending the day in conversation and drink.
It was terribly cold, and up at Minard's house more than
fifty voters were lacing themselves with whisky against the
weather, for those who came to vote spent the day in order to
defend the ballot-box if occasion arose. Naturally enough the
conversation in the grocery began to turn on the subject of
the impertinent Free State election which meant an armed
invasion of the town, and the talk at Minard's was more than
a little concerned with the gang of cutthroats and Border
Ruffians who most certainly were lurking at the grocery until
they were drunk enough to make a try for the ballot-box.

Just as the early, winter darkness was beginning to fall,
R. P. Brown with two companions walked down to Dawson's
and stopped in the road before the grocery. A Dr. Motter,

desirous of preventing any trouble, went out to him and said: " Mr. Brown, I think it would be advisable for you to return with your men." " By God," answered Brown, " you think I am not armed. My men have sixty-eight shot ready to fire and I've got sixteen on myself." He tore open his coat and Dr. Motter had a look at the pistols. " That makes no difference to me," said the doctor, and walked away. Later in the evening a party of the men from the grocery rode the quarter of a mile to Minard's and stopped some hundred yards from his house. The defenders ran out and arranged themselves in line for the fight which didn't come off. Both sides were getting drunker and aching for trouble. By nine o'clock Brown was ready to assert himself again, and so took fifteen of his companions down to the grocery to get a jug of liquor and a fiddle; the voters were obviously going to make a night of it. He fulfilled his errand without any difficulty beyond hard language passed on both sides.

After Brown's men returned from the grocery the remainder of the evening went by peacefully enough, with only a few insulting messages sent back and forth between the two strongholds. Big talk was a Kansas habit; in a new country men have a tacit agreement to bluster in order to reassure themselves that man is important after all. But by two in the morning things seemed quiet and Stephen Sparks, a legislator elect, started home with his son and nephew. They passed the grocery where the pro-slavery men were still keeping their late hilarity alive. Somebody saw them and called out: " There goes old man Sparks with his rifle on his shoulder," and immediately ten or a dozen of the loiterers by Dawson's fire jumped up and ran out after Sparks, hallooing for him to stop. The old fellow kept tramping doggedly on through the snow, in the moonlight; the boys stayed close to his side. In the corner of a rail fence beside a lane they were brought to bay. Perhaps the mob didn't intend much more than some drunken heckling. When Sparks belligerently answered the rough invitation to come in and drink with them, that invitation was replaced with a command to surrender his gun. Much debate followed, with Dr. Motter on a stump urging that since Mr. Sparks had gotten so far on his way home they should let him continue, and that it would look bad to commit any violence on him. The mob didn't quite comprehend Dr. Motter's logic.

But the matter was taken beyond the mob's generosity. R. P. Brown appeared at the head of the lane with a cocked double-barrelled gun in his hand and men at his back. Mr. Brown came immediately to the point: " You God-damned lousy niggardly pro-slavery sons-of-bitches, we demand old man Sparks." Sparks came out to them, and shook the leader's hand with considerable relief. Brown then ordered the pro-slavery men to march ahead up the lane. They flatly refused to do it; they had no idea of turning their backs on fifteen men who had guns, liquor, and short tempers. And so the two irregular gangs straggled together up the lane to the point where the road branched to Dawson's grocery. There they separated. The inevitable happened. A shot was fired — by whom no one knew — and every man jumped for cover. A fast exchange was kept up for some ten minutes, but the bright moonlight glittering on the gun-barrels made it hard to take aim. Brown's men retreated toward Minard's. Before they went in they could see the men at the grocery congregating about one spot, but at the distance it was impossible to discover the cause. They themselves had one casualty; the son of old man Sparks had suffered two slight wounds.

Jones Gets Slapped

By nine o'clock the next morning Brown's men were loaded into the wagon, a little sleepy and cold, but well pleased with their behavior of the day before. They had easily gotten the best of the affair, defended their ballot-box, elected their candidates, rescued old man Sparks, and fought a smart skirmish, with only a scratch or two for the company. During the night news had come that added, perhaps, to their general contentment; at least one fellow at the grocery was mortally wounded or dead. They jolted on to the juncture of the Kickapoo and Fort Kearney roads, where they would turn off.

Over the brow of a hill, up which their mules were walking, appeared a party of men in two wagons. The strangers ran their teams down the rough road from the hill-top with a great clattering. They drove past Brown's wagon, and stopped beyond down the grade, where one division of the party turned and came back to intercept the men bound for Leavenworth. One of the men in the wagon called to Brown: " How do you do, gentlemen? Is the difficulty at Easton over? Tell us the news." There was no answer, for Brown silenced his people with a motion of his hand; they were in a tight place and knew it. If the strangers took them for pro-slavery people, such wouldn't be long the case. Jareau, the French driver, kept the team plodding up the grade. " Gentlemen, won't you tell us the news? We have started to Easton and if there isn't any difficulty at Easton we want to go back home." Again Brown commanded his men to silence with a wave of his hand. " They are a set of Abolitionists and won't give a man an answer when he asks them in that gentlemanly kind of style." That idea started the men in the two wagons clamoring. Somebody called out the question as to how they were on the goose. " It's no time to answer such

133

questions," was the reply from one of Brown's men. That settled the matter. The strangers got out of their wagons and began to close in. Brown and his people climbed down and stood in pretty good order, shoulder to shoulder, with their backs to the wagon. The attackers kept their distance, while the whole group moved slowly to the top of the knoll. Jareau stayed in his seat and held the team to a slow walk. At the top of the rise they knew the game was up. Just below, blocking the road, was another party of mounted men.

Brown surrendered. " We want to be treated as prisoners," he said; " none of your Kickapoo Rangers' treatment." Captain Martin promised to do what he could to keep his men in order. They were not the Kickapoo Rangers — just some private citizens riding over to Easton to investigate the rumor that Free State voters had killed a man there. Some of them were already drunk. A brutal fellow named Gibson was waving his hatchet about and threatening murder; Captain Martin had some difficulty in beating him back into obedience. But even among the soberest there was talk of hanging if they could fix on the man who had shot Cook at Easton. Brown's men were put in two wagons, and Martin ordered a few of the sober and more discreet captors to ride with them to prevent some random shot into the groups of prisoners.

The conclusion could have been predicted. The prisoners themselves, during the cold ride for the six or seven miles back to Easton, must have foreseen it clearly. They were herded into Dawson's grocery, and Brown was singled out for a sort of mock trial. The Kickapoo men got drunker and drunker, and Dawson sold them a coil of rope as well as liquor. Captain Martin and a number of the more decent members of his party tried to save the prisoners and carry them to the Territorial authorities for a proper trial. The best they could do was to let all except Brown escape just as darkness was beginning to fall. Only the teamster, Jareau, waited faithfully for his employer, who was still in the grocery, with bound arms, waiting for his captors to make up their minds.

Martin gave up in disgust. The men were not the Kickapoo Rangers and he had no authority over them. Brown himself told Martin that if they killed him his blood would not be on Martin's head. With that comforting reflection, Martin left the grocery. "If any of these drunken sons-of-bitches want to stay, let them stay." Most of them stayed to see Brown and Gibson carried outdoors and made to fight, to see Brown knocked down while the crowd cheered, and to see him struck on the temple with Gibson's hatchet.

A sort of quietness fell over the party after they saw the lath-hatchet flash in the moonlight. Justice — the justice they had ridden so far to see — was done. They loaded their victim into the wagon and wrapped him in a blanket. At Hefness' store, a little way out of Easton, they stopped. One of them went up to the wounded man. "Brown, how do you feel? Are you badly hurt?" "I think I am not very badly hurt, but I am very cold." "Here, take my buffalo-robe," said the questioner. "I've already got a blanket over me; you'll get cold yourself," was Brown's reply. The fellow insisted. "No, no," Brown repeated, "you need it." Perhaps he knew that a buffalo-robe would do no good; he died a little while after some of the men laid him on the floor of his own house. Back at Easton, Cook was dying of the bullet wounds received the night before when Brown's people fired their volley toward the grocery.

It was a miserable business. A tooth for a tooth, an eye

for an eye. "They killed one of the pro-slavery men, and
the pro-slavery men killed one of the others, and I thought it
was about mutual," an eye-witness told the politicians who,
six months later, came to investigate Kansas affairs. What
did Calhoun sitting in his last Senate, or Garrison burning
the Constitution, or Webster speaking at Syracuse know of
this sort of thing? That generation-long debate between two
orders of living, two sets of ideas, two philosophies, was find-
ing strange and brutal repercussions along the frontier
country, where men needed peace and all their energies to
dig in and live before the harshness of nature. The issues and
ideals which to Calhoun, to Garrison, to Webster, were so
passionately clear, were very vague here, but what they
lacked in clarity was made up for by violence and savagery.
Perhaps it is the Gibsons, the R. P. Browns, the Collins', and
the Sheriff Jones' who, after all, must settle such issues. It
is not a happy thought. But the end, in Kansas and in the
nation, was not yet. Over at Osawatomie was old John Brown,
wondering what the spring would bring.

After the affair at Easton many people in the Territory
feared trouble on a large scale. They were not as sure as
John Brown that peace would prevail until the spring had
come and the water subsided. In Lawrence there was great
apprehension, for another attack was expected. Their only
comfort was from a letter in which Eli Thayer described a
new gun he was having made for use in Kansas. It was a
breech-loading affair, with a bore of about an inch and
a half, and would carry two or three miles as accurately as a
rifle at short range. The letter had a very cheering effect.
If Missouri was active, so was Massachusetts. Massachusetts
was a trifle more subtle; furthermore, it had a better idea of
the value of mechanism, advertising, and principle.

JONES GETS SLAPPED

Greater than the fear of trouble from over the line was the fear of Franklin Pierce. The Free State men in Kansas felt that the Government was against them, and they were not so confident that at the next crisis they could keep from involving themselves with the United States troops. Shannon was in Washington, where he had gone to explain himself and the Wakarusa war. Conflicting rumors and newspaper reports carried the excitement over the Government's attitude to a pitch of extreme excitement. President Pierce issued a proclamation on the eleventh of February which was intended to allay the agitation and put an end to movements in other sections to interfere in Kansas affairs. All persons in the Territory " engaged in unlawful combinations *against the constituted authority of the Territory of Kansas, or of the United States,*" were commanded to disperse peaceably to their respective abodes and the United States troops were pledged to effect this or repel any foreign interference. Shannon got the power he had so desperately wanted in December — that of calling out the United States troops.

John Brown, among others, was cynical about the good faith behind such a proclamation. In March, after the Free State government had met for the first time, and after a committee had been appointed at Washington to investigate Kansas affairs, John Brown received a letter from Mr. Giddings of Ohio.

HALL OF REPRESENTATIVES, U. S.,
March 17, 1856.

MY DEAR SIR:

We shall do all we can, but we are in a minority, and are dependent on the " Know-Nothings " for aid to effect anything, and they are in a very doubtful position; we know not how they will act. All I can say is, we shall try to relieve you. In the meantime you need have no fear of the troops. The President never

137

will *dare* employ the troops of the United States to shoot the citizens of Kansas. The death of the first man by the troops will involve every free State in your own fate. *It will light up the fires of civil war throughout the North, and we shall stand or fall with you.* Such an act will also bring the President so deep in infamy that the hand of political resurrection will never reach him. Your safety depends on the supply of men and arms and money which will move forward to your relief as soon as the spring opens. I am confident there will be as many people in Kansas next winter as can be supplied with provisions. I may be mistaken, but I feel confident there will be no war in Kansas.

Very respectfully,

J. R. GIDDINGS.

JOHN BROWN, ESQ.

Just a little before John Brown received Mr. Giddings' letter, Major Clark, who was one of the claimants to the honor of shooting Thomas Barber, also got some information from Washington. It was from Whitfield, the Territorial Delegate under the Shawnee Mission Government. " Shannon is with you, I hope, before this with full and ample power to put down the abolitionists in the Territory. We think here that Mr. Pierce comes up to the scratch nobly. Your humble servant is charged with figuring in getting up the message. One thing certain, Clark, if they attempt to fight Uncle Sam's boys, the ball is open and civil war is inevitable."

Thus at Washington there were people who felt that Kansas was the turning point in political affairs. If Mr. Giddings and Mr. Whitfield were right and if the Free State men pushed their policy, the ball would be open with the Northern sympathizers of Free State Kansas in the rôle of rebels and the Washington governmental machinery safely in Southern hands. Aside from any question of constitutionality it was merely a political accident that turned the defenders

of the faith into the protestant rebels. And when the time
came for the trial, apparent orthodoxy carried its usual
prestige.

Meanwhile the present technical rebels of Kansas were
hastening to give themselves the forms of legality. The Free
State Legislature assembled on March 4 and drew up a
memorial to Congress asking for admission as a State. Lane
and Reeder were elected to take office as Senators if Kansas
should be admitted. John Brown Jr. was there as a member
of the Legislature. But the Territorial laws were still in force
and a more pressing question was what attitude to take in
regard to them. By the middle of April a meeting was called
of the settlers in the Osawatomie neighborhood to discuss
the matter of taxation under the Shawnee Mission laws. The
temper of the settlers was against the payment of taxes,
but opinion was divided on the point of armed resistance.
The Reverend S. L. Adair, John Brown's brother-in-law,
stood for nonpayment and nonresistance, and the Browns,
under the leadership of their father, stood for armed resistance. But there was a more militant clergyman present
than the Reverend Adair. The Reverend Martin White rose
and spoke in behalf of the Territorial Legislature. " I went
to one of their meetings," he later said in regard to the Free
State men, " and tried to reason with them for peace, but in
so doing I insulted the hero of the murder of the three
Doyles, Wilkinson, and Sherman, and he replied to me that
he was an ' Abolitionist ' of the old stock — was dyed in the
wool and that negroes were his brothers and equals — that
he would rather see this Union dissolved and the country
drenched with blood than to pay taxes to the amount of one-
hundredth part of a mill." The Reverend Martin White was
not a peaceful man, and it is doubtful if his efforts could

have contributed much to that end. The Browns knew him; he was one of the men who had ridden up to the Brown claim when the sons had first come to Kansas and asked them how they were on the goose. Now he knew how they felt. The debate in the settlers' meeting was not the last time their trails would cross.

The Reverend Martin White's reasoning for peace did not sway the sentiment of the meeting, which adopted four resolutions declaring its attitude toward the Shawnee Mission Government. The resolutions could not be mistaken: " we utterly repudiate the authority of that Legislature as a body, emanating not from the people of Kansas, but elected and forced upon us by a foreign vote," and " the officers appointed by the same, have therefore no legal power to act." That was not all, for the members set out in writing their determination to forcibly resist any attempt to compel obedience to the enactments of the Legislature. " Let that attempt come from whatever source it may," was what they said. This could mean only one thing — a willingness to oppose the United States troops if occasion arose. For the settlers of the district the tight-rope walking act was over. It was probably well for the success of the Free State cause that men of such color had not been in the saddle at the first siege of Lawrence. But these fellows had the courage to declare themselves, and their last resolution read: " That a copy of these resolutions with the proceedings of this meeting be furnished to the several papers of Kansas with a request to publish the same."

There is no doubt that John Brown was also ready to subscribe himself to these things, and there is as little doubt, after all, that he hoped for a test of their consequences. Mr. Giddings had said that the death of the first man by the troops would light up the fires of civil war throughout the North, and that half a nation would stand or fall with him who struck the first blow in Kansas. The man who had *not* mounted the soap box at Lawrence to damn the signers of a compromising treaty and had *not* played the frontier Gideon with tin lanterns and Sharpe's rifles was now ready to fight, not the Missourians, but the United States troops. At Lawrence the principle behind an attack on the Missourians after the treaty would have been a little obscure and hard to explain. And John Brown always knew the value of a principle. But here the principle was clear enough. The first Captain John Brown had died while fighting for the catchword of "no taxation without representation"; the Kansas Captain John Brown did not intend to die for that catchword or any other, but he was desperate enough to take his chances if the fires of civil war should be lighted up. Anything might happen in such a shuffle. A new deal with higher stakes.

The settlers' meeting and their resolutions had little effect on the course of events. The spring was opening up and the fear of Missouri increased daily. There was already talk of taking the signers of the Lawrence treaty at their word and seeing if they would help serve on the Branson rescuers the old writs which had waited for months. But worse for the Free State cause than writs and Missourians was the fact that the South at last seemed to have awakened to the need for organized immigration to Kansas. Jefferson Buford had already arrived with his party of several hundred settlers; the Bibles they had received at McIlvaines' book store in Montgomery, Alabama, were long since in the trash-bins of the river boats where the crusaders had honestly tossed them. The Southern immigration to Kansas had poor organization.

In the North they published circulars telling of the rich and money-making land of Kansas and the glory of voting or shooting in the cause of freedom; in the South they talked about a question of political expediency.

John Brown had stated his position in the resolutions passed by the settlers' meeting, but he was not content to wait for results until assessors and sheriffs tried to collect taxes in the district. Opportunity for forcing the issue came when Sterling G. Cato held his court at Dutch Henry's Crossing on the Pottawatomie Creek. Judge Cato's court was well situated for the peaceful conduct of its business. In the first place the people on the creek were pro-slavery. There were the blustering and successful Sherman brothers who dealt in stock and supplies with immigrant parties, buying or trading for lame and sick animals which could be sold when they had recovered for a sound profit. There were James Doyle and his sons, Allen Wilkinson, who was a member of the Territorial Legislature, and a pro-slavery man named McMinn. In the second place this section had been troubled by none of the violence which had been common about Lawrence, Franklin, and Lecompton, during the past year and a half. Here the Judge could charge his court under the Shawnee Mission laws without fear of disturbance.

John Brown wanted " to hurry up the fight — always," his son Salmon said of him. The settlers' resolutions of a week before had not yet brought the desired results, but if people who were known to favor them were brought before a Territorial court the ball might be opened in good earnest. John Brown sent Salmon and Henry Thompson to Dutch Henry's in the hope that Judge Cato would arrest them. It was not that they were to be offered up as a sacrifice; the arrest would merely give an excuse for an armed rescue. The young men were against it, for they were somewhat afraid that there would be no ram in the bushes, but John Brown was determined, and so they went as he commanded. They returned in peace to their own relief and the certain disappointment of the old man.

The device of the arrest was not the last trick in his bag. He himself paid a visit to Cato's court, and John Brown Jr., now Captain of the Pottawatomie Rifle Company, led his men to the Crossing for a drill. The rifles were stacked in a cabin nearby and a number of the men filed into the courtroom to hear what the Judge had to say to his Grand Jury. The next day John Brown wrote a letter concerning the result.

Brown's Station, 22nd April, 1856

Dear Brother Adair —

. . . Many of the volunteer co. went in without show of arms to hear the charge to the Grand Jury. The Court is *thoroughly bogus* but the Judge had not the nerve to avow it openly. He was questioned on the bench in writing civilly but plainly whether he intended to enforce the Bogus Laws or not; but would give no answer. He did not even mention the so called Kansas *Legislature or name their acts* but talked of *our* laws; it was easy for any one conversant with law matters to discover what code he was charging the jury under. He evidently felt much agitated but talked a good deal about having criminals punished, &c. After hearing the charge and witnessing the refusal of the Judge to answer, the volunteers met under arms passed the Osawatomie Preamble Resolutions, every man voting aye. They also appointed a committee of Three to wait on the Judge at once with a coppy in full; which was immediately done. The effect of that I have not yet learned. You will see that matters are in a fair way of comeing to a head.

Yours sincerely in haste,

JOHN BROWN.

143

The effect was simple. By dawn Judge Cato and his helpers were well on their way to Lecompton, the pro-slavery stronghold, where they knew they would be safe. It was the first and last time a Territorial court tried to hold session in that region. But John Brown's object had not been to clear the county of Territorial officials; he had scored a victory but it was not the sort of victory he contemplated.

It was not this bloodless victory and peace to put in the spring crop that John Brown desired. He had come to Kansas to see if "something would not turn up to his advantage," but with the opening of spring he had decided that this advantage was not to be derived from homesteads and crops on the free soil of Kansas; pioneering here was as unprofitable as at Richmond or North Elba. Back in January the wife of John Brown Jr. had written to Mary Day Brown some news which carried more than an echo of critical feminine prudence: "our men have so much *war* and *elections* to attend to that it seems as though we were a great while getting into a house." By April John Brown himself was thinking of Brown's Station as merely a sort of bivouac. The improvement of a claim, a decent cabin, and crops for the coming year were nothing. On the seventh he wrote to his wife:

. . . We do not want you to borrow trouble about us, but trust us to the care of "Him who feeds the young ravens when they cry." I have as usual little to write. We are doing off a house for Orson Day, which we hope to get through with soon; after which we shall probably soon leave this neighborhood, but will advise you further when we do leave. It may be that Watson can manage to get a little money for shearing sheep if you do not get any from Connecticut. I still hope you will get help from that source. We have no wars as yet, but we still have abundance of "rumors." We still have frosty nights, but the grass starts a little. There are none of us complaining much just now, all being able to do something. John has just returned from Topeka, not having met with any difficulty but we hear that preparations are making in the United States Court for numerous arrests of Free-State men. For one, I have no desire (all things considered) to have the slave-power cease from its acts of aggression. "Their foot shall slide in due time." No more now. May good bless and keep you all!"

Several facts about John Brown emerge from the incidents of the spring. Money matters were no better, and thirty dollars was all he could spare to help the wretched circumstances of the family at North Elba. He had deliberately resigned the leadership of the local Free State militia, which was now commanded by his son John. He did not intend to work the Kansas claim to help his fortunes, for he planned to leave the neighborhood. His object in leaving Osawatomie was not definite or it was such that he did not care to put it down in black and white for his wife to read. He had been content with a peaceful solution of the political troubles in the preceding fall but now he wanted to provoke the pro-slavery faction, the Territorial officials, and even the United States troops. "Their foot shall slide in due time," was the pious sentence. He was even ready to trust his son to the dubious device of a rescue to bring about the desired collision. If he had wanted merely an open fight he would not have resigned his command of the Liberty Guards, and would not have planned to leave the neighborhood. He did not intend to return to North Elba. He simply wanted to be free to move on a moment's notice for some obscure reason which he did not care to confide to his wife. He was a secretive man, and probably none of his followers knew precisely what he had in mind. The gentle and indecisive Jason had certainly not risen into his father's confidence. John Brown Jr. was the most trusted son, but Henry Thompson had at least an inkling that some new and big project was up. A few weeks after John Brown's letter to North Elba concerning the move, Henry Thompson wrote his own wife the same sort of hint about a mysterious future for the Kansas adventurers: " upon Brown's plans will depend my own until School is out." Whatever those plans were they had to be remunerative, for spring found the settlement down-at-the-heels and knowing little more than where the next meal would come from.

Despite his anxiety for action, John Brown was to have nothing to do with the reopening of violence in the Territory. Had he but known it, circumstance was playing directly into his hands. The ink was scarcely dry on the resolutions adopted by the settlers' meeting before Sheriff Jones appeared again at Lawrence with the old warrants for the Branson rescuers. S. N. Wood, who had played a leading part in the rescue, was back in Lawrence after a lecturing trip East in the Free State cause. Jones managed to find him easily enough and to execute the arrest. Keeping the prisoner was a different matter, for a crowd quickly gathered, and in the tumult Wood escaped. The next day Jones violated the Sabbath and tried again with unexpected success. A fellow named Tappan slapped his face, and such resistance to an officer was certainly a sound reason for appealing to Governor Shannon for troops. Jones was delighted. A tingling cheek was a small price to pay for such satisfaction.

It required three days for Sheriff Jones to get himself clothed with the new authority and return to Lawrence. With Lieutenant McIntosh and the regulars at his back he set about serving his writs. Wood, the man he most desired, was not in town, but before dark he had collected six prisoners of minor importance. That night he sat in his tent, with the

lantern light outlining his shadow on the canvas. The logical
event followed. There was the flash and report of a gun in
the darkness, the troopers rushed out, and a crowd gathered.
Jones was lying on the floor of his tent, wounded in the back.
Nothing could have been more unhappy for the Free State
cause and for Lawrence. A slap on the sheriff's face had
brought Lieutenant McIntosh and his troopers; the shot
would certainly bring a good deal more.

Sheriff Jones was an able servant of the pro-slavery
cause, but the Sheriff dead was worth much more than Jones
alive. The news spread like wildfire. The newspapers announced his death and called for revenge. " In a fight let
our motto be, ' War to the knife, and knife to the hilt '; asking no quarter from them and granting none. *Jones' Murder
Must Be Revenged!!* " This was the slogan of the pro-
slavery *Squatter Sovereign* as late as May 6, when Jones was
well on the way to mending from his wounds. The soberer
people of the town of Lawrence knew that the long dreaded
direct collision with the United States troops was imminent.
They held meetings and denounced the cowardly crime, offered a reward of $500 for the man who fired the shot, and
protested the innocence of the community. Colonel Sumner
wrote to Dr. Robinson a day or two after the incident:

The recent attempt made upon the life of Sheriff Jones will
produce great excitement throughout the Territory and on the
Missouri frontier, and I consider it of the utmost importance
that every effort should be made by your people to ferret out
and bring to justice the cowardly assassin. It is not too much
to say that the peace of the country may depend on it, for, if he
is not arrested, the act will be charged by the opposite party
upon your whole community. This affair has been reported to
Washington, and whatever orders may be received will be instantly carried into effect. The proclamation which requires

obediance to the laws of the Territory as they now stand until legally abrogated, will certainly be maintained, and it is very unsafe to give heed to people at a distance who counsel resistance. If they were here to participate in the danger, they would probably take a different view of this matter.

Colonel Sumner had stated the situation well, and he had also given some good advice. Dr. Robinson could only send a copy of the Lawrence public meeting's proceedings by way of answer.

The criminal was not brought to justice. The incident itself and the fact that no one was brought to punishment for it released a new period of violence in the Territory. There were murders and reprisals on both sides, with little to choose between them on the score of humanity or justice. Those things — humanity and justice — were a little too much to expect at such a time. Meanwhile, the people of Lawrence waited in apprehension for the machinery of legal retribution to get in motion against them; they knew well that their protestations of innocence were in vain at the very moment they voted on them and wrote them down.

It was early in May when Judge Lecompte put that machinery in motion by charging his Grand Jury:

This Territory was organized by an act of Congress, and so far its authority is from the United States. It has a Legislature elected in pursuance of that organic act. This Legislature, being an instrument of Congress by which it governs the Territory, has passed laws. These laws, therefore, are of the United States authority and making; and *all that resist these laws resist the power and authority of the United States, and are therefore guilty of high-treason.* Now, gentlemen, if you find that any persons have resisted these laws, then you must, under your oaths, find bills against them for high-treason. If you find that *no such resistance has been* made, but that combinations have been formed for the purpose of resisting them, and individuals of influence and notoriety have been aiding and abetting in such combinations, *then you must still find bills for constructive treason.*

Reeder, Robinson, Lane, and S. N. Wood were among those indicted. If the chief Free State leaders could be put under lock and key on a charge which did not admit of bail, a good deal would be accomplished. The jurymen did not trouble themselves much about the definition of treason; they were willing to take the word of the Judge. John Brown was later to say of Judge Lecompte: " If the Lord Almighty had seen fit to deliver Judge Lecompte into my hands, it would have taken the Lord Almighty to get him out again." The unhappy Judge did much to make " Kansas treason " a fashionable thing to profess; it was especially fashionable in Boston, which, incidentally, lay many miles from Kansas.

The Grand Jury's indictments accomplished their end. Robinson was arrested and held for four months before being released on bail, Reeder escaped from the Territory in disguise, and Lane simply happened not to be available at the time. But the work was not done by halves; the jury recommended that *The Herald of Freedom* and *The Kansas Free State*, the Lawrence newspapers, and the Free State Hotel at Lawrence be abated as nuisances. The stone Free State Hotel was far too much like a small fortress; that subject had been on the minds of various pro-slavery men for some time.

The posse began to gather under the leadership of I. B. Donaldson, United States Marshal for the Territory. There were men from Kansas and from Missouri, and then there were Colonel Buford's men who had come all the way from Alabama to combat the organized immigration of the North. They probably had not expected action so early or

action of such a decisive nature. The game, indeed, seemed
to be up for Lawrence. Their " impregnable moral position "
since the shooting of Sheriff Jones was a trifle battered. But
it would have been well for the pro-slavery cause if Donaldson, Buford, and the rest had refrained from pressing their
new advantage.

Meanwhile, the people of Lawrence were writing more letters and making less preparation toward defense than in the
days before the Wakarusa war. They wrote desperately to
Shannon, enclosing one set of resolutions after another. " We
have the most reliable information from various parts of the
Territory, and the adjoining State of Missouri, of the organization of guerilla bands, who threaten the destruction
of our town and its citizens." The Governor made the
proper answer: " Your note of the 11th instant is received,
and in reply I have to state that there is no force around or
approaching Lawrence except the legally constituted posse
of the United States Marshal and Sheriff of Douglas
County, each of whom, I am informed, has a number of writs
in his hands for execution against persons now in Lawrence.
I shall in no way interfere with either of these officers in the
discharge of their official duties." The futile correspondence
dragged on. They wrote to Donaldson and declared themselves " order-loving and law-abiding citizens," who only
waited an opportunity to testify their " fidelity to the laws of
the country, the Constitution, and the Union." Donaldson's
answer was lengthy and ironical; he had obviously enjoyed
the writing of it. The shot at the shadow on the tent wall
seemed to have been forgotten by the people of Lawrence.
They expected a simple lawyer who happened to be Governor and a simple Marshal to discriminate between an individual act of violence and the communal sentiment. It was

scarcely fair; they themselves insisted in regarding Jones and Atchison as representing all that the South stood for.

On May 19 a last attempt was made to save the town by the Messrs. Eldridge who personally appeared before Shannon. It was the same story rehearsed face to face. Shannon refused to interfere with the posse, and he would not call out the troops under Sumner, who was now in his command. " I could call them out if I chose," he said, " but I shall not do so." The unhappy Governor tried to be just; he now felt that there was, as there had not been in the preceding autumn, a necessity for entering Lawrence. The emissaries said their last word: " If the posse goes into Lawrence the people may be maddened to resistance, and we'll have civil war." " War then it is, by God! " he replied, and left the room.

On the next evening Deputy Marshal Fain entered the town and made two arrests without meeting any show of resistance. It was too late for submission to be of any good. When morning came the people of Lawrence could see a body of horsemen on the hill commanding the town. Soon other men could be seen planting cannon on the height. A white flag waved for a time above the guns, and then the watchers saw a red one spread with the motto " Southern Rights." At length the flag of the Union rose into the breeze beside it.

Under the cover of the guns on the hill Fain again came into the town. His posse consisted of less than ten unarmed men, but he summoned the Messrs. Eldridge and three other citizens to serve with them. This was considerable humiliation for people who had made sport of Jones and his writs only a little while before, but they submitted in hope that cheerful obedience would placate the Marshal's men. They assisted in arresting three of their fellow-partisans on the charge of treason, but even this was in vain; outside Lawrence Sheriff Jones, his wounds healed, was restlessly waiting with seven hundred men at his back.

While Fain was in the Free State Hotel, where he was treated to the best meal that establishment could provide, he received a final statement from the Committee of Public Safety for Lawrence. At last they agreed to a complete submission to the laws, national and territorial, but it was perfectly useless. Fain made his arrests and turned his men over to the Sheriff's posse, and by three o'clock Jones with a body of heavily armed horsemen had drawn rein in front of the Hotel. He demanded of the citizens the surrender of their cannon and rifles. The delivery being made, it was announced that the printing presses and the Hotel itself must be destroyed. The Eldridge families were given until five o'clock to remove their belongings. The rest of the posse, with fixed bayonets, moved into the town and began the work of demolishing the printing offices. The red flag waved over the office of the *Herald of Freedom* and the Hotel. Type, presses, paper, books, and other equipment of the offending newspapers were broken and scattered in the streets or dumped into the river. At the appointed time the cannon were turned on the Hotel at a point-blank range and the bombardment began. If the building had been erected as a fortress the work was well done, for the cannonshot had little effect upon it. In the end it was reduced to ruin by fire and gunpowder. Pillaging continued until after dark.

The number of men in the posse, such as Colonel Buford and Colonel Zadock Jackson of Georgia, who desired to maintain order and prevent a wanton destruction of property, were absolutely powerless in the face of their followers. As for Jones, he declared that it was the happiest moment of his life; he had what he wanted at last. Atchison, also, joined with that sentiment in the exhortation he had made to the Rangers in the morning. "Boys, this day I am a Kickapoo Ranger, by God! This day we have entered Lawrence with 'Southern Rights' inscribed upon our banner, and not one damned Abolitionist dared to fire a gun. Now, boys, this is the happiest day of my life. We have entered that damned town, and taught the damned Abolitionists a Southern lesson that they will remember until the day they die. And now, boys, we will go in again, with our highly honorable Jones, and test the strength of that damned Free-State Hotel, and teach the Emigrant Aid Company that Kansas shall be ours. Boys, ladies should, and I hope will, be respected by every gentleman. But when a woman takes upon herself the garb of a soldier by carrying a Sharp's rifle, then she is no longer worthy of respect. Trample her under your feet as you would a snake! Come on, boys! Now do your duty to yourselves and your Southern friends. Your duty I know you will do. If one man or woman dare stand before you, blow them to hell with a chunk of cold lead."

Atchison was somewhat of an orator; he had been Senator from Missouri and Vice-President of the United States, and had addressed more august bodies than the Kickapoo Rangers. No wonder that back in the South, which Atchison claimed to be defending, Lewis Washington threw a newspaper aside without reading whenever he saw the name "Kansas."

6

"A LITTLE COMPANY BY OURSELVES"

THE report of the taking of Lawrence caused immediate action in the Brown settlement. Such an alarm had been expected for some time and the family was ready. John Brown Jr. left his business of planting a patch of corn, saddled his horse, and rode to Osawatomie with the news. The word was carried to the members of his company, the " Pottawatomies," and by evening thirty-four men gathered at the fork of the Osawatomie and California roads. The companies from Osawatomie, the " Marion Rifles " and the " Pomeroy Guards " were also to appear at this rendezvous, but they sent word that the report of the attack on Lawrence had been contradicted by a later messenger. The men under the leadership of John Brown Jr. pushed on toward Lawrence and learned the truth before they reached Marais des Cygnes. A courier hurried back to Osawatomie to ask for reënforcements. At Prairie City, where the march was next broken, they were informed that there were no Free State defenders at Lawrence, and that the pro-slavery forces were in possession of the important Blanton's bridge. There was nothing to do but wait until the Osawatomie men joined them, and so the party pitched camp. With them that night, there bivouacked another little company which was not under the command of John Brown Jr. and which bore no relation to the militia. Old John Brown was its leader, and under him were Owen, Frederick, Oliver, Salmon, Henry Thompson, and Theodore Weiner.

This party had no connection whatsoever with the " Pottawatomies "; John Brown had been commander of the local rifle company, but he had seen fit to disband it and form a smaller, more mobile force, which would be more in sympathy with his ends and would offer no question or scruple to his commands. John Brown Jr. was not in the force, for it was necessary that some member of the family have charge of the militia. Jason was not a member for he lacked the resolution of his father and brothers, and possessed far too much humanity of heart. Weiner possessed practically no humanity of heart; as Salmon described him he was a " big, savage, bloodthirsty Austrian " and a fellow who " could not be kept out of any accessible fight." He owned a store in the region and was accounted a very successful man; he had at least one willing henchman in the person of a man named Benjamin, who was a helper and partner in the business. All in all, Weiner was a man after John Brown's own heart, and the two had recently formed a partnership for a more ambitious piece of business than keeping a frontier store. Salmon's description is probably accurate enough; the members of the little company by themselves must have understood each other very well indeed.

The next morning, the morning of Friday, May 23, 1856 the militiamen could see John Brown cooking breakfast for his party and talking earnestly with Weiner and a member of the " Pottawatomies," James Townsley by name. John Brown confided to Townsley that he had just received news of impending trouble on the Pottawatomie Creek, and wanted to know if Townsley would take the independent company back with his wagon to keep watch on matters there. Weiner joined in the request, professing grave fear for the safety of families left behind without proper protection. Townsley agreed readily enough.

Salmon Brown once related that the plan for the next two days of action was matured in a common council consisting of the leading men from John Brown Jr.'s company and of the entire body that was to act under the old man himself. According to Salmon's account, the Lieutenant for the " Pottawatomies," H. H. Williams, made out a list of men in the region who had been prominent in enforcing the Border Ruffian laws and who, by consequence, should be picked off " to prevent the utter destruction of the whole community." If such a council was called it certainly did not learn of the real purpose behind the new expedition which the little company contemplated. Townsley, who was to go with John Brown, did not understand the nature of the project, and the Lieutenant, H. H. Williams, who Salmon said was the principal man in the council, would certainly not have succeeded John Brown Jr. as Captain if he had advised the raiders in the course which they pursued. John Brown was no man to tell his secrets; he carried many of them to the grave with him.

After the council John Brown Jr. and Jason were busy at a grindstone, sharpening those straight two-edged swords which had been brought to Kansas in John Brown's wagon in the preceding fall. Bain Fuller, a mere boy, turned the instrument, while the other two pressed the old steel blades of the " Order of the Grand Eagles " against the stone. " That looks like business," said one fellow to Frederick Brown.

"Yes, it does," answered Frederick. Jason, pressing the steel against the stone to give it a sharp, true edge, had not a notion of the purpose behind all this preparation. The oldest brother, who stood there beside him, was one of the few men in the camp who knew precisely what was to be done, what was the motive behind it, and how long the idea had been in the mind of his father. The time had come at last. "We shall probably soon leave this neighborhood," John Brown had written to his wife six weeks before. It was a blessing for the poor woman in the New York mountains that she could not read between the lines.

While the old artillery sabres were getting their edge on the stone, John Brown packed up his camping equipment in the usual neat bundle. He was an orderly man by nature, and he probably guessed that his days of living in houses might be over for a time. Whatever story was circulating in the camp concerning the business which was taking John Brown away, there were some who feared that he would not act with sufficient caution for his own good and the good of the Free State cause. A fellow interrupted him at his packing to say as much. He suddenly rose erect and faced the speaker. It must have irritated him strangely to hear such words when his mind was made up to act, for with him the intention was equivalent to the deed. "Caution, caution, sir. I am eternally tired of hearing that word caution. It is nothing but the word of cowardice." There was an impatient scorn at the innocence of the man who dared to offer him advice. What could that fellow know of his purposes. He had taken every step beforehand, had balanced the chances and the odds, and if his plans miscarried he had faith enough in his own resources. And John Brown was no coward.

The wagon was loaded. All of the party except Weiner

climbed in and the driver whipped up the team of greys. Weiner rode beside on his pony. As they passed out of the camp the men behind gave them cheer after cheer. They were going out to strike some sudden blow of vengeance for Lawrence, perhaps to fall on stragglers from Buford's company. In any case it was to be a blow for safety of their homes and for the free soil of Kansas. As the cheers rose from the ragged, excited crowd, John Brown Jr. knew that the blow was to be for freedom but he knew that freedom was not all. The heavily burdened wagon, with its single outrider, passed back along the road which the militia had covered the preceding evening. It disappeared from sight in the direction of Pottawatomie. The cheers in the camp died down.

All afternoon the wagon creaked slowly along behind the team of greys. As it reached the top of the high ridge just south of the Wakarusa, a horseman stopped the party. He told them the latest news from Washington: how the young Congressman Brooks of South Carolina had avenged the honor of his uncle and his State by clubbing Senator Sumner with a walking stick and had thus given another valuable martyr to the Free State cause. " At that blow the men went crazy — crazy. It seemed to be the finishing, decisive touch," was Salmon Brown's reminiscence of the incident at a time when the surviving Browns were sadly in need of recalling any extenuating aspects of the expedition. Again near the house of Ottawa Jones, a friendly Indian, they were hailed by a group of Free State men under Captain J. M. Anthony, who asked where they were going. With an equivocal answer and a promise to join the Free State forces at Lawrence later, the raiders pushed on about their secret errand. Late in the afternoon when they had almost reached their destination they saw a mounted man approaching. When he was nearer to them, John Brown stood up in the wagon and cried " Halt! " There followed a short parley between John Brown and Blood, the man he had stopped. The news about the sack of Lawrence was passed. " Cowards," was the word John Brown had for the men who had not fired a shot for the town. He was in a sort of cold frenzy; the first strain of waiting quietly with that decision he had made would tell on any man. The members of the group crouching in the rough wagon-bed hung on every word and gesture with excited eagerness. Blood rode away with John Brown's last admonition in his ears: not to mention the meeting by the road, for the party was bound on a secret expedition and did not want anyone to even know that they had been in the neighborhood. Blood was left to his own conclusions; in a few days he would be able to guess the truth clearly enough.

When they had gotten within two or three miles of Pottawatomie Creek the party turned off to the right from the main road and drove to the edge of the timber between two deep ravines. There they made camp for the night, and waited.

If Townsley had been a very acute man he would have guessed by this time that the excuse John Brown used in asking him for his wagon and team had little to do with the real purpose of the expedition. John Brown had said that the settlement was in danger and that the return was for its defense. But here they were camping quietly in the woods by the creek and completely out of touch with events at their homes. Their leader had not even troubled to get news from Blood of the conditions in the neighborhood. He knew that the families left behind would be safe enough; there had never been any difficulty or violence in this part of the Territory south of Douglas County and Lawrence. Furthermore, if news had come of an impending attack by pro-slavery forces, it was strange that it should have been confided to John Brown alone when there were many others in camp whose homes were equally unprotected. But Townsley did not trouble his head about these matters. Old Brown had a strange power of making people believe what he said; finally Old Brown himself believed many things which he had once stated merely as a means to some end of his own.

But now in the camp by the stream, Townsley learned the truth — or part of the truth. When the team had been fed and the men had gotten their scanty supper, John Brown explained his project to Townsley. He wanted Townsley to guide the party up to the forks of the creek, some five or six miles above in the neighborhood where Townsley lived, and point out to them the homes of all the pro-slavery families, so that they could sweep the creek as they came back down to the camping place. Townsley had no stomach for such a piece of work. All he wanted now was to take his wagon and go home, but John Brown was far too wise to permit any such thing. What Townsley did not learn was one of John Brown's primary reasons in executing his present plan. He didn't need Townsley's help in pointing out victims, for they had probably been settled upon some time before by a simple question: was the man known to be pro-slavery and did he have good horses?

That night and all of the next day the party rested quietly in their camp. Only a mile or so down the creek was Dutch Henry's Crossing with the several pro-slavery families of Doyle, Wilkinson, and the others. It would not do to excite curiosity by moving about when the company was supposed to be far away on the road to Lawrence; the ruffianly Sherman brothers might take action to investigate or at least pass on the news. Furthermore, the men were tired out from the long march of Friday night, and all their strength and nerve would be needed for the work in hand when darkness again came. Whatever curiosity John Brown may have had about the way the unprotected people at his settlement were faring was not sufficient to make him break cover. It was no time to run unnecessary chances.

The spot was well chosen for such secrecy. The usual open prairie land of the Territory was broken here by hills and precipitous ravines, and along the steep, winding banks of the Pottawatomie Creek, now discolored by the mud and wastage of spring rains, stood a broad border of heavy timber. Down stream was the Sherman ford and further on was Osawatomie, where the Pottawatomie joined the Marais des Cygnes to form the Osage River. And the season was also ripe; the spring was far advanced and the grass was good. Men on the move would not have to carry provender for their horses.

A short while after dark John Brown gave the order to march. The company moved rapidly and quietly northward toward Mosquito Creek. They forded the creek above the Doyle place and soon reached the first cabin. One of the men knocked on the door, while the others stood by waiting. Everything was silent for a moment and then they heard the sound of a gun being rammed through the chinks of the cabin wall. The raiders scattered on the instant; they had not come for a stand-up fight. If that was all they wanted they could have gotten it quickly enough without leaving the militia. " We did not disturb that man. With some candle wicking soaked in coal oil to light and throw inside, so that we could see within while he could not see outside, we would have managed it, but we had none," Salmon Brown related of the incident. " It was a method much used later," he innocently added. So the night of May 24 did not end such adventures for the Brown gang.

They next reached the Doyle cabin, which stood on Mosquito Creek, only a mile or so from where it emptied into the Pottawatomie. As they cautiously approached, two large and savage watchdogs leaped up at them. Frederick swung his short two-edged sword at one of the beasts and Townsley stepped in to despatch it with a blow of his sabre. The first of the Bierce swords was stained with blood. Townsley, Weiner, and Frederick stopped a little way from the house, while John Brown, Thompson, and three of the sons went up to the door and knocked. Doyle's voice answered. There was no saving sound of a rifle being rammed through the cabin chinks, and the gleam of a newly lighted candle shone within. " We want to know where Mr. Wilkinson lives," one of the men said. Doyle replied that he would tell them the way and then opened the door. John Brown and his men pushed inside. " We are from the Northern army. You and your boys must surrender. You are our prisoners." Mahala Doyle cried out in protest; she saw the meaning of the business. Old Doyle must also have understood, but he only said, " Hush, mother, hush." The prisoners of the Northern army were marched out of the house — the father Doyle, the twenty-two-year-old William, and Drury who was only twenty. Mahala Doyle's tears prevailed a little, for the next son, John, was left in the cabin with her and the younger children.

The three victims were hurried a short distance down the road toward Dutch Henry's and there the party halted. John Brown set the example. He presented a revolver to the forehead of old Doyle and fired. It had begun; there was no turning back now. The Brown sons fell on William and Drury Doyle and hacked them down. Drury tried to flee but they pursued and overtook him. In the young grass near a ravine they left his mangled body. The other two lay in a bloody heap by the roadside where they had fallen.

The killing at Doyle's was perforce one of principle, for the family's horses had been out on the prairie. The little group, with their stained swords, hurried forward on foot to Wilkinson's. It was not yet midnight; and the business was far from finished.

Again at Wilkinson's cabin a dog gave the alarm. Again there was a knocking at the door and a request for directions. Wilkinson began to tell the men outside the way to Dutch Henry's, but one of them called to him, " come out and show us." At the entreaty of his sick wife, Wilkinson objected; he answered that it was hard to find his clothes and could give the direction just as well without going out. The waiting men retreated a little from the door at that and held a hurried conference in whispers. They gave up the subterfuge and directly asked, " Are you a Northern armist? " " I am," replied Wilkinson. " You are our prisoner. Do you surrender? " Wilkinson made no defense: " Gentlemen, I do." When he wished to make a light before opening the door one of the men called out, " If you don't open it now we'll open it for you." Wilkinson complied immediately, and five men entered — the same five as at Doyle's. They seized their prisoner and began to ransack the house for arms and supplies. They took all they could find, a gun and powderflask.

The sick woman begged that her husband be permitted to remain with her and he himself only asked for delay enough to call someone to attend his wife. The thin-faced old man, with a dirty straw hat pulled low over his eyes, looked at the little children and the woman who was pleading with him. " You have neighbors," he finally answered. " So I have," she protested, " but they aren't here and I cannot go for them." The old man looked at her again: " It matters not," was all he said.

They hurried Wilkinson from the house, without giving him time to get his boots or a little clothing against the damp and the night air. One of the party went back in the cabin and took two saddles. Again the woman begged that someone stay with her. " I would," the fellow said, " but they wouldn't let me." He, too, left her. Once or twice she faintly heard her husband's voice raised in complaint. Finally she crept to the door and listened intently. All was still.

Wilkinson was killed in the roadway, to the south of his house. The murderers dragged his body a short distance to one side and left it in some dry brush. It was over neatly and quickly; they proceeded in the direction of Dutch Henry's Crossing. They must have gone along more rapidly now. The saddles could not have been taken from the house for nothing, but at that most of the company had to ride bareback.

About two o'clock on Sunday morning they reached the place of James Harris, with whom the Shermans were staying. John Brown and four of his men got into the cabin and with drawn sabres went up to the bed where Harris and his wife and child were lying. " The Northern army is here. It's useless to resist. Do you surrender? " It was the same formula. Harris and three other men, who were sleeping in the single room of the cabin, gave themselves up to the mercy of the Northern army. One of these men was Dutch Bill Sherman, one was John Whiteman, and the third was a stranger unknown even to Harris. The raiders then ransacked the house and took such arms and ammunition as they could find. The stranger was led outside, but his answers to their questions must have satisfied the Browns, for he soon came back into the cabin. It was Harris' turn next. They demanded if there were any other men about the place besides the four already found. A search revealed no others. " Where is Dutch Henry," old Brown asked. " He's out on the plain hunting some lost cattle of his." They questioned Harris on his own account. " Have you ever taken any hand in helping pro-slavery men to come into the Territory of Kansas? Did you have any hand in the last troubles at Lawrence? Have you ever done the Free State Party any harm and do you ever intend to do that party any harm. What makes you live at such a place as this? " " I can get higher wages here than anywhere else," was the simple reason Harris gave. He was a poor day laborer. Then the questioners got down to business. " Are there any bridles and saddles here." They stood by while Harris saddled Dutch Henry's shave-tail pony and added it to their plunder. Harris had to do a very simple thing to earn his own safe release; it was merely to answer " no " to all the first set of questions. Old Brown and Owen then took him back into the cabin.

" Come outside with me," was John Brown's order to Dutch Bill. Sherman went out with his captor to join the silent group waiting for them. A man came in to assist Owen in guarding the other prisoners who huddled in the cabin's one room. For fifteen minutes the people there, guards and prisoners alike, and the puzzled child, strained to hear what was passing in the darkness. At last they caught the sudden noise of a bursting cap. It was the recall signal for the two men who kept watch inside. The work was done. To the ears of those just released came for a moment the faint receding sound of hoofs thudding on the soft spring earth.

John Brown and his party returned to their camp between the two deep ravines. The old blades, stained with the blood of five men, were washed in the waters of Pottawatomie Creek. But there remained more important evidence of the crime to be effaced before the gang could confront the world again. Before dawn they were in possession, not of the murdered men's horses, but of fast running horses brought to them and exchanged by their confederates. The terms of the transaction will never be known. The sons who survived John Brown even denied for years his presence on the Pottawatomie on the night of May 25. When the truth was out at last and the world had prepared a motive — a motive which would fit the martyr — there were confessions from the sons. The world had justified the murderer; the Browns knew that it is a little more difficult to justify a horse thief. When daylight came the evidence was gone, for the stolen horses were well on their way north to be sold. The sons had only to guard a short time longer the secret motive which had caused the disbanding of the Liberty Guards, the letter of April 7 to Mary Day Brown, the organization of the little company by themselves, and the raid along the Pottawatomie. They kept the secret well.

John Brown met the two sons who had stayed behind with the " Pottawatomies " late on the night after the massacre when they were camping near the Ottawa. News of the happenings along the creek had preceded him. On Saturday after John Brown Jr. had led a scouting party into Lawrence and had discovered the complete lack of resistance by the inhabitants, the " Pottawatomies " and the three other militia companies with them decided to disperse to their homes. A little later Second Lieutenant Church with a cavalry detachment of regulars came upon the camp and ordered the militia to disband. On the next day John Brown Jr.'s company was on the Ottawa Creek ready for its easy march back home. It was there that news of the massacre came. A horseman dashed into the camp, his mount winded and lathered with sweat, and shouted out: "Five men have been killed on Pottawatomie Creek, butchered and mangled, and old John Brown has done it!" For the poor Jason this was the worst shock of his life. To John Brown, Jr., it came as no surprise, for he had known very well what to expect from the secret expedition. But the reality was worse than he had imagined.

In the camp of the "Pottawatomies" there was no exultation or satisfaction at the vengeance for Lawrence. There may have been cheers when Townsley's wagon lumbered away behind the team of greys, but now there were none. The repudiation of John Brown and all the tribe of Browns was swift and unmistakable. John Brown Jr. was abruptly left without his command and even the innocent Jason shared in the disgrace. H. H. Williams, who had been, according to Salmon's story, an influence behind the massacre, now gained from it the incidental profit of becoming John Brown Jr.'s successor as Captain, and the fact of his election does much to establish his innocence of Salmon's charge. John Brown Jr. once claimed that he lost his captaincy because he liberated two slaves. Jason was more candid concerning the effect from the news of the butchery: "This information caused great excitement and fear among the men of our company and a feeling arose against John and myself which led the men all to desert us."

When John Brown and his gang slipped back to join the militia camp there was no friendliness and no applause. In-

stead there was the reproachful face of the trembling and
overwrought Jason to confront him. " Did you have anything to do with the killing of those men on the Pottawatomie? " " I did not do it," John Brown answered, " but I
approved of it." " I think it was an uncalled for, wicked act,"
Jason said. " God is my judge," replied John Brown, who
was more ready to trust the judgment of his own peculiar
God than the common humanity of his son's heart. A question to Frederick only confirmed Jason's most horrible suspicion. " Frederick, do you know who the murderers were? "
" Yes, I do, but I can't tell you." " Did you kill any of them
with your own hand? " Frederick wept as he answered: " No;
when I came to see what manner of work it was, I could not do
it." Jason was afraid to hear more. All of the sons had
not inherited the iron of their father and their father's
willingness to pay any price for his immediate desire.
Furthermore, none were as clever as Old Man Brown
himself.

The party scattered from the camp on Ottawa Creek.
The militia proceeded homeward under Williams, but John
Brown and his men had no desire for their company, which
might prove dangerous as well as unfriendly. They crossed
Middle Creek and struck off toward the claims of Jason and
John Brown, Jr. Those two sons went on alone, not toward
their homes but to Osawatomie. A few miles south of Ottawa
Jones' place John Brown Jr. received his unearned share
of the Pottawatomie booty. It was a valuable running horse,
which the new owner described as having been " taken by
Free-State men near the Nebraska line and exchanged for
horses obtained in the way of reprisals further south." It
was a rough account of the business transaction after the
massacre.

"A Little Company by Ourselves"

Jason and John sought protection in Adair's cabin where their wives had fled before them. Already the hunt was up for the murderers, and the road from Palmyra to Osawatomie was full of men on the lookout for John Brown. By nine o'clock in the evening they reached the place where they hoped to find refuge. Adair himself came to the door with his gun and called, " Who's there? " " John and I," answered Jason. " Can't keep you here," was Adair's immediate reply. " Our lives are threatened. Every moment we expect to have our house burned over our head." The two fugitives were almost desperate. " Here are we two alone. We have eaten nothing all day. Let us lie on your floor till morning — in your outhouse — anywhere." It was their aunt who finally let them in. " Did you have anything to do with the murders on the Pottawatomie? " she asked. The two protested their innocence. " Then you may stay, but we risk our lives in keeping you."

Jason and John were given a mattress on the floor near the Adairs' bed. Jason rehearsed the whole story — the departure from the camp, the words of the excited horseman who had brought the news, the hurried court-martial of John, and the secret return of the raiders. When the tale was finished there was still no sleep for the four who waited in the dark for the noise of horses and a fusillade on the cabin. For hours John lay groaning. At last he spoke to his aunt. " I feel that I am going insane," he told her. Near three o'clock they heard a knocking at the door. It was Owen seeking shelter like his brothers. Adair called to him: " Get away, get away as quick as you can! You endanger our lives. You are a vile murderer, a marked man! " " I intend to be a marked man! " Owen shouted back as he rode away from the cabin. Everything was quiet again except for the groans of John. Jason, despite the burden on his mind, managed to sleep a little. When daylight came John was quite mad.

The two fugitives could not stay longer at Adair's cabin. Jason decided that the safest course for him was to give up to United States authorities rather than trust himself to the mercies of outraged neighbors or Buford's men. John kept enough sanity to hide, with his horse and rifle, in a ravine on Adair's land. The wives remained at the cabin, not knowing whether they would ever see their husbands again.

Since the Sunday afternoon when the courier had dashed into the camp of the " Pottawatomies " and shouted out his news, the whole region had been in a tumult of indignation. Old Doyle had been found in the road with a pistol shot in his forehead and his breast hacked by the sabres, but his death had been more merciful than that of his sons; Drury's fingers and arms had been completely severed and the head and body slashed, and the corpse of William was similarly mutilated. Everyone knew by this time how Harris had found the gigantic body of Dutch Bill lying in the creek, whose waters had washed out some of the brains from the clefts in his skull and carried the blood away from the stump of his left arm.

Party feeling for the moment vanished in a general sense of horror. At Osawatomie, within three days after the massacre, there was a meeting to consider the crime. There were the usual resolutions.

Whereas, An outrage of the darkest and foulest nature has been committed in our midst by some midnight assassins unknown, who have taken five of our citizens at the hour of midnight from their homes and families, and murdered and mangled them in the most awful manner; to prevent a repetition of these deeds, we deem it necessary to adopt some measures for our mutual protection and to aid and assist in bringing these des-

peradoes to justice. Under these circumstances we propose to
act up to the following resolutions:

Resolved, That we will from this time lay aside all sectional
and political feelings and act together as men of reason and
common sense, determined to oppose all men who are so ultra
in their views as to denounce men of opposite opinion.

Resolved, That we will repudiate and discountenance all
organized bands of men who leave their homes for the avowed purpose of exciting others to acts of violence, believing it to be the
duty of all good disposed citizens to stay at home during these
exciting times and protect and if possible restore the peace and
harmony of the neighborhood; furthermore we will discountenance all armed bodies of men who may come amongst us from
any other part of the Territory or from the States unless said
parties shall come under the authority of the United States.

Resolved, That we pledge ourselves, individually and col-
lectively, to prevent a recurrence of a similar tragedy and to
ferret out and hand over to the criminal authorities the perpe-
trators for punishment.

	C. H. Price, President	
	R. Golding, Chairman	
H. H. Williams	R. Gilpatrick	
Secretary	W. C. McDow	Committee.
	S. V. Vandaman	
	A. Castele	
	John Blunt	

If this attitude had persisted things might have been different for the Territory, but within a few weeks party sympathies had reasserted themselves and the old struggle was
begun anew on a more direct and brutal scale. One settler
even testified, when time and history had given the butchery
a certain respectability, that Free State men sympathized
with the murderers, but that " policy dictated that the deed
should be disavowed as having general disapproval." But
the reaction did follow in part because of the attitude taken
by the pro-slavery newspapers of the border. When Free

State settlers read such things as the following lines in the *Border Times* of Westport, Missouri, they must have felt a little on the defensive.

WAR!   WAR!

Eight Pro-Slavery men murdered by Abolitionists in Franklin County, K. T.

LET SLIP THE DOGS OF WAR!

We learn from a despatch just received by Col. A. G. Boone, dated at Paola, K. T., May 26, 1826, and signed by Gens. Heiskell and Barbee, that the reported murder of eight pro-slavery men in Franklin County, K. T., is but too true.

Back in the States the Democratic press made no capital of the incident. At last they had a retort to the catalogue of crimes which the Free State agitators in the Northern newspapers laid at the door of the South, but, strangely enough, the retort was not used. Meanwhile, the Republican press from ignorance or policy was giving a false and garbled version of Pottawatomie and crying up its own latest martyr, the violent, short-sighted Senator Sumner, who had done a little, perhaps, to earn the stick of Congressman Brooks about his ears. John Brown's part in that bloody night's work was not known and by consequence the North was ready to receive him a little later as the hero of Kansas. But now in that Territory groups of heavily armed horsemen — Free State and pro-slavery — scoured the roads and countryside for Old Man Brown and his gang.

It was one such group under the command of the Reverend Martin White that fell in with Jason as he fled to seek the protection of United States troops. Jason did not recognize the fighting preacher, and innocently asked him the way to Ottawa Jones'. Martin White looked the questioner over. "You are one of the men we are looking for!" he shouted. "Your name is Brown. I knew your father. I knew your brother!" Up came all the guns with the clicking of hammers. "You are our prisoner," White added more quietly. "Got any arms?" "A revolver," Jason answered. "Hand it out. Now go ahead of the horses," he was ordered. Jason knew that the order was practically the order for his death. He leaped backward, still facing the horsemen. His usual stammering speech left him. "My name is Jason Brown. I am a Free State man and what you call an Abolitionist. I have never knowingly injured anybody. Now if you want my blood for that, there's a mark for you." He tore open his shirt and waited. One by one the guns dropped down and rested across the saddle-bows. He had won. "We won't kill you now," Martin White said, "but you are our prisoner and we hold every man a scoundrel till he is proven honest."

For four miles they drove him at a fast walk. Just as Jason's ague came on they stopped at a cabin and store by the roadside and gave the prisoner a sack of coffee for a pillow. One fellow, dissatisfied with the way things were falling out, stood over him with an unsheathed bowie knife. "Do you see anything bad about me," Jason asked. "I don't see anything good about ye!" he snarled and then turned away leaving the sick man alone. After a little time they put him on horseback, tied his arms behind his back and his feet beneath the mount's belly, and, with a guard of twenty men, rode to Paola.

The place was crowded with men organized in search for the Pottawatomie murderers, and now that a prisoner was in their hands the idea of a speedy hanging appealed very strongly. While the end of a new hemp rope dangled from a branch, three men, not dressed in the usual frontier fashion, stepped out of the crowd and approached Jason who huddled under the tree. One of the strangers tapped him on the shoulder and showed a scrap of paper in the palm of his hand. " Whose writing is that? " he asked. " My father's," replied Jason. " Is old John Brown your father? " " Yes." The questioner did not say another word, but stepped back into the crowd. He seemed to be arguing with them, but Jason could not hear what he said. In a short time he returned and quietly said: " Come with me to my house and I will treat you like my own son, but we must hold you prisoner." The man was Judge Jacobs of Lexington, Kentucky, and one of his two companions was that same Judge Cato, whose court the Browns had broken up. Jason had a large measure of gratitude in his nature, for in remembrance of the incident he could say: " Then came what changed my whole mind and life as to my feeling toward slave-holders. I can't see a Southerner or a Southern soldier, now, whatever he thinks of *me*, without wanting to grasp his two hands." But the stay under the protection of Judge Jacobs was not one to make the poor fellow forget those horrible events which had made him a fugitive: every day Mrs. Doyle sat down at the same table with Jason and the people of the house. She never spoke a word.

On the third night John was brought in. He had been captured at Adair's and hurried to Paola, where Jason and a number of other prisoners were being held. After a few days the brothers were separated, to be reunited about the time of their removal to Osawatomie. John was more sane now, but the harsh treatment by his new captors made his derangement a sort of blessing. They tied his arms tightly behind him with small hard hemp rope, and attached a longer one by which he was driven. Captain Wood himself saw that the turns of the rope were brutally secure. Jason was carried in a wagon as far as Osawatomie, but John was driven on foot ahead of the horses, while the cords cut into his upper arms and the hot summer sun beat down on him.

At the new camp on the Ottawa Creek John's situation was no better. He was chained by his ankles with an ox-cart chain to the center pole of the guard tent. The close turns of the rope on his arms had never been loosened and the flesh was terribly swollen. They had driven him through the waters of Bull Creek whose sharp yellow flints had lacerated his feet despite the boots. The maniac leaped about within the span of his chain, shrieking military orders to the encampment in the delusion that he commanded all whom he saw about him. Finally Captain Wood went up to Jason. " Keep that man still," he said. " I can't keep an insane man still." " He is no more insane than you are. If you don't keep him still, we'll do it for you." Jason could do nothing with his brother and Wood's threat was fulfilled. One of the troopers knocked John down and beat him into unconsciousness. For three or four hours he lay still in the sunshine before the guard tent.

For two weeks Captain Wood encamped near the Ottawa Creek, only a mile or so from the Adair cabin, while his men beat the bush for the Brown gang. Word would be brought in that John Brown had been seen somewhere in the rough country along the Marais des Cygnes, and the troopers would turn out to scour the river bottoms and the timbered ravines, but they never raised their quarry. He was lying with his party in a safe hiding place, so close to the camp of the troops that night and morning he heard the notes of their bugles. He hoped to make an attempt at rescue, but perhaps he could guess what had been resolved upon in Wood's camp: if the attack came the Brown brothers were to be disposed of before the fight commenced.

When the unsuccessful hunt finally ended the prisoners were chained two by two, and the long march to Lecompton began. Mrs. Adair saw her nephews being driven past in the midst of the other men chained with them. All she could do was give them a little food and her prayers. It was gruelling business — twenty-five miles a day, under the blazing sun of early summer, while the chains dragged at their ankles. Wood did nothing to alleviate the special severity which had been visited on the Browns, but his motives could scarcely have been political, despite the charge of pro-slavery sympathy which was brought against him; only a few years later, he was to command a Federal division in the Army of the Cumberland. This severity had some justification, for it was the general belief in camp that they held two of the Pottawatomie murderers. Jason was an innocent victim, but in John, who suffered more, they did have one of the criminals. He was an *accomplice before the fact.*

By this time John Brown had fought and won what he called " the first regular battle fought between Free-State and pro-slavery men in Kansas," had gotten himself an able press agent, and had become to some people, who could forget or excuse Pottawatomie, or deny his share in it, a sort of hero and defender. Before the end of June he wrote home the first letter since the night of May 24. It was his official announcement:

Dear Wife and Children, Every One, --
    It is now about five weeks since I have seen a line from North Elba, or had any chance of writing you. During that period we here have passed through an almost constant series of very

trying events. We were called to go to the relief of Lawrence, May 22, and every man (eight in all), except Orson, turned out; he staying with the women and children, and to take care of the cattle. John was captain of a company to which Jason belonged; the other six were a little company by ourselves. On our way to Lawrence we learned that it had been already destroyed, and we encamped with John's company overnight. Next day our little company left and during the day we stopped and searched three men. . . .

On the second day and evening after we left John's men, we encountered quite a number of pro-slavery men, and took quite a number of prisoners. Our prisoners we let go; but we kept some four or five horses. We were immediately after this accused of murdering five men at Pottawatomie, and great efforts have since been made by the Missourians and their ruffian allies to capture us. John's company soon afterward disbanded, and also the Osawatomie men.

That was all he had to say about Pottawatomie. It was the story he wanted the world to accept. To get it before the world as quickly as possible and in the most profitable fashion, he added, after much other news and the account of his "first regular battle," a paragraph of directions for his wife.

If, under God, this letter reaches you so that it can be read, I wish it at once carefully copied, and a copy of it sent to Gerrit Smith. I know of no other way to get these facts and our situation before the world, nor when I can write again.

Pottawatomie opened a new life for John Brown; it showed him how one thing might be done as well as another. It also opened a new life for the Territory, for success breeds imitation and masters are entitled to disciples. " The disorders in the Territory have, in fact, changed their character, and consist now of robberies and assassinations, by a set of bandits whom the excitement of the times has attracted hither." Such was the official report of a high military officer in the Territory. In the disturbances before May 24 some sort of issue had existed between two parties. Now the principle meant nothing except an excuse for plundering and banditry by gangs of ruffians — the scum and backwash of frontier life. For a time at least the prejudices and fears of their more honest neighbors gave them protection and free rein. The massacre on the Pottawatomie had set the example; it had shown how the trick might be turned, how ineffectual any forces of justice were, and how quickly partisan feeling would rally to condone such a deed.

When the Pottawatomie militia peremptorily disposed of John and Jason on the day after the murders, old Brown could not be sure that things would fall out so well for him. He counted strongly on just such a turn of affairs in the Territory, but he realized after the conduct of his neighbors in the militia, that a little time would be needed to bring to fruit his hope of vindication. H. H. Williams had led the disgruntled riflemen back to their homes, John and Jason had struck off by themselves for Osawatomie, and John Brown with his men had dropped from sight into the timber and broken country.

The fugitives hid themselves on Jason's claim. Owen, on a mate to the fast running horse which John had received, was despatched to Osawatomie for supplies. Only the speed of the new mount saved him, for when he was only a mile or so west of the Adair cabin on his return trip a party of men sighted him and gave chase. His own fast horse was winded and lathered with sweat before he shook off the pursuers and took refuge in the brush. There he found his brother John in hiding. He tried to persuade him to join their father's camp, but John refused and remained in the ravine on Adair's land. Owen took John's fresh horse and pushed on. The next morning John was taken prisoner.

When Owen finally reached the camp after his narrow escape, the gang under his father was reënforced by a certain O. A. Carpenter and by an Austrian Jew, Bondi, who was an associate of Weiner, the murderer, and of Benjamin. They sadly needed backers at the present crisis, but Carpenter was of far more value than a mere rifleman. He knew of a place where Brown and his men could lie in safe hiding from the bodies of searchers who patrolled the roads and scoured the country; John Brown leaped at the opportunity of such protection until the storm released by Pottawatomie should blow itself out, and a revival of the old party prejudices make it possible for him to confront the world again.

That night the flight toward the new hiding place began. They cautiously left the the Middle Creek region and moved toward the Ottawa. The order of the march was dictated by John Brown. Frederick rode first, followed by Owen and Carpenter, their guide. Ten paces behind them was old Brown, and back of him the others, riding two by two. The three youngest of the company, Salmon, Oliver, and Bondi, rode without saddles, for the spoils of Pottawatomie did not include equipment for all the horses taken. There were ten men now in the company — well mounted, well armed, and nerved by the desperate necessities of the game they were playing. A dangerous lot if they were cornered: they knew that they could expect little quarter.

After several hours of the secret flight, when they neared the ford of the Marais des Cygnes, they heard a noise in the dark path ahead. For a moment the riders hesitated; by the fitful light of a dying campfire they could just discern the tents of a cavalry patrol. The sentry's challenge rang out. There could be no turning back; only boldness could bluff things through. John Brown pushed to the head of the party and answered the challenge, while the others huddled their horses together to appear in the obscurity of the path as a small company. Their leader was equal to the moment. He called for the Captain of the troop. After a little time he appeared in front of his tent. " Who are you," he demanded. " Some Free State farmers going back home toward Lawrence," was the cool reply. The Captain regarded the speaker. He looked the part he played: a stooped man wearing a tattered straw hat, dirty frayed trousers, and old boots. " All right," the Captain said; " pass on." His duty had nothing to do with honest law-abiding men. He was out on the hunt for a gang of criminals.

By the next day they reached the hiding place to which Carpenter was leading them. It was in the depth of the untouched timber, a half-mile from Ottawa Creek. An enormous oak had fallen there and by the protection of its trunk they pitched the rough camp. The horses were tethered in the underbrush. John Brown quickly inspected the locality and posted guards. The place looked safe enough, but the life here was to be a hard one. John Brown prepared two meals a day for his men from the coarse flour baked in skillets. Creek water, with a little ginger and a spoonful of molasses to each pint, washed down the food. They slept on the ground under the unhealthy mists that rose from the Ottawa. And always there was the strain of perpetual vigilance.

It was here on May 30 that the press-agent found John Brown. James Redpath was correspondent for the *Tribune* and the St. Louis *Democrat*, and his sympathies were strongly with the Free State faction. In fact, Redpath was

a "Union-splitter" and he saw John Brown as a possible
tool to the desired end of civil war. He had come to Kansas
for that purpose: "I believed that a civil war between the
North and South would ultimate in insurrection, and that
the Kansas troubles would probably create a military conflict of the sections. Hence I left the South, and went to
Kansas; and endeavored, personally and by my pen, to
precipitate a revolution."

He claimed that he simply stumbled on the Brown camp
by accident. In any case it was a happy day for both him
and Old Brown. But Redpath may have been enterprising
enough to find his man and the necessary information may
well have come from Lehnart or Cook or some more immediate accomplice. Those two were men of the stamp John
Brown found useful, and in Kansas they struck up an early
if obscure contact with him. After the attack on Lawrence
they had ridden off to make reprisals. "Reprisals" in
Kansas was a word that might mean anything.

Redpath knew that he was in doubtful territory when he
wandered into the wooded country along the creek bottom.
A powerful looking fellow suddenly appeared before him,
and Redpath's hand dropped to his gun. Indeed, the
stranger looked wild enough: his hair was matted and
tangled and he had been unshaven for many months, his
pantaloons were tucked in old red-topped boots, and from
a broad belt several pistols and a large Arkansas bowie
knife protruded in easy reach of the hand. The fellow's
eyes had the hard glint of a madman. "Hello," he shouted,
"you're in our camp!" Redpath took no chances. "Halt!
or I'll fire," he answered, and his eight-inch Colt covered
the man. A short parley followed to the eminent satisfaction of the correspondent. The wildman was Frederick

Brown, son of old John Brown. He had seen Redpath in Lawrence and recognized him as a friend. " You're all right," he said.

The walk to the camp was a strange one. Frederick hurried ahead, swinging the empty water pail he carried, and talking madly about Pottawatomie — how his family was accused of it and how they were innocent of any blood. His excitement and vehemence increased momently. He led Redpath many times back and forth across the creek and through the brush, still waving the empty pail and turning about at every few paces to gaze at his listener. In the end Redpath lost all patience and pluntly told the mad guide that he would hear no more until he had found old John Brown himself. At that Frederick's wits seemed to return a little. He quietly filled his pail and with no further words led the visitor down a devious path toward the camp. Twice they were challenged by sentries who slipped suddenly out from the timber and as suddenly disappeared again.

They reached a sort of opening, in the center of which a great fire was blazing beneath a pot. Three or four armed men lay on red and blue blankets on the grass, and to one side Oliver Brown and Charley Kaiser, a recent recruit, leaned on their guns. The other rifles and the sabres were stacked in a half-military fashion against a tree, and a dozen horses, ready saddled, were picketed on the edge of the camp. Near the fire Redpath saw for the first time old John Brown himself, busy about the matter of cooking a pig to supplement the skillet-bread and creek water diet.

He received Redpath with considerable cordiality. Here, indeed, was an opportunity. The interview lasted for an hour, and a more profitable hour John Brown never spent.

There was a touch of genius in his words to the reporter:
" I would rather have the small-pox, yellow fever, and
cholera all together in my camp, than a man without principles. It's a mistake, sir, that our people make, when they
think that bullies are the best fighters, or that they are the
men fit to oppose these Southerners. Give me men of good
principles; God-fearing men; men who respect themselves,
and with a dozen of them, I will oppose any hundred such
men as these Buford ruffians." Only the subject of Pottawatomie was barred from the conversation by John Brown's
definite command. " I shall as Captain communicate whatever is proper about the conduct and intentions of this
company." And so he did; he communicated precisely what
was proper.

The hour passed and Redpath went on his way. He was a
good reporter and a man of cleverness and convictions. He
knew that what the Free State cause needed to consolidate
Eastern sympathy, as well as its Kansas position, was a hero.
A fellow like Robinson — cool, sagacious, seeing the whole
situation — was not that sort of a hero. In simpler terms he
was not good copy. Old John Brown would do admirably.
A grey-haired old man, dirty and poorly dressed, with toes
sticking out of broken boots, leaning over a pot and clutch-
ing a greasy iron fork.

The pendulum was swinging back and the old prejudices
were at work again. Another recruit, Benjamin Cochrane,
brought news that Bondi's cabin had been burned and his
cattle run off, and that Weiner's store had been ransacked
by way of vengeance for Pottawatomie. The United States
troops had watched the whole affair without lifting a hand
to interfere. There was a considerable degree of justice perhaps, in the vengeance, but its way was bad. Two wrongs

did not make a right and some people began to look to John Brown as a possible ally in preventing the spread of such depredations into the Free State community. Captain Shore, who commanded the Prairie City Rifles, and a Dr. Westfall found their way to the camp by the fallen oak, and a sort of alliance was struck up for the benefit of all concerned. The butchery on the creek might bring reprisals from men who would not trouble themselves to hunt down the true criminals. The union with an alleged murderer was better than submission to possible outrage from Missourians and the pro-slavery men of the Territory. At least the murderer could shoot straight and ride hard, and no one, neither enemy nor friend, had ever questioned his courage. The ethics of the alliance could be temporarily shelved.

The day after Redpath's visit John Brown learned from Captain Shore that the time had come to strike. A large force of Missourians were camping at the Black Jack spring on the Santa Fe trail. It was John Brown's opportunity and he seized it. Shore was to fight as a preventive measure, because Free State men did not feel safe with the Missourians in the neighborhood; his ally was to fight for his vindication, for the chance to leave the outlaw camp in the bush, for his very life. Redpath and Shore were his salvation.

The company camping by the black jack oaks on the Santa Fe trail had one errand in the Territory; it was to hunt down the Pottawatomie murderers. Already it had assisted in the capture of Free State men at Paola, including Jason and John Brown Jr. and now it was on the track of the main gang under the old man himself. At its head was Henry Clay Pate, a one-time student at the University of

Virginia, who had come to Kansas to write and fight for Southern rights. He had arranged to do both with the greatest degree of efficiency and authority, for he was a correspondent of the *Missouri Republican* at St. Louis, and a Deputy United States Marshal. Eight years later at Yellow Tavern he died in the same cause, as Colonel of the Fifth Virginia Cavalry. Now his business was that of chasing an outlaw, with men of little better stamp at his back.

By ten o'clock the next morning, Sunday morning, the outlaw and his party were in Prairie City. They kept the Lord's day by listening to the sermon of a wandering preacher until the order came to move. In the very midst of the sermon someone caught sight of three strangers passing in the direction of Black Jack. Devotions were interrupted. Two of the strangers were captured, and at the muzzle of a gun confessed that they were from the camp of Captain Pate. John Brown got all the information he needed. The plan he devised was simple and efficient: a night march and a surprise attack at dawn.

The enthusiasm at Prairie City was considerable. Some forty men started out with John Brown's party when the march began, but during the silent hours on the road to Black Jack they had time for reflection. Enthusiasm dwindled mile by mile. When the first streaks of daylight came only seventeen of the volunteers remained. The horses were left at a sheltering clump of oaks under the care of one of Shore's men and Frederick Brown, whose unbalanced mind made him unfit for fighting.

Cautiously the twenty-six men moved over the ridge. A half-mile away was Pate's camp, just beginning to stir into life. In the distance they saw the covered supply wagons standing as protection before the tents, and beyond the tents on a rise of ground the picketed horses and mules.

The two companies under Shore and John Brown deployed briskly for the attack. A Missouri sentinel fired and fell back on his camp. Shore's men scattered to the left in a thin line. On the exposed slope of the prairie they halted and opened fire with their Sharpe's rifles at the range of three hundred yards. Without pausing for a single shot on the enemy John Brown led his people in to close quarters. They gained the sheltering rim of a ravine, near enough for their short range guns to cope with the Sharpe's rifles of Pate's men. The position was perfect; from it they could lay an enfilading fire on the startled camp.

The short dawn passed and the hot summer sun climbed higher. The end was not in sight. John Brown could see the grey puffs of smoke from Shore's line on the uncovered eastern slope becoming less and less frequent. One after another those raw fighters crept back out of range and gave up the business. Some few came around to join Brown's own dwindling ranks on the ravine's rim. Shore himself had gone to rouse help. Brown managed to persuade six of the frightened deserters to keep a safe position and make some show by firing on Pate's horses. Only eight men remained in the ravine. It was now broad noon.

Suddenly from behind the ridge a single horseman appeared. He galloped in a close circle about the camp, flourishing his sabre as he stood in the stirrups, and shouting wildly. The words drifted indistinctly between the cracking of rifles: " Come on boys, come on! We've got them surrounded! We've cut off communications!" Shot after shot was fired at the lone fellow, but he kept on his mad circuit. It was the "flighty" Frederick mounted on Owen's Ned Scarlet.

The ruse worked. Two men came out from the camp, holding up a ramrod from which a white handkerchief fluttered. John Brown, alone, walked out to meet them. The three came together at a spot between the lines. "Are you the Captain of that company?" John Brown demanded of the flag-bearer. "No." "Then stay with me and send your companion back to call the captain out. I will talk with him and not with you." In a little while Pate joined them. "I am a Deputy United States Marshal, acting under the authority of the General Government," he explained. John Brown was not impressed: Washington was very far away from Black Jack. "I will listen to nothing of that kind. If you have any proposal to make, make it here and now. If you haven't got one for me, I have one for you. It is unconditional surrender!" He took out his pistol and held it ready. The callow young fellow did not understand the odds against him in the person of the cornered, desperate old man, who stood there so cool in his desperation.

They walked in the direction of the camp. The eight attackers who had maintained the fight filed down the ravine in front of the camp to receive the unexpected surrender. As the leaders approached the defenders' line, where Lieutenant Brockett commanded, John Brown called out for him to lay down arms. Brockett did not obey. "Give the order," John Brown said to Pate. Pate hesitated; he began to sense the ruse and the real strength against him. In a flash the pistol was at his head. "Give the order!" the old man's voice rang out.

The surrendered weapons were piled into a wagon. The twenty-odd prisoners — some cursing their own stupidity

for falling into the trap and some heartily glad to be out of
the affair — were marched down to the captors' position.
There a sort of agreement and terms of surrender were prepared and signed by the leaders of both parties. The
prisoners were to be exchanged for Free State men taken
by the recent Paola round-up in which Pate had assisted.
John Brown Jr. and Jason were to be exchanged for
Pate and Brockett, respectively. Arms, especially side-
arms, and horses " so far as practicable " were to be
returned at the release of each man. Shore, with reënforcements, was back on the field in time to put his name to the
document.

Pate's pride was sorely hurt, and before the close of the
month he was apologizing for himself in the columns of the
New York *Tribune*. " Had I known whom I was fighting I
would not have trusted to a flag of truce. . . . Captain
Brown commanded me to order my company to lay down
arms. Putting a revolver to my breast he repeated the command, giving me one or two minutes to make the order. He
might have shot me; his men might have riddled me, but I
would not have given the order for a world, much less my
poor life." But the order seems to have been given. In July
John Brown answered Pate's charge of treachery in the
Tribune by a letter which was a model of soldierly dignity,
magnanimity, and innuendo. The impulsive, too heroic,
young Virginian was to learn much about soldiering and
other matters before the fatal day at Yellow Tavern. In
Kansas he was no match for Old Brown.

So ended what John Brown complacently termed the
" first regular battle " of the Territory. It was not a very
impressive engagement; fifty men, most of them frightened
by what they were doing, lay on the prairie and shot at each

other. The business lasted for five hours and when it was all over no one had been killed and only two or three were wounded. But for the fugitive and outlaw it was a great victory; it made all of his later ones possible. And then there were Pate's horses and mules, which were to be returned "so far as practicable."

After Black Jack, recruits crowded in. "Some of them," John Brown recorded, "were very busy, not only with the plunder of our enemies, but with our private effects, leaving us, while guarding our prisoners and providing in regard to them, much poorer than before the battle." John Brown never missed a chance to refer to his poverty, and few chances to alleviate it. There was considerable alleviation the day after the battle when he pillaged the store and corral of J. M. Bernard, a pro-slavery sympathizer, and added several thousand dollars' worth of booty to the spoils of Black Jack. The cause of freedom and the plunder business were thriving side by side.

John Brown pitched his camp on a small island of Middle Creek and fortified it by earthworks. He commanded a hundred and fifty armed men. His name was cleared and he could act in the open. He was the recognized Free State champion.

News of the battle flashed over the Territory. It was only a matter of hours before Whitfield, the Delegate to Congress, was raising a force at Westport to march to the rescue of Pate, and before the United States troops were on the move to break up the lawless gangs of both factions. Colonel Sumner and his cavalry intercepted Whitfield's men and read them the President's despatch and the Governor's proclamation concerning Kansas disorders. They listened respectfully; the dust had scarcely settled behind Sumner's dragoons before they were again on the march. Sumner himself was rather cynical about the effect of the President's message.

At the fortified island in Middle Creek Colonel Sumner and Major Sedgwick had found John Brown before the meeting with Whitfield. " I started with a squadron of cavalry," Sedwick reported, " to go about forty miles to break up an encampment of free-soilers who had been robbing and taking prisoners any pro-slavery man they could meet." With some hundred and fifty men at his back the commander of the encampment felt himself entitled to consideration; he came out from the island and demanded terms. Colonel Sumner would hear none of it. The officers of the General Government were not there to treat with "lawless and armed men." The order was given to occupy the camp. Among the troops who marched in was Lieutenant J. E. B. Stuart. The young Lieutenant got a good look at Old Brown of Osawatomie; the face was not one to be easily forgotten.

The Black Jack prisoners were released and the captors were commanded to disperse. Sumner looked over the men before him, and turned to Preston, a Deputy United States Marshal, who accompanied the troops. " Is there anyone here for whom you have a warrant? " he asked. Brown, the Pottawatomie murderer, and the Marshal with a warrant in his pocket stared each other in the eye. In that moment Preston's courage melted away. Colonel Sumner waited. " I do not recognize anyone for whom I have warrants," he said. " Then what are you here for? " retorted Sumner in disgust.

7

LETTERS OF MARQUE FROM GOD

WITHIN an hour after Sumner's order the island camp was empty. The Free State men who had rallied to expel the Missourians scattered to their own homes, very well pleased with the short campaign. The Brown gang had no homes. The cabins on their claims lay in ashes as a result of that night's work on Pottawatomie. There was nothing for them now but the life of wanderers, existing on the country — the life of hidden camps and meager foraging and night rides. Two of the Brown family were suffering from wounds; Henry Thompson had been hit at Black Jack, and Salmon had accidentally shot himself a short while after the battle. Salmon was removed to Carpenter's cabin in the neighborhood and left in the charge of Bondi for a few days. Only a half-mile away from the deserted " Camp Brown " on Middle Creek, a new camp was pitched in the thick underbrush.

No project of real importance could be undertaken until the wounded men were again on their feet. It was a time of recuperation, rest, and planning. It was a time of waiting until circumstances again would permit them to become active. On June 10, a general council was called. There was no prospect of any business in the near future to hold the gang together; there was not even the fear of punishment or the desire of mutual support, for a week earlier they had won their fight. Henry Thompson, still suffering from the wound in his spine, was carried to Carpenter's cabin. Some obscure affairs called Weiner away from the scene where services of a true lover of freedom were needed most. He left for Lousiana, where John Brown himself had once thought of acting " to make a diversion in favor of Kansas." Weiner and his Captain had probably discussed the matter of opportunities in Louisiana. Now they settled their accounts and parted. Bondi went along with Weiner as far as Leavenworth. The remnants of the organization remained in their hiding place.

What happened during the following weeks was never known. Only one thing is certain: John Brown was not the sort of man to sit down in idleness under any circumstances. The question is: what was the precise nature of John Brown's business during this period of strict secrecy?

Plundering, raiding, and murder were still going on unchecked in Kansas, for the troops were far too few to adequately police the Territory. Whitfield's men looted Osawatomie, immediately after Sumner's order to disperse, and then safely escaped into Missouri. The Lawrence militia made a successful attack on Franklin and took considerable plunder. Numerous gangs, small enough to move without attracting attention, roved about the region, living on what they could steal under the pretext of " reprisals." In one such gang were Lenhart and Cook, who had before this fallen into accord with John Brown and who was to show himself more to his liking as time passed. Cook, indeed, had been an honored guest in " Camp Brown " the very day before Colonel Sumner's appearance. Major Sedgwick with considerable degree of reason had put the matter: "One of these things must happen: either it will terminate in civil war or the vicious will band themselves together to plunder and murder all whom they meet."

The first part of Major Sedgwick's prophecy seemed on the verge of fulfillment for the nation just as the latter part had already come for Kansas. Within a few days after Congressman Brooks' walking stick fell about the ears of Senator Sumner and paid him for the mixture of truth, untruth, and insult which composed his "Crime Against Kansas" speech, the new Republican Party nominated its first Presidential candidate at Philadelphia. John Frémont, the "Pathfinder," the frontiersman, the land speculator, was the candidate; the party platform declared it both "the right and duty of Congress to prohibit in the Territories those twin relics of barbarism, polygamy and slavery." The old lines of party cleavage were changing, and as early as the summer of 1856, before the election, the change was evident. The division was more nearly sectional than ever before in the half-century since the "irrepressible conflict" first began to develop.

Over against the "Black Republicans" with their slogan of "Free soil, free speech, and Frémont," stood James Buchanan. Fillmore was also in the field as the choice of the Know-Nothings, but he and his party were equally colorless and irrelevant to the main issue. This issue was sharply drawn between the Republicans and Democrats; the Know-Nothings were caught between the upper and the nether millstone. Behind Frémont was the new-born enthusiasm and sectional consciousness of the North and West, and behind Buchanan the political expertness, the tenacity, the habit of leadership, and the prestige of victory of the Democratic

Party. But beyond these things was the single high card of the South: *the threat of secession.* A certain Virginia politician, Governor Wise, expressed a general sentiment of his contemporaries. " To tell me we should submit to the election of a Black Republican is to tell me that Virginia and the fourteen Slave States are already subjugated and degraded; that the Southern people are without spirit and without purpose to defend the rights they know and dare not maintain." His contemporary, J. M. Mason, said the same thing in a letter to Colonel Jefferson Davis. " I give it as my judgment, in event of Frémont's election, the South should not pause, but proceed at once to 'immediate, absolute, and eternal separation.' So I am a candidate for the first halter." There was no secrecy about these things. In the public print it was asserted that measures had been perfected " to withdraw from the Union before Frémont can get possession of the army, and navy, and the purse-strings." In other words, if Frémont had been elected, the capital of the Southern Confederacy would probably have been at Washington, D. C., and its flag the Stars and Stripes. But *secession* was not a new word to the ears of Northern voters, and many who cast their ballots for free soil, free speech and Frémont, believed it to be a word and nothing more. Four years later, it was the word which echoed in the first gun fired on Fort Sumter.

Even in the summer of 1856, as the campaign waxed more violent, a man like Gerrit Smith, who had been a non-resistant, could unwittingly repeat the prophecy of Major Sedgwick: " You are looking to ballots when you should be looking to bayonets. . . . There was a time when slavery could have been ended by political action. But that time has gone by — and, as I apprehend, forever. There was not virtue enough in the American people to bring slavery to a bloodless termination; and all that now remains for them is to bring it to a bloody one." And before the mutilated bodies along the Pottawatomie were hurried underground, Garrison had called for a convention " for the purpose of taking measures to effect a peaceable withdrawal from an alliance which an experience of more than three-score years has demonstrated to be as impracticable as it has been disastrous to genuine republicanism and a pure Christianity." For him the Union was a covenant with death. It was simply a question as to how long the center could hold against the whirl of those violent forces.

July 4 was the day appointed for the meeting of the Free State Legislature at Topeka. Colonel Sumner had his instructions from the office of the Territorial Governor and he had the proclamation of the President which he interpreted to mean that the Legislature should not assemble. " I am decidedly of the opinion that that body of men ought not to be permitted to assemble. It is not too much to say that the peace of the country depends upon it." There could not be two governments in the Territory. But only a little earlier the Republican National Convention had made the admission of Kansas with the Free Constitution a part of their program. On July 1, the same day that the report of the Howard Committee on Kansas troubles was submitted, Charles Robinson and other leaders wrote a letter to members of the waiting Legislature. Resistance to any Federal interference, they said, was justifiable. " You have met for the purpose of doing what other new States have done, and what you have a constitutional right to do, and no man or class of men have a right to interfere, not excepting even the President of the United States." The last of the six signatures to this letter of advice was that of John Brown Jr.

JOHN BROWN

Just two days before the date of the Legislature's assembly, John Brown suddenly appeared in the town of Lawrence, where he found Colonel W. A. Phillips, the correspondent of the *Tribune*. He gave the correspondent a statement of his intentions; he was going to Topeka to help defend the Legislature if any effort should be made to disperse it. That would be a respectable service to the cause of freedom, but, unhappily, he could not give a statement of services to the cause in the recent past, for if he had accomplished anything it was of such a nature that he did not care for it to have publicity. But he did need Phillips' help in a private matter dealing with ancient history; he had prepared an answer to Pate's accusations in the *Tribune* and this he confided to the correspondent. If one press-agent was good, he had decided that two would be better.

Phillips saddled up that evening and rode towards Topeka with John Brown's company. In a bivouac some ten miles from the town the two men spread their blankets on the damp grass and rested with their saddles for pillows. For hours they talked. John Brown had criticism for both parties in Kansas: slavery brutalized all men of that faction, and the Free State people had too many broken-down politicians from the East, who would rather pass resolutions than act, and who criticized all who did real work. John Brown had a very definite idea of what was real work; generally speaking, it was whatever he himself did. There were reminiscences of his trip to Europe and his visits to fortifications there in the days when he had been a peaceful wool-merchant. " Modern warfare does away with those things," he said; " a well-armed brave soldier is the best fortification. The way to fight is to press to close quarters." He deplored the basis of society in selfishness. " There are an infinite number of wrongs

196

to right, but in our country slavery is the sum of all villainies." The talk drifted on. " Now," he said, " it is midnight." His hand pointed to the clear summer stars. " How grand the symmetry of the heavens is. Everything there moves in harmony with the government of God. It's not that way with us poor creatures." They fell into silence.

When the shift of the stars told that it was nearing two o'clock, John Brown rose from the blanket and called his men. Within ten minutes they had saddled, packed, and mounted, to ride on their way across the rough country, fording the streams to avoid the road. It was hard going in the dark and when daylight came the company was floundering in the dense thickets of the creek bottom still some miles from Topeka. When they rode finally along the freer slopes in the early sunshine the notes of a bugle came drifting to them in the thin morning air. Beyond the stream they saw the distant tents of the United States soldiers.

Phillips entered Topeka with one of the men who was to bring news when the company was needed. John Brown's parting words were that the Legislature should meet, resist all who interfered with it, and fight, if necessary, even the United States troops. The correspondent carried with him the impression of an iron-willed old man, who was at the same time a philosopher, a grim fighter who would " press to close quarters," a child of nature listening to the whisper of wind on the prairie, and a prophet pointing to the stars. At least, such is a rough paraphrase of Mr. Phillips' rhetoric. He did not see the blood already on those hands or know why it had been spilled.

John Brown had given out that he was going to Topeka for action, but all day he lay in the timber that fringed the creek. In the town the legislators gathered despite Colo-

nel Sumner's order to disperse. The companies of United
States troops marched in and halted before the building where
the Legislature had assembled. The untrained Free State
militia wavered. Colonel Sumner's order was obeyed. " Gentlemen, this is the most disagreeable duty of my whole life," the
Colonel had said; but he saw it as his duty and fulfilled it with
dignity. As the column of dragoons moved off, cheers, Free
State cheers, were raised for Colonel Sumner.

The men whom Phillips left in the cover of the timber
dropped out of sight, and the secrecy of the past weeks again
enveloped them as completely as before. Only a few hints of
their life during the ensuing period have ever emerged. Salmon Brown gave out that in the end they left their hiding because Lucius Mills insisted that the invalids should be
moved and because they were " a drag on the fighting men."
But the nearest that John Brown had come to a public fight
was on July 4 when he lay in the creek bottom outside Topeka. If " fighting " did occur, as Salmon implied, that
fighting was of a strictly private nature — the side of his
endeavors which John Brown consistently failed to mention
in his copious accounts of his services. And the night ride to
Topeka proves clearly enough that the invalids could not
have been such a drag that no action was possible. There
happens to be further evidence that violent events occurred
in John Brown's lack of esteem for Mills because he "had
no desire to fight and was content to play nurse and doctor."

The attitude toward Mills came to a head when Oliver
offered him a fine revolver, which was part of the spoils of
Black Jack. John Brown ordered his son to keep the weapon,
for Mills would never use it. Oliver's mind was made up, and
John Brown simply tried to take the pistol by force. Salmon
snatched it from Oliver's belt, saying, " Now you fellows

fight it out!" The two men grappled — father and son. The old man was like a child in the hands of his powerful son. His arms were crushed to his sides and he was jammed back against the wagon. "Let go of me! Let go of me, I say!" he shouted in rage. "Not till you behave yourself!" Oliver had his way. The iron family discipline of the old days had broken a little now.

The end of the month found the party of seven on the road to the East. There were John Brown, the four sons, Henry Thompson, and Lucius Mills. The sons and Thompson were "sick of trouble and fighting" which they had found in Kansas under the leadership of John Brown. But the decision to leave was a sudden one, for at that very moment Henry Thompson's brother William was on his way to join the Browns. The Territory was somewhat quieter now, but the quiet was not that of a Free State victory. The proslavery men were tightening their hold after the disorganizing results of Pottawatomie and Black Jack; a blockhouse stood in John Brown's own region near Osawatomie; the Legislature had been dispersed; and all in all the need for Free State men was as great as ever. Did John Brown leave the Territory because he agreed with the disgust of the Free State Party which his eldest son expressed? "They, as a party, are guided by no principle but *selfishness*, and are withal most arrant *cowards* — they deserve their fate." Or did he leave because he felt that he could not serve the Free State cause in his own especial fashion, when Georgians were building blockhouses and Federal troops kept up a patrol for marauding bands?

At Nebraska City John Brown made a discovery which changed the complexion of Kansas affairs for him. At that gateway to Kansas by the overland route he found an encampment of six hundred Free State settlers ready to move in and fight or vote. Most of these immigrants had come under the auspices of the recently organized National Kansas Committee, but a hundred or so had been raised by James Lane, who opened the overland road when the Missourians blockaded the river. Now Lane was in command of the motley and poverty-stricken camp; in other words, he was "General" of the new army of occupation. Lane was impulsive, vindictive, vain, selfish, and confident, with a certain streak of immediate effectiveness which, more than once, did more harm than good to the general cause for which he was engaged. Furthermore, he had a taste for melodrama and gesture; in his vanity he felt that every proslavery man thirsted for his blood and so he took cover under a stage name. He was known as "General Jo Cook" and the deception would not have taken in a child. Back in the days of the Wakarusa war he and John Brown had met, and now John Brown received his confidence. All in all they had much in common.

But there was another man in the camp who was destined to play a far more intimate part in the affairs and fate of John Brown. This man was a certain "Colonel Whipple." Aaron Dwight Stevens had a much sounder reason for an alias than did Lane: he had been a soldier in the Mexican War and later a bugler-orderly to Colonel Sumner in the far West, but insubordination and mutiny made him a prisoner under a commuted sentence of death. After a daring escape he took up a claim in Kansas, and here what he had learned of soldiering in Mexico and in the Indian campaigns gave him a rank equal to that of the officer who had once commanded him and who was now aligned against him. Stevens learned, among other things, that he could get along faster elsewhere than in the strict organization of the army or under the conventions of ordered society. He was an efficient irregular fighter and he had the temperament for the life. The tight-lipped old man who had already made some reputation in that line interested him considerably. And so here was another recruit ready when the time should come — a violent, generous, brown-bearded young fellow of twenty-five, who hated authority and restraint, took no stock in religion, believed in spiritualism, wrote verses sometimes, and who sat by the campfire at night singing " Just As I Am " or " Eden Shore " in a rich baritone voice.

John Brown thought it better to throw in his lot with these men in the impending invasion than to go on East to a more uncertain future. He walked toward Nebraska City beside his plodding ox team, wearing the dingy, threadbare clothes of a hard-working old farmer; but with his change of plans came a change of costume. The people in the camp saw him mounted on a splendid horse, scrupulously clad in white summer dress, and with a broad straw hat protecting his lined, determined face from the sun. The man who had been " tasty in his dress " back in Hudson thirty years before was still so when opportunity offered, but dress, like other things, was a means to an end with him now. Not a few of the company thought, " he must be some distinguished man in disguise."

If there was any doubt in John Brown's mind concerning the wisdom of his decision, it must have been put away by news of Free State success at the blockhouse of New Georgia. On August 5 the Lawrence militia and some few volunteers from Osawatomie drove out the pro-slavery settlers, looted the place with admirable thoroughness, and burned the blockhouse. John Brown's especial stamping ground was once more free from interference, and he could return to the district in safety. Furthermore, there was a circumstance about the affair which could tickle his vanity: pro-slavery rumor had credited him with the job.

The sick and wounded members of the Brown party were carried to Tabor, Iowa, in the ox cart and left until they would be well enough to move. Owen, upon recovery, returned to Kansas, but Oliver, Salmon, and William and Henry Thompson made their way back East to drop again into the ways of peace for a while. William Thompson was instructed in the business which the others had learned so well by their Kansas life, and soon was ready enough to assist in a holdup when the four young men decided that they needed horses. Long afterwards, Salmon insisted that the horses were pro-slavery horses; but the holdup was on a peaceful Nebraska road where pro-slavery men in pursuit of the Brown boys would scarcely have ventured.

The plans of " General Jo Cook " received a great setback. He intended to march into Kansas at the head of his " army," but the arrival of S. G. Howe and Thaddeus Hyatt as representatives of the National Committee put an abrupt end to this pleasant idea. The Committee's methods were very direct; if Lane did not give up his command there would be no more supplies. The reasons the Committee advanced were courteous but also direct; " various considerations," they reported, " conspired to create a well-grounded apprehension in our minds that, by some hasty and ill-timed splurge, he would defeat the object of the expedition if suffered to remain even in otherwise desirable proximity." They understood their man very well, and so " General Jo Cook " took horse and rode into Kansas. With him rode a Captain Samuel Walker and Captain John Brown.

" Captain Brown, I wouldn't have your thoughts for anything in the world." John Brown started out of his deep absorption and turned to Walker. " I suppose you are thinking about that Pottawatomie affair? " " Yes," Walker admitted. John Brown's nervous, bony hand tightened on the reins, drawing his horse to a full stop. He looked intently at his companion for a moment. " Captain Walker," he said at last, " I saw that whole thing but I did not strike a blow. I take the responsibility. But there were men who advised doing it, and afterwards failed to justify it." Thus Lane and Robinson were marked as the men behind Pottawatomie. Walker was a thoroughly militant Free State man, and he already understood the massacre: an admission of complicity would do no harm here, especially when the buck could be passed up the line to such important persons as Robinson and Jim Lane. And John Brown always managed delicately to adjust the extent of his connection with Pottawatomie to the stomach of his audience. A little later the Boston people could swear to his complete innocence.

John Brown dropped from the party at Topeka, while Lane and Walker rode on toward Lawrence. The very day after Lane's arrival there, the campaign for driving out proslavery men began. At the end of the moonlit march the militia attacked Franklin. For three hours there was sharp firing, and then the Free State men ran a wagon load of burning hay against the blockhouse. The town was taken at the small cost of one man dead and six wounded, and the plundering began in good earnest, for the men had not given up a night's sleep for nothing. They marched back home loaded down with loot, and in their midst was a fine six-pounder which had once belonged to Lawrence. The type of the *Herald of Freedom* was now melted to make balls for it.

JOHN BROWN

John Brown was not present when the Free State companies took Fort Saunders on Washington Creek, nor did he have a hand in the business-like assault on the blockhouse of Colonel Titus, where Captain Shombre was killed and Captain Walker wounded, at the head of their men. " This is the second edition of the *Herald of Freedom!* " the cannoneer shouted as he touched off the Franklin six-pounder against Fort Titus, but John Brown was taking no risks in the cause of freedom at this time. He was far too busy maturing plans for a new project of his own to waste his efforts in matters such as those at Franklin, Fort Saunders, and Fort Titus. Lane sent an urgent request for his help, but there was no response from the man who was getting ready to play his old game on a bigger scale. " I will still work with you," he had said, " but under no commander but Old John Brown."

Now when everything was over and the wounded Colonel Titus with the other prisoners from his fort were safely under guard in Lawrence, John Brown came out of his week· of hiding. " Titus surrendered to me. I promised him his life, and I will defend it with my own," Captain Walker said to the Committee of Safety who were for hanging the prisoner *they* had not taken. Captain Walker was a determined man, and the Committee of Safety gave him his way. Just as Walker reached the house where Titus was held he heard shots from within. He rushed in, fearing that all his arguments and threats with the Committee had amounted to nothing. Just beyond the door stood a frontier desperado named " Buckskin," firing over the guard's shoulder at Titus who lay wounded on a cot. One blow from the butt of Walker's heavy dragoon pistol sent Buckskin tumbling heels-over-head down to the bottom of the stairs.

The desperado Buckskin was not the only man whom

Walker had to fight to save the life of his prisoner. Outside, in front of the building, Captain Brown and a Doctor Avery were haranguing the restless mob to hang Titus at any cost and despite anyone's protests. " Walker himself," they declared, " has resisted the Committee of Safety and is a public enemy." Three companies of Walker's men stood in close rank before the building; the orators talked on but talk was the sum of it, for they did not dare an attack on the solid line of three hundred fixed bayonets. And so Titus was saved. There was an unhappy harmony between the attitudes of Captain Brown and Buckskin, both of whom tried in their individual ways to kill an unarmed prisoner. John Brown might have recalled how the Border Ruffian, Judge Cato, saved Jason Brown from the rope, or how the Kickapoo Ranger, Captain Martin, did what he could for R. P. Brown, and protected Dr. Robinson from just such a mob as that which now clamored for the death of Titus. But too often the " Buckskins " had their way.

The exchange of Free State prisoners, taken because of the attack on Lawrence, for Titus and his men was the last official act of Governor Shannon. He was sick of his job as the executive of the troubled Territory, and, furthermore, his incompetence and temporizing had robbed him of confidence at Washington. The resignation came at a new crisis, when the whole region was in a tumult and the earlier disorders were revived on a larger and bloodier scale. There had been smaller successes for the Free State cause than those of Franklin and Fort Titus, but they likewise added to the general rancor and violence. Some of John Brown's associates, Bondi, Holmes, and probably Frederick Brown, raided the Reverend Martin White's home, stealing ten horses and a considerable amount of general plunder. Meanwhile the pro-slavery faction was gathering itself for a last campaign to dislodge its enemies. At Westport and New Santa Fe large numbers of men collected under the leadership of Atchison and John W. Reid. On August 26 began the march to sweep Kansas.

A day or two after Walker's bayonets had quieted the enthusiasm of John Brown's mob, Brown himself was in Osawatomie ready to begin his private campaign. The last time the people of the settlement had seen John Brown he had been a penniless and desperate man, waiting for the opportunity to better his condition by the butchery on the creek. Now they saw him as the owner of a spic and span four-mule team, a wagon heavy with provisions, and plenty of money. The money, like the five dead men in the shallow graves along the Pottawatomie, told no tales. Bondi, a follower and accomplice, reported that the " plenty of money " came from Northern sympathizers, such as Thaddeus Hyatt. In any case the man who had entered the Territory with sixty cents in his pocket, to see if something would not turn up to his advantage, now rode a fine blooded horse, dressed himself in spotless white summer clothing, and possessed a full wallet. Pottawatomie, Black Jack, and the summer in the secret camps was behind him; something had turned up at last.

The sons who had followed their father during the summer, except Frederick, were " sick of trouble and fighting," but within a week, John Brown led a new gang of nine members, equipped with stolen goods and mounted on stolen horses. Jason, who had been released from his confinement, was the only son among them, for Frederick, along with Bondi, seems to have been acting in the Holmes' band of raiders, which looted the home of Martin White. But there was another man in the neighborhood with precisely the same sort of followers — homeless, reckless fellows, with stolen shirts on their backs and stolen horses between their knees. His name was Captain Cline; John Brown called him "a very active young man." John Brown saw no reason why three men acting with the same end in view should not act together. The upshot was that the three gangs came to an agreement whereby John Brown was the real leader of all, with Cline and Holmes nothing more than his Lieutenants. It was a triumph of tact and business instinct.

The motive behind John Brown's new organization differed in no way from that of the past, but with his more ambitious scale of action he gave a new dignity to the business by drawing up a Covenant for the men of his own company. First, the Covenant declared that the members were enlisted "as a regular volunteer force for the maintenance of the rights and liberties of the Free State citizens of Kansas." This was all very good, so long as no one asked what the volunteers considered those rights and liberties to be. Now, "the rights and liberties of the Free State citizens" seem to have been understood as the right and liberty of these especial "Free State citizens" to take whatever "valuable property" satisfied their needs or pleased their fancy. The Covenant was fairly plain on this point: "All valuable property taken by honorable warfare from the enemy, shall be held as the property of the whole company or companies as the case may be, equally, without distinction; to be used for the common benefit, or be placed in the hands of responcible agents for sale: the proceeds to be divided as nearly equally amongst the company or *companies* capturing it as may be." "Honorable warfare" was the violent acquisition of "valuable property." "The enemy" were the people, preferably pro-slavery people, whose valuable property was to be acquired. John Brown understood the value of a big name for a simple thing. (The program was ambitious; " all acts of petty theft " were piously declared " disorderly." No prisoners were to be executed without a fair trial.)

Business began immediately. Within four days after he and Captain Cline came to their agreement, they made a clean sweep of the valley of Sugar Creek, took supplies, clothing, and one hundred and fifty head of cattle, and were slowly on their way north to Osawatomie with the herd before them. John Brown justified himself very simply; he assumed that all the pro-slavery cattle in the Territory had been originally lifted from Free State men and should come back to him, their acting representative. The idea of returning cattle to original owners was, of course, never entertained; it was all in the family of Freedom anyway.

On the night of August 28, the companies were back in Osawatomie with their fruits of honorable warfare. Early the next morning the spoils were divided, and John Brown drove his herd to the rise of ground just north of the town. He did not like to camp with Cline's company, for he feared that their riotous ways might corrupt the manners of his own men. The Covenant permitted neither strong drink nor profanity to the followers of John Brown. But rest, as well as the relaxation of swearing and drinking, was forbidden them in the new camp. John Brown rode off with Holmes and some of his men along the Pottawatomie valley which he knew so well. They were in the saddle all day, rounding up the cattle owned by settlers on the creek. It was the third of John Brown's Pottawatomie raids, for not a week earlier the last of Dutch Henry's horses had been driven in; the very horse that John Brown rode, a fine blooded bay, belonged to Henry Sherman.

It was a good day. In the afternoon they rode up the Fort Scott trail toward Osawatomie with the herd before them. The yellow dust from the hooves of the cattle rose in swirls, hung suspended for a while in the late sunshine, and slowly settled, when the herd and riders passed, to the dry grass of the prairie. Far away another swirl of dust marked a group of men galloping toward them down the trail. It was Frederick and four other men with news from Lawrence; Atchison's force was moving into the Territory at last, and General Lane urgently wanted John Brown's party for the defense of Lawrence. John Brown postponed an answer to the call. His men were tired, and the cattle which had cost five days of hard riding could not be turned loose again without some wrench to the economic conscience.

They reached Osawatomie toward sunset and John Brown with his men retired to the camp on the hill. There was plenty of time; no immediate danger was felt from Atchison, and the fighting, if fighting had to be done, could be delayed until the " valuable property " taken during the past week was well on its way to a safer region. Frederick said good-bye to his father and rode off down the road to Lawrence. The men in the camp on the hill saw the few lights of the town go out, and then turned themselves to sleep. Far out to the northeast on the prairie two sentinels kept a drowsy watch for an enemy they did not expect to see. Frederick Brown lay sleeping in a cabin by the Lawrence road.

" They've killed Frederick Brown! And yonder they come! " a man shouted as he rushed up the trail to the camp. John Brown leaped up from beside the fire where he was preparing breakfast. " Men, come on! " he cried, and rushed downhill toward the Osawatomie ford. All, except a fellow named Parsons, waited to gulp their coffee before following down the slope. They overtook their leader before he crossed the river. Already the sound of firing could be heard, for a Dr. Updegraff and Holmes, who was saddling up for a day after cattle when the alarm was given, had ridden out to engage the point of the advancing force. The thin crackling of rifles became more frequent as they neared the river. The fight had begun in earnest.

"Parsons, were you ever under fire?" John Brown asked as the two men hurried to the ford. "No. No, but I will obey orders. Tell me what you want me to do." "Take more care to end life well than to live long." Parsons was impressed; John Brown had a genius for saying the impressive thing, at the impressive moment.

When they crossed over into the town, John Brown's orders were more practical. "Parsons, take ten men, get in that blockhouse, and hold it as long as you can." The rest of the group with some men from the town scattered into the fringe of underbrush and timber along the river. From the second storey of the blockhouse, the defenders saw Reid's mounted men advancing in a long double line from the West. The light glittered on their brass cannon. Against cannon the blockhouse would be a deathtrap, and the sight of it sent the men piling out to join John Brown, in the shelter of the woods. They met Cline's horsemen retreating through the town, their ammunition exhausted and one of their number dead on the field behind them.

The attackers advanced under sharp fire from the cover by the river. For a moment their order broke. They rallied, dismounted, and charged. The cannon was unlimbered, and levelled. Grape-shot tore through the trees, snapping off branches and whipping the underbrush. The first line of attackers broke into the protecting timber. The fight was over.

Now it was every man for himself. There was no order, no discipline in the desperate endeavor to get over the deep stream before Reid's riflemen reached the southern bank. Partridge was picked off in the river. Holmes saved himself by diving while the slugs slapped into the water above him. Just as a man took careful aim at the far bank a lucky shot from Austin brought him crashing from his saddle. John Brown himself waded safely over at a shallow place — a harried old man in a white linen duster and broad straw hat, holding two revolvers above his head, while the coattails floated ridiculously out behind him like the wings of a crippled duck.

The fugitives scattered in all directions. Slowly the sound of firing died down behind them. After a while a thin column of smoke rose in the air; then a tongue of pale flame lifted beneath it. Osawatomie was burning. The column spread and blackened, and hung like a cloud above the valley at the fork of the streams. For good or bad, John Brown had brought it there — for, as Reid said, Osawatomie was "the headquarters of Old Brown." The flame consuming the one-time peaceful town had sprung from the flash of that pistol lifted against Doyle's forehead. And somewhere, back across the river, lay the dead body of John Brown's own son.

In the early evening John Brown and Jason crept back toward the Adair place to find Frederick's body. There was no time for mourning. John Brown looked at the corpse, took the dead man's cap to replace the fine straw hat he had lost during the day's flight, and disappeared in the darkness. The first blood of the Brown family had been shed in the fight for freedom, for cattle and horses, for plunder.

Much more was to follow. Frederick came back, it was said, because he felt that the murders of Pottawatomie bound him to Kansas; but the business of lifting cattle also bound him to the lawless country. The Reverend Martin White claimed that when he met Frederick Brown on the road near the Adair cabin in the early morning he recognized Frederick's boots as a pair taken in the Holmes raid on the White cabin, and that Frederick, realizing the situation, had reached for a revolver. " The same day I shot Fred," White said, " I would have shot the last devil of the gang that was in the attack on my house, if I had known them and got the chance." And so the madman, Frederick Brown, came back, perhaps to live out a great crime, to lift cattle, and to die with his boots on. The boots, if Martin White is to be believed, were stolen boots.

Utter ruin enveloped John Brown as he walked away from the Adair cabin in the night with the sight of the dead man's face fresh in his mind, and the dead man's cap on his head. His own men and the two accessory bands were melted away and scattered. All the plunder, the large herd of stolen cattle, the stolen mounts of his company, the wagon with its spick and span four-mule team, and Osawatomie's confidence in him were gone. There was now not even the hope, which he had been sure of after Pottawatomie, that circumstance would play into his hands again. He did not even dare to join the Free State men at Lawrence, where defenders were so sorely needed; there was no guarantee that any kindly reception would await him there. He had involved the cause, and the homes of his one-time neighbors, in his own ruin. Nothing was left except secrecy of the friendly brush under whose cover he could lick the wounds of his fortunes, of his vanity, of his egotism.

General Reid fell back to the camp on Bull Creek which he had left the night before on the forced march to attack Osawatomie. He was proud of himself and jubilant at his success. His report read: " I moved with 250 men on the Abolition fort and town of Osawatomie — the headquarters of Old Brown — on night before last; marched 40 miles and attacked the town without dismounting the men about sunrise on yesterday. We had a brisk fight for an hour or more and had five men wounded — none dangerously — Capt. Boice, William Gordon, and three others. We killed about thirty of them, among the number, *certain,* a son of Old Brown, and almost certain Brown himself; destroyed all their ammunition and provisions, and the boys would burn the town to the ground. *I could not help it.*" He was wrong in his estimate of the enemy's losses; Frederick and another man were killed before the fight began, two men were killed in the actual fighting, and one unhappy fellow, whom neither faction claimed, was shot in the occupation of the town. John Brown himself had only been struck by a spent ball during the fight in the timber, but the report of his death spread through the region. In St. Louis, the *Morning Herald* wrote, in reference to Pottawatomie, that " his death and the destruction of his family would, for that reason, be less a matter of regret even with men of the humanest feelings." Later when everyone knew that John Brown himself had escaped, General Persifer Smith could report in regard to the deaths in his gang, " there is nothing to regret as to those who suffered, yet the act was a grossly unlawful act, and deprives those who took part in it of all consideration for the future." General Smith obviously thought the matter to be a case of dog eating dog and good riddance. But in Lawrence the followers of John Brown did themselves and their leader a good turn; their stories made him out as the hero of Osawatomie, and the man whose presence had attracted its ruin became ironically associated with its name forever. Thereafter he was not Old Brown, or Captain Brown, but Old Osawatomie Brown. Indeed, he paid something for the title.

Lane moved tardily into action. He marched out from Lawrence with his force, sighted the Osawatomie raiders on Bull Creek, and discreetly retired into camp eight miles away. " Fighting " Jim Lane marched back home without losing a man and without firing a shot. Reid retreated safely into Missouri. Immediately there was another wild goose chase — to Lecompton this time to release Free State prisoners there and break up the militia which acting Governor Woodson had gathered in support of his pro-slavery opinions. But the vigilant Colonel Cooke was on hand with the regulars, and he had his way; all of the profit Lane and Harvey got from their march was some extremely sound advice from the Colonel. It was the integrity and impartiality of the army men that gave the distraught Territory such little peace as it enjoyed.

On September 7, a week after Osawatomie, the Lawrence commanders sat in council to consider leading a reprisal force to Leavenworth to avenge the murder of a Free State man. Distant cheers began to rise from the outskirts of the settlement. The clamor and shouting spread, as people filled the street. Lane, Harvey, and the rest leaped up from their debate and ran outside to join in the excitement. They saw, over the heads of the shifting crowd, a lean old man riding a grey horse slowly down the street toward them. His gun lay across the saddle bow before him, jerking up and down in time to the tired pace of the horse. He gave no heed to the welcoming cheers; his shoulders bent forward and his eyes seemed to gaze fixedly at some goal that vanished beyond the end of the straggling dusty street. John Brown came back to find that Holmes, Bondi, and his other men had done well their work at Lawrence. The shouts rose up for him, for the hero, for Osawatomie Brown. He took no apparent pleasure in them, as he rode slowly, abstractedly, through the crowd, for he was not the man to show the concession of pleasure when he only received what he felt to be a just reward of his worth. In the times when there were no cheers, his pride and egotism had fed on a great secret reserve of certainty and self-approbation; in short, they had fed on themselves, and fattened. But the applause of other people, the strict and forced obedience of his own family and followers, the cringing, half-fearful devotion of the fine sheep-dog he had shot when it followed another man were all necessary to him; they filled a profound need and supported him, but they gave no pleasure, just as the coarse loaf of a workman keeps up the necessary life but gives no pl asure to the palate. In the past when there were no cheers, John Brown had held his children, and sung to them, " With songs and honors sounding loud." Since those days he had once or twice heard cheers lifted in his honor — in the camp two days before Pottawatomie, from the handful of ragged settlers at Prairie City, and now from the excited crowd that pressed around his grey horse on the streets of Lawrence. He paid no attention. He heard remotely, as an echo, the shouts from many people, thousands of people, who filled the paved streets of cities far to the East, the well-mannered applause of great men sitting in large, richly furnished rooms. That echo rose and multiplied in his mind, as the cheering rose between the poor, unpainted shacks and dwindled out into the wide silence of the prairie.

JOHN BROWN

In Lawrence John Brown lost no time in appealing as well as he could to that greater, more influential public which lay eastward across the Mississippi. The picture of the hero which Bondi and Holmes had created for Lawrence, he now attempted to create for the world at large. His newspaper story of Osawatomie carefully focused the whole event upon the writer and at the same time maintained a certain impersonal decorum. John Brown knew well enough that the pen was mightier than the sword, but he saw no reason why one should not use both; and the battle he lost by the sword was converted magically into a victory won by the pen. The enemy's losses were multiplied to seventy or eighty, killed and wounded, and their total number was raised to four hundred. It was a hard-fought battle, lost against tremendous odds; General Reid described it as " driving out a flock of quail."

On the same day John Brown wrote to Mary Day Brown the news of Frederick's death. It was merely another item in the complacent detailed account of Osawatomie: " our dear Fredk was shot dead without warning." That was all. A week elapsed after the death before John Brown told his wife; he had spent that week in hiding, not knowing whether he would emerge as a fugitive or as a hero. He came out as the hero, and in that rôle he wrote his letter.

The Leavenworth expedition was determined upon at Lawrence. There was considerable sentiment in favor of offering the leadership to John Brown. But Osawatomie Brown had enough of fighting for the time; he not only declined the command, but he declined to go on the expedition at all. " I will fight under no command except that of Old John Brown," he had said; as a matter of fact, he would not even command an expedition that promised to be as profitless as a

216

march to Leavenworth. He served in his own way, and that way was not to fight pitched battles with large companies of men on each side. He was a raider who only fought battles when there was no help for it. Colonel Harvey, with two companies, took the road into Leavenworth County. Meanwhile, Colonel " Whipple " was on an expedition with which John Brown would have found more sympathy. " Whipple " raided the pro-slavery settlement of Osawkee and got eighty horses and other "valuable property." In "Whipple's" company was a young man of twenty-one, named John Henry Kagi. He was a studious fellow, rather slight and stooped in figure, with thin brown hair and lean face. Under well-arched brows his cold, veiled eyes, hazel-grey in color, indicated the reserved, unemotional nature. After a schooling in Virginia he taught at Hawkinstown in that state until too many discussions on the subject of slavery made it best for him to leave for his home in Ohio. He studied Latin, law, and history, wrote for newspapers, and went West to Nebraska. There he was admitted to the bar. On July 4 he saw Colonel Sumner's dragoons drawn up before the meeting house of the Legislature at Topeka, and that sight caused him to join the militia which " Whipple " commanded. From that day on he was ready to fight as well as write for the Free State cause. He was a man with convictions but with no enthusiasms; furthermore, he possessed a strong logical sense. It was that logic which made him argue and write tirelessly, somewhat arrogantly but without passion, made the schoolteacher leave slave-holding Virginia, converted the young lawyer into the militiaman and raider, and which, in the end, carried him stoically, indifferent to success or failure, and with the calm of a syllogistic conclusion, to his death at Harper's Ferry. But in the fall of 1856, in Kansas, it sent him to jail as a horse thief and highwayman. All in all he was the victim of his logic; because of it he never saw men as men, motivated by a confusion of passions, desires and beliefs; he saw them as ciphers. Because of it he was a thorough agnostic to whom God was a " useless problem."

The arrival of the newly appointed Governor Geary on September 9, introduced a new sense of reason and humanity into Kansas affairs. " Men of the North — men of the South — of the East and of the West *in Kansas* — you, and you alone, have the remedies in your own hands. Will you not suspend fratricidal strife? Will you not cease to regard each other as enemies, and look upon one another as the children of a common mother, and come and reason together? " Behind the appeal to humanity and reason stood the reënforced Federal troops in the Territory, and behind them and Geary the determination of Fillmore and the Democrats to have peace at any price in Kansas. The troubles there were jeopardizing Buchanan's chances of election.

Lane knew that his game was up. He started for Nebraska, taking a small force with him, but even now their march was broken by a desultory attack on pro-slavery settlers. Fear of Geary and the troops caused him to move on, but Colonel Harvey arrived to finish what Lane had begun. Harvey's attack on the pro-slavery people was successful enough but most of his men ended their expedition as prisoners of Captain Wood of the United States Army. The campaign for peace in Kansas was on in earnest.

But before Lane's flight Atchison was ready to move on Lawrence with twenty-seven hundred well-equipped men. Geary arrived on the morning of September 13, with Cooke's regulars, determined to put a definite end to any disturbance

218

in the Territory. There was not a Missourian in evidence, but Geary found the town in a turmoil of anxiety, for most of the Free State militia were away under Colonel Harvey. The new Governor promised protection, but at the same time he made his policy perfectly clear. He and Lieutenant-Colonel Cooke got three cheers for their pains as they rode out of Lawrence.

Before the dust had well settled along the trail from town, Dr. Robinson, now free and back at his post in Lawrence, wrote to John Brown.

Captain John Brown.
Dear Sir:
Governor Geary has been here and *talks very well*. He promises to protect us, etc. There will be no attempt to arrest any one for a few days, and I think no attempt to arrest you is contemplated by him. He talks of letting the past be forgotten, so far as may be, and of commencing anew. If convenient, can you not come to town and see us? I will then tell you all that the governor said, and talk of some other matters.
Very respectfully,
C. ROBINSON.

John Brown was prompt. On the very next day, when Atchison had already occupied Franklin and shots had been exchange with Free State pickets, Captain Brown called on Governor Robinson. The visit was an occasion which the Governor who had no State to govern celebrated in his most moving style.

Captain John Brown.
My Dear Sir:
I take this opportunity to express to you my sincere gratification that the late report, that you were killed, at the battle of Osawatomie, is incorrect. Your course, so far as I have been informed, has been such as to merit the highest praise from every patriot, and I cheerfully accord to you my heartfelt thanks for your prompt, efficient, and timely action against the invaders

of our rights and the murderers of our citizens. History will give your name a proud place in her pages and posterity will pay homage to your heroism in the cause of God and humanity.

Trusting that you will conclude to remain in Kansas, and serve during the war, the cause you have done so much to sustain, and with earnest prayers for your health, and protection from the shafts of death that so thickly beset your path, I subscribe myself,

Very respectfully,
your obedient servant,

C. ROBINSON.

This letter was all very fine, with its tribute which was only qualified with the clause, " so far as I have been informed," but it was not the precise sort of letter John Brown most desired. He wanted a letter that could be *cashed in*, and he got it.

To the Settlers of Kansas:

If possible please render Captain John Brown all the assistance he may require in defending Kansas from invaders and outlaws, and you will confer a favor upon your co-laborer and fellow citizen.

C. ROBINSON.

John Brown Jr. who was there to watch his father fold up the precious paper and put it in his pocket, once made the charge that Robinson discussed the Pottawatomie murders, and suggested that John Brown undertake similar work in other districts. " If you know of any job of that sort that needs to be done, I advise you to do it yourself." Such were the words that the son righteously placed in the mouth of his father. When John Brown had been in his grave for nearly twenty years Charles Robinson could still say of him: " I never had much doubt that Captain Brown was the author of the blow at Pottawatomie for the reason that he was the only man who comprehended the situation and saw the absolute necessity of some such blow, and had the nerve to strike it." But as John Brown's motives in Kansas became clearer to him, Robinson changed his mind; then he could define his Captain Brown as a mere " Union-splitter " and a common " jay-hawker." Perhaps he could reflect with comfort on the careful clause, " so far as I have been informed." Robinson did not betray Brown; he merely learned more about him.

John Brown left the profitable interview and went out into the town. Atchison was at Franklin, ready to begin the assault on Lawrence; only a few hundred defenders, hastily collected, were there, and victory was sure. It would be merely another case of " driving out a flock of quail." John Brown, with the honors of Osawatomie fresh on him, was offered the command of a company, but his character was not changed in a week and he had no intention in the world of fighting. He walked about, making himself conspicuous, giving advice. " Be sure you see the hind sight of your gun, then fire. . . . Be sure of the hind sight of your gun . . . if all the bullets which have ever been aimed at me had hit me I would have been as full of holes as a riddle." The defenders in the pitiful earthworks were much encouraged. The next morning John Brown was gone; when there was no profit in sight he would run no chance of being shot " as full of holes as a riddle."

John Brown might have stayed for the fight and saved his face. The first light of dawn divulged to the anxious Lawrence pickets, not the enemy, but the national flag floating in the wind above Mount Oread. The guns of Lieutenant-Colonel Joseph E. Johnston's troops covered the town from the height. Governor Geary had kept his promise.

The Missourians sullenly withdrew. The troops rode back and forth across the Territory. Within a month complete peace was established, several hundred armed Free State immigrants were imprisoned, and many of Harvey's men.

whom Captain Wood had brought in, were tried and received long sentences at hard labor. For the first time Kansas was free of the cutthroats, the jay-hawkers, and the "reprisal men" who had made life impossible for the honest settler who merely wanted peace and a home.

John Brown's days of usefulness in Kansas were over. Sick and weak from fever and dysentery, he lay in the wagon as it jolted along the rough trail toward Iowa. Beside the wagon walked three of his sons — John, Jason, and Owen. A fourth son lay in the shallow grave at Osawatomie. Along the valley of the creek that flowed by the ashes of the town the early frost bit the grass above five other unmarked mounds. John Brown had come to Kansas to see if something would not turn up to his advantage. There was not much to show for the troubled year. He was older, much older, and his health was breaking. His moment of prosperity, the big herd of cattle, the splendid blooded bay, the wagon with its spick and span four-mule team, and the life of his son had all been exchanged for the mere name, Old Osawatomie Brown. The name was not quite all he had from the bargain; he could reach into his pocket and feel the two pieces of folded paper. "Your course, so far as I have been informed, has been such as to merit the highest praise from every patriot. . . ." It was a few years later when John Brown received higher endorsement than a Governor's letter of credit. A certain self-conscious liberal and self-conscious aristocrat, Wendell Phillips of the silver tongue, struck one of his best phrases on this subject. "He sails with letters of marque from God," said Mr. Phillips.

8

PASSING THE HAT

SALMON and Watson were digging potatoes on the high field at North Elba. The early Northern winter was near, and every potato that they tore from its hill and shook clean of the crumby earth was precious. It was just so much warmth, just so much more strength, against the rigor of the descending season; it meant the support of life itself until the spring should open again. Someone called to them from the house and they raised up from the furrow. News had come from Kansas.

It was important news for the family in the wretched draughty house at North Elba. Frederick was dead, and the fight of Osawatomie had been lost. Her son's death was one more thing for Mary Day Brown to endure. But she was stoic; she had borne and lost other children. That was not all the news. The Reverend Martin White had boasted of killing Frederick. The Reverend Martin White was simply a name to Mary Day Brown; to her he was one of the wicked people in Kansas who fought her husband and the right. But Salmon remembered him well enough; the armed horseman who galloped up to the new Brown claim in Kansas and demanded, " How are you men on the goose? ", the speaker at the Osawatomie settlers' meetings, the owner of the house that was twice raided and robbed. In the morning Salmon and Watson had gone; they were on the road to Kansas to kill Martin White and avenge their dead brother.

They travelled fast. Gerrit Smith, the fugitive slave Frederick Douglass, and other Free State sympathizers, gave them money, not guessing the secret personal intention that was taking them back to Kansas. At Chicago Sharpe's rifles were put into their hands from the stores of the National Kansas Committee, and they joined the Committee's train of supplies and arms that was ready to move West under the leadership of Dr. J. P. Root. Packed in long heavy boxes in the covered freight wagons were two hundred fine Sharpe's rifles. They never reached Kansas. The slow journey westward was but a stage on their longer circuitous journey into Virginia, into Harper's Ferry.

John Brown travelled eastward on the Chicago road from Tabor, in Iowa, and missed his sons with the wagon train. In Chicago he was well received by the National Committee, and so impressed them with his knowledge of Kansas affairs that he was sent in the wake of the Root party to advise concerning the disposition of the arms and supplies. He wrote Owen to intercept Salmon and Watson at Tabor until his own arrival, and again took the road to Kansas. Before leaving, however, he gave some advice to the Committee; the immediate introduction of the supplies, he said, was not of much consequence compared with the danger of losing them. Governor Geary's program of suppression was becoming more and more effective.

The easy westward trip of the wagons ended at Tabor and the arms were stored. Watson waited for his father, but Salmon went on into the Territory, hunting for the Reverend Martin White. At Topeka he heard a report that the fighting minister of the gospel was dead. The report was false but it relieved Salmon of the responsibilities of revenge, and so he retraced his path. His adventure, financed by Free State sympathizers, was a purely personal one, and he felt no obligation to his generous friends to substitute an impersonal one which would be more in harmony with the supposition on which the money had been given. He simply bought a horse, a stolen horse, and set out for Ohio.

John Brown himself had no further business in Kansas, for he was in a great hurry to get back East and put into action a program of exploiting sympathy with the Free State cause. He had not forgotten how Gerrit Smith read John Brown Jr.'s letters to the Anti-Slavery Convention at Syracuse, how every eye was wet with tears, and how every pocketbook was opened. He had two items of capital for this program; Robinson's letters and the name, Osawatomie Brown. At Chicago those items procured for him a new suit, a fine and deacon-like suit befitting his station. In Ohio Governor Salmon P. Chase gave him twenty-five dollars and a letter of introduction. The Governor's signature at the bottom of the sheet was worth considerably more than twenty-five dollars. At Peterboro, Gerrit Smith received a call from his old friend and debtor; he expressed his pleasure in noble terms.

Captain John Brown:—

You did not need to show me letters from Governor Chase and Governor Robinson to let me know who and what you are. I have known you many years, and have highly esteemed you as long as I have known you. I know your unshrinking bravery, your self-sacrificing benevolence, your devotion to the cause of freedom, and have long known them. May Heaven preserve your life and health, and prosper your noble purposes!

GERRIT SMITH.

JOHN BROWN

John Brown was far too busy collecting his letters of introduction and esteem to have time for his family on the North Elba farm. The time he spent with them had become less and less in the recent years; there had always been some new project, some new hope, some new speculation that took him away for long periods and left Mary Day Brown to bear and bury children, and hold things together against the perpetual poverty. She managed, uncomplaining, for she had never known a different sort of existence. And so it was only logical now, that John Brown, with a pocket full of letters and his head full of schemes, should turn, not to the unboarded farm house at North Elba, but to the houses of wealthy, prominent men, where the letters would insure consideration and honor. Early in January he reached Boston.

The letters opened all doors. He met many people who had followed the Free State struggle in Kansas with intense interest. They had preached for the cause, had formed committees, had written for newspapers, and had given money, and now they were glad to meet a man who had fought at close quarters in the prairies and river bottom of Kansas. They were not disappointed in him; he provided all the materials for the making of a hero.

Immediately after his arrival John Brown met Frank B. Sanborn. Sanborn, just out of Harvard, was a very young man, who had given up schoolteaching in order to follow God's will and work for the Massachusetts State Kansas Committee. He was an excessively earnest young man, confident of himself, and confident that he knew God's will; beyond this he possessed to a considerable degree that tight especial brand of New England romanticism which manifested itself in stealing Guinea niggers, making money,

226

wrestling with conscience, hunting witches, building tea-clippers, talking about Transcendentalism, or being an Abolitionist. Stealing Guinea niggers and hunting witches, were out of date now, and the habit of wrestling with conscience was somewhat on the decline; it was the period of clipper ships, money making, Sunny Brook Farm, and Abolitionism. Money making and Abolitionism were still to a certain degree mutually exclusive, but times had changed since the broadcloth mobs and Thompson riots, and Free State sentiments, if not downright Abolitionism, were certainly respectable. Very shortly the Reverend Henry Ward Beecher would put one aspect of the sentiments quite concretely: " That nation is the best customer that is freest." Meanwhile, Frank B. Sanborn was a militant Abolitionist, and into the bargain he was romantic enough to expect a hero who would embody all of his ideals. John Brown provided the hero. He always exercised a particular fascination and conviction on the young; the people who died with him at the Ferry were very young men.

John Brown immediately confided in his new disciple. Sanborn put the idea in this way: " He wishes to raise $30,000 to arm and equip a company such as he thinks he can raise this present winter, but he will, as I understand him, take what money he can raise and use it as far as it will go." Sanborn understood his hero perfectly: " he will, as I understand him, take what money he can raise and use it as far as it will go."

When John Brown ate a good Sunday dinner at the table of the wealthy George Luther Stearns, he recognized an opportunity to consolidate his position as the fighting hero of Kansas. He told about Black Jack. The influential Mr. Stearns was much impressed. John Brown exhibited a remarkable piece of audacity: in a few pointed sentences he demolished the reputations of the important Free State leaders in Kansas. With Governor Robinson's letters in his pocket, he tactfully demolished Governor Robinson's reputation. Martin Conway, he said, was the best of the politicians, but Conway, unhappily, was lacking in force. The conclusion which Mr. Stearns should draw was very simple; if the best of the Free State leaders lacked force, what Kansas needed was a fighter. In short, Kansas needed John Brown. Mr. Stearns drew the conclusion.

Stearns was completely won to the support of John Brown, and he was not alone in his conviction. Theodore Parker, the radical clergyman, S. G. Howe, who had been instrumental in disposing of " General Jo Cook," and Amos A. Lawrence, once a powerful rival of " Perkins & Brown," were among the number of converts to the support of John Brown. Stearns, Lawrence, and Howe, as well as many other backers of John Brown, were hard-headed, successful men who merely wanted to see Kansas a Free State. They disliked slavery for a variety of reasons and were against its extension into the Territories, but they were not necessarily Abolitionists; there was a sharp distinction between the two groups. The Abolitionists were *Disunionists,* burned the Constitution, and spat on resolutions and platforms. Their nature had not changed since the day, seventeen years earlier, when old John Quincy Adams made this entry in his diary: " Garrison and the non-resistant Abolitionists, Brownson and the Marat Democrats, phrenology, and animal magnetism all come in, furnishing each some plausible rascality as an ingredient for the bubbling caldron of religion and politics." To a man of John Quincy Adams' experience, statesmanship, and downrightness of intellect the

Abolitionists were simply another brand of " cranks." The other group were interested in a practical, legal solution of the problem under the terms of the Constitution. For them disunion meant, not the destruction of slavery, but the creation of a separate, slave-holding nation to the South. " Owing to a variety of causes, the Abolitionists have received," as Theodore Roosevelt put it, " a vast amount of hysterical praise, which they do not deserve, and have been credited with deeds done by other men whom they in reality hampered and opposed, rather than aided. After 1840, the professed Abolitionists formed but a small and comparatively unimportant portion of the forces that were towards the restriction and ultimate destruction of slavery; and much of what they did was positively harmful to the cause for which they were fighting." Abolitionism was froth on the wave and not the wave itself. The men with a practical sense and a respect for the letter of the law and the Constitution were the people who saved Kansas; they were the people who ran the Emigrant Aid Company or who broke the market for Missouri State bonds and made investors shout for an end to Missouri aggression into Kansas. And the man whose editorials broke the bonds was a poet, William Cullen Bryant by name, and he had once studied at the Reverend Moses Hallock's school, where John Brown had presented himself as a tall, dignified, and sedate young man with ministerial ambitions.

John Brown met all types. He spent one pleasant Sunday evening in Theodore Parker's parlor arguing with William Lloyd Garrison on the subject of resistance and non-resistance. The vocabularies of the two disputants were primarily biblical; either Brown or Garrison had difficulty in saying the simplest thing without an appeal to scriptural dignity. Any topic with either of them was liable to infinite inflation; when they discussed the same topic, at the same time, and with each other, the result must have been a marvel of biblical rhetoric. Mr. Garrison talked of peace and quoted the New Testament; Captain Brown talked of war and had the chance to repeat his favorite text: "without the shedding of blood there is no remission of sins." His present business in the East was to get $30,000, ostensibly to equip a company whose purpose, among other purposes, would be the shedding of blood. Mr. Garrison was a relatively harmless fanatic with a simple and, abstractly considered, laudable purpose; Captain Brown was less simple, less fanatical, and less harmless. There is scarcely need to add that he was, all in all, somewhat less laudable.

The first week of John Brown's stay in Boston saw business on foot. The Massachusetts State Kansas Committee, with Mr. Stearns as chairman, voted to turn over to him, as an agent of the Committee, the two hundred Sharpe's rifles and ammunition which were stored in Tabor, Iowa. Furthermore, they handsomely voted him five hundred dollars for expenses. The deal was not closed, however, by the action of the Massachusetts Committee, for some confusion of ownership existed with the National Committee. John Brown went to New York and appeared before them; he wanted the rifles, some general supplies, and $5,000 in cash. The rifles were voted back to the Massachusetts Committee, but the money was a different matter. The National Committee had more immediate information concerning matters in Kansas and they were more inquisitive than the Massachusetts gentlemen. They asked some presumptuous questions as to Captain Brown's intentions. Captain Brown was of no mind to answer questions:

" I am no adventurer. You all know me. You are acquainted with my history. You know what I have done in Kansas. I do not expose my plans. No one knows them but myself, except perhaps one. I will not be interrogated; if you wish to give me anything I want you to give it freely. I have no other purpose but to serve the cause of liberty." Now, as a matter of fact, the gentlemen of the Committee did *not* know what John Brown had done in Kansas. For that reason they voted $5,000 to " aid Capt. John Brown in any *defensive* measures that may become necessary." Only $500 could be collected until *defensive* measures became necessary, and defensive measures were certainly not in John Brown's calculations. He was greatly chagrined at what he interpreted as the Committee's lack of appreciation for his past services, and he was even more chagrined when as late as the summer he had managed to get his hands on only a hundred and fifty dollars. But well before the summer he could write: " *I am prepared to expect* nothing but bad faith from the National Kansas Committee at Chicago, as I will show you hereafter." But he was not quite ready to kill a goose that had laid even a deplorably small golden egg, and so he added: " *This* is for the present *confidential*."

When the meeting was over John Brown made the gesture of preparing a list of supplies and equipment necessary to outfit a company of fifty volunteers for Kansas service and handed over the list to Mr. White, the assistant secretary. The total cost of the equipment came to $1,774, which left, as has been ungraciously pointed out, a comfortable profit from the former estimate of $30,000, or even from the $5,000 demanded from the National Committee. But even then the sum of $1,774 was not turned over to John Brown in cash; a part of the Committee's bad faith was in buying the equipment and having it stored at Tabor until defensive measures should become necessary.

After a hurried trip to Gerrit Smith's home for business and a more hurried one to North Elba for pleasure, John Brown was back in Massachusetts. The young Mr. Sanborn was making himself very useful; he had been instrumental in presenting before the Massachusetts Legislature a bill to appropriate $100,000 to relieve Kansas distress and compensate those who had suffered for the Free State cause. On February 18, Mr. Sanborn introduced Captain John Brown to the Joint Committee on Federal Relations, not as an advocate, he said, but as a witness for the case. " We have invited Captain Brown and Mr. Whitman to appear in our behalf, because these gentlemen are eminently qualified either to represent Massachusetts in Kansas, or Kansas in Massachusetts. The best blood of the ' Mayflower ' runs in the veins of both, and each had an ancestor in the army of the Revolution. Mr. Whitman, seventh in descent from Miles Standish, laid the foundation of the first church and the first schoolhouse in Kansas; John Brown, the sixth descendant of Peter Browne, of the ' Mayflower,' has been in Kansas what Standish was to Plymouth Colony." Mr. Lawrence had already called John Brown " the Miles Standish of Kansas," but the Plutarchian parallel was scarcely exact; anyway, it bore as little on the case as did the mistake concerning John Brown's genealogy. But the Mayflower descent was as good a reason for voting the $100,000 as some of the other reasons advanced; it had also as little foundation in fact. Mr. Sanborn continued his rhetoric and inaccuracy: " Ask this gray haired man, gen-

tlemen — if you have the heart to do it — where lies the
body of his murdered son — where are the homes of his four
other sons, who a year ago were quiet farmers in Kansas."
Quiet farmers in Kansas. Did the question echo in John
Brown's mind as he rose to speak? "And where lie the
bodies of the murdered Doyle and Wilkinson and Sherman,
who a year ago were farmers in Kansas?" John Brown's
speech was not remarkable; in substance it was a recital of
what the Brown family had lost and suffered in Kansas and
a plea for compensation. He mentioned the insanity of
John Brown Jr. "A maniac — yes, a maniac!" he said,
and wiped a tear from his eye. In his hotel room, he added,
lay the very trace-chain which his son had worn under the
summer sun of Kansas, and any members of the Committee
might see it if they so desired. From the catalogue of suffering and service of the Brown family in the cause of freedom, he moved to a vague criticism of the Free State
leaders. He himself had been asked to take command, but refused, and only acted as "adviser." Happily, the gentlemen of the Committee did not know the emphatic opinion of
Colonel Cracklin, commander of the Lawrence Rifle Company: "John Brown had nothing to do with either building
or commanding any fort or breastwork about Lawrence, or
with the defense of Lawrence against any attack whatever."
John Brown had not even been present to "advise" at the
crisis. The speech concluded with a definition of the sort of
immigrants Kansas needed: "We want good men, industrious men, men who respect themselves; who act only from the
dictates of conscience; *men who fear God too much to fear
anything human.*" And the man who feared God too much
to fear anything human took his seat.

The speech was not a great success. The Committee declined to recommend the passage of the bill, which, as they made have suspected, would amount to a practical endowment of the Brown family. The failure of the bill was a considerable blow to John Brown, for it was a scheme which he had nurtured carefully. Back in the summer before leaving Kansas he prepared a detailed claim for compensation and turned it over to Mr. Whitman. It was entitled "the names of sufferers and persons who have made sacrifices in endeavoring to maintain and advance the Free-State cause in Kansas, within my personal knowledge." The sufferers were simply members of the Brown gang. The paper said much about the Brown's sacrifices; it said nothing about their profits.

The failure of the $100,000 coup sent John Brown scurrying about New England in a desperate endeavor to raise money by personal appeals. Returns trickled in slowly, but their total, not a small sum, was far from satisfying John Brown. He published appeals in newspapers: "I ask all honest lovers of *Liberty and Human Rights, both male and female,* to hold up my hands by contributions of pecuniary aid. . . . It is with *no little sacrifice of personal feeling* that I appear in this manner before the public."

Mr. Lawrence published an offer to be "one of ten, or a smaller number, to pay a thousand dollars per annum till the admission of Kansas into the Union, for the purpose of supporting John Brown's family and keeping the proposed company in the field." John Brown did not miss the possibilities in this idea, but he believed a bird in the hand to be worth two in the bush. Doing business on credit had ruined his previous speculations, and now he was out for immediate cash. He wrote Mr. Lawrence:

PASSING THE HAT

The offer you so kindly made through the *Telegraph* some time since emboldens me to propose the following for your consideration. For One Thousand Dollars cash I am offered an improved piece of land which with a little improvement I now have might enable my family consisting of a Wife & Five minor children (the youngest not yet Three years old) to procure a Subsistence should I never return to them; my Wife being a good economist, & and a real old fashioned business woman. She has gone through the Two past winters in our open cold house; unfinished outside; & not plastered. I have no other income or means for their support. I have never hinted to anyone else that I had a thought of asking for any help to provide in any such way for my family; & *should not to you*, but for your own suggestion. I fully believe I shall get the help I need to operate with West. Last Night a private meeting of some gentlemen here; voted to raise one Thousand Dollars in New Haven for that purpose. If you feel at all inclined to encourage me in the measure I have proposed, I shall be grateful to get a line from you; Care Massasoit House, Springfield, Mass; & will call when I come again to Boston. I do not feel disposed to weary you with my oft repeated visitations. I believe I am indebted to you as the *unknown giver* of One share of Emigrant aid stock; as I can think of no other so likely to have done it. *Is my appeal right?*

To say the least, the letter was artful.

Mr. Lawrence replied immediately. He had just given $14,000 to a Kansas school fund, and was short of cash, but he could offer the assurance that the " family of ' Captain John Brown of Osawatomie' will not be turned out to starve in this country, until Liberty herself is driven out." There was a postcript which exhibited the thin pretext on which Brown's request was made: " I never saw the offer to which you refer, in the ' Telegraph,' and have now forgotten what it was." However, a subscription was begun to raise the $1,000 to pay the Thompsons at North Elba for John Brown's farm. All of the money was not in by May, and the suppliant wrote a dictatorial, sullen demand, which contained at least one obvious lie: " I must ask to have the $1,000 made up at *once;* and forwarded to Gerrit Smith. *I did not* start the measure of getting up *any subscription for me;* (although I was sufficiently needy as God knows). . . ." John Brown had a genius for putting other people in the wrong: It was that trait of character, perhaps, which made many of John Brown's one-time friends and supporters reflect on him with peculiar bitterness. " John Brown had no enemies in New England, but many friends and admirers. He was constantly receiving money from them. They little knew what use he was making of it, for he deceived everybody." Such was one of Mr. Lawrence's reflections.

In Collinsville, Connecticut, one of the major deceptions began. One morning in early March John Brown rehearsed the story of Black Jack to a group of loungers in the village drug store. Among the fly-specked glass jars of quinine and peppermint, the loungers listened to the story of things quite different from the stuff of their own well-ordered existence in Collinsville: " deployed for the attack . . . moved to the flank . . . close quarters . . . a wooded ravine . . . mounted on Ned Scarlet . . . a white handkerchief tied to a ramrod." All those things were very far away on the dry prairies of Kansas under the blazing sun, but for that reason they listened more intently; this stooped, farmer-like old man, so much like themselves, had been there, had seen those things, had walked out alone to meet the fellow with the white handkerchief on the ramrod. At the end of his tale John Brown reached down and drew from his boot-top a broad, two-edged dirk, which was part of the Black Jack spoils. He turned the weapon over meditatively in his large knotted hand. " If I had a lot of these things fastened to poles about six feet long they would make a capital thing for the settlers to keep in their log cabins to defend themselves against any sudden attack." Among the people who crowded about to look at the Missouri dirk was a certain Charles Blair, a blacksmith and forger. " Mr. Blair," John Brown said, " what would you make such things for? Say five hundred or a thousand? " " I could make five hundred, I suppose, for a dollar and a quarter apiece," " Blair calculated, " or if you want a thousand, for a dollar apiece." " I'll want them made," answered John Brown. On March 20 Blair shipped a dozen sample pikes, and by the end of the month a contract was signed.

Obviously, the use of the pikes as defensive weapons in Kansas cabins was no reason for their manufacture. In the first place there were plenty of guns in Kansas, too many, in fact, and the introduction of a thousand pikes would be a sort of joke. In the second place, it would be absurdly poor judgment to manufacture the pikes in Connecticut if they were for use in the West; their construction was so simple that any village blacksmith could do the job. The region where they were to be employed lay much nearer to hand than Kansas. John Brown's remark was simply intended to pull the wool over the eyes of people whose money would pay for the pikes.

John Brown chose a strange fellow in whom to confide the purposes of his pikes. In New York there was a man named Hugh Forbes, who titled himself " Colonel," as a relic of the days when he had been a conspirator and a soldier in the Garibaldian revolution of 1848. He was an Englishman by birth and an adventurer by profession. He was a person of some education, spoke French and Italian fluently, professed a knowledge of military matters, exhibited radical republican convictions, and presented an urbane, confident front to the world despite the slick elbows of his coat and run-down heels of his boots. The failure in Garibaldi's revolution left Forbes without a job; Paris proved unprofitable, and he drifted to New York, where his smooth manners, ability at fencing, and knowledge of foreign languages gave him a precarious living. Teaching the art of the foil and rapier or translating for the *Tribune* merely occupied the gentleman adventurer until an adventure should turn up.

When he met John Brown he thought that he had found the adventure. The adventurers of John Brown's acquaintance were very different from this one, whose subtlety, urbanity, and impressive knowledge of military science quickly won Brown's confidence. Here was a man who had actually lived and acted in the world which John Brown only laboriously touched when he scrawled in his crabbed hand such notes as this in his memorandum-book: " Guerilla warfare see Life of Lord Wellington, Page 71 to Page 75 (Mina). See also Page 102 some *valuable hints* in same Book. *See also* Page 196 some most important instructions to officers. *See also* same book Page 235 these words Deep and narrow defiles where 300 men would suffice to check an *army*." The Colonel simply charmed the secret out of John Brown's breast. Part of the secret was that the project got its backing from wealthy and prominent men of the East. Forbes allowed himself to be persuaded to accept the rôle of John Brown's drill-master at the salary of one hundred dollars a month. Until there were officers to train and soldiers to drill his duty was to prepare a manual of guerrilla warfare following a foreign book of the type with which Forbes was acquainted. It was to be called, " The Manual of the Patriotic Volunteer." A hundred dollars a month was not much in consideration of his great talents, but it would relieve his immediate needs; he had high hopes for the future. As for John Brown, he merely saw in Forbes an able and impressive subordinate, who possessed a certain technical training; he did not recognize, as yet, the unpleasant trait of ambition.

April was another month of effort to raise money. He continued his soliciting in the old fashion and added a dash of drama to revive the interest of his chief backers. He wrote to Eli Thayer: " One of the U. S. Hounds is on my track; & I have kept myself hid for a few days to let my track get cold. I have no idea of being taken; & *intend* (*if ' God will ';*) to go back with Irons *in* rather than *uppon* my hands." While he lay in hiding from the U. S. Hounds in the comfortable house of Judge Russell, he took out his two revolvers and repeater every night to make sure of their loads. The family looked on with awe and apprehension. " Here are eighteen lives," he would grimly say as he put the weapons back in his pockets. " If you hear a noise at night," he once advised Mrs. Russell, " put the baby under the pillow." And then he appealed to the distressed woman's housewifely instincts: " I should hate to spoil these carpets, too, but you know I cannot be taken alive." The clergyman, Theodore Parker, thought the carpets might be well sacrificed in a crisis, for he wrote to Judge Russell concerning his fugitive guest: " If I were in his position, I should shoot dead any man who attempted to arrest me for those alleged crimes; then I should be tried by a Massachusetts jury and be acquitted." The clergyman gave strangely practical advice. The joke of the matter was derived from the simple fact that there were no U. S. Hounds on John Brown's trail. The spectacular renegade from Kansas could not have been seriously disturbed even when he held up the Russells' little girl and said: "When I am hung for treason, you can say that you used to stand on Captain's Brown's hand."

One morning Mrs. Stearns received an invitation to call on Captain Brown at the Russell house; the lady could not help being flattered, and no sooner was dinner over than she got in her carriage and drove away on her very pleasant errand. Captain Brown received her with dignity. He wanted her private opinion on a little address which he had prepared for Theodore Parker to present to his congregation the next morning. Slowly and with emphasis he began to read. " Old Brown's Farewell to the Plymouth Rocks, Bunker Hill Monuments, Charter Oaks, and Uncle Tom's Cabins," was the title. " He has left for Kansas. . . . And he leaves the States with a feeling of deepest sadness, that after having exhausted his own small means, and with his family and his brave men suffering hunger, cold, nakedness, and some of them sickness, wounds, imprisonment in irons, with extreme cruel treatment, and others death. . . ." John Brown lifted his eyes now and then to watch the effect on Mrs. Stearns. The slow, emphatic voice proceeded: " . . . that after all this, in order to sustain a cause which every citizen of this ' glorious republic ' is under equal moral obligation to do, and for the neglect of which he will be held accountable by God, — a cause in which every man, woman, and child of the entire human family has a deep and awful interest, — that when no wages are asked or expected, he cannot secure amid all the wealth, luxury, and extravagance of this ' heaven-exalted ' people, even the necessary supplies of the common soldier. 'How are the mighty fallen!'" While the words echoed in the flattering intimacy of the Russell parlor, Mrs. Stearns felt that she sat in the presence of true greatness.

In all probability Mrs. Stearns was the entire audience for which John Brown intended his farewell. That audience was completely converted and completely ashamed of its immoral " wealth, luxury, and extravagance." Mrs. Stearns was in the mood for selling all her goods and giving the money to the poor Captain John Brown. The exalted mood persisted next morning, and Mrs. Stearns did an unfair thing. She attacked Mr. Stearns on the subject before breakfast. Mr. Stearns was not quite prepared to sell his estate, as she suggested, and so he compromised by writing a check for $7,000. The two paragraphs of "Old Brown's Farewell" are one of the highest paid literary productions on record.

Mr. Stearns' generosity had one unhappy condition attached to it. The order for $7,000 could not be touched except for the support of a volunteer company on active service in Kansas. The equipment provided by the National Committee was stored in Iowa, and two hundred revolvers, acquired through the generosity of Eli Thayer and the Massachusetts Arms Company, were to be shipped West. The Arms Company expressed a hope that " there may be no occasion for their service in securing rights which ought to be guaranteed by the principles of justice and equity." On the other hand, John Brown sincerely hoped that if he did have to go to Kansas there would be trouble. The Arms Company continued: " We have no fear that they will be put to service in your hands for other purposes." John Brown must have paused over that sentence; it might mean but a polite profession of faith in Captain Brown's integrity, and then, again, it might mean something quite different. When Mr. Stearns wrote that the revolvers would be given, he added a remark which showed how well John Brown's criticism of Free State leaders had taken effect: " I think you ought to go to Kansas as soon as possible and give Robinson and the rest some Backbone." That was flattering enough in itself, but it also meant that John Brown's eastern public was worn out with the begging campaign; they had paid their money and now they wanted to see the show.

John Brown's campaign for raising money in the East came at a very fruitful time. Buchanan had defeated the Republicans, and on March 4 he became President. Two days later the Supreme Court of the United States gave its decision concerning Dred Scott, a slave who sued his master on the ground of having been twice resident on free soil. Dred Scott had been taken to Illinois and then to the unorganized territory north of 36° 30', but had been brought back to the slave-holding State of Missouri, where the suit was originally filed. For ten years the case had dragged on from court to court; the decision published by the Supreme Court that Dred Scott could not be emancipated was the final legal word on the subject of slavery. The reasons for the decision made it clear that far more than the fate of a single black man and his wife were at stake. In the first place, Dred Scott, being a negro, could not be a citizen of the United States and consequently could not bring suit in a Federal Court. In the second place, he brought the suit in Missouri, where the laws of Illinois could no longer affect his condition. But the third reason carried with it a dreadful weight of consequence, for it declared the one great attempt to compromise the slave problem unconstitutional and void: Dred Scott, as a resident of the territory north of 36° 30', was not emancipated because Congress, despite the Missouri Compromise Act, had no right to deprive citizens of their property without due process of law. The decision defined the Missouri Compromise in the way which the South had always regarded it; the Compromise was the *voluntary concession of a legal right* made for the sake of peace. The decision echoed the words of Calhoun, that prophetic enemy of all compromise: " Slavery follows the flag." Squatter sovereignty was disposed of by the same stroke that demolished the Missouri Compromise. The Supreme Court pointed out the letter of the Constitution; some other people pointed out that Chief Justice Taney and four of his Associate Justices were Southerners.

The Dred Scott decision did much to focus attention on the Kansas issue. Governor Geary's policy of impartial suppression had in the end cost him his political neck, and Robert J. Walker was now the successor to an unenviable position. Walker was a Southerner and this fact made many Free State men sure that their battle in the Territory was far from conclusion. And John Brown everywhere proclaimed that the quiet of the Geary regime was deceptive. Dred Scott and Robert J. Walker helped to swell the subscriptions to support Captain Brown's " Volunteer Company," but most of those subscriptions bore the unpleasant label, " for defensive measures only." It was not the sort of money John Brown liked best — money " for secret service and no questions asked." But his public was tired of giving any sort of money, and to realize on what had been given he had to go to Kansas and engage in " active service." Kansas, in the spring of 1857, was not the place where John Brown's especial variety of " active service " would be welcome; people were more interested now in a settlement by the ballot-box than by " Beecher's Bibles." Even some of John Brown's own backers would have agreed with a certain raw-boned, Western politician concerning the Dred Scott decision: " We shall do what we can to have it overrule this. We offer no resistance to it." The raw-boned Western politician was named Abraham Lincoln.

It was with a burden of apprehension that John Brown turned from the East to the more inhospitable frontier across the Mississippi. " I expect to return West; & to go back without even securing an outfit. I go with a *sad heart*, having failed to secure even the means of equipping; to say nothing of feeding men." Now the actual amount of money and supplies raised by John Brown in his Eastern campaign came very close to the sum which he had set for his goal. The amount was sufficient to equip the company which had served as his pretext. He was sad of heart simply because the money and supplies could be used *only* in Kansas. His mind was fixed on another arena and another plan. He was also sad of heart because the Massachusetts State Legislature had not seen fit to endow the Brown family. However, the devoted Mr. Sanborn and other friends hoped to persuade the State of New York to such generosity.

John Brown secured something near his $30,000 in the East. But more significant for him and for his future was the honor and consideration which he had found in the houses of rich, prominent people. He had eaten pulse at rich men's tables, for, as he always said to his hosts, a fighting man must keep accustomed to coarse fare. At the very moment when he refused the satisfactions of the well-furnished tables, his vanity was fattening as it never had before. He was enjoying something that simple money could not buy; he was a hero.

Passing the Hat

Men such as Stearns, Lawrence, Howe, Parker, and Thayer had entertained him and given him money, but they were not the men who did the most for him. At Concord John Brown and Ralph Waldo Emerson met as the guests of Henry David Thoreau. Thoreau and Emerson took John Brown at the value he set on himself. They didn't give him money, but in 1859 they gave back to the world his own definition of himself. Emerson possessed a set of ideas which have been given the interesting name of Transcendentalism; he spent his life trying to find something in man or nature which would correspond to the fine ideas and the big word. In John Brown, Emerson thought that he had found his man. " For himself, Brown is so transparent that all men see him through. He is a man to make friends wherever on earth courage and integrity are esteemed, — the rarest of heroes, a pure idealist, with no by-ends of his own. Many of us have seen him, and every one who has heard him speak has been impressed alike by his simple, artless goodness and his sublime courage. He joins that perfect Puritan faith which brought his ancestor to Plymouth Rock, with his grandfather's ardor in the Revolution. He believes in two articles — two instruments, shall I say? — the Golden Rule and the Declaration of Independence; and he used this expression in a conversation here concerning them: ' Better that a whole generation of men, women, and children should pass away by a violent death, than that one word of either should be violated in this country.' " That is a big value to place on a " word," but Emerson was a man who lived in words, big words, and not in facts. Before this Emerson had proclaimed in one of his exalted public moments that the sum of all the lives of men, women, and children in the South was not worth one hair of Senator Sumner's stricken holy head. It is only natural that once or twice when he tried to deal with matters of fact words made him a common demagogue. And it is only natural, that Emerson, in his extraordinary innocence, should have understood nothing, nothing in the world, about a man like John Brown to whom vocabulary was simply a very valuable instrument. "For himself, Brown is so transparent that all men see him through," said Emerson. He could not realize that John Brown's words, " Better that a whole generation . . ." simply echoed the words spoken a year before to Louisa Wilkinson, when she pled with him. " It matters not."

9

THE BIRTH OF A NATION

WILL you buy something — a pair of shoes, or something — for one of those little Kansas children? " John Brown's hands were full of the small coins just dropped there by Harry Stearns, the thirteen-year-old son of his chief benefactors. Then the child added: " Captain Brown, won't you write me, sometime, what sort of a little boy you were? " And Captain Brown made the promise.

During the slow, almost purposeless trip westward with his wagon and team, John Brown kept his word. By the dirty oil lamps in hotel rooms, by his campfire, by the hot summer sunlight when he sat on the roadside, John Brown filled page after page with his tight, nearly illiterate handwriting. It was also the handwriting of an old man — cramped, irregular, painful — but it told what sort of a little boy " John " had been. " This story will be mainly a narration of follies and errors; which it is to be hoped *you may avoid;* but there is one thing connected with it, which will be calculated to encourage any young person to persevering effort; & that is the degree of success *in accomplishing his objects* which to a great extent marked the course of this boy throughout my entire acquaintance with him; notwithstanding his moderate capacity; & still more moderate acquirements." The golden text of the document was underscored: "the degree of success *in accomplishing his objects.*"

It told how John lost the precious yellow marble given him by the Indian boy, the little pet bob-tailed squirrel caught in the woods, and the ewe lamb. "These were the beginning of a severe *but much needed course* of discipline which he afterwards was to pass through." It showed how the deprivations and rigors of a frontier childhood made John precocious, self-reliant, and resourceful, and gave him confidence in the face of distress. And it did not neglect to mention Plymouth Rock; Plymouth Rock was a piece of John Brown's capital. But more important still, there appeared the circumstantial story how John, years and years ago, was led to "declare, *or Swear: Eternal war* with Slavery." All in all, the letter was not written to please little Henry Stearns; it was written to tell Mr. and Mrs. Stearns that Captain John Brown was such and such a kind of man. Captain Brown was a man on whom they could depend.

But there was another meaning to the letter; a meaning more profound, obscure, and necessary. In New York Colonel Forbes was working on his "Manual of the Patriotic Volunteer"; the blacksmith in Collinsville had a contract for a thousand heavy, broad-headed pikes; in Tabor two hundred accurate and deadly Sharpe's rifles lay stored in their long boxes. And John Brown's head was full of a scheme whose magnitude and consequence no one but himself could guess. At last things were moving toward the fulfillment of that scheme; for the first time it seemed near and possible, and with this new possibility came the first dubieties and waverings. And so he wrote: "He followed up with *tenacity* whatever he set about so long as it answered his general purpose: & hence he rarely failed in some good degree to effect the things he undertook. This was so much the case that he *habitually expected to succeed* in his undertakings. With this feeling *should be coupled;* the consciousness that our plans are right in themselves." John Brown had always had the consciousness that his plans were "right in themselves," but the rest sounds a little strange after the long history of so many failures. The letter was John Brown's letter to himself, written to wipe out just that history. What it said was this: "Those old failures are no matter, for I was *right*. And now, *now at this last, I am still right and I will not fail.*"

John Brown and Owen drove their two wagons from town to town, still trying to raise money. They were at Cleveland, Akron, Hudson, Chicago to work the same appeals that had been so successful in New England. News from Kansas gave no hint that further troubles would break there to give him an opportunity to uphold his carefully nourished reputation as the fighting leader. A letter from John Brown Jr. gave some astute advice on this point: " place it out of the power of Croakers to say that the ' peace ' had been broken only in consequence of the advent there of such disturbers as ' Jim Lane ' and ' Old Brown.' And further, when war begins, if the people there take the right ground, you could raise and take in with you a force which might in truth become a ' liberating army ' when they most stood in need of help." But odds were against the rôle of liberator on the one hand, and, on the other, they were against the chance of cashing any of the financial pledges except by " active service " in Kansas. He could write to Kansas and ask Wattles, Holmes, Conway, Cochran, and others to meet him in

Tabor for some vague conference, which was to settle the
political destinies of the Territory, or he could send encouraging and ambiguous messages back to Boston, but
that was the sum of it; nobody felt like turning up for the
conference and no more money came from Boston. John
Brown realized the embarrassment of the dilemma. His policy was one of politically honorable wisdom; it was one of
watchful waiting, of writing notes, of hope, and, perhaps,
of prayer. In other words, he took his time about getting to
Kansas.

"It seems as though if you return to Kansas this Spring
I should never see you again." Such was the mournful and
foreboding text which John Brown Jr. set on his father's
westward journey. When John Brown was in Hudson, and
saw around him the altered background of his hard childhood, the same ominous sense possessed him. "If I should
never return, it is my particular request that no other
monument be used to keep me in remembrance than the
same plain one that records the death of my grandfather
and son; and that a short story, like those already on it, be
told of John Brown the fifth, under that of grandfather. I
think I have several good reasons for this. I would be glad
that my posterity should not only remember their parent-
age, but also the cause they labored in." That very spring
he had made arrangements for the stone to be sent from the
old family home in Connecticut to North Elba. There it
waited until the chisel cut in the names of John Brown and
of the sons who died with him far to the south in Virginia.
But now there were only the irresolutions and vague distress which ended the letter to his wife: "I am much
confused in mind, and cannot remember what I wish
to write. May God abundantly bless you all!" Did

the words, " hence he rarely failed in some good degree to effect the things he undertook," put to rest all his doubts?

It was August 7 before John Brown reached Tabor. His first care was to account for his past delay and for the indefinite delay which he knew would follow. " In consequence of ill-health," he wrote Mr. Stearns, " and other hindrances too numerous and unpleasant to write about, the least of which has *not been* the lack of sufficient means for freight bills and other expenses, I have never as yet returned to Kansas." Then came a rehearsal of financial disappointments and a veiled rebuke for the failure to pay for the North Elba farm. " *Have not given up*," was the vague and encouraging sentiment which closed the letter. To Mr. Sanborn he said: " I am now, at last, within hailing distance of our Free-State friends in Kansas." But a remark made to his wife carried the substance of the situation which the cleverest of the New England correspondents could not guess: " Should no disturbance occur, we may possibly think best to work back eastward."

Two days after John Brown's arrival in Tabor Colonel Forbes reported for duty. The Colonel's conduct, since their private understanding in New York, was one of the things which preyed most on John Brown's mind. Forbes had promised to make short work of his " Manual " and hurry westward to join his leader, but the middle of June found him still in New York engaged in an effort to raise funds on the basis of his connection with John Brown. He wanted the money for the strictly private reason of paying his wife's fare from Paris to New York. But more grievous than this private exploitation of John Brown's own source of revenue was another fault: Forbes was presuming to have opinions of his own. To Joseph Bryant, John Brown's agent, he said that there was little need of going to Kansas for no difficulties could be expected before winter. Now this was the unhappy contrary of what John Brown wanted all of his Eastern supporters to believe; every letter was calculated to give the impression that a crisis might break at any moment and that he, John Brown, was merely waiting until the blow could be struck with the most disastrous effect to all enemies of freedom. He was, he insisted, " though faint, yet pursuing."

Forbes, with all of his loose talk, was decidedly dangerous, and, furthermore, he was an expense; already he had received an order for $600. John Brown made up his mind to dispose of such a general inconvenience as his drill-master. A peremptory order was mailed under care of Mr. Bryant in late June.

Sir:
If you have drawn on W. H. D. Callender, Esq., cashier at Hartford, Conn., for six hundred dollars, or any part of that amount, and are not prepared to come on and join me at once, you will please pay over to Joseph Bryant, Esq., who is my agent, six hundred dollars, or whatever amount you have so drawn.

When Mr. Bryant called with his order, the Colonel was so charming and convincing that he could not be so impolite as to take it out of his pocket. He carefully endorsed the order, when he was again alone, with his two reasons, one practical and one ethical: " I did not present this to the colonel, as I presumed it would be of no use; and then he is, I am persuaded, acting on good faith." Of course, the Colonel had long since drawn and pretty well used up the $600.

When Forbes reached Tabor he quickly lulled John

Brown's distrust and established the old confidence. The "Manual" was finished and the troublesome family situation solved by sending Miss Forbes to join her mother in Paris. Forbes professed himself to be ready for active service, and suppressed such private opinions as he may have cherished; he was not yet ready to play his own hand. The Captain and the Colonel amicably settled down to see what Kansas would offer to further their scheme.

Kansas did not have much to offer. The great majority of people were heartily sick of disorder, and looked forward to the October elections to settle the matter once and for all by a Free State majority in the Territorial Legislature. The policy of non-voting in Territorial elections was superseded by this more conservative and practical arrangement, and the matter of the Topeka Constitution and State machinery was, temporarily at least, in abeyance. Governor Walker had pledged himself to protect the election against fraud, and only a few anticipated any overt difficulty. With those few, such as James Lane, this idea was more of a hope than a conviction.

James Holmes was one man who sympathized with Lane's point of view. John Brown wrote immediately to his "little hornet," whose expertness in cattle-lifting had so endeared him to the leader's heart in the days before Osawatomie. Holmes was now settling on a peaceful claim but his reply showed that he kept an eye open. "I do not know," he said to John Brown," what you would have me infer by 'business.' I presume, though, by the word being emphasized, that you refer to the business for which I learn you have a stock of material with you. If you mean this. I think quite strongly of a good (?) opening for this business about the first Monday in October next." That Monday was the date set for the election, and the " materials " were the Sharpe's rifles at Tabor. But the " little hornet " was not quite sure whether his chief's concerns were purely political, and so he added: " If you wish other employments, I presume you will find just as *profitable* ones."

But John Brown had no idea of horse-stealing or cattle-lifting except, of course, under peculiarly favorable circumstances. He preferred trouble in Kansas for the simple reason that it would permit him to cash his $7,000 draft from Mr. Stearns and get his hands on supplies. Horses and cattle would, however, be welcome as pleasant unearned increment, but John Brown's primary interest now lay in the larger aspects of the situation. James Lane seemed to be the man on whom he could depend to develop these larger aspects.

During these days James Lane was busy in his endeavor to bring the old days of bloodshed back to the Territory. This was to be accomplished under the pretext of defending the Territorial elections by force and in this contingency he looked longingly across the line into Iowa where the Sharpe's rifles lay under the eye of John Brown. Lane had opposed taking any part in the Territorial elections, but when the reactionary peace sentiment of the majority turned in that direction, he, as an opportunist, was ready to take advantage of it. Back in the spring John Brown had confided to Augustus Wattles a similarly violent distaste for mixing in the conduct of the Territorial Government: " I bless God that He has not left the Free-State men of Kansas to pollute themselves by the foul and loathsome embrace of the old rotten whore." The idea now was that the foul and loathsome embrace of the rotten whore might be sanctified by a proper sacrament of blood and fire. John Brown, as an opportunist, was willing to assist in administering that sacrament, on the nuptial morning of the first Monday in October.

"We want you and all the materials you have," Lane wrote him on September 7. Lane realized the vanity of the man with whom he was dealing, and, to clinch the bargain, made him a Brigadier General in his army; there were, of course, a number of brigadier generals. Despite the sane statement from Wattles that "those who had entertained the idea of resistance have entirely abandoned the idea," John Brown recognized possibilities in Lane's suggestion. He wrote in answer: "As to the job of work you inquire about, I suppose that three good teams, with well-covered wagons, and ten *really ingenious, industrious* men (*not gassy*), with about $150 in cash, could bring it about in the course of eight or ten days." But when the "Quartermaster-General of the Second Division," a Mr. Jamison, appeared at Tabor with no wagons and only $50, John Brown declined to enter Kansas. He returned the $50, referred to his poor state of health, and added that "he was disappointed in the extreme."

The election came off very peacefully with success to the Free State ticket. There were, naturally, some false returns, but the Governor was willing to see fair play, and the Free State men elected their Congressional Delegate and secured a majority in the Territorial Legislature. Meanwhile, John Brown gave Sanborn a long and artful account of affairs. He was nearly penniless, even being unable to pay his board bill in Tabor, and so he confessed to the Collinsville contact for pikes on which he had already paid $150. "Wise military men may ridicule the idea; but ' I take the whole responsibility of that job.' " With the letter was his Kansas correspondence to give an idea of affairs. "I will not say," he added in an heroic strain, "that Kansas, watered by the tears and blood of my children, shall yet be free or I fall." The quiet result of the election which followed a day or two afterwards would have made this and the Lane correspondence look a little bit ridiculous to any other eyes than Mr. Sanborn's.

As matters stood it came to Mr. Sanborn's portion to quiet the irritation that some Eastern supporters felt with John Brown's delay. He had been sent to Kansas to " give Robinson and the rest some Backbone," and here was Robinson with his wiser faction deliberately piloting the Territory into an efficient and undramatic solution of its difficulties. People like Thomas Wentworth Higginson could not understand and Mr. Sanborn instructed them. " You do not understand Brown's circumstances," he wrote early in September. " He is as ready for a revolution as any other man, and is now on the borders of Kansas safe from arrest but prepared for action, but he needs money for his present expenses, and *active* support. I believe he is the best Disunion champion you can find, and with his hundred men, when he is put where he can raise them, and drill them (for he has an expert drill officer with him) will do more to split the Union than a list of 50,000 names for your Convention, good as that is." So that was the game — Union-splitting. To some men John Brown stood for Disunion, but to others he presented himself, with characteristic tact, in quite a different light. Emerson, for instance, made this informing comment. " There is a Unionist, there is a strict constructionist for you! He believes in the Union of the States, and he conceives that the only obstruction to the Union is slavery; and for that reason, as a patriot, he works for its abolition."

The comfortable results of the election did not diminish Lane's desire to get John Brown, and more especially John

Brown's " materials " into Kansas. Behind Lane was a secret order, the " Danites," and by its means Lane contemplated a widespread massacre of pro-slavery sympathizers. In the light of Pottawatomie, he could not feel that John Brown would be averse to such business. He approved of John Brown's aid, but he did not approve of John Brown's characteristic desire to run whatever show was in progress. The election was to have served as a pretext to begin violence, but after its failure in that respect another pretext was not lacking. On October 19, a pro-slavery convention was to meet at Lecompton to frame a constitution for the admission of the Territory. It was Lane's idea to start the massacre then and there with the party leaders. Two days before that date, when Lane was in Lawrence organizing his men for the slaugter, the cat was out of the bag. At a meeting packed by " boys," the riffraff and scum of the region, Lane rose to speak in the midst of cheers. But in the meeting was one of his subordinates who had come under order to bring supplies for three days' service. " General Lane tells us that further peaceful measures are out of the question; that our only remedy for this new trouble is by shedding blood. I fully agree with him! " There were more cheers. Then Mr. Goodin continued. " But I may differ with some of you as to the proper place to begin this blood-spilling business. No person has occasioned more strife, or been the more fruitful cause of our disturbances than — James H. Lane! He demands blood! We all want it; but it is his blood that is demanded at this time; and if he presses on his assassination project, I propose he shall be the first person to contribute in that direction." That settled the matter; Lane gave up the idea of blood-spilling. If news of the meeting reached Tabor, John Brown must have blessed the luck which had kept him out of him out of Kansas. Rather, he must have blessed his own judgment.

It was at the end of October, when the Lecompton Convention had prepared its Constitution, that Whitman and Lane raised $150 for John Brown's expenses. A council of all the leaders, the Vigilance Committee, and the officers of Lane's organization was to be held, and John Brown had a right to expect interesting developments. He put the money in his pocket, along with another hundred dollars from the Reverend Adair, and set out for Kansas. In flat defiance of instructions from Lane and from Whitman, he left the arms at Tabor; he had no intention of letting them out of his own hands. The money he simply regarded as part of what the Kansas Committee owed him. Since the unhappy Whitman had raised the money by a personal loan, it is no wonder that he felt a little dissatisfied with the situation. When John Brown left Kansas he was even more dissatisfied.

John Brown appeared at Whitman's home on November 5, two days late for the important council but ready to profit by its consequences. The council, unfortunately, had no consequences, and John Brown consoled himself by collecting from Whitman $500 and some of the equipment pledged by the Massachusetts Committee. All seemed quiet even in the storm center of Lawrence and a trip to Topeka gave no more promise than John Brown's forecast of "interesting times" would be fulfilled. From Topeka he wrote to Mr. Stearns: "I find matters quite *unsettled;* but am decidedly of the opinion that there will be no use for the Arms or ammunition here before another Spring. I have them all safe, *& together unbroken: & mean to keep them so:* until I can see how the matter will be finally terminated. I have many calls uppon me for their *distribution;* but shall do no such thing until I am satisfied that they are *really needed*. I mean to be busily; but *very quietly* engaged in perfecting my arangements during the Winter." This was the alibi for disregarding the order of Mr. Whitman, the Committee's representative, to bring in the arms.

Meanwhile, John Brown was very quietly engaged in Kansas in perfecting his arrangements. He got in touch with certain old friends, such as Cook, Colonel Whipple, and Parsons, whose manners and ideas of the proper conduct of life were somewhat like his own. The pretext John Brown used for calling these men together was the old one of organizing a company for " the purpose of putting a stop to the aggressions of the pro-slavery forces." In the minds of most of those who got the messages this was simply a convenient synonym for anything, just as " business " had been in the mind of the " little hornet."

On the prairie to the northeast of Topeka John Brown camped with four of his recruits. There " Colonel Whipple," Cook, Kagi, and Charles Moffet learned that their business was to spend the winter at a " military school " in Ohio. That was all their leader had to offer by way of explanation. In the morning Cook was sent back to Lawrence to cash a draft for John Brown and to pick up two other students for the military school. The rest of the party left for Tabor.

Kansas, " watered by the blood and tears " of John Brown's children, meant nothing to him now. He was anxious to get about business of his own; Kansas had served his turn and was behind him. The separation was so complete that in the winter Whitman could not restrain his irritation in a letter to Mr. Stearns: " he then left, declining to tell me or anyone where he was going or where he could be found, pledging himself, however, that if difficulties should occur he would be on hand and pledging his life to redeem Kansas from slavery. Since then nothing has been heard of him and I know of no one, not even his most intimate friends, who know where he is. In the meantime he has been much wanted, and very great dissatisfaction has been expressed at his course and now I do not know as even his services would be demanded in any emergency." John Brown simply disappeared from the knowledge of Kansas and left no address.

"*I do not mean* to 'trouble Israel,'" John Brown had written to the Reverend Adair during his short stay in Kansas. When the new party of " eleven desperadoes," as Owen called them, reached Tabor, their leader felt that it was time to speak out. He told them what land he meant to trouble. The land was Virginia. The immediate reaction of some of the men was against the business. The opportunities of Kansas, they felt, were good enough for them. They had good reason to believe that the old days of jay-hawking and raiding would come back soon, and that " Union-splitting," if " Union-splitting " was the game, could be managed just as well in Kansas as in Virginia. And there was the perfectly human resentment at being tricked by a pretext. Cook especially was opposed to the new idea: " Some warm words passed between him and myself, in regard to the plan, which I had supposed was to be entirely confined to Kansas and Missouri. Realf and Parsons were of the same opinion with me. After a good deal of wrangling we consented to go on, as we had not the means to return, and the rest of the party was so anxious that we should go with them." And so Cook was hanged at Charlestown simply because two years earlier he did not have a few dollars in his pocket.

John Brown revealed to some chosen ones of his men a prospect which made all their Kansas life — the conventions, the constitutions, the cattle-lifting, the raiding, the skirmishes — seem very trivial and childish and unimportant. After the first irritated surprise had passed the prospect confounded and dazzled them by its very magnificence. A thing less brilliant, less ambitious, might have evoked a thousand objections and cautions, but the splendor here silenced every wise doubt or fear and intoxicated every heart. They trusted Old Brown to show them how the trick could be turned, for he knew the rich, complicated world which their lives had never touched, he had experience and reputation, and then he was so sure, so confident, of final success. He simply gave them of the insane root which he himself had eaten years before; he taught them the meaning of ambition and the meaning of imagination. They were very young, very impressionable, very ignorant men, and, after all, they didn't like slavery. John Brown told them that God had created him to be the deliverer of the slaves, just as Moses was of the children of Israel; they did not much discuss that point.

On December 4 they left Tabor and set out for Ashtabula where the military school was to be established. They walked along beside the wagon of arms and supplies, with heads bowed to the wind and snow. Despite the harshness of the western winter, they circled about the few towns on their road and slept in the open, without protection. Food was short and they shot what game they could find on the way. At night, before they wrapped up in their blankets, they sometimes sang; and the songs were those which John Brown suggested. When the songs were over, and the voices, led by Stevens' baritone in " The Slave has seen the North Star," died away, and the men were dropping off to sleep, they could hear remotely the prairie wolves howling in the cold night.

A new seriousness lay over the men. Their schooling was

intended to make them not only into soldiers, but into leaders, organizers, and politicians. The training began on the slow journey across Iowa, for every day was filled with talk and debate about matters which would help them in the new career. Owen put down in his diary some of the talk: " warm argument upon the effects of the abolition of slavery upon the Southern States, Northern States, commerce and manufactures, also upon the British provinces and the civilized world; whence came our civilization and origin? Talk about prejudices against color; question proposed for debate, — greatest general, Washington or Napoleon." There is something both absurd and a little pathetic about the awkward earnestness of those debates — ignorant, reckless, inexperienced fellows talking themselves into a new sort of world where they intended to cut a figure. They were going to learn in a few months all the things necessary and they were very eager. But in their ignorance, their recklessness, and their lack of experience lay the force which fed their ambition and made them ready to go on. They were not fools but they were going to do what angels might fear to do; what John Brown held out for them seemed so easy to accomplish. When some of them finally sat in the dark engine house at the Ferry and listened to the rifle shots and shouts all night long they overheard one of their prisoners say to John Brown; " You men have committed treason against the State and the United States." Two of the raiders asked: " Are we committing treason against our country by being here? " " Certainly," replied Brown. " If that's so we don't want to fight any more. We thought we came to liberate the slaves, and didn't know that was committing treason." These two, like many others, did not realize what they were to do. And when morning came these two fellows, who didn't want to fight any

more, died before the assault of Colonel Bob Lee's
marines.

The school was to be established in Ashtabula County,
Ohio, but by the time the party of scholars reached Springdale, supplies and money were running so low that to go on
would have been madness. And so they stayed in Iowa, in
the quiet Quaker settlement, to set up their military school,
to argue about war, and the Bible, and politics, and history,
and to make scandalous love to the girls of the neighborhood.
After a week or so, Brown found a farmer who was willing to
give board to his men in exchange for the teams and wagons
and so the party left the house of the Quaker John Painter
and moved out to William Maxson's farm.

The training for the adventure was soon in full progress.
The "expert drill-master," Forbes, was now alienated from
the conspiracy, and Stevens took his place. The drilling was
perfectly open, but the neighbors simply understood it to
mean that there would be more excitement in Kansas. The
men flourished their wooden swords under the commands of
the deserter, Stevens, and only one or two of the people who
watched the spectacle realized what the sabres, that some
day would replace those wooden swords, were expected to do.
Maxson, Painter, and perhaps a few others had a little of
John Brown's confidence, but they kept the secret. The training went on; they read Forbes' "Manual," they took walks
into the country to study natural fortifications and the means
of defending or taking them, they talked about Washington
and Napoleon, and they debated statecraft. A mock legislature was formed to draw up laws for a "State of Topeka."
In the farm house or in the town school they met and prepared
themselves for the time when all this debating, the bills, and
laws, and amendments would be in sound earnest. "I want

to put into the hands of my young men," John Brown wrote to Sanborn a little later, " copies of Plutarch's ' Lives,' Irving's ' Life of Washington,' the best written Life of Napoleon, and other similar books, together with maps and statistics of States."

The winter was not a complete idyl of high-minded earnestness. There was quarrelling sometimes among the men, and passionate wrangling and arguments on purely personal matters which had nothing to do with Napoleon's strategy or the " State of Topeka." Some of the men were insubordinate in the face of John Brown's rigid and often pettish discipline; Owen Brown and Stevens, who had wills of their own, were especially troublesome. Stevens, as was reported, more than once " gave the old man merry hell." And parents of the region were alarmed, not without some justice, for the good names of their daughters. The scholars considered themselves soldiers, and they assumed the soldierly prerogatives in more ways than one.

All in all the school had little importance in the final summary of events. The school which did prepare these men for John Brown's purposes was the school of Kansas. There they learned the sight of blood, they learned the ways of violence and got the feeling that they were above law. They learned, above all, what virtue can lie in a word; the word " Freedom " obscured every selfish motive, and transformed, in the public mind if not in the recesses of their own more realistic minds, every act of criminality or violence into something worthy and excellent. And to some of them — to Kagi, the stooped young schoolmaster, or Realf, the half-insane, persecuted renegade who wrote bad verses and had one time been a pensioner of an aristocratic English family — the word must have been a real and passionate justification for all things. It

THE BIRTH OF A NATION

is hard to know precisely. But all the men shared one characteristic in common; they all were restless, they all had acquired a taste for excitement, and they were utterly unable to go back to the repose of common life. They were adventurers, and John Brown promised to provide the adventure.

In discussing this adventure with his followers, John Brown seems to have kept to safe generalities. He did mention Harper's Ferry as the point where operations would probably begin, but the critical details of the affair and its eventual reach were obscure in the minds of at least some members of the company. To the doubtful Parsons, for instance, John Brown, declared that he merely intended to release some slaves with as little fighting as possible, and give them arms to defend themselves on their flight to the North Star. In other words, Parsons was being lured on into the project just as Cook had been lured to the military school — a step at a time, with pretext after pretext gradually cleared away. With exquisite tact John Brown let each man know, or surmise, just what it was best for him to know about the total adventure. The adventure was the *conquest of the South*.

The soldiers who were to execute the conquest were the slaves themselves. John Brown knew so little about actual conditions in the South that he believed every negro was only waiting the chance to rise and cut his master's throat. He would provide the organization to harness this energy and hate. The great need was for officers to keep this vast potential army under direction and control. The men at William Maxson's farm were the nucleus but many more were necessary, and John Brown had a scheme to get them. The operations would in the beginning be confined to a single

State, so that a collision with the United States troops would be postponed until the insurrection and conquest were well under way; he was sure that the State militia would lack the decision and organization necessary to make them a major obstacle. The actual course of events proved this to be true. And John Brown had a scheme which would take care of the crisis when the General Government intervened.

In these schemes Colonel Forbes played an important rôle. It was John Brown's idea to corrupt the soldiers of the regular army, and from these men to provide the officers for his own army of conquest. Besides gaining trained men who could drill and direct the liberated negroes, he would, by the same blow, paralyze the United States Government, and give time for the disunion sentiment in the North to be transformed into action. The North would be convulsed with its own revolution, the central Government would be but a word, and he would have his own army behind him and a collapsing South at his feet. Colonel Forbes, with his superior education, was to put into practice the idea of seducing the private soldier of the army. The New England disunionists, who had contributed money to John Brown in the past, would concoct the Northern revolution.

The means of tampering with the army were as ridiculously inadequate as the means of rousing the slaves. When Forbes came to Tabor in August he brought with him a tract written under John Brown's direction, which was the first of a projected series entitled, " The Duty of the Soldier." Beneath the title was the sentiment: " Presented with respectful and kind feelings to the Officers and Soldiers of the United States Army in Kansas." The tract referred to the ancient republics where the word soldier was synonymous with *freeman*, it described legitimate and illegitimate authority, and it pointed out that there can " exist no moral obligation to do that which is immoral." But it asked one significant question: " Will the soldiery of a Republic consent to become *living machines,* and thus sustain Wrong against Right? " It asked this significant question several times.

The tract with its talk about ancient republics was not precisely the sort of thing which the ordinary soldier would read with interest. But the tract might provide a means of getting contact with that ordinary soldier, and laying before him a project which would interest him: that project would be the conquest. John Brown realized that he already had one deserter, Stevens, in his company. The word *Kansas* in the dedication was merely a blind and nothing more. In the summer of 1857 John Brown was intent on making his Eastern friends believe that he was embarking on a Kansas campaign, and, furthermore, if the tract should fall into unsympathetic hands in its distribution the one word " Kansas " would put investigation on a cold scent and not endanger his main scheme.

However futile and absurd the tract seems as an appeal to the hard-bitten rank and file of the regular army, John Brown put great store by it. On a copy which he sent to Augustus Wattles, he wrote out an addition to the text: " It is as much the duty of the common soldier of the U. S. Army according to his ability and opportunity to be informed *upon all subjects* in any way affecting the political or general welfare of his country; & to watch with jealous vigilance, the course, & management of all public functionaries both civil and military: *and to govern his actions as a citizen Soldier accordingly: as though he were President of the United States.*" Theodore Parker, Sanborn, Governor Chase, and Gerrit Smith also received copies, for John Brown was anx-

ious to get money for distributing the tract. " My particular
object in writing," as he put it to Parker, " is to say that I
am in immediate want of some five hundred or one thousand
dollars for secret service, and no questions asked." The bland
and vague-headed Gerrit Smith was the only person really
impressed, but even Sanborn, who disapproved of the scheme,
contributed seventy-two dollars.

Six months later, in the spring of 1858, when the conspiracy had lost Forbes, John Brown still believed in the general
idea. He appealed to Theodore Parker to act as the author,
and his instructions made it clear that he now realized the
defects of the old tract. " I want you to undertake to provide
a substitute for an address you saw last season, directed to the
officers and soldiers of the United States Army. The ideas
contained in that address I of course like, for I furnished the
skeleton. I never had the ability to clothe those ideas in language at all to satisfy myself; and I was by no means satisfied with the style of that address, and do not know as I can
give any correct idea of what I want. . . . In the first place
it must be short, or it will not be generally read. It must be in
the simplest or plainest language, without the least affecta-
tion of the scholar about it, and yet be worded with great
clearness and power. . . . The address should be appropriate, and particularly adapted to the peculiar circumstances
we anticipate, and should look to the actual change of service from that of Satan to the service of God." Theodore
Parker declined the honor, but to show his appreciation he
forwarded John Brown the report of General McClellan on
the European armies. Perhaps a minister of the gospel had
the right to be cynical about the written or spoken word causing many people to change service from Satan to God.

Meanwhile, the original author of the first tract of " The

Duty of the Soldier " had, from his employer's point of view, changed his service from that of God to Satan. When Forbes left for the East early in November, John Brown's confidence in him was still strong and the Colonel went away with a letter of introduction to Frederick Douglass. Forbes quickly wore out Douglass and the friends of Douglass by his persistent begging, and when that source of supply failed he turned to more vigorous measures. In December John Brown's various supporters began to receive letters threatening disclosure of the conspiracy if money was not forthcoming to fulfill John Brown's own contract with Forbes. Now the people who received these letters knew little about Forbes and nothing about any contract he had with Brown. They looked upon the Garibaldian Colonel as a common blackmailer who was simply trying to work a bluff on their pocketbooks. They themselves did not fear any disclosures for *they were not in Brown's confidence and knew nothing about the ambitious extent of his scheme.* In the winter of 1857–58 they still believed that their money was only to be used in Kansas. They treated him as an impostor, and expressed polite sympathy with the poverty of his family; Mr. Sanborn gave the further insult of contributing ten dollars.

In writing abusive letters to those people, whom he ironically termed the " Humanitarians," Forbes was simply acting on the same error which had involved him with John Brown in the first place. In the light of his experience with European revolutions, he interpreted the network of committees to mean only one thing — a widespread and highly organized conspiracy. He did not realize until too late the casuistry which some of John Brown's supporters practiced and which John Brown himself encouraged when he demanded " money with no questions asked." But after the fiasco was over, the whole issue was lost in a welter of casuistries; Gerrit Smith, in his injured innocence, went insane, everybody wrote letters, Dr. Howe wrote his letter and took a trip to Canada, and a certain Mr. Andrews, later Governor of Massachusetts, manfully expressed the supreme piece of casuistry when he declared, " whatever may be thought of John Brown's acts, *John Brown himself was right.*" In other words, there had never been a conspiracy, and John Brown was an innocent man. Forbes didn't realize that John Brown stood absolutely alone; John Brown had been too deep for him just as for the New England friends. But the day came when the friends were exceedingly glad that John Brown had been so deep, for it gave them their cue of graceful exit.

John Brown's own method of dealing with Forbes was not exactly straightforward. He instructed his son, John, to write the following letter to the trouble-maker:

Your letter to my father, of 27th January, after mature reflection, I have decided to return *to you*, as I am unwilling he should, with all his other cares, difficulties, and trials, be vexed with what I am apprehensive he will accept as *highly offensive and insulting*, while I know that he is disposed to do all he consistently can for you, and will do so, unless you are yourself the cause of his disgust. I am trying to send you a little assistance myself, — say about forty dollars; but I must hold up till I feel different from what I now do. . . . Now, you in your letter undertake to *instruct* him to say that he had positively engaged you for one year. I fear he will not accept it well to be asked or told to state what he considers an *untruth*. Again, I suspect you have greatly mistaken the man, if you suppose he will take it kindly in you, or any living man, to assume to instruct him how he should conduct his own business and correspondence. And I suspect that the seemingly spiteful letters you say you have written to some of his particular friends have not only done you great injury, but also weakened his hands with them. While I have, in your poverty, deeply sympathized with you and your family, *who*, I ask, is likely to be moved by any exhibition of a wicked and spiteful temper on your part, or is likely to be dictated to by you as to their duties? . . .

The letter itself and the backhand method of its delivery show that John Brown had lost nothing of his old astute talent for putting other people in the wrong; it echoes that masterpiece of almost twenty years before, the letter to Mr. Chamberlain. The question of real right and wrong, however, did not exist in the quarrel between John Brown and his Lieutenant; each man was playing his own game in the most expedient style. But the letter gives one interesting commentary by the author on himself: " Again, I suspect you have greatly mistaken the man, if you suppose he will take it kindly in you, or any living man, to assume to instruct him how he should conduct his own business and correspondence." And that was perfectly true; Forbes had mistaken his man.

Early in February John Brown presented himself at the door of Frederick Douglass at Rochester, New York. While the scholars were having the debates and swinging the wooden swords under Stevens' instruction, their leader had business in the East. " I will not stay unless you allow me to pay board," he said to Douglass, and Douglass promised to accept three dollars a week for the pleasure and inspiration of Captain Brown's company. All day long the guest sat in his room, preoccupied and intent, while the his bony fingers gripped the pen-staff and filled page after page with his ragged, old man's script. Every post carried off letters addressed in that ragged, old man's script to all sorts of people who might give money. Money was all important now — it was everything. That six hundred dollars thrown away on the scoundrel Forbes would have gotten his " scholars " and his " materials " together, and would have turned the trick. The night march into Virginia, the sudden blow, the rallying slaves, riflemen holding the defiles in the hills, revolution to the North, and to the South insurrection spreading, spreading like fire in dry prairie grass of Kansas. The time was near.

The letter writing went on day after day. One to Colonel Higginson read: " I have been told that you are both a true man and a true Abolitionist, and I partly believe the story. Last fall I undertook to raise from five hundred to one thousand dollars for secret service, and succeeded in getting five hundred dollars. I now want to get, for the perfecting of by far the most important undertaking of my whole life, five hundred to eight hundred dollars within the next sixty days." The same direct appeal and promise ran through all the letters. " I have nearly perfected arrangements for carrying out an important measure in which the world has a deep interest, as well as Kansas: " he wrote to Theodore Parker, " and only lack from five to eight hundred dollars to enable me to do so, — the same object for which I asked for secret-service money last fall. . . . Do you think any of my Garrisonian friends, either at Boston, Worcester, or any other place, can be induced to supply a little ' straw ' if I will absolutely make ' bricks '? " Every letter was cunning and each made the demand peculiarly personal. To Parker he said, " none of them understand my views as well as you do," and to Colonel Higginson, " I do not know as either Mr. Stearns or Mr. Sanborn are Abolitionists."

Excited, curious letters came to the Douglass house in Rochester addressed to " N. Hawkins." Sanborn, Higginson, Parker, Stearns and the rest realized that some big project was about to break; a slave stampede in Missouri was their wildest guess. John Brown invited them to a conference at Peterboro, and declined their pressing invitations to come to Boston with expenses paid; Captain Brown was supposed to be in hiding on the Kansas border and it would not do for " N. Hawkins " to be seen in Boston. And so they had to wait longer for the truth. Only Frederick Douglass, remembering how, ten years before, the bony, nervous finger had crept down the map and rested on the mountains of Virginia, could understand what was the truth. Then one day his guest showed him a long paper written out in the ragged, old man's script. It was the " Provisional Constitution And Ordinance For The People Of The United States."

On February 18, Gerrit Smith wrote in his diary, " Our old and noble friend Captain John Brown of Kansas arrives this evening." It was the time and place for the conference to which Higginson, Stearns, and Sanborn had been invited. Sanborn, impelled by his curiosity in Brown's plan and a desire to see Edwin Morton, an old friend who was a tutor in Smith's household, was the only one of the three to appear. He arrived on Washington's birthday. That evening the men sat before the fire in Morton's room upstairs and listened to the astounding revelation. Its audacity filled them with dismay and apprehension, but to every objection John Brown had an answer. He was positive and terribly in earnest. Everything depended on winning the support of these men who could give the money he needed. Gerrit Smith, already convinced by discussions of the past few days, walked nervously in and out of the room, while the argument proceeded. When the time came to read the Provisional Constitution he sat down with the others and heard it out. That strange, ineffectual lot of conspirators listened to the intent voice reading the paper whose very title meant treason. Smith, a bland

and impressive elderly man, filling the chair with his large complacency; Sanborn, the worthy, sincere young school-master (always the important young schoolmaster), with romantic notions and a taste for busy detail; — in disturbed silence they heard the voice reading each word with slow emphasis. " Whereas, slavery throughout its entire existence in the United States, is none other than a most barbarous, unprovoked, and unjustifiable war of one portion of its citizens upon another portion, . . ." Past midnight the conference broke up.

Next day the discussion went on. Point by point John Brown beat down their objections. He described the method of attack, the details of organization and fortification, the campaign in the South, and the retreat, if such were necessary, through the North to safety. More than that, he could predict what the reaction in the nation at large would be. Some of this they did not understand, for they were not fighting men, and not very clever politicians, but they understood, or thought they understood, John Brown's recurring argument; " If God be for us, who can be against us? "

While the remote winter sun was setting, Smith and Sanborn walked for an hour in the snow-covered fields. All those fields and woods had been bought from the Indians by Gerrit Smith's father; many things had come to pass in the country since that time. At last Gerrit Smith spoke. " You see how it is. Our old friend has made up his mind to this course, and he cannot be turned from it. We cannot give him up to die alone; we must stand by him now. I will raise so many hundred dollars for him, and you must lay the case before your friends in Massachusetts." They walked slowly back to the house in the diminished light.

Sanborn returned immediately to Boston where he placed

the plan before Higginson and Theodore Parker. John
Brown realized the value of Sanborn as an organizer and
financial backer, but he realized that the prestige of such
a man in his actual fighting ranks would mean much more.
Sanborn had scarcely reached Boston before he received a
letter. " What an inconceivable amount of good you might
so effect by your counsel, your example, your encouragement, your natural and acquired ability for active service!
And then how little we can possibly lose! Certainly the cause
is enough to *live* for, if not to . . . for. I have only had this
one opportunity, in a life of nearly sixty years; and could I be
continued ten times as long again, I might not have again an
equal opportunity. God has honored but comparatively a
very small part of mankind with any possible chance for such
mighty and soul satisfying rewards. But my dear friend if
you should make up your mind to do so, I trust it will be
wholly from the prompting of your own spirit after you have
thoroughly counted the cost." Sanborn waited for the
prompting of his own spirit and waited with no result. " Long
accustomed to guide my life by leadings and omens from that
shrine whose oracles may destroy but can never deceive," he
finally apologized, " I listened in vain, through months of
doubt and anxiety, for a clear and certain call." Poor Mr.
Sanborn! He did admire heroes so much, and he was so sincere, so upright, so worthy, and so important. He was all of
those things, but he was not the stuff from which heroes are
made. He could work day and night at the busy details of
the cause, but he could not die for it — or even run the chance
of dying for it. It is not probable that he was disappointed in
himself; it was not his fault that he received no clear and certain call. When the terrible and bloody collapse came, he kept
as much of his dignity and self-possession as most of the

others. And afterwards he spent many years writing about himself, about other worthy, sincere, and important men of his circle, and, with a sort of academic passion for heroism, about his one great hero.

John Brown left Peterboro for Brooklyn, where he stopped with some wealthy negroes by the name of Gloucester. Here his business was to enlist support among the free negroes, and to this end he probably revealed his scheme in a much greater degree than to his New England friends. He secretly visited Boston and in his room at the American House discussed the details of the news which Sanborn had brought back. Theodore Parker was ready to lend his energies to the enterprise, but he was not too hopeful about its practical success. His attitude was qualified somewhat like this: "I doubt whether things of the kind will succeed. But we shall make a great many failures before we discover the right way of getting at it." Higginson was more militant and more sanguine, and Dr. Howe and Mr. Stearns made promises of aid. They understood the general idea of the attack and were only ignorant of the place and manner of its opening; the thought of taking Harper's Ferry and the United States arsenal, the thought of treason, might have caused them to hesitate. This plea of ignorance was all that was left to them when the end came. They were stunned and bewildered then, for, being peaceful men, they had not been able to visualize the spectacle of innocent people shot down in the streets and riddled corpses lying in the shallows of the river. The real business of violence and blood-spilling seemed very remote as they now made their promises of money. John Brown was well pleased with the promises, for, on March 6, he wrote to John Brown Jr.: "My call here has met with a most hearty response, so that I feel assured of at least tolerable success."

With this encouragement John Brown continued his campaign. At Philadelphia John Brown Jr. met his father and took part in a conference with various prominent negroes. Then followed a rapid tour including New York, New Haven, North Elba, Peterboro, and Rochester. From there the son was to move southward, hunting for people of " the right stripe " at " Bedford, Chambersburg, Hagerstown, Md. *or even Harper's Ferry.*" Despite his shrewd reticences in Room 126 of the American House, John Brown knew quite definitely where and how his attack would begin. In letter after letter of instruction to his son, the name of the town occurred, and always it was underscored.

From Rochester John Brown went to St. Catherine, Canada, with a negro by the name of Loguen, who was in his confidence. There he met Harriet Tubman, a negro woman, who by her courage and ability as an " underground railway " worker had earned the name of " Moses of her People." With such sponsors, John Brown quickly gained the confidence of the large colored colony in the region, and was sure that these people would provide a considerable number of recruits. But most of the negroes here had known a taste of slavery, and however enthusiastically they might listen to John Brown's plans they were of no mind to risk themselves again. Negroes, after all, were human.

John Brown, in keeping with the magnitude of his intentions, wished to give them all the pomp and form of authority. He determined nothing less than a constitutional convention to be held at Chatham, Canada, among those very free negroes whom he had so recently impressed. A constitutional convention to authorize a mere foray and the liberation of a few slaves would have been almost a humorous performance. But the business planned for the middle of May was no simple raid; and there was not, necessarily, any humor in a convention held to authorize a " conquest." Whatever humor there was, lay in the discrepancy between the means and the proposed end. Let us suppose that by some wild trick of circumstance the adventure did not miscarry — Would the Provisional Constitution and the convention appear quite so ridiculous?

On May 25, John Brown arrived in Springdale to collect his scholars for the convention, and four days later he was in Chatham ready to begin. Cook prepared a noncommittal form for notifying interested persons of the convention. " We have issued a call for a very *quiet* Convention at this place, to which we shall be very happy to see any true friends of freedom and to which you are most earnestly invited to give your attendance." And at Chatham the news circulated that a colored Masonic lodge was being organized. But the pomps of a Masonic lodge were pale beside those which the rhetorical Cook described in one of his indiscreet letters to two young women of Springdale: " I can almost hear the swelling anthem of Liberty rising from the millions who have but just cast aside the fetters and the shackles that bound them. But ere that day arrives, I fear that we shall hear the crash of the battle shock and see the red gleaming of the cannon's lightning." On May 8, the " Provisional Constitutional Convention " came to order in the wooden schoolhouse on Princess Street in Chatham. None of John Brown's New England supporters appeared for the convention which was to authorize the battle shock and the cannon's lightning. There were twelve white men beside the leader: Kagi, Leeman, Tidd, Gill, Parsons, Taylor, Moffet, Cook, Realf, Owen Brown, and Stevens. Thirty-four negroes were present, one of whom, a preacher by the name of Munroe, presided over the proceedings.

John Brown rose before the little group in the schoolhouse. He told them how the idea of giving liberty to the slaves had possessed him like a passion for the preceding twenty or thirty years; how during his trip to Europe he had inspected fortifications with the intention of applying the knowledge to mountain warfare in the South; how he had studied guerrilla warfare from the days of the Roman conquest of Spain to those of Mina in Spain and of Toussaint L'Overture in Hayti; and how the result of all this was a completed plan of action. The plan, he added, was entirely his own. He explained it in detail. The first blow would rally the free negroes of the North as well as the slaves. These would be the fighting men. The slaveholders who refused to release their chattels would be taken and held as hostages for the safety of any of the attackers who might be captured. Nonslaveholders would be protected, for, in fact, John Brown looked to the poor white class in the South for considerable support. The insurrection would spread rapidly southward with the backbone of its defense in the impregnable mountains, and the territory occupied would be organized under the regulations of the Provisional Constitution. As soon as the slave States, under the pressure of the insurrection, bought their peace by wholesale abolition, a new election of officers under the Constitution would take place. This, presumably, was a statement that John Brown, since he had no selfish interests, would resign any power as soon as the final object was achieved. The particular issue is not one that demands discussion.

An oath of secrecy was voted and administered despite John Brown's protest of religious scruples. The Constitution was read and laid down for debate. Only one Article, number XLVI, provoked objections. It read: " The foregoing Articles shall not be construed so as in any way to encourage the overthrow of any State Government of the United States: and look to no dissolution of the Union, but simply to Amendment and Repeal. And our flag shall be the same that our Fathers fought under in the Revolution." The article was carried despite the objection, but it is pleasant to reflect that there was at least one logician in the convention.

With the adoption and signing of the Constitution and with appropriate " congratulatory remarks," the Provisional Convention came to an end. The evening of the first day, a new body gathered according to the regulations of the Constitution itself. John Brown was elected Commander-in-Chief, with Kagi as his Secretary of War. At the following meetings held in the First Baptist Church and " No. 3 Engine House," Realf was elected Secretary of State, George Gill, Secretary of the Treasury, Owen Brown, Treasurer, and Osborn P. Anderson and A. M. Ellsworth, members of Congress. The other officers, that of President among them, were to be filled by the decision of a committee of fifteen of which John Brown was chairman. The business was over and the Provisional Government was established. It had its beginnings, as it was to have its end, in an engine house.

Whereas, slavery throughout its entire existence in the United States is none other than a most barbarous, unprovoked, and unjustifiable war of one portion of its citizens upon another portion, the only conditions of which are perpetual imprisonment and hopeless servitude or absolute extermination; in utter disregard and violation of those eternal and self-evident truths set forth in our Declaration of Independence: Therefore "We, citizens of the United States, and the Oppressed People, who, by a recent decision of the Supreme Court are declared to have no rights which the White Man is bound to respect; together with all other people degraded by the laws thereof, Do, for the time being ordain and establish ourselves, the following PROVISIONAL CONSTITUTION and ORDINANCES, the better to protect our Persons, Property, Lives, and Liberties; and to govern our actions."

Such was the preamble of the document. Its most remarkable feature, as has been pointed out, was John Brown's statement of slavery as a " most barbarous, unprovoked, and unjustifiable war." Being war, and being a righteous war, it vindicated everything. Robbery became, under its terms, confiscation, and murder became execution. And so, a little tardily, the events of Pottawatomie received their definition. " Better that a whole generation of men, women, and children should pass away by a violent death . . . ," he had said to Emerson. The game now involved a generation and a state and not five men and a herd of horses. The comparison almost tricks one into acquiescence: to steal a horse is immoral, but to steal a state is neither moral nor immoral; it simply succeeds or fails. It is well to be realistic for a moment and remember how ghastly would have been the way of its success.

One intention of the Constitution was to check that very aspect of especial horror, and ruthless despatch which characterizes a racial struggle. But the threat of that horror would have remained, as Gerrit Smith pointed out, to unman and disorganize the defenses against insurrection. The threat, in itself, was a powerful weapon; the actuality might have been the ruin of the insurrection, for it cannot be supposed that the Northern States would have permitted without interference a protracted period of bloodshed, anarchy, and violation. Having that in mind, one can almost regret the failure at Harper's Ferry. The North and the South might have learned that blood is indeed thicker than water, and a solution might have been reached without the convulsion of the four terrific years from 1861 to 1865. Of course, there were issues other than slavery.

But John Brown had no intention of letting the insurrection get out of hand, so that there could be any appeal to such sympathies. The Provisional Constitution offered a system whereby the movement could be held under control and direction. Arrangement was made for the ordinary legislative, executive, and judicial branches of government. There was to be a Congress composed of not less than five or more than ten members, elected by all citizens of mature age and sound mind connected with the organization. A President and a Vice-President were to be elected in the same way, as well as one Chief Justice and four Associate Judges. The Commander-in-Chief was to be elected by the President, Vice-President, and majority of the Provisional Congress and of the Supreme Court. During the first three years the Commander-in-Chief was to have, like the President, a working veto over all legislative enactments. No officer should be entitled to any salary " other than a competent support of himself and family," except in case of an equal division of public property on the establishment of peace or in case of special provision by treaty.

All persons who voluntarily delivered up their slaves and had their names registered on the " Books " of the organization were to be protected and not treated as merely neutral. The persons and property of all non-slaveholders who remained absolutely neutral were to be respected in so far as circumstances would allow. But Article XXXVI read: " The entire and real property of all persons known to be acting either directly or indirectly with or for the enemy, or found in arms with them, or found willfully holding slaves, shall be confiscated and taken, whenever and wherever it may be found, in either free or slave States." All property so confiscated, as well as " all property the product of the labor of those belonging to this organization and of their families," was to be held for the benefit of the whole. There is no evidence to show that this communal conception of property was not something more than a war measure. The negroes, as the experience of emancipation was to show, could not work for themselves. They had been accustomed to explicit directions as to when, where, and how they should employ themselves, and John Brown must have realized this fact. The abolition of private property would accomplish two expedient ends: it would throw the wealth of white, non-slaveholding citizens into the common treasury, and it would permit the irresponsible negro labor to be kept under direct control. The communal arrangement did not necessarily imply a purely idealistic basis; it was rather an astute practical adjustment for peculiar circumstances. The negro, like the soldier of the regular army, was to perform an exchange of his service from that of Satan to that of God, in so far as God was embodied in the Provisional Government.

The Constitution arranged for the reunion of families separated by slavery and by the excitement of the insurrection, for the establishment of schools and churches, for the keeping of the Sabbath, and for personal cleanliness. At no time was there to be swearing, " filthy conversation, indecent behavior, or indecent exposure of the person, or intoxication, or quarrelling." " Unlawful intercourse of the sexes " was forbidden by the Constitution, and the violation of any female prisoner was punishable by death. In other words the whole plan of the Constitution looked beyond the period of actual fighting to the establishment of a stable state; but the existence of this state was assumed in the provisions for making treaties. " Before any treaty of peace shall take full effect, it shall be signed by the President and Vice-President, the Commander-in-Chief, a majority of the House of Representatives, a majority of the Supreme Court, and majority of all general officers of the army."

In the light of the intentions stated and implied by the Constitution and in the light of John Brown's conduct, the debated article, Article XLVI, appears as nothing but a piece of dishonesty — a piece of expedient dishonesty. John Brown was not temporizing to deceive himself; the article was a sop to timid spirits. When he sat on the floor of the dark engine house, he answered the question of treason explicitly enough. " Certainly," he said.

The men left Chatham on May 11, to hunt work for their support in neighboring Ohio towns until they should receive the signal that the conquest was on. Everyone expected action in the very near future — as soon as a little money could be had — and they were all impatient with the delay. In fact, there was some talk, in which Cook led, of making an independent raid to the South if the promised funds were not immediately forthcoming. Cook always talked a good deal — especially to women. The idea of an independent raid does something to define the mixed motives behind the business; these fellows would rather fight than earn a living.

The postponement of the movement southward came, not as a result of financial distresses, but by reason of Colonel Hugh Forbes. The subterfuge of John Brown's letter, and Sanborn's ten dollars, had accomplished nothing. The Colonel was intent on becoming the active leader of the conspiracy, and his attempt at blackmail was combined with one to undermine John Brown's position with his supporters. He described a plan, which he attributed to his employer, to "beat up a slave quarter in Virginia," run off some hundreds of slaves, arm others, destroy the Harper's Ferry arsenal, and maintain a force in the mountains until a Northern Convention had restored tranquillity and overthrown the proslavery administration at Washington. Forbes' criticism of this hypothetical proposition was an instructive one, and showed that the fellow himself was not without certain abilities. "This, I contended would be a merely local explosion. A slave insurrection, being from the very nature of things deficient in men of education and experience, would under such a system as B. proposed be either a flash in the pan or would leap beyond his control, or any control, when it would become a scene of mere anarchy and would assuredly be suppressed. On the other hand, B. considered foreign intervention as not impossible. As to the dream of a Northern Convention, I considered it as a settled fallacy." To supplant this scheme Forbes outlined "The Well-Matured Plan," to which, he said, John Brown had agreed the previous autumn. This was a series of well-prepared slave stampedes in the border states, each stampede being conducted independently so that one failure would not jeopardize the project. The anticipated result would be to force the borders of safe slaveholding gradually southward and to "impel the proslaveryites to commit some stupid blunders." But if the matter were left in Brown's hands it would end in some fiasco or in a tragedy, for Brown was a vicious, unreliable, and unprincipled man. Such was Forbes' description of his erstwhile friend and employer.

Even as late as May 14, when Forbes wrote the preceding statement to Dr. Howe, he had not despaired of succeeding John Brown in the confidence and generosities of the con-

spirators. He did not expose what he certainly knew to be
the real plans which he and John Brown had discussed, and
it is more than probable that he contemplated, if he could
dispose of that vicious and unreliable man, a program more
ambitious than slave stampedes. But "The Well-Matured
Plan" would suffice as a beginning. The most important
thing was to get a hand into the Bostonian purses and flesh-
pots. Even when he buttonholed Senator Wilson of Massachusetts in Washington and denounced John Brown, he was
so astute in his accusations that the essential plot was not
jeopardized. Forbes, in some respects, was a very clever man.

Six months earlier, when the first appeals and threats were
made, the men who received Forbes' letters were merely bewildered, for then they had not risen to the dignity of conspirators. Now they were distinctly alarmed. The weaker
souls, such as Gerrit Smith, whom John Brown a little scorn-
fully referred to as a "timid man," favored indefinite postponement. Higginson was of sterner stuff. "*If the thing is
postponed,*" he wrote to John Brown at Chatham, "*it is postponed forever* — for H. F. can do as much harm next year
as this. His malice must be in some way put down or *out-
witted* — & after the move is *once begun,* his plots will be of
little importance." Higginson was a man after John Brown's
heart.

But Forbes' little colloquy with Mr. Wilson in the corridors
of the Capitol put an end to the hopes of Higginson and
John Brown, for the Senator wrote to advise Mr. Howe to get
the arms contributed for defense in Kansas out of John
Brown's hands. "*If they should be used for other purposes,
as rumor says they may be, it might be of disadvantage to
the men who were induced to contribute to that very foolish
movement. If it can be done, get the arms out of his control*

and keep clear of him at least for the present. This is in confidence." But a solution of this difficulty was at hand. Mr. Stearns had at various times during the preceding year advanced money to the Massachusetts Kansas Committee, and the arms, as well as notes given by Kansas citizens to the Committee for supplies, stood as security for the loans. Mr. Stearns, acting in his capacity as chairman of the Committee, wrote to John Brown at Chatham concerning the arms: " In consequence of the information thus communicated to me, it becomes my duty to warn you not to use them for any other purpose, and to hold them subject to my order as chairman of said committee." Meanwhile, acting in his capacity of simple Mr. Stearns, the business man, he forclosed on the arms, and received their ownership *without the knowledge of the full Committee*. Still acting in his capacity of simple Mr. Stearns, he transferred the arms to John Brown. And the alarmed Senator received this comforting letter from Dr. Howe: " Prompt measures have been taken and will resolutely be followed up to prevent any such monstrous perversion of a trust as would be the application of means raised for the defense of Kansas to a purpose which the subscribers of the fund would disapprove and vehemently condemn." What Senator Wilson did not learn was that the arms were no longer the possession of the Kansas Committee. " It is still a little difficult," Mr. Sanborn wrote years afterwards, " to explain this transaction concerning the arms without leaving a suspicion that there was somewhere a breach of trust." Mr. Sanborn was generous with his friends. The conspirators were " honorable men," and they saved all the honor they could out of a trying business.

The question of honor and of conscience was still uppermost in their minds when they met to consider the next step in the conspiracy. John Brown was to be sent to Kansas to quiet any suspicions raised by Forbes' revelations; the details of the more important attack on Virginia should be left entirely to the discretion of their " agent." The common sentiment of these men — Smith, Parker, Howe, Stearns, Higginson, and Sanborn — was that they wanted no report except by action. They were entirely in accord with Gerrit Smith's feeling: " I do not wish to know Captain Brown's plans; I hope he will keep them to himself." They did not want to be embarrassed by knowledge, and when the telegraph wires hummed with tidings of insurrection and savage fighting at Harper's Ferry, and when the big print of the newspapers announced the lamentable end, they must have fervently thanked God for the foresight which had kept them so innocent, so technically innocent. This was the fashion in which, as Gerrit Smith said, they could not give John Brown up " to die alone "; in a sense, they simply passed the buck on down to him. Now, so long after, one can scarcely restrain the regret that these men, very good and, in most ways, such admirable men, should not have owned more courage and more essential honesty rather than so much of the sort of honesty which permitted them to answer a Senatorial Committee's questions " truthfully " and which kept their skirts and consciences clean. The clergymen, Parker and Higginson, were somewhat more honest with themselves; being clergymen, they possibly remembered how Pilate called for the basin and washed his hands.

The casuistry practiced about the arms soothed Senator Wilson's fears, and the decision to send John Brown to Kansas would render all of Forbes' disclosures and threats somewhat ridiculous. " It was hoped that by this delay," as Frederick Douglass put the matter, " the story of Forbes would be discredited; and this calculation was correct, — for nobody believed the scoundrel, though he told the truth." John Brown himself toyed at one time with a more drastic suppression of the troublesome fellow. He had just seen adopted the Provisional Constitution which authorized the execution of anyone who deserted to the " enemy," and he was on fire for the immediate fulfillment of his scheme. Forbes was a preliminary inconvenience to be disposed of. And so he wrote to Sanborn on May 14: " We have those who are thoroughly posted up to put on his track, and we beg to be allowed to do so." But the committee decided on a more judicious solution and John Brown, somewhat unwillingly, was packed off to Kansas. Dr. Howe wrote the traitor a stinging letter disclaiming any responsibility on his part or the part of the Kansas Committee for John Brown's actions. " You are, sir, the guardian of your own honor; but I trust that for your children's sake, at least, you will never let your passion lead you to a course that might make them blush." After John Brown's departure from New England Forbes still had hopes of success: " Let them not flatter themselves that I shall eventually become weary and shall drop the subject; it is as yet quite at its beginning." But the game was up, and so he passed off the scene, still muttering, still threatening, and wondering, with a little contempt perhaps, how he had been worsted by the ignorant, intent old man, — the strangest adventurer he had ever known. The Garibaldian Colonel gave no further trouble; he disappeared, with his soldierly bearing, his grace at fence, his impeccable manners, his ambitions, and his shabby coat, to some obscure destiny of his own.

10

DO YOU BELIEVE QUETELET?

I AM now writing in the log-cabin of the notorious Captain James Montgomery, whom I deem a very brave and talented officer, and, what is infinitely more, a very intelligent, kind, gentlemanly, and most excellent man and lover of freedom." Thus John Brown wrote to his son John on July 9. His trip to Kansas had been in instructive contrast to the indecisions and procrastination of the preceding summer; now his mind was made up and he did not have to play for time. After a hurried visit to North Elba, he reached Cleveland, Ohio, on June 20, where he assembled his men, gave them a cut of the war committee's advance payments, and released them to their own devices until the great moment should come. Kagi and Tidd went directly to Kansas with him, where they were joined later by Stevens and Gill. Cook was already at Harper's Ferry, spying out the region and the people, and Realf had been assigned to a similar espionage job in New York on account of Forbes. The other men drifted away on their private concerns. Five of them, including Realf and Gill, the Secretary of Treasury, were lost to the conspiracy. Parsons, who never relished the idea of running up against the United States Government, came at last to accept his mother's solicitous advice. " They

290

are bad men," she put it. " You have got away from them, now keep away from them."

Kansas at the time of John Brown's arrival was in the midst of great political excitement. The members of the pro-slavery Lecompton Convention, whom Lane would have massacred, had drawn up their Constitution the preceding fall and submitted it to the people with alternative slavery and non-slavery provision. The non-slavery provision was simply a political trick, for even under this arrangement slaves and their children already in the Territory should remain. The Free State men understood the situation thoroughly, and when the Constitution was placed before the citizens they refrained from voting. The Constitution with slavery was carried, and, as usual, there were some false ballots. A counterstroke of the Free State majority in the Territorial Legislature, returned the entire Constitution for a popular yes-or-no vote, and not, as formerly, to decide merely whether it should be adopted without the slavery provision. This time the pro-slavery men refused to vote, since the issue, to their minds, was already settled. Of course, the Constitution was rejected. But humorously enough, both parties voted for officers under the Constitution; the Free State faction won the contest and placed a handsome majority in the hypothetical Legislature. On February 2, 1858, the President submitted to Congress the question of Kansas admission under the Lecompton Constitution, and the final political crisis for possession of the Territory was at hand.

While John Brown travelled anxiously back and forth across the East in preparation for his conquest, the conflict over the Lecompton Constitution was at its height. Douglas, the man whose doctrine of " squatter sovereignty " had once been held as a Southern victory, desperately opposed its passage. He was too honest to permit even the cause which claimed his sympathies to be victorious by such a shabby piece of chicanery and fraud as the Lecompton Constitution undoubtedly was, and his honesty, in a sense, was his political ruin. The two Houses of Congress disagreed, and a compromise was reached under a bill devised by W. H. English of Indiana. The English Bill provided that Kansas should be admitted at once as a slave State, and if the people of the Territory declined, the question should be laid aside until there was a population of ninety-two thousand. The acceptance of the arrangement by the people, however, would carry with it an impressive grant from Government lands. " The right of property is before and higher than any constitutional sanction," read one section of the Bill; " and the right of the owner of a slave to such slave and its increase is the same, and as inviolable, as the right of the owner of any property whatever." The question was whether the Free State majority in Kansas would adopt this doctrine, sell out its principles, and accept the offered bribe.

Despite the apprehension and excitement with which the struggle in Congress was followed, violence had been confined to a comparatively small area in the south. This was the stamping ground of James Montgomery, whom John Brown pronounced so " intelligent, kind, and gentlemanly." He was the self-appointed guardian of freedom, but one act of his guardianship, even before John Brown's arrival, had resulted in the greatest atrocity ever committed in the Territory except that of Pottawatomie. Montgomery ordered a certain Georgian, Charles Hamilton, to leave the region. Hamilton and other pro-slavery settlers complied, but while Montgomery was absent on a raid, they returned, took eleven men, marched them into a ravine, and shot them down. Five were killed outright, and five were severely wounded. It was the signal for a revival of all the old hatred and outrage which had marked the years of 1855 and 1856. The personal intervention of the new Governor, Denver, temporarily pacified the region with a treaty which promised that the past should be forgotten. Montgomery disbanded his men, and, for a time at least, honestly turned his efforts toward establishing peace.

John Brown was inevitably attracted to the region where there was most likelihood of disturbance. That troubled region then knew another captain of raiders — Captain Shubel Morgan. In July Mr. Sanborn received a copy of the "Articles Of Agreement For Shubel Morgan's Company." It was practically a repetition, somewhat less elaborate, of the "Covenant" under which John Brown had recruited his men before Osawatomie. It contained the same paradox. Article V read: "All acts of petty or other thefts shall be promptly and properly punished, and restitution made as far as possible." It was preceded by another Article, no less enlightening: "All property captured in any manner shall be subjected to an equal distribution among the members." Among the members of Shubel Morgan's gang were the kind and gentlemanly James Montgomery, Kagi, Tidd, William Partridge, Wattles, and the Snyder men, who had only saved themselves from the Hamilton firing squad by a desperate defense. All told, there were fourteen "hands."

The record of their services to Freedom during the summer has remained in the same obscurity which wrapped John Brown in the days after Black Jack. In July John Brown reported to his Eastern friends: "I have concealed the fact of my presence pretty much, lest it should tend to create excitement; but it is getting leaked out, and will soon be known to all. As I am not here to seek or secure revenge, I do not mean to be the first to reopen the quarrel." At this time, shortly after the organization of the gang, the nature and profits of its future activities were in doubt, and John Brown appealed for money to feed his men, for, as he put it, they could " not work for wages." By the time the money came, the band was self-sufficing, and, since they could not work for wages, they must have worked for something else. John Brown could then spare Gerrit Smith's draft for the use of the family at North Elba.

Whatever the efforts may have been that played substitute for work for wages, it is known that they were arduous. Several of Shubel Morgan's men let drop at one time or another references to the life of that summer. The nature of their enterprises kept them in small groups of two or three. Kagi and Gill were Brown's usual companions, for Stevens was characteristically insubordinate, and the leader had no great liking for Tidd. He reported to Sanborn in August that he had lain " every night without shelter, suffering from cold rains and heavy dews, together with the oppressive heat of the days." Despite these hardships there must have been certain things which rendered the business attractive, for John Brown could boast that several men under the command of Governor Denver's officer had secretly offered him their services. In any case, before this stay in Kansas was concluded, several avowed and prominent horse thieves offered their services and were accepted by Shubel Morgan. " It seems strange in a Christian country," he remarked to the Wattles family about this time, " that a man should be called a monomaniac for following the plain dictates of our Savior." Perhaps it is not too cynical to speculate

as to how Christ-like were the endeavors of Shubel Morgan
and his company in the summer and fall of 1858.

In any case the authorities of the National Kansas Committee had reason to conclude that some of John Brown's
business principles were not in strict accord with the plain
dictates of our Savior. Mr. Stearns, chairman of the Massachusetts State Kansas Committee, had made considerable
advances to that organization, and held, as security for his
money, a lien on a certain lot of arms and a number of promissory notes given by Kansas settlers to the Committee for
supplies. Mr. Stearns' foreclosure on the arms was the
readiest scheme to get them in John Brown's hands and quiet
Senator Wilson's mind; to help finance John Brown in Kansas he turned over to him some of the promissory notes. John
Brown proceeded with a high hand. The conduct of Mr.
Whitman, the regular agent for the Committee, did not
satisfy him, and he proceeded to make his own collections
from the signers of the notes, giving his receipt as agent.

Furthermore, he felt that the resolution passed in the New
York meeting of the National Kansas Committee to appropriate $5,000 " for necessary defensive purposes " could
now be fulfilled, for he considered himself to be on active
service. With this slim justification he gave receipts for
supplies as the agent of the National Committee. His claims
were not modest. " Sir: — You are hereby notified that I
hold claims against the National Kansas Committee which
are good against them and all persons whatever; and that
I have authority from said Committee to take possession,
as their Agent, of any supplies belonging to said Committee,
wherever found." And: " You will therefore retain in your
hands any monies or accounts you may now have in your
custody, by direction of said Committee or any of its Agents,

and hold them subject to my call or order, as I shall hold you responsible for them, to me as Agent of said Committee." The communication of the Secretary of the Committee to Mr. Whitman, its Kansas Agent, was particularly explicit on the subject of John Brown's pretensions. " Capt. John Brown has no authority to take, receive, collect or transfer any notes or accounts belonging to the National Kansas Committee, nor has he ever had." But by that time the self-appointed " agent " had acquired a pleasant sum, which, of course, the Committee never recovered. " Mr. Whitman acted as agent both for the National Committee and for the Massachusetts Committee; and the business had become so complicated in one way and another that when Brown levied upon the agents for money claimed by him under votes of the Committees, it excited a lively dispute in Kansas." This is Mr. Sanborn's apology for the business; the least that can be said is that John Brown's conduct certainly did not solve any of the complications.

The exposures of the summer and early autumn told heavily on John Brown's health. It would have been a hard life even for a much younger man, and he was now verging toward old age. Sustained by will alone, he travelled back and forth across the Territory on the secret expeditions with his men and on the business of collecting his notes. By the end of October there was every prospect that the rigors of a border campaign were at hand. " The Captain has shown," Kagi wrote, " that he *can* be in the Territory without making war. He will now, if necessary, take the field in aid of Montgomery." The Denver truce was broken. Montgomery raided the grand jury at Fort Scott and destroyed their papers. A week later there was firing on his cabin to further annoy the sturdy Mrs. Montgomery. " I do get plumb tired of

being shot at, but I won't be druv out." Despite persistent
ill-health John Brown responded.

His men fortified a cabin in Montgomery's neighborhood,
and on November 13 John Brown himself took a modest hand
in another investigation of court records. Montgomery got
news that a jury at Paris had indicted him, and promptly
raided the place. John Brown hung about on the outskirts
of the town while his friend sorted the jury's papers, for it is
doubtful if he took much interest in Montgomery's legal
experiments. This was too much. On December 2, a sheriff
and posse appeared with the purpose of taking Montgomery
and his accomplices. Montgomery captured the sheriff.

John Brown was in Osawatomie, but some of his men
shared in the honor of discomfiting Sheriff McDaniel. When
their leader reappeared in the southern counties a few days
later, he came in the awkward rôle of peace-maker. At Sugar
Mound Montgomery presented to a joint conference of Free
State and pro-slavery men the draft of a treaty prepared by
John Brown. By its provisions all criminal processes against
Free State men were to be quashed and all prisoners released;
all pro-slavery men, " *known* to have been actively and crimi-
nally engaged in the former political difficulties of the Territory," were to be expelled; and all acts of " *robbery, theft,
or violence* against others, on account of their *political differences,*" were to be discontinued. The arrangement was decidedly a Free State victory.

The peace was of short duration. On the excuse that a Free
State prisoner was still in confinement, Montgomery and
Brown organized a considerable force and planned a decisive
raid on Fort Scott. When it was decided that Montgomery
should lead the expedition, John Brown immediately lost
all interest in the affair and refused to go farther than the

rendezvous; he would, as he had declared, serve only " under the command of Old Brown." Montgomery claimed after the event that it was absolutely imperative that John Brown should not be in control, for he was determined to destroy the town, root and branch. The consequences, even under the boasted restraint of Montgomery, were grave enough, one man being killed and the settlement systematically looted.

It is unnecessary to question John Brown's sincerity when he offered his treaty at Sugar Mound, just as it is unnecessary to question Montgomery's when he agreed to the arrangement. They could claim a technical excuse for the Fort Scott raid, but they were well paid for their pains; one store, the store owned by the murdered man, provided $7,000 worth of plunder. Whatever may have been the motives in theory, the motives in practice were those of wholesale robbery. In so far as John Brown was concerned, the matter of his good faith is not left to speculation. On December 2, before he knew of the posse's attack and four days before he presented his treaty, he declared his intentions to his family: " When I wrote you last I thought the prospect was that I should soon shift my quarters somewhat. I still have the same prospect, but am wholly at a loss as to the exact time." One cannot refrain from comparing this with the similar remark as to his plans just before the Pottawatomie raid: " We are doing off a house for Orson Day, which we hope to get through with soon: after which we shall probably soon leave this neighborhood, but will advise you further when we do leave." A rough paraphrase of both remarks would go something like this: Just as soon as opportunity offers I shall do a job I have in mind; unhappily, the nature of the job is such, that the country will be too hot to hold me when it is done. To God and his infinite grace I commend you.

On December 20, four days after the Fort Scott raid, he did the job. John Brown divided his men into two companies. Under his own command went Gill, Kagi, a well-known horse thief called "Pickles," Charles Jennison, who was a horse thief and a clever man, and several other enterprising young fellows; Tidd and Hazlett were among the men led by Stevens. At least one member of this company, Hazlett, was not particular about clear titles to his mounts; John Brown bought from him a fine stallion which he had picked up down in Missouri.

Under cover of darkness the gangs crossed over into Missouri. John Brown led his men to the Hicklan plantation, entered the house at pistol point, ransacked the place, and "liberated" the few slaves on the premises. At the home of John Larue nearby the party "liberated" five slaves, six horses, harness, a wagon, bedding, clothing, provisions, and such incidental pieces of property as came most readily to hand. Mr. Larue and another man were made prisoners and carried back to Kansas. The whole matter was managed so adroitly that no blood-letting appeared necessary. Stevens was less adroit. He liberated a negro girl only after he had shot her master. According to his story, he demanded the girl from her master, David Cruise, who invited him to come into the the cabin. The moment he entered, Cruise quickly bolted the door and reached for a pistol. Stevens beat him to the draw by a satisfactory margin, and shot him dead. Stevens left the ethical question open: "You might call it a case of self-defense, or you might also say that I had no business in there, and that the old man was right." There is no doubt as to what a court of law would call it.

The two raiding parties meet at their rendezvous and together took up the march into Kansas. When daylight came they pitched a camp in a heavily timbered ravine and waited for the safety of darkness. By midnight on December 22, they reached the Wattles home where Montgomery was staying at the time. After a few hours of rest the eleven negroes were hurried into the wagons, and put on the road again, but John Brown was not with them nor any member of his gang except the solitary driver of the slow ox-team. The undefended fugitives reached Osawatomie on Christmas Eve. No preparations had been made for receiving them, but Mrs. Adair, who once turned her nephew, Owen Brown, from the protection of her door, had not the heart to reject these forlorn, irresponsible creatures. When the Reverend Adair reminded her of the heavy penalty imposed by the Fugitive Slave Law, she only replied: " I cannot turn them away." Here they remained until the middle of January, hidden in an abandoned shack, while Missouri posses beat the wooded land along the Pottawatomie.

The general sentiment in Kansas concerning the raid was a decided disappointment to John Brown. Even Wattles, who gave him the shelter of his cabin for a short time, disapproved of going into Missouri contrary to the agreement. But while John Brown lay hiding in his camp on Turkey Creek, many other men besides Wattles, Free State men, were swelling the general condemnation of the act. " Little did I think, in '56," wrote one correspondent of the Lawrence *Herald of Freedom*, " that professedly Free-State men would be guilty of the same crimes for which we denounced the pro-slavery men of that year, and which raised such a storm throughout the nation." Captain Samuel Walker, a Free State man who knew Brown well, was sent by the Governor to investigate the difficulties in the southern counties. The same newspaper summarized his report: " Outrages, he states, have been committed by those desperadoes equalling in atrocity those of the vilest border ruffians in the campaign of 1856. Captain Walker states that there has been a great revulsion public sentiment there within the last few weeks. Everywhere he met men who had sustained Montgomery in the past, who now say they can do it no longer. He has gathered about him all the desperadoes of the Free-State party, and they live by plunder and crime. . . . We hear from other sources that Captain Brown is a compeer of Montgomery, and that only a few days ago he made a marauding expedition into Missouri, and after commiting various ' excesses,' armed a party of slaves, mounted them on horses, and marched them over into Kansas." Public sentiment was decidedly disappointing.

The reason for such general feeling was not far to seek. The English Bill had been defeated months before, despite the heavy bribe of public land, and everyone seemed fairly confident that the matter of a Free-State Kansas was settled. Much remained to be done, but the essential crisis was past. The controversies in the Territory were now more specifically " political " — minor issues drawn between factions of the Free-State party itself. But all men, regardless of party or faction, wanted peace, and except in the southern counties of Linn and Bourbon they had it. And even Linn and Bourbon and border Missouri lay under the guarantee of the Denver treaty and the later agreement drafted by John Brown himself. It was only natural that people reflected on John Brown's hand in the peace agreement and felt that there had been, somehow, an inexcusable breach of faith. And it was on them, not on the true aggressor, that the retaliation from Missouri would fall.

It was to repel the certain pursuit that John Brown appealed to Montgomery to organize his men, but Montgomery washed his hands of the whole transaction. All of his energies were turned to an attempt to pacify the border, in which he was assisted by William Hutchinson, correspondent of the *Times*, and by Wattles. " For Brown's doings in Missouri I am not responsible," Montgomery wrote to Lawrence. " I know nothing of either his plans or intentions. Brown keeps his own counsels, and acts on his own responsibility. I hear much said about Montgomery and his company. I have no company. We have had no organization since the 5th day of July." Montgomery, of course, had forgotten Fort Scott, but he was ready to back up his general protestation of innocence by surrendering to the authorities. On January 18 he gave himself up at Lawrence and was released on $4,000 bail. Two weeks later he brought in six of his own former colleagues who followed his example.

To meet the prevalent criticism against him John Brown had one weapon — his pen. While in hiding in the South, he prepared his " Parallels " to vindicate the Missouri raid. One case was the Hamilton massacre, concerning which he inquired: " What action has ever, since the occurence in May last, been taken by either the President of the United States; the Governor of Missouri, or the Governor of Kansas, or any of their tools; or by any pro-slavery or *administration man?* " The other " parallel " was the Missouri raid, in extenuation of which he cited two things. The first was the " Jim Daniels story." " On Sunday the 19th of December a negro called Jim came over to the Osage settlement from Missouri & stated that he together with his Wife, Two Children, & another Negro man were to be sold within a day or Two & beged for help to get away." The second was the claim that property taken from a man who had no interest in the raided estate was returned to him. Hicklan's own statement on this point is emphatic: " Nothing that was taken was ever recovered. I learn that it was stated by John Brown that he made his men return all the property they had taken from me. This is not true." The " Jim Daniels " matter, which was also reported by the faithful Gill, bears likewise the color of an *ex post facto* decoration; it is astonishingly similar to the numerous stories in justification of Pottawatomie, such as the reported plot of the Shermans to kill or drive out the Brown family. In summary of his own case, John Brown concluded: " Eleven persons are forcibly restored to their *natural; & inalienable rights,* with but one man killed; & all ' Hell is stirred from beneath.' " Charles Robinson once pointed out a more accurate parallel than this to the Hamilton outrage: it was the outrage of Pottawatomie. There was one essential difference, for Hamilton killed his five men in revenge and Brown killed his five in robbery and in the cause of liberty. It was now time to leave Kansas. John Brown had accomplished in a certain measure, that which Cook once gave out as his intention. " In his trip East he did not realize the amount of money that he expected. The money had been promised *bona fide,* but owing to the tightness of the money market they failed to comply with his demands. The funds were necessary to the accomplishment of his plans. I afterwards learned that there was a lack of confidence in his scheme. It was therefore necessary that a movement should be made in another direction, to demonstrate the practicability of his plan. This he made about a year ago, by his invasion of Missouri, and the taking of about a dozen slaves, together with horses, cattle, etc., into Kansas, in defiance of the United States marshal and his posse." In simpler terms, John Brown had to do something to justify himself in the eyes of the people who filled his purse. The most desirable thing to do was something which would also fill his purse; the Missouri raid served the purpose. In the end it was to serve another purpose as well, for it supported the comfortable idea that all John Brown intended in Virginia was just such another raid on a larger scale.

The march began on January 20, when the prairie winter was at its worst. The departure from Osawatomie was hastened by the fact that Tidd and Stevens succeeded in stealing a span of horses, which, naturally enough, had to be gotten out of the district as soon as possible. " I had learned of a span of horses held by a Missourian stopping temporarily a few miles from Osawatomie, and the suspicion was well grounded that he had appropriated them from them free state owners." It is unnecessary to comment on this apology which Gill made for the affair; lone Missourians did not penetrate into Free State Kansas and appropriate anything, for the Free State men of Kansas had spent the last three years in demonstrating that they were perfectly able to take care of themselves. It is a pity that Mr. Gill didn't have the courage to say; there was a good span of horses in the neighborhood, we wanted them, and we took them. There is an adage to the effect that a man who will lie will steal; it may be remarked that a man who steals will, frequently, lie.

John Brown and Gill with their slow ox-cart full of shivering negro fugitives could not keep pace with the span of " replevined " horses which the comrades were hurrying on to the rendezvous at Topeka. The flight was another mark of John Brown's audacity and fortitude, for both he and Gill suffered greatly from the bitter cold. But the very elements which froze their feet through the broken boots was a cover and a defense against pursuit. After four days on the road, penniless and dog-tired, they reached the protection of Major Abbott's home near Lawrence.

The question of finance was, as usual, pressing. The stolen cart and oxen were sent into Lawrence to be sold, and Tappan, the fellow who once slapped the jaws of Sheriff Jones, now gave a more subtle blow to the institution of slavery by lending a wagon and team. Despite his previous conduct about the Kansas Committee's notes, John Brown still seemed to hope for money from Whitman. But on the very day before the arrival at Lawrence, Judge Conway wrote a confidential note to John Brown on this point: " I am of the opinion that you will not be able to get any funds from him. He expressed himself to me since his return from the East as dissatisfied at your proceedings in Lawrence when you were here before." When the party drove away on the next leg of the journey, however, John Brown had plenty of money; the plausible suggestion has been made that he received settlement for more Missouri plunder than the oxen and cart.

The rigors of winter weather persisted after they left Lawrence for Topeka, where Gill dropped out to recover from his exposures and Stevens took his place. It was the old man, weakened by sickness and fatigue, who pushed on; he had to see this business through to its very end, or every hope and plan was a failure. But all this endurance and courage seemed to be spent for nothing, when they reached the predetermined resting place of Fuller's cabin on Spring Creek. The stream was in flood.

News of the passage of the suspicious " emigrant wagon " had reached the Territorial authorities and a posse from Atchison was already on its track. John Brown sent a hurried appeal to Topeka for aid and waited for the waters to subside. Meanwhile Governor Medary ordered Colonel Sumner to capture the outlaw and telegraphed his pleasure to President Buchanan. There is no doubt that President Buchanan, likewise, was pleased.

"What do you propose to do, Captain?" one of the men from Topeka asked. "Cross the creek and move north," was John Brown's answer. Across the still swollen stream of Muddy Creek lay eighty men of the Atchison posse, but Colonel Sumner's regulars had not arrived. John Brown ordered his twenty-odd men into a double file in front of the wagon. "Not go straight at 'em, boys! They'll be sure to run." The first men in the file plunged into the waters of the ford. Mr. Wood, marshal and commander of the posse, was distinctly surprised at such unorthodox behavior; he had come to attack, not to be attacked. But Mr. Wood intended to be party to no such lack of orthodoxy; with agitated fingers he unpicketed his horse, mounted, and hastily rode away. The example was popular. Every man ran for his horse, and if a comrade-in-arms managed to snatch his bridle free of the bush or stump to which it was tied, he leaped on behind. One poor fellow disappeared from sight desperately clinging, in great distress of mind, to the tail of a horse which a friend was spurring for dear life. Those of the attackers who had mounts pursued and harried the routed enemy. When they returned to the ford with a few prisoners and horses they found that the wagons had been drawn over by ropes and the cavalcade was ready to move on. So ended the interesting engagement of Muddy Creek, which was known to Kansas in later times as the "Battle of the Spurs." It was a battle won by the terror of John Brown's name; John Brown trusted much in that weapon.

The real crisis of the march was past. John Brown was free to go on about his business, and the boys from Topeka were rewarded by ownership of the captured horses, which had been retained for " prudential reasons." Sheer good fortune and Gill's quick wits saved the fugitives from another posse near Nebraska City, where they crossed the Missouri River to the free soil of Iowa. Their leader hurried them on to Tabor, where he felt sure of public commendation, prayers of thanksgiving to the Lord, and a general collection.

A great shock was in store for the successful raider. There were no cheers to greet the tired and self-satisfied men who stopped their horses on the Tabor common on Saturday, February 5. John Brown did what he could to arouse the good people of Tabor from their astonishing apathy when so obviously confronted with the goodness of God. A note was thrust into the hand of the Reverend John Todd as he entered his church the next morning. " John Brown respectfully requests the church at Tabor to offer public thanksgiving to Almighty God in behalf of himself, & company: *& of their rescued captives in particular* for his gracious preservation of their lives, & health; & his signal deliverance of all out of the hand of the wicked, hitherto. ' Oh, give thanks unto the Lord; for he is good; for his mercy endureth forever." The Reverend John Todd was frankly puzzled; the poor man was not quite sure as to the decorum of thanking the good Lord for success in horse stealing and murder. He turned for advice to a Dr. King who occupied the pulpit with him. Dr. King was not puzzled. " Brother Todd," he counselled, " this is your church, but if I were you I would not make a prayer for them. Inasmuch as it is said that they have destroyed life, and stolen horses, I should want to take the charge under examination before I made a public prayer." And so there was no collection.

General sentiment was even more emphatic at the public

meeting held the next day to investigate the charges. John
Brown was allowed to speak for himself. A fortunate incident
saved him that embarrassment; he recognized in the audience
a certain Dr. Brown, a slaveholder. " One has just entered
whom I prefer not to have hear what I am going to say. I respectfully request him to withdraw." There was a hubbub,
and when it was over, the Captain Brown and not the Dr.
Brown withdrew. " We had better look to our arms," he said
to his men when they stood outside the church building. " We
aren't yet among friends." He was quite right, as the resolution adopted by the meeting demonstrated plainly enough.
" *Resolved,* That while we sympathize with the oppressed, &
will do all that we conscientiously can to help them in their
efforts for freedom, nevertheless, we have no sympathy with
those who go to Slave States, to entice away Slaves, & take
property or life when necessary to attain that end."

It was with a profound sense of disappointment, of resentment, and of self-pity that John Brown shook the ungracious
dust of Tabor from his feet for the last time. " There are
those who would sooner see me supplied with a good halter
than anything else for my services," he wrote a little later,
when the memory of Tabor's ingratitude still rankled. But
before that time he had the satisfaction of sending to his one-
time friends there a statement of the pleasant welcome which
greeted him at Grinnell, Iowa, where, it seems, three Congregational clergymen held another conception of the good
Lord's attitude toward horse rustling and murder as well as
nigger stealing. At Grinnell both Brown and Kagi spoke and
were loudly cheered; the whole party and teams were kept
for two days with no charge; bread, meat, cakes, and pies
were prepared for the journey; cash contributions amounted
to twenty-six dollars; and there was " last but not least Pub-

lic thanksgiving to Allmighty God offered up by Mr. Grinnell in the behalf of the whole company for His great mercy; & protecting care, with prayers for a continuance of those blessings." There is no record that the people of Tabor revised their theology.

From the hospitality of Grinnell John Brown moved on to Springdale, the old seat of his war college, where the negroes remained until March 10. There were various threats of trouble and interference for the fugitives, and the Quakers no doubt had some fears that blood would be spilled in the midst of their rural peace. But the threats and rumors came to nothing, for the reputation of Old Brown was enough to deter the ill-organized enthusiasm of the pro-slavery people of Iowa City, and the Government itself took no hand in the matter. The Fugitive Slave Law, in practice, was a ticklish principle.

The generosity of the right-thinking Mr. Grinnell did not end with the consumption of the meat and cakes and pies, which had been prepared under his auspices. When, on March 10, the eleven o'clock train left for Chicago it carried away, safely housed in a box-car, the escaped slaves whose adventures were nearly at an end. Mr. Grinnell had engaged the car at Chicago, and the poor station agent in Iowa assumed that the railway officials understood the purpose when a draft for $50 made out to John Brown and signed by the superintendent of the road, was thrust under his nose. Naturally, the fellow was impressed.

At Chicago Allan Pinkerton completed the work which Grinnell had begun. His good will was not diminished by being roused at four-thirty in the morning, he gave the negroes a breakfast, raised $500 for their leader, and arranged for another box-car to take them on to the freedom of Canada.

JOHN BROWN

At Detroit John Brown, who had hurried on from Chicago to meet Frederick Douglass, saw his charges put on the ferry and carried away from the inhospitable shore of the United States. On the boat was the twelfth fugitive, a two months old negro baby, who bore the name of his liberator. John Brown turned away from the ferry's slip and hurried about his arrangements for leaving Detroit. That job was done, he had won out despite sheriffs and Missourians and marshals and dragoons. . . . " Oh, give thanks unto the Lord; for he is good; for his mercy endureth forever." The adventure was closed, and these things, except in so far as they could be transposed into terms of the supreme adventure, were put away . . . the kind and gentlemanly James Montgomery, the prairie snowstorm, frost-bitten feet inside broken boots, the patient, puzzled gratitude of the slaves, the dead body of old man Cruise, and the black baby whose name was John Brown. They were not items of contented reverie, for John Brown never looked back; his past and history were simply an instrument for framing astounding future.

When John Brown reached Cleveland on March 15, he auctioned off two horses and a mule for which, as he admitted, he could give no clean bill of sale. However, they were " Abolition " stock; " I converted them," he explained.

He is a medium sized, compactly-built and wiry man, as quick as a cat in his movements. His hair is of a salt and pepper hue and as stiff as bristles; he has a long, waving, milk white goatee which gives him a somewhat patriarchal appearance. A man of pluck, is Brown. You may bet on that. He shows it in his walk, talk, and actions. He must be rising sixty and yet we believe he could lick a yard full of wild cats before breakfast and without taking off his coat. Turn him into a ring with nine Border ruffians, four bears, six injuns and a brace of bull pups and we opine that " the eagles of victory would perch on his banner."

Do You Believe Quetelet?

We don't mean by this that he looks like a professional bruiser, who hits from the shoulder, but he looks like a man of iron and one that few men would like to "sail into."

It was thus that "Artemus Ward" in the Cleveland *Plain Dealer* characterized the man who was auctioning off converted live stock and giving lectures. In the lecture of March 21, John Brown's remarks did a little to justify "Artemus Ward's" high opinion. "I have never by my own action driven any pro-slavery men out of the Territory, but if occasion demanded such a thing, I would use them like fence-stakes — drive them into the ground to make permanent settlers." And again: "I never killed anybody, although on some occasions I have shown my young men with me how some things might be done as well as others, and they did the business." Or perhaps, the Cleveland newspapers libelled the distinguished lecturer and man of iron. If so, an even grosser libel was being spread in the streets of Cleveland by certain posters, put up by the United States marshal, which announced a reward offered by the President of $250 and by the Governor of Missouri of $3000 for the arrest of John Brown. But the outlaw, with such a price on his head, safely walked the city streets, gave his lecture, auctioned his horses, and made his boasts. And it is doubtful if he paid for this increased security by the cynical reflection that the farther he got from Kansas the more general was the approbation of his services there.

Despite the public sentiment which guaranteed his immunity from marshals and deputies, not a great many people in Cleveland were ready to pay a quarter of a dollar to hear John Brown lecture and even fewer were ready to make outright contributions. At Jefferson, where he went by the invitation of Congressman Giddings, he found more enthusiasm and a ready answer to Mr. Giddings' appeal for a collection. John Brown assured the audience gathered in the Congregational Church that he held to "the doctrines of the Christian religion as they were enunciated by the Savior," and such faith was rewarded, for " every Democrat as well as Republican present gave something." Good people so fuddled in their politics could not be expected to have much clearer views in their theology. Mr. Giddings, whose ardor compensated a little for whatever statesmanlike vision he lacked, gave his guest three dollars.

The days in Ohio were anxious and busy ones. It was time to begin recalling the scattered members of the Provisional Army, to raise money, and to make preparations for the forwarding service in Ohio which John Brown Jr. would direct. All of these preliminary cares were complicated by recurrent poor health, the result of the exposures on the prairie, or of a "righteous visitation for their fanaticism." By April 10, however, his sufferings abated and he was ready to leave for Gerrit Smith's home at Peterboro.

" Capt. J. B. of Kansas and his friend Mr. Anderson came at 11 A.M." This was the entry in Gerrit Smith's diary which recorded his welcome of the old friend. The gentle, aged philanthropist was moved to tears when his guest rose to speak at a public meeting and told his audience of the raid into Missouri, the rescue of the eleven pitiful slaves, and the suffering on the long flight out of the ungracious country of Kansas. Gerrit Smith once said; " No man out of Kansas has done so much as Eli Thayer to save her; no man in Kansas as John Brown — Old John Brown, the fighter." He was more extravagant now when he stood up with tears in his eyes. " If I were asked to point out — I will say it in his presence — to point out the man in all the world I think most truly a Christian, I would point out John Brown. I was once doubtful in my own mind as to Captain Brown's course. I now approve of it heartily, having given my mind to it more of late." His thoughts flew southward to some indeterminate defile in the mountains. When he first heard news of the Missouri foray he had written: " The topography of Missouri is unfavorable. *Would that a spur of the Alleghany extended from the east to the west borders of the State!* "₁ And now he began the meeting's contributions to the man whom he thought most truly a Christian by putting himself down for $400. If he had some illusions about John Brown, that Christian had none about his benefactor. " I know Gerrit Smith to be a timid man." And so he was.

Encouraged by the success at Peterboro, John Brown proceeded to Westport, New York, and from there to North Elba. He was still a sick man, as he wrote to Kagi, but Smith's $400 and his urgent advice to Eastern friends to make up $2,000 seemed to bring the goal of the conquest within sight. Despite the ague and a troublesome gathering in his head he promised his Lieutenant not to remain idle. His word was good, for he soon left North Elba and began the last tour of New England to complete his preparations. At Concord he joined Sanborn and made a speech in the Town Hall which greatly impressed Bronson Alcott.

He seemed superior to any legal traditions, able to do his own thinking; he was an idealist, at least in matters of State, if not on all points of his religious faith. He did not conceal his hatred of Slavery, and less his readiness to strike a blow for freedom at the fitting moment. I thought him equal to anything he should dare: the man to do the deed necessary to be done with the patriot's zeal, the martyr's temper and purpose.

It was a repetition of the story of the year before.

313

The stooped but still rigid old man with his neat rural dress, his talk about bayonets and bullets and God's will, his immense awkward dignity, immense egotism, his white beard and hard grey-blue eyes which glittered, as one host put it, with a "little touch of insanity," moved impressively about the albums and pleasant china of those New England parlors. Most of the the people who sat about him in those parlors, and gave their earnest attention to his words, found something peculiarly congenial to their own prejudices and beliefs. Captain Brown was a "higher law man." He was "superior to any legal tradition" — just as most of these people felt themselves to be — and if he claimed to have a divine commission, they could understand what he meant, for they too were privy to God. The Southerner pointed to the Constitution and said: "There is the law and the bargain; keep them and give us justice." Garrison burned the Constitution as a "covenant with Hell" and many other countrymen of his, if they were not ready to do this, could still call on conscience and the higher law. Unhappily, a corollary of this divine revelation was to make the South pay, and pay again. The disagreement might conceivably have been settled under terms of law, but when it was transposed into terms of theolgy there was no hope of settlement. There is only one way to conclude a theological argument: bayonets and bullets. And in that last appeal God's hand reached down to prove the "higher law men" perfectly right; as events demonstrated, God was, obviously, not on the side of the South. By the same logic, it may be added, God was not, personally, on the side of John Brown.

Not everyone whom John Brown met could give him Alcott's praise as "the manliest of men and the type and synonym of the just." A. A. Lawrence, who once had referred to John Brown as a "true representative of the Puritanic warrior" now gave a slightly different description of him. " He has been stealing negroes and running them off from Missouri. He has a monomania on that subject, I think, and would be hanged if he were taken in a slave State. He has allowed his beard to grow since I saw him last, which changes his appearance entirely, as it is almost white and very long." And then Mr. Lawrence appended a comment of some theological interest: " He and his companion both have the fever and ague, somewhat, probably a righteous visitation for their fanaticism." When John Brown was introduced to Senator Wilson of Massachusetts he was very direct. " I understand you do not approve of my course," he remarked to the Senator in a calm but firm tone. " I do not," was the reply. " I understand that you have spoken in condemnation of it." " I have," Mr. Wilson answered with equal firmness; " I believe it to be a very great injury to the anti-slavery cause, just as I regard every illegal act, and every imprudent act, as being against it." Being a " higher law man " John Brown could not comprehend such an objection, and so he simply declared that he believed that he was right. Not being a " higher law man " Mr. Wilson had no answer at all to that. It is too bad that the Senator did not realize, as he carried on his little debate with John Brown, how outrageously he himself had been duped by his friends, Howe and Stearns, in the matter of the rifles, and how outrageously his fears and his opinions were to be justified by this same farmer-like old fellow who stood before him. He might not have known better what to say to John Brown's last remark, but he would have known what to do. There would have been no attack at Harper's Ferry.

From the argument, reminiscence, and deference of the parlors and platforms, John Brown moved to his more serious business. At Collinsville he called on the blacksmith, Blair, and asked about his pikes. Blair knew enough about the political situation to put one very pertinent question. "What good can they be if they are finished; Kansas matters are all settled, and of what earthly use can they be to you now?" John Brown met the question with an evasion, and the prospect of this tardy payment for his contract kept the blacksmith from smelling a rat — or from admitting that he did. He got $300 more in cash on the contract and hired a workman to finish the job of making the broad, murderous heads and preparing the stout staves to season for handles. And so in this common blacksmith shop of a peaceful, common village a workman turned innocently to the business of manuacturing these barbarous fasces of the higher law.

"We are getting on slowly, — about fifty dollars per day; and if Gerrit Smith accepts, we will send the old man off early next week." It was in this fashion that Mr. Stearns announced at the end of May the impending departure of John Brown from New England. Mr. Stearns himself paid in $1,200 of the $2,000 demanded by John Brown, for he was a man, as Sanborn remarked, who " having put his hand to the plow turneth not back." The conspirators apprehensively watched John Brown depart; they could only wait for time to tell them where and how the affair would begin, for they, perhaps from a desire for their own comfort, were not in his confidence. Now when he took leave of them he could not tell them where he would be for the next few weeks; they were to send his mail in care of John Brown Jr. in Astabula County, Ohio, which was near the scene where he intended to begin operations. All else that they knew was that there was some scheme for sending a man to Canada to recruit, probably in the company of Harriet Tubman, and that Brown would soon be at the place of action ready to strike. The blow, they vaguely expected, would fall on the anniversary of the signing of the Declaration of Independence. They must have felt that it would be peculiarly appropriate.

" Now is the time to help in the movement, if ever," Sanborn wrote to Higginson," for within the next two months the experiment will be made." That was what it was — an experiment — in the eyes of the men who were providing the materials to John Brown. They maintained something of the detachment of the experimenter; they knew what John Brown intended, they put in his way the money and rifles and pikes, and they waited, with the sense of not being too much involved, for the result of the experiment. Theodore Parker had said that many things would have to be tried before a solution could be found and that John Brown might as well be one of them. For a long time before this, he felt as he wrote when he was in Europe, near death, and when John Brown was already in the grave: " We must see much darker hours before it is daylight — darker, and also bloody I think, for nations don't settle their difficulties without passion, and so without what comes of passion." But he and the others were willing to utilize that passion despite its train, which they might prevision, of rapine and violence and recrimination. They could not understand, any more than could John Brown, the attitude of a man like Senator Wilson: let us do what we can with the law. Nor could they understand the feeling of a man like Lincoln, humane, wise, and fallible, but learning from his own failings. Lincoln had said of the Dred Scott decision that the Supreme Court had sometimes overruled its own decisions and that citizens should merely work to have it overrule this one. " We offer no resistance to it." They could not understand the philosophy that one must live

317

in an imperfect world and should try to do what one can with the imperfect institutions devised by other imperfect men; they were so sure that they knew the truth. Theodore Parker quoted what Cromwell said in the House of Commons: "There is one general grievance, and that is the law!"

The conspirators were willing to utilize violence because they felt that the divinely inspired end justified all means and because, after all, they could not really visualize the barbarous and pitiful consequences. They could not see the dead man lying in the street of the Virginia town while the hogs tore at the entrails of the body, and death as an idea is so greatly different from that sort of thing. It was Dr. Howe, who had witnessed something of European revolutions, who suffered a change of heart in regard to the Virginia plan. While Sanborn was important and busy about his details and Gerrit Smith had tears in his eyes as he pointed out John Brown as the Christian, and Parker was going abroad to die, Howe paid a visit to South Carolina and lived for a time on a plantation, where he saw a little of Southern society from a new point of view. He was not so sure of himself then, and as the months passed he withdrew more and more from the conspiracy. The fact is instructive, but his friends did not understand the moral of the incident, any more than most Southerners understood the general sentiment of the North. The friends persisted in their conviction of knowing the truth, and if they felt any pinching of the heart they quieted it by reflecting on their detached position as experimenters. "Superior to any legal traditions" was the phrase Bronson Alcott had used. Culpability, if there was culpability in their action, was shifted by another reflection which Morton indicated to Sanborn. "' L'expérience démontre, avec toute l'évi-

dence possible, que c'est la société que prépare le crime, et
que le coupable n'est que l'instrument que l'exécute.' Do you
believe Quetelet? " It might be interesting to know whether
Sanborn did or not.

11

THE SUMMER IDYL

GOOD-morning, gentlemen; how do you do?" Mr. Unseld regarded the four men in the road before him with the easy, half-kindly curiosity which greeted all strangers in that rural neighborhood. One was an old fellow, stooped and bearded, and the other three were young men. The old fellow introduced himself and his companions; he was a Mr. Smith, two of the young men were his sons, Oliver and Watson, and the last was named Anderson. "Well, gentlemen," the planter said, still curious about the stranger's business, " I suppose you are out hunting mineral, gold and silver?" " No, we are not, we are looking for land; we have a little money but we want to make it go as far as we can. What does land sell for about here?" " It runs in price," Unseld answered, " from fifteen to thirty dollars in the neighborhood." "That's high; I thought I could buy land here for about a dollar or two the acre." " No, sir," the planter replied emphatically enough, not liking to have the worth of land in his section run down in any such fashion; " if you expect to get land for that price you'll have to go further west, to Kansas, or some of those Territories where there is Congress land." It was a home shot and the old man must have looked sharply at the friendly Mr. Unseld; but Mr.

Unseld was apparently innocent of the impertinence of knowing too much. They talked on a little longer; Mr. Smith told how he had been a farmer in northern New York State, but had sold out there because the heavy frosts always kept him from making anything, and how he was determined to try farming and the cattle-buying business farther south. They said good-bye, and Mr. Unseld took his way down the road to the Ferry. Mr. Smith and his young men turned up the Maryland mountain about their business. It was the morning of the Fourth of July, in the year 1859.

When Mr. Unseld finished his morning in the town, crossed the bridge over the shallow Potomac, and again climbed the road up Maryland Heights, he found the four strangers back at the same place. " I have been looking around your country up here," said the old fellow," and it is a very fine country, a very pleasant place, a fine view." Below them lay the easy stream of the Potomac, broken by the shifting sand-spits and wooded islets that now reflected a rich midsummer green in the water. To the left the Shenandoah River debouched in a slow curve from its valley to join the flow of the Potomac, and beyond the stream precipitously rose the rocky and heavily wooded Loudon Heights where a tangle of foliage half sheathed the rigor of its slopes. On the narrow neck of land between the two rivers lay the busy town of Harper's Ferry whose houses straggled up the steep rise of Bolivar Heights behind it. It was a very pleasant place, a fine view; it was a fine country — comfortable but not smug, for the mountains prevented that, and rich but strong and unsuspicious. Mr. Smith continued; " the land is much better than I expected to find it; your crops are pretty good." He pointed to a field nearby where a few white men and negroes worked side by side cutting grain. " Do you know of any farm in the neighborhood for sale? " he asked. Mr. Unseld knew of one that belonged to the heirs of a Dr. Kennedy. But the stranger thought it might be best to rent for a little while and get better acquainted, so that he could not be taken advantage of in his deal.

"Boys," said the old man, "since you are not very well, you had better get back and tell the landlord at Sandy Hook that we won't be there to dinner, that we'll go on up and look at the place; but you can do as you please." But the boys decided that they would go on with their leader, and the whole party walked on up the road with Mr. Unseld in the direction of his home. He asked them to come in to have dinner with him, and when they declined, he hospitably suggested that they come in anyway for a drink. They did not drink, they said. The conversation drifted on for a little while about the topics of farming. "You can't do much more than make a living up at the Kennedy place," Unseld warned his new acquaintances, who replied that their chief interest, after all, was in buying fat cattle and driving them north for sale. "Well," Unseld directed since they seemed to be willing to take their chances at the Kennedy farm, "if you follow up this road along the foot of the mountain, it is shady and pleasant, you will come out at a church up here about three miles, and then you can see the house by looking from that church right up the road that runs to Boonesborough; or you can go right across and get into the country road and follow that up." They gave their thanks and departed, leaving him a little puzzled, perhaps, about people who wouldn't have dinner with you at dinner time and wouldn't even drink with you.

The Kennedy house, which Mr. Smith found according to his directions, stood about five miles from the Ferry — a distance which the prospective tenant considered convenient for his purposes. It was not a pretentious place, but from the public road, three hundred yards away, it made a very pretty show for a small house. On the other side of the road on a piece of swamp ground was a rough one-room cabin which the thick foliage almost hid from the sight of a passer-by. The place suited the farmer whose crops the northern frosts had killed, and a few days later he got the address of Dr. Kennedy's widow and executor from the useful Mr. Unseld. When he met that new friend on the road the next week he could contentedly remark; " Well, we've got the houses and paid the rent; we pay thirty-five dollars for the two houses, pasture for a cow and horse, and firewood from now until the first of next March, and here is the receipt." John Brown was almost too clever in his methods of putting suspicion to sleep. " I don't want to see the receipt," replied Mr. Unseld, " it's nothing to me." If he had only known the truth, it was a great deal to him.

Long before this John Brown had prepared for the strange household which was to spend its summer on the Kennedy farm. On the day following his first meeting with Mr. Unseld he wrote his wife: " I would be most glad to have you & Anne come on with Oliver, & make me a visit of a few weeks while I am prepareing to build. I find it will be indispensable to have some women of our own family with us for short time. I dont see how we can get along without, & on that account have sent Oliver at a good deal of expence to come back with you; & if you cannot come, I would be glad to have Martha & Anne come on." Mary Day Brown did not feel that she could do as her husband requested, and in her stead went her daughter Anne and her daughter-in-law Martha. By July 19, the two girls were keeping their respective places in the life on Kennedy farm — Martha as the manager of the household duties, and Anne as sentinel against the mixed kindliness and curiosity of the neighbors.

It was only the screen of Anne's constant vigilance and tact which kept the secret of the Kennedy farm. Mail and freight, such as the arms which John Brown Jr. forwarded from Ohio, were received by Kagi in Chambersburg under the name of Henrie, but the recurring sight of the small covered wagon on the road to Chambersburg, escorted by one horseman, roused suspicions; and later a more dramatic disclosure became imminent when Shields Green was pursued as a runaway slave after his companion, Owen Brown, had disposed of impertinent questioners at the point of his revolver. Toward the end of summer when the number of men at the farm increased, Anne's task grew more and more difficult; the mere presence of women gave an added color of peace and respectability to the household, but there was always the peril that someone would discover the real number of persons in hiding or would attempt to investigate the heavy boxes of unopened " furniture " which sat in the bare rooms of the house. Mr. Unseld frequently rode up during the lazy summer afternoons to talk to the old man for whom he seemed to have a certain liking, and he noticed the changes in the personnel of the farm. " Where are the boys? " he would ask, and Mr. Smith would offer the studied reply, " Oh, they have gone off somewhere." To the easy-going and loquacious visitor the answer was always satisfactory. Once or twice he found no one about except the women, and so he stayed in his saddle and talked in his casual, friendly fashion to Anne and Martha who sat on the high porch of the dwelling. But Anne's chief trial was a Mrs. Huffmaster, who had once rented the garden and still felt the ease of possession when she came over. The little barefooted woman with her four children tagging at her skirts had the feminine gift of observation and the feminine tenacity in following up her curiosity. She noticed everything. Once she saw Shields Green sitting in the obscurity of the " dining-room," and after that the poor negroes were never allowed downstairs except after nightfall. She noticed the unusual amount of washing drying in the garden that had once been hers, and remarked enviously and questioningly, " Your men folks has a right smart lot of shirts." She noticed the mysterious boxes, but always had to be content with Anne's explanation; "mother is coming soon and she's very particular and doesn't want us to unpack her furniture until she gets here." And so the summer passed, and the men came and went, intent on their business, and Anne sat on the high porch during the day, reading or sewing while she kept glancing up at the road some three hundred yards away. When she stood before the open window washing the dishes or when she carried the platters of victuals in to the hungry men, she never forgot that her main business was to be watchful — always watchful — to guard her father's secret. After sunset she would return to the porch or sit on the high steps, straining to see the road and listening for the movement of strange feet above the small noises of a summer night. At last the sound of voices in the house died away, the men tramped off upstairs to bed, and she was left alone.

The fulfillment of the plans developed painfully and slowly. Some men on whom John Brown had counted became involved in their own concerns, feared to trust the issue, or lost all confidence in the scheme, and dropped away from the conspiracy. Parsons, who had proved himself at Osawatomie, Moffet, a certain Henry Carpenter, and George B. Gill, the Secretary of State of the Provisional Government, all failed to appear. Realf, who said noble things in his bad verses about Liberty and Tyrants and Brotherhood, was somehow not ready to die for those things; instead, he went to England to lecture and raise money for the cause. He returned to testify before the gentlemen of a Senate Committee. A year and a half earlier John Brown had written to his daughter Ruth concerning further service of her husband, Henry Thompson, as a member of the Springdale military school. "O my daughter Ruth! could any plan be devised whereby you could let Henry go ' to school.' . . . I would rather have him ' for another term ' than to have a hundred ordinary scholars. . . . God forbid me to flatter you into trouble! I did not do it before. My dear child, could you face such music if, on a full explanation, Henry could be satisfied that his family might be safe? " Ruth could not face such music, and only replied; " When I think of my poor despised sisters, that are deprived of both husbands and children, I feel deeply for them." The decision did not change with the passing of time, and Henry Thompson, like Jason and Salmon, was sick of fighting and trouble. Two of his brothers, William and Dauphin, went in his stead to Virginia. " I shall rejoice over ' one that repenteth,' " wrote the leader in the face of his disappointments, and settled himself to the task of filling his depleted ranks.

To John Brown Jr. was delegated the duty of organizing reënforcements in Canada and the States, of raising further funds, and of forwarding the arms. He was an unhappy choice for such responsibilities. His mind was never quite clear after the terrible night in Kansas when he lay on the floor of the Adair cabin, and now this defect probably contributed to the failure at Harper's Ferry. He made a trip to Rochester to confer with Douglass, whom he missed there, to Boston to speed Harriet Tubman on the Canadian project and to see members of the war committee, and to Syracuse, the home of the colored man Loguen, whom he hoped would accompany him north. He also had on his New England visit the instructions from his father to sound out friends in regard to further financial help. " It is terribly humiliating to me to begin soliciting of friends again; but as the harvest opens before me with increasing encouragements, I may not allow a feeling of delicacy to deter me from asking the little further aid I expect to need." It was the freight bills on the arms which prompted this demand for money, and it was their arrival which prompted the further remark to John Brown Jr.: " will you please expect something quite definite very soon." Despite such explicit evidence of impending action and his own references to it, the son made a comment to Kagi in early September which only too plainly indicated his failure as an agent: " I had supposed you would not think it best to commence opening the coal banks before spring, unless circumstances should make it important." Not a word was ever heard from the organizations in Canada to supply fighters for the conquest, and the Ohio negroes likewise failed at the crisis. One of their own number, two months before the climax, expressed in violent language his complete disgust with the situation at Cleveland. The vague directions and misapprehensions of John Brown Jr. may have had something to do with the final disappointment of his father when he watched the cordon tightening about the death trap of the arsenal and waited, and waited in vain, for the Northern reënforcements. In any case, certain white men, such as Hinton and Gill, claimed later that they were not properly notified as to the date of attack. All in all, the deranged son was a perilous link in the intricate chain of the conspiracy.

JOHN BROWN

On August 19, Frederick Douglass reached Chambersburg, called at the shop of a negro barber who was an Underground Railroad agent, and from him learned where he was to meet Isaac Smith of Harper's Ferry. At a deserted quarry he found an old man dressed in clothes which time and hard usage had made as grey and colorless as the weather-beaten walls of stone behind him. A battered hat shaded his bearded lean face, worn by anxiety and exposure. In his hands was a fishing tackle, but the visitor saw no fish. The men passed their greetings.

Among the rocks Douglass, John Brown, Kagi, and Shields Green, whom Douglass had brought with him, sat down and began their discussion of the hazardous future. When " N. Hawkins " sat in the Douglass house at Rochester writing his letters and drawing up the Constitution, his host had not believed that more was intended than an ambitious program of stampeding slaves — or at least, Douglass in the face of later development always maintained that such was his belief. He now discovered his error. John Brown intended to occupy Harper's Ferry and capture the rich store of arms and munitions there; there was to be much more than any slave stampede. Even now Douglass did not suspect the full intent of the man who sat before him, but he learned enough to make him flinch at the issue. It would be fatal to the original plan of running off slaves, he said, and fatal to all engaged. It would be an attack against the Federal Government and would align the whole country against the emancipation movement. While the argument proceeded, Kagi and the slow, inarticulate Green held their peace. John Brown met every point of the objections; he wanted to rouse the nation, and the capture of the Ferry would show all the slaves that a real blow had been struck for them and would give them a rallying place. "Captain Brown," protested Douglass, "the place is a perfect steel-trap; you'll be surrounded and cut off and taken." Again, as ten years before in the same argument with the same man, John Brown leaned forward and the eyes darkened intently and glittered: "Let them surround me; I could cut my way out!" The voice was metallic and vaulting. "I would have prisoners, hostages, and could dictate my own terms of escape." "Captain Brown," pleaded Douglass, "Captain Brown, don't you know that Virginia would blow you and your hostages sky-high rather than let you hold that arsenal for one hour?" "I could cut my way out," said Captain Brown. Then Douglass must have comprehended at last the sort of fatality which once led the tip of the bony, nervous finger down the map — New York, Pennsylvania, Maryland — and brought it to rest above the mountains of Virgina.

The debate was not concluded that day, but its issue was determined beforehand. Douglass was beaten and knew it; the old plan was changed and he was going back home, despite the Captain's plea to remain and fight for his people. At the moment of parting, John Brown put his arms about Douglass, and made his last request: "Come with me, Douglass; I will defend you with my life. I want you for a special purpose. When I strike, the bees will begin to swarm, and I'll want you to help me hive them." But Douglass' mind was made up; like Sanborn, he received no clear and certain call. It is not kind to condemn him, to say that he lacked heart and courage. Perhaps he was perfectly honest in feeling that there had been a change of plan which released him from obligations; certainly, he was wise. He turned to go. "Shields," he said to his companion, "Captain Brown's plan has changed since he talked to us last. You have heard him. If you want you can come back with me." And "Emperor" Green replied in his broken fashion, "I b'leve I go wid de ole man."

The defection of Douglass was a considerable disappointment to John Brown, but he did not immediately give up hope that his friend would repent and return to the fold. In September, Douglass received a letter signed by a number of Philadelphia negroes who felt that their class ought to be represented in a " convention " which was to come off " right away near Chambersburg." "We think," they said, " you are the man of all others to represent us. . . . We are ready to make you a remittance, if you go. We have now quite a number of good but not very intelligent representatives collected. Some of our members are ready to go on with you." It seemed that agitations among the free negroes in the region about Harper's Ferry were having gratifying results; the bees were swarming already, but Douglass had no mind to help hive them. A copy of the letter in John Brown's papers indicated that he, or possibly Kagi, had a hand in the moving appeal of the Philadelphia negroes. Those people, like their Ohio and Canadian brothers, failed to appear when the final moment came; it is doubtful if they had the same excuse of being misinformed as to the time of attack, for they were in more direct contact with Kennedy farm and did not have to depend on John Brown Jr.

In regard to the slaves of the region, John Brown adopted a course of doubtful wisdom. The whole success of the project depended on the immediate, unified, and violent rising of the slaves themselves; it was imperative that they escape, over the dead bodies of their masters if necessary, and gather at the arsenal or the farm to be armed and organized into companies commanded by the original attackers. Cook

wanted to go out among the plantation negroes and give
them some exciting hints of what was to be expected, but
according to Anne Brown's testimony her father, fearing
betrayal and Cook's loquacity, positively forbade any such
scheme. However there is evidence that contact was made
with a certain number of field-hands. And a short time
before the attack Cook was ordered to discover without
creating any suspicion exactly how many male slaves there
were on or near the roads leading into town and to make such
memoranda as would be unintelligible to any except the
members of the company. He got two dollars for expenses,
and under the pretext that he was deciding a bet between
Mr. Smith and himself he took a census of the negro men
held along the Charlestown road. But it is certain that preparations were inadequate and no negroes voluntarily took
part in the affair; if promises had been made they remained
unfulfilled. The possibility of betrayal played a considerable
part in the excessive caution with which this aspect of the
conspiracy was managed; field-hands might be counted upon
to hold their counsel, even if they did not take an actual part,
but there was an especial danger from house-negroes, whose
situation was comfortable and who held to a great degree
the confidence of their masters. In regard to the negroes, the
Harper's Ferry region was particularly ill chosen, for there
were no extensive agricultural interests and by consequence
only a small number of slaves; and a disproportionate number of those were house or body servants.

But there was another fundamental error in the plan of
conquest. John Brown, along with the greater number of
Abolitionists, thought of slavery in terms of abstract moral-
ity, and never in the more human terms of its practical
workings. They saw a situation which violated all justice,

and they firmly believed that every victim of the situation was ready to avenge himself by cutting a throat. The slave himself was at the same time more realistic and more humane; he never bothered his kinky head about the moral issue, and for him the matter simply remained one of convenience or inconvenience. Since the system did not involve that absentee ownership, which had caused the horrors of West Indian slavery, and since immediate contact existed between master and slave, an exercise of obligation reached downward as well as upward and the negro's condition was tolerable enough. The system was subject to grave abuse, but economic considerations bolstered whatever little decency the slaveholder possessed, for the slave was very valuable property and it was only natural that the master would take care to give his property such treatment as would not jeopardize its value. There was, by consequence, no great reservoir of hate and rancor which at the least opportunity would convert every slave into a soldier; when the war came the masters marched off, leaving their families and estates in the care of those same negroes for whose liberty, presumably, the North was fighting. If John Brown did not understand the system he might have received a little instruction on the Monday morning of the attack when Cook went to the house of a certain Mr. Byrne. " We want your slaves," he stated. Mr. Byrne's reply told something about the South's peculiar institution. " Mr. Cook, if you want my slaves, you will have to do as I do when I want them — hunt for them. They went off Saturday evening and they haven't gotten back yet." It was, however, too late for Cook or Brown to profit by any instruction.

As great a danger as betrayal by house-negroes or by curious neighbors was the indiscretion of some of the conpirators themselves. Necessarily a large number of people throughout the North and Canada had some inkling of the project, and it is only surprising that serious consequences did not follow from such knowledge on the part of men who were themselves not involved in the affair. They had no stake in it except a possible sympathy and in some cases not even that was present to deter exposure. Most of the men at Kennedy farm wrote letters which would have afforded damning evidence as to the intentions of these " miners " in Virginia. In late September Jeremiah Anderson wrote to a brother in Iowa: " Our mining company will consist of between twenty-five and thirty well equipped with tools. . . . At present I am bound by all that is honorable to continue in this course. We go in to win, at all hazards. So if you should hear of a failure, it will be after a desperate struggle, and loss of capital on both sides. But that is the last of our thoughts. Everything seems to work for our hands, and victory will surely perch upon our banner. . . . I expect (when I start again travelling) to start at this place and go through the State of Virginia and on south, just as circumstances require; mining and prospecting, and carrying the ore with us." It would not require much ingenuity to read between the lines of such a letter, but Leeman, in writing to his mother at about the same time, was even more explicit. " I am now in a Southern *Slave State* and before I leave it, it will be a *free State*, Mother. . . . Yes, mother, I am waring with Slavery the greatest Curse that ever infested America; In Explanation of my Absence from you for so long a time I would tell you that for three years I have been Engaged in a Secret Association of as gallant fellows as ever puled a trigger with the sole purpose of the *Extermination of Slavery*." Realf confided his own connection with the Virginia campaign to

JOHN BROWN

Mr. Arny of Kansas, and his friend's urgent advice to keep himself clear of John Brown may have helped to send him packing off to England. As early as August John Brown was enraged by the tactlessness of his men, and expressed himself to Kagi. "I do hope all correspondence except on business *of the Co: will be droped for the present.* If everyone must write some *girl;* or some other *extra* friend telling, or shoing our location; & telling (*as some have done*) all about our matters; we might as well get the whole published *at once,* in the New York Herald. Any person is a *stupid Fool* who expects his *friends* to keep *for him;* that which he cannot keep himself. All our friends have each got *their special friends;* and they *again have theirs;* and it would not be right to lay the burden of keeping a secret on any one; at the end of a long string." John Brown was a tight-lipped man, and that virtue, cultivated through years of secret-keeping, may well have made him impatient with the lesser cynicism of other men. It was Cook, suffering from what Realf pedantically described as *cacoethes loquendi,* who most merited his leader's wrath. In Cleveland, a year earlier, he boasted of his Kansas exploits, of having killed five men, and of being employed on a secret expedition. During the long period while he was spying out the land about Harper's Ferry he had taken a wife and settled down as a lock-tender and there may have been fear that some Delilah would get hold of the loquacious Samson. In any case, it was Cook's especial failing that he owned the habit of talking too much to women, and women, we are told, have the habit of talking too much to anybody. And so John Brown, who at this time did not doubt Cook's good intentions or honesty, lived in apprehension that he would fall in with some unfortunate confidant.

Perhaps John Brown need not have been in such fear of exposure. Could any person who heard the rumor of an attack on a United States arsenal believe it? Could anyone in his right senses believe that a handful of men had organized a Government, an army, and by a slave insurrection hoped to set up a new nation in the heart of peaceful Virginia? John B. Floyd, the Secretary of War at Washington, could not believe it. On August 25 he received a letter, which the postmaster of Cincinnati forwarded to him. " Sir: " the letter ran, " I have lately received information of a movement of so great importance that I feel it my duty to impart it to you without delay. I have discovered the existence of a secret organization, having for its object the liberation of the slaves at the South by a general insurrection. The leader of the movement is *Old John Brown*, late of Kansas. He has been in Canada during the winter, drilling the negroes there, and they are only waiting his word to start for the South to assist the slaves. They have one of their leading men (a white man) in an armory in Maryland — where it is situated I have not been able to learn. As soon as everything is ready, those of their number who are in the Northern States and Canada, are to come in small companies to their rendezvous, which is in the mountains in Virginia. They will pass down through Pennsylvania and Maryland, and enter Virginia at Harper's Ferry. Brown left the North about three or four weeks ago, and will arm the negroes and strike the blow in a few weeks; so that whatever is done must be done at once. They have a large quantity of arms at their rendezvous, and are probably distributing them already. As I am not fully in their confidence, this is all the information I can give you. I dare not sign my name to this, but trust you will not disregard the warnings on that account." Mr. Floyd seems to have possessed a strange faith in human nature. " I was satisfied in my own mind," he later said, " that a scheme of such wickedness and outrage could not be entertained by any citizen of the United States." Furthermore, there was no arsenal in Maryland. And so Mr. Floyd pigeonholed the letter and banished it from his thoughts.

Perhaps Mr. Floyd does not deserve too much criticism for his simple faith in the good nature of United States citizens. After the grass is green it is easy to say that one heard it growing. Superficially, the political situation seemed no more grave than it had been for years past. The Kansas troubles, which had threatened to precipitate a conflict, were adjusted at last. And most people, with eyes to the concerns of their own communities, must have agreed with the answer of Senator Douglas to Lincoln: " If each State will only agree to mind its own business, and let its neighbors alone . . . this republic can exist forever divided into free and slave States, as our fathers made it and the people of each State have decided." His opponent, the shambling, awkward Cassandra of Illinois, might prophesy that " a house divided against itself cannot stand," but people who live by compromises find it hard to accept an issue as irrevocable as that. But politicians, North and South, were busy in the unconscious fulfillment of the prophecy. Buchanan asked Congress for money to buy Cuba, and rebuked William Walker for filibustering in Nicaragua because it jeopardized the destiny of the United States to spread itself " over the continent of North America, and this at no distant day should events be permitted to take their natural course." Prime field-negroes were keeping pace in price with the rising prosperity of the South, and the demand for an outside supply was greater than the extensive illicit trade could meet. Of course, some

Northern capital had an interest in the illicit trade; New
England skippers did not break so easily with an honorable
tradition. But there was agitation in the South for legalizing
the importation of slaves. "If it is right," said William
Yancey of Alabama, "to buy slaves in Virginia and carry
them to New Orleans, why is it not right to buy them in
Cuba, Brazil, or Africa, and carry them there?" It would
be difficult to logically confute Mr. Yancey from his premises, but one practical answer lay in the position of Virginia: to open the trade and cut the price which Virginia
negroes fetched in New Orleans would alienate the sympathy
of Virginia from the Southern policy. And certainly most
Southerners, who were not as logical as Mr. Yancey, did not
agree with him. Meanwhile, the Democratic administration
sat serenely in Washington with the white-haired, pleasant
Mr. Buchanan at its head, and the lines of cleavage within
that Party were imperceptibly widening toward the day, not
so far distant, when they would destroy the powerful, easy
machine and put the shambling Cassandra in the chair which
Mr. Buchanan was filling so urbanely and so ineffectually.
But for the present Mr. Lincoln had the answer to his prophecy, and Mr. Douglas was his victorious rival for a senatorship.

The letter, which the Secretary of War put aside and only
published after Colonel Bob Lee's Marines had ended the
episode, was not the work of an enemy. One of John Brown's
Springdale friends confided the secret to friends of his own
in the hope that something could be done to save the old man
from the fatal consequences of his scheme. Two letters were
written and mailed from different points in Iowa to Mr.
Floyd in care of the postmasters at Cincinnati and Philadelphia. It was hoped that an increased guard at Harper's

Ferry would be noticed by Cook and cause John Brown to give up his project. Only the letter from Cincinnati reached its destination, and the weight of evidence in two letters coming from different places and presumably from different hands was lost. But the trusting Mr. Floyd would probably not have acted otherwise in any case.

Meanwhile another friend of John Brown gave a public warning. Of the attitude of the negroes themselves toward slavery Gerrit Smith wrote, after pointing out the failure of politicians and parties to deal with the problem: " No wonder they are brought to the conclusion that no resource is left for them but in God and in insurrection. For insurrection then we may look any year, any month, any day. A terrible remedy for a terrible wrong! " And he continued in terms which clearly indicated his knowledge of Harper's Ferry. " And is it entirely certain that these insurrections will be put down promptly and before they can have spread far? Will telegraph and railroads be too swift for even the swiftest insurrection? They can be rendered useless in an hour. Remember too, that many who would be glad to face insurgents, would be busy transporting their wives and daughters to places where they would be safe from that worst fate which husbands and fathers can imagine for their wives and daughters."

Meanwhile the men who were going to solve the problem where parties and politicians had failed were gradually gathering in the region and getting ready to begin the insurrection which would prove too swift for telegraph and railway. John Brown realized that it would be " distressing *in many ways* " to have his turbulent men about with nothing to occupy them. " We *must* make up our lot of hands as nearly *at one, & the same time;* as possible." He probably remembered that after the Chatham convention his men, under the leadership of Cook, had talked about raiding independently in the South if action should be longer delayed. The temptation would be much greater now when they were on the ground, well-armed, and nerved to the dangers of their enterprise.

Their faith in their leader was not implicit. In declining to take part in the business Salmon Brown had said to his brothers; " You know father. You know he will *dally* till he is trapped." In explaining himself later Salmon remarked that his father had a peculiarity for insisting on order. " I felt that at Harper's Ferry this very thing would be likely to trap him. He would insist on getting everything arranged just to suit him before he would consent to make a move." Some of the other men expressed more definite objections to the plan. They agreed with Frederick Douglass that to occupy the town of Harper's Ferry was sheer madness. All the white men except Kagi, Cook, and Meriam, who did not arrive until just before the moment of action, strenuously opposed the plan for a time; the negroes, knowing nothing of Harper's Ferry, naturally had no opinions. At one time Tidd was so enraged at the idea that he left the farm and spent three days at Cook's house to let himself " cool off." John Brown met the opposition by offering to resign his place as commander; " we will choose another leader, and I will faithfully obey, reserving to myself the privilege of giving counsel and advice when I think a better course could be adopted." On August 18 Owen put a paper into his father's hand.

JOHN BROWN

Dear Sir,

We have all agreed to sustain your decisions, until you have *proved incompetent*, & many of us will adhere to your decisions as long as you will.

Your Friend,

OWEN SMITH.

The men had wisely determined that *one* bad plan was better than several good ones; furthermore, they did not understand how irrevocable was the throw John B. contemplated.

The criticism of the generalship in occupying the Ferry was not to end with Frederick Douglass and the fighters on Kennedy Farm. It has persisted in most estimates of the attack. John Brown cut himself off from his base of supplies, the farm house, placed a river at his back which could be crossed by only one undefended bridge, and divided his small force. The criticism is based on the simple premise that John Brown intended to raid the town, gather up a few slaves, and escape with them into the hills. His answer lay in his intentions. The farm house was his base of supplies only until the moment of the attack on the town, for it certainly could not have been defended against the superior forces which would pursue fleeing raiders. The arsenal and the town itself would become the base of supplies where the revolting slaves were to be armed and organized. The stores at the farm were to be used merely to equip the slaves who would gather on the Maryland side, and that would solve the question of the bridge, for any forces attempting to cut off the men in the town at that point could be pocketed between two fires. Thirteen of the twenty-two men in the force which John Brown divided against military principles were officers, and their troops were to be the slaves who would rally in the

first few hours of the excitement. The separated officers were
placed in positions of strategic importance, and there is
little doubt that had the slaves appeared these commanders
could have established contact, have occupied the Ferry to
better equip and organize their men, and when the time came
have cut their way out through the untrained ranks of the
militia. And their progress would have been *southward*, probably along the rich valley of the Shenandoah, where the
topography offered possibility of defense and food could be
easily obtained. Everything depended on the insurrection of
the slaves themselves; that was the chance of failure John
Brown was taking, but he felt confident that it was a slight
one. If the revolt did not occur, he relied on his hostages, as
he said to Douglass, to insure his own safe egress from the
town. He probably did not consider that side of the question
much: the boy John " followed up with *tenacity* whatever
he set about so long as it answered his general purpose: &
hence he rarely failed in some good degree to effect the things
he undertook. This was so much the case that he *habitually
expected to succeed* in his undertakings." If the revolt did
turn out to be a flash in the pan, and he did have to buy an
immediate escape by hostages not much would be left to him
and his men but a few harried days or weeks of hunger and
sleeplessness in the Maryland mountains while the ring of
marshals and posses and militia drew closer. It was unthink-
able; if he mentioned hostages and retreat to Douglass and
to his men it was only to stay their doubts and lead them to
the step from which they could not turn back. With the
slaves in arms, he could have no thought of retreat into those
Maryland mountains where provisions would be hard to
obtain for a considerable body, where there would be no
possibility of reënforcements from the increasing number

of negroes who would break for freedom, and where the whole moral force of an offensive movement would be lost. Necessarily his plans could not be developed in detail beyond the occupation of the arsenal and town, the arming of the slaves, and a general movement southward; he could trust God and himself for the further contingencies. The slaves would rise, he was sure the slaves would rise, and his face was southward. That was enough.

August passed and the time had not yet come. In early September the pikes arrived and the men at Kennedy Farm had the new task of fixing their blades to the stout seasoned staves. They were a strange and diversified lot of men brought together by equally strange and diversified motives. Anne Brown could write of them: " It is claimed by many that they were a wild, ignorant, fanatical, or adventurous lot of rough men. *This is not so*, they were sons from good families well trained by orthodox religious parents, too young to have settled views on many subjects, impulsive, generous, too good themselves to believe that God could possibly be the harsh unforgiving being He was at that day usually represented to be. Judging them by the rules laid down by Christ, I think they were uncommonly good and sincere Christians if the term Christian means follower of Christ's example, and too great lovers of freedom to endure to be trammeled by church or creed." It is of no use to dwell on the theological points raised by Anne Brown's description. Christ scourged the money-changers from the temple, but he also remarked that those who live by the sword shall perish by the sword. And so they sometimes do. The principles of the Reverend Henry Ward Beecher and his Sharpe's rifles to the contrary, it is hard to visualize the Nazarene in the Kennedy farm house, sitting on a box of revolvers, and fixing a pike-head to its stave or leading a rabble of blood-crazed slaves down the Shenandoah valley. Worse things have been done in His name.

The picture, one may safely surmise, was not as simple as Anne Brown painted it; some of the men were wild, some ignorant, a few fanatical, but all adventurous. They had learned how to spill blood in Kansas, some of them had seen their names in the newspapers, they were spoiled for a common, decent life, and if John Brown did not lead them, and that soon, they would " raid by themselves." And all except some two or three were " rough men." Meriam, the last arrival, was a weak, earnest, fanatical young man. Watson Brown seems to have followed his father trustingly and blindly; he himself was a rather gentle fellow, much like his brother Jason, and he was a great deal in love with the young wife he left in North Elba. Hazlett and Leeman, who were " rough men," could say of Barclay Coppoc and Dauphin Thompson that they " were too nearly like good girls to make soldiers; that they ought to have gone to Kansas and ' roughed it ' awhile to toughen them, before coming down there." Hazlett was rough enough to steal a fine stallion, and Leeman, according to Anne, " smoked a good deal and drank some times." There was Stevens, the deserter; Kagi, who could read Latin, who looked like a " melancholy brigand " and some of whose statements had seemed to " Artemus Ward " " no doubt false and some shamefully true "; and Cook, the expert marksman, who talked too much to women and boasted of having killed five men. There was the free negro, Dangerfield Newby, who was taking the most direct way to get his wife and children out of slavery. " Oh, Dear Dangerfield," she wrote to him, " come this fall without fail, money or no money I want to see you so much: that is one bright hope I have before me." There were four other negroes, likewise the ignorant victims of the conspiracy; Copeland, Leary, O. P. Anderson, and "Emperor" Green had said the fatal words, "I b'leve I go wid de ole man."

It was a trying existence in the cramped quarters of the small farm house. During the hours of daylight the negroes were confined to their garret, for fear of detection, and the other men sat about downstairs oiling revolvers, browning rifle-barrels, and fixing the pike heads to the staves. The same debates which had begun on the march through Iowa to Springdale continued now while the time for action rather than talk drew on. Editions of the *Baltimore Sun*, bought at the Ferry, told the men what was going on in the world beyond the four walls of the farm house, and they must have realized with some pride that their own doings would soon be the thrilling news for this as well as all other papers. The present restraints wore on the men, and made Anne's task doubly hard. Hazlett and Leeman were the most insubordinate of all her "invisibles," for they would wander off to the woods or to Cook's house at the Ferry in broad daylight. When one of the late summer thunderstorms broke over the valley, all the men would take advantage of the protecting tumult outside to leap about and scuffle and shout to their heart's content. The days passed slowly in overhauling the arms, in arguments, in playing cards and checkers, in studying tactics or drilling, and in singing the same songs which Stevens had sung by the prairie campfires. Sometimes Watson would slip over to the cabin across the road and write to his wife. "I think of you all day, and dream of you at night. I would gladly come home and stay with you always but for the cause which brought me here, — a desire to do something for others, and not live wholly for my own happiness. . . . We have only two black men with us now; one of these has a wife and seven children in slavery. I sometimes feel as though I could not make the sacrifice; but what would I want others to do, were I in their place? . . . Oh, Bell, I do want to see you and the little fellow very much, but I must wait. There was a slave near her whose wife was sold off South the other day, and he was found in Thomas Kennedy's orchard, dead, the next morning. Cannot come home so long as such things are done here. . . . I sometimes think perhaps we shall not meet again. If we should not, you have an object to live for, — to be a mother to our little Fred. He is not quite a reality to me yet. We leave here this afternoon or tomorrow for the last time." And so the preparations went on around Watson while he thought of Bell, whom he was not to see again. In the mornings, his father read a chapter from the Bible and stood up to pray, just as he had stood behind his chair, gripping its back, and prayed among his family and workmen in the house at Richmond many years before. In the evenings he sat on a stool in the kitchen where it was warm and where he would not disturb the " boys " who never felt quite free when he was about. And Anne kept her place on the porch, listening and peering into the dark.

On September 29, she and Martha left the farm for good. The time of acting had almost come. The great difficulty was the recurrent lack of funds, but this was relieved by the arrival of Francis Meriam on October 15. This grandson of the Abolitionist agitator, Francis Jackson of Boston, had been interested in John Brown for some time and a year before had offered to join him " in any capacity," as he said, " you wish to place me, as far as my small capacities go."

When he arrived now, after having heard by accident in
Boston of the financial troubles, he supplemented his small
capacities with about $600 in gold. The poor fellow was not
cut out for the work in hand, as Stevens, who well understood such work, realized from one glance at the frail, colorless recruit. But the money was welcome; it removed the last
delay.

It was high time to begin. Five days earlier Kagi informed
John Brown Jr. that they had not five dollars left, and " the
men must be given work or they will find it themselves."
The men felt as they had after the Chatham Convention;
they wanted to put their philanthropy on a paying basis as
soon as possible. He further instructed the Ohio agent that
no more recruits could be received for weeks or perhaps
months to come; " they must keep off the border until we
open the way clear up to the line (M. & D's) from the
South." There was no talk of the attackers themselves retreating northward with liberated slaves; they were full of
confidence and their faces were southward. Kagi continued:
" This is just the right time. The year's crops have been
good, and they are now perfectly housed, and in the best
condition for use. The moon is just right. Slaves are discon-
tented at this season more than at any other, the reason for
which reflection will show you. We can't live longer without
money, — we couldn't get along much longer without being
exposed. A great religious revival is going on, and has its
advantages. Under its influence, people who are commonly
barely *unfavorable* to Slavery under religious excitement in
meetings speak out boldly against it. In addition to this and
as a stimulant to the religious feeling, a fine slave man near
our headquarters, hung himself a few days ago because his
master sold his wife away from him. This also arouses the

slaves. There are more reasons which I could give, but I have not time."

John Brown wrote his last instructions home — how the stock was to be cared for during the winter, how the four pairs of blankets he was sending should be allotted in the household, how the daughters-in-law, Martha and Bell, were to have a home with his family, and how Anne should keep a letter to remember her father by. That was the only reference to a doubtful conclusion for the Virginian venture. For the present he could send no money, but he gave his blessing; "try to commend you always to the God of my fathers."

It was Sunday, October 16. The men who knew nothing of the full scope of the project were called together and it was explained to them. The two Coppoc boys, Edwin and Barclay, Copeland, Leary, and, of course, Meriam, were among those who had been kept in such ignorance until the last moment. Stevens read aloud the Constitution of the Provisional Government of the United States. John Brown administered the oath to that symbol of the new revolution. Some miles away, in the house of Colonel Washington, was another symbol of the revolution — the pistols given to General Washington by Lafayette and the sword given to him, as tradition had it, by Frederick the Great. Cook knew the very cabinet where they lay. In the evening John Brown spoke the final instructions to his men and a final admonition. "And now, gentlemen, let me press this one thing on your minds. You all know how dear life is to you, and how dear your lives are to your friends; and in remembering that, consider that the lives of others are as dear to them as yours are to you. Do not, therefore, take the life of anyone if you can possibly avoid it; but if it is necessary to take life in order

to save your own, then make sure work of it." And in that
spirit the revolution was baptized.

Night drew on and the hour came to go. The rewards which
these men hoped for at the end of the road to the Ferry were
as various as the men themselves. The more able and intelligent among them, who were to some degree in John Brown's
confidence, undoubtedly saw themselves in places of high
command in the campaigns and in the state which those
campaigns would create. They didn't like slavery, and they
hoped that their attack would wreck the institution forever,
but they were ready to capitalize the process and profit from
the wreckage; like many staunch Free State men whom they
had known in Kansas they were not averse to lining their
own pockets in the cause of liberty. Indeed, the laborer is
worthy of his hire.

For the most part they were daring and very brave men;
they knew that they were taking their lives in their hands —
but every robber and bandit knows the same thing. Action
in the face of such knowledge does not necessarily constitute
heroism, and the risk which these men were taking was not
commensurate with the dazzling stake; they intended to
steal a state. And each one felt that though his neighbor
might fall he himself would survive and enjoy the fruits.
Only Taylor, who like Stevens and Stewart believed in " spiritualism," lacked such faith in his own safety. He coolly
predicted his own death, and when the time came, he marched
off in the autumn darkness down the road to the Ferry. With
him down the road marched the others — restless, daring
men — on their way to be shot and bayonetted and hanged.
It is hard to believe that any of them could have completely
answered the question; " My friend, why are you here? "

John Brown, leading them down the road, might have

found a readier answer, but it, like the other answers, would not have told the whole story. George Gill once gave a part of the answer which John Brown could not have given:

> It seems that all great men have their foibles or what we in our differences from them call their weaknesses. "A man is never a hero to his valet" and I am about to give you an expression of truthfulness which I have never given to any one yet. . . . I admit that I am sadly deficient as a God or hero worshipper. . . . And the man who may do his fellows the most good may be far from the goody-goody, but may be personally absolutely offensive.
>
> My intimate acquaintance with Brown demonstrated to me that he was very human; the angel wings were so dim and shadowy as to be almost unseen. Very superstitious, very selfish and very intolerant, with great self esteem. . . . He could brook no rival. At first he was very fond of Montgomery, but when he found that Montgomery had thoughts of his own, and could not be dictated to, why, he loved him no longer. Montgomery, Lane, and all others went down before his imperial self. He was intolerant in little things and in little ways, for instance, his drink was tea, others wanted coffee. . . . He was iron and had neither sympathy or feeling for the timid or weak of will. Notwithstanding claims to the contrary, he was essentially vindictive in his nature.

Gill, as Secretary of Treasury for the Provisional Government, knew John Brown very well and he also knew that human motives are not usually pure and simple. John Brown, according to Gill, might *do* good, but it was not because he *was* good; it was because he was strong. He marched down the road to Harper's Ferry because he could not do otherwise. "Mr. Brown," questioned Congressman Vallandigham of the wounded prisoner on the pallet, "who sent you here?" "No man sent me here," Mr. Brown replied; "it was my own prompting and that of my Maker, or that of the Devil, whichever you please to ascribe it to. I acknowledge no master in human form." John Brown was there because it was the will of God — or the will of the Devil; it was his name for that profound compulsion with which his own will was identified. He somehow felt, by reason of its very strength, that it was outside himself, but he was identified with it and acquiesced in it. As his brother-in-law, Milton Lusk, had said of him years before in Hudson, John Brown doted too much on being head of the heap. As the years passed he had tried many ways to get to the head of the heap and had failed and failed again, but with each failure the desire had become more insatiable, more absolute. The desire was susceptible to meanness, to chicanery, to bitter, querulous intolerance, to dishonesty, to vindictive and ruthless brutality. He laid open his Old Testament on his knees and read: " I hate vain thoughts, but thy laws do I love "; " Except the Lord build the house, they labor in vain that build it; except the Lord keepeth the city, the watchman waketh in vain "; " Remember them that are in bonds as bound with them "; and then at last, " And almost all things are by the law purged with blood; and without shedding of blood is no remission." It was all there — the Word, the Law. And his own will and God's will were one. Hypocrisy is too easy a word to use here, and too simple. If John Brown had no scruple at deception it was because the end justified the means. The end had justified so much in his life — embezzlement, theft, lying, cruelty, murder. That end, that goal, which beckoned year after year, seemed to float and shift and change its shape like some mirage. In other words, John Brown's enormous egotism expressed itself in one set of terms after another, and after Harper's Ferry there would be a final transposition of this egotism into new terms. In his past history these terms had become larger, more impersonal, more dignified, and justification under them had become easier. It is hard to justify the embezzlement of the New England Woolen Mills' twenty-eight hundred dollars and the prayerful letter to his wife on the subject, just as it is hard to justify any piece of vulgarity. It was necessary to invoke "Liberty" in Kansas; in Virginia it was almost gratuitous to do so, for the theft of a state justifies itself. Does man's will need justification beyond the will of God?

"Men, get on your arms," came the order; "we will proceed to the Ferry." It was Sunday night, October 16, 1859.

12

THE SWORD OF
FREDERICK & WASHINGTON

THE wagon, with its load of pikes, sledge, crowbar, and
fagots, creaked down the grade. Behind it marched
eighteen members of the Provisional Army, two by
two, with their rifles hidden under coats and the long grey
shawls which they wore. They met no one on the road, for it
was a raw, damp night when few people would be tempted
out-of-doors. Well before they reached the covered bridge,
which connected the Maryland and Virginia banks of the
Potomac, Captains Cook and Tidd moved ahead of the wagon
and began their work of cutting the telegraph wires. Back
at the farm house Captain Owen Brown and two privates,
Barclay Coppoc and Meriam, remained to keep watch and
arm the slaves who would appear as soon as the alarm was
struck. Now they could only wait.

In the shadow of the bridge entrance the men came to a
halt, took the rifles out from the concealment of their shawls,
and buckled on the cartridge-boxes, heavy with each man's
forty rounds of ammunition. Captains Kagi and Stevens
fell out of the ragged line and slipped ahead to dispose of
the bridge watchman. "You are our prisoner," they said to
the astounded fellow. William Williams, who had watched
in vain through many nights for the something to happen

on his bridge, thought it was just a good joke. In the group
of men that joined his captors he recognized Mr. Cook, the
lock-keeper, and the old gentleman whose name was Mr.
Smith. And then, looking down the barrels of the rifles, he
realized that it was no joke. He was not the last man to make
such a mistake that night. Captain Watson Brown and
Private Stewart Taylor were detailed to guard the Potomac
bridge, and the others proceeded with their prisoner.

They passed the railway hotel and station, which was
called the Wager House, and went as quietly as possible
toward the armory yard on the Potomac bank. But Daniel
Whelan, the armory watchman, heard the rattle of their
wagon and came a little way out from his watchhouse door
to see what was going on in town at such a late hour. For a
moment he thought it was the head watchman, but on approaching the locked gate of the yard he realized that the
group of men who clustered about were strangers and on no
proper errand. "Open the gate!" "I couldn't if I was
stuck," answered Dan Whelan, faithful to his job. One of
the strangers leaped on the gate pier and another snatched
hold of Whelan's coat. Several others clapped their guns to
his body, but he refused to give up the key. "We haven't
got time to bother with the key," said one, and with the
crowbar twisted in the chain of the gate they quickly opened
it and drove the little wagon into the yard. By the light of
their torches they peered into the watchman's face. "I was
nearly scared to death with so many guns about me. I didn't
know the minute or the hour I should drop; they told me to
be very quiet and still and make no noise, or they would put
me to eternity." Dan Whelan was more frightened than
ever in his life, but he had kept the key in his pocket.

John Brown ordered his men about their business. Two of

them remained with him to guard Williams, Whelan, and the few young fellows who were later picked up from the streets. Finally the captor explained himself to the two puzzled and frightened prisoners. " I came here from Kansas, and this is a slave State. I want to free all the negroes. I have possession now of the U. S. armory, and if the citizens interfere, I must only burn the town and have blood." There would be blood, much blood, before it was all over.

These were much the same words which Captain Stevens used when the startled Colonel Lewis Washington stood in nightshirt and slippers at his own door and saw by the light of a crude flambeau four armed men with their guns levelled at him. " Possibly you will have the courtesy to tell me what all this means? " said the Colonel with a dignity which transcended danger and nightshirt and slippers. Stevens answered him: " We have come for the purpose of liberating all the slaves of the South, and we are prepared to do it." When Colonel Washington had dressed himself, and Cook had taken Lafayette's pistols and Frederick's sword which their prisoner had once shown him in courtesy, a little more of Stevens' purposes became apparent. " Have you a watch, sir? " he demanded. " It is on my person," stated the prisoner. " I want it." " You shall not have it," was the cool refusal. " Take care, sir! " threatened Stevens, and then added the question, " Have you any money? " " It is very comfortable to have a good deal of it in these times," remarked the Colonel; " money is rather scarce." " Take care, sir! " Stevens reiterated, but with less confidence in his position. But Colonel Washington's dignity and courage must have been further increased by the act of putting on his breeches. " I am going to speak plainly," he said; " you told me your purpose was philanthropic, but you did not mention at the same time that it was robbery and rascality. I do not choose to surrender my watch. There are four of you here with guns, and you may take it, and my money, but I will not surrender it." In the walks of his daily life Captain Stevens had not had the opportunity of knowing many gentlemen such as Lewis Washington; here was a peculiar situation with which the odds of four men and four rifles somehow could not deal. He waived the point of watch and money and fell back on the moral weight of terror and philanthropy connected with the name of his chief. "I presume," he said with an ominous inflection, "you have heard of Osawatomie Brown?" "No, I have not," replied Colonel Washington, who was not properly impressed. "Then, you have paid very little attention to Kansas matters." The answer to that remark would have explained a great deal in recent history; "I have become so disgusted with Kansas and everything connected with it, that whenever I see a paper with ' Kansas ' at the head of it, I turn over and do not read." "Well," Stevens retorted with an air of glorification, "you will see him this morning." Colonel Washington was still unimpressed.

When the few Washington negroes had been roused out and a carriage and four-horse wagon prepared, the captors retrieved their loss of prestige by sarcasm. "Your carriage waits at the door," they said to Colonel Washington. It is easy to believe that he took his seat now in the same manner with which he always stepped into his carriage. On the way back to the Ferry the party stopped at the Allstadt place and repeated the former procedure. With a heavy fence rail they burst in the door, seized Mr. Allstadt and his eighteen-year-old son, and ordered them into the wagon with their own and the Washington slaves. A little before daylight the wagon and carriage drew into the armory yard, where Stevens introduced the prisoners to John Brown. "Osawatomie Brown of Kansas," added the Commander of the Provisional Army, who must have forgotten for a moment that Kansas and Kansas fame were very distant things. Then he fell into his rôle as host and adopted a courtesy appropriate to the importance of his guest. "You will find a fire in here, sir," he remarked, indicating the watch house. "It is rather cold this morning." After a little he came back for a parley. "It is too dark to see to write at this time, but when it has cleared off and become lighter I shall require you to write some of your friends to send in a stout negro as a ransom." Then he added reflectively: "I shall be very attentive to you, sir, for I may get the worst of it in my first encounter, and if so, your life is worth as much as mine. I shall be very particular to pay attention to you. My particular reason for taking you first was that, as the aid to the Governor of Virginia, I knew you would endeavor to perform your duty, and perhaps you would have been a troublesome customer to me; and apart from that, I wanted you particularly for the moral effect it would give our cause having one of your name, as a prisoner." With that Washington and the other prisoners were left alone to wander in the yard on the side away from the gates or sit in the watch house, where the slaves would come, furtively trailing their pikes, to warm themselves against the cold of dawn.

By this time the first blood had been spilled. The watchman who came to relieve Bill Williams met the guard on the bridge, struck Captain Owen Brown, and tore himself away from the men who seized him. "I didn't know what 'Halt' mint then any more than a hog knows about a holiday," once explained Patrick Higginson, but he understood better when the rifle ball furrowed his scalp as he dodged into the safety of the Wager House. At 1:25 A.M. the train to Baltimore drew up at the Harper's Ferry station. Patrick Higginson in great excitement told the conductor all about the trouble on the bridge — the very bridge over which the train would have to pass. Almost disbelieving such a thing, the baggage-master and engineer walked up the tracks to investigate; rifle-fire from the bridge convinced them, and the train was backed away out of danger. At 1:25 in the morning Shephard Hayward always got up and came out on the station platform to take care of any baggage from the Baltimore train. Being baggage-master was a good job for a free negro, and Shephard had made the most of it; he was respected and liked by all the white people, had money in the bank, and enjoyed the friendship of Mayor Beckham, who took considerable interest in the well-being of the section's negroes. This morning, as always, Shephard came out to attend to his business on the platform. He didn't see the watchman, and walked toward the bridge to hunt for him. There was a command, and as he turned back to the Wager House, a shot from the obscurity of the bridge. Shephard Hayward, free negro, property owner, respected citizen, fell at the impact of that rifle ball which had been fired, perhaps, for the word of liberty. Shephard would have found the whole affair very hard to understand, but death, some twelve hours later, released him from the great pain of his wound and from any speculations about liberty and justice.

The shot from the bridge and the cry of the wounded negro woke Dr. John D. Starry from his warm bed. He rushed out into the street, but found that Shephard was beyond all his professional aid. He did what he could to quiet the apprehensions of the passengers who filled the station's waiting room, and then set them an example of self-possession by boldly walking up to the armory yard. He was challenged but not arrested at the armory, and later, when he talked with the guards of the bridge, the same Providence seemed to protect him. Until daylight he stayed near the station, watching and trying to puzzle out the meaning of the unpredictable events before him. He saw the Washington carriage and wagon drive into the armory yard, and again, just after five o'clock, he saw the same wagon move out of the yard and over the covered Maryland bridge. In the wagon he could make out three men, armed with pikes, and walking beside it two more who carried rifles. It was a detachment under John Cook on the business of bringing in slaves and slaveholders from the Maryland side. With the coming of dawn Dr. Starry made up his mind. He saddled his horse, rode to the home of the acting superintendent of the armory, and then carried the alarm up the steep slopes of Bolivar Heights. Back at the rifle works below the hill he found three strangers on guard; he rode directly toward them, only halting within some twenty-five yards, but his especial Providence was still vigilant, and he returned without hindrance to his self-appointed business of organizing the townspeople for their defense. " I went back to the hillside then," he related, " and tried to get the citizens together, to see what we could do to get rid of these fellows. They seemed to be very troublesome." There he learned that another citizen was dead. The new victim of those troublesome strangers was Boerley, the good-humored, hearty Irishman who could take the two ends of a whiskey cask in his powerful hands and swing it up on the counter to be bunged. He had walked out in the street, unarmed, to take a look at the excitement. The invading riflemen, still so sure of success, asked no questions about any man's errand; a man showed himself as a fair target and that was enough.

Already the bell of the Lutheran church was tolling the alarm. The people who gathered in perturbed groups in answer to the summons were woefully unready for the deadly business in hand. The only weapons which Dr. Starry could find among them were one or two squirrel rifles and a few shotguns. The Doctor was so disheartened by the inadequate state of things at the Ferry that he hurried on the heels of his own messenger to Charlestown, eight miles away, to bring the Jefferson Guards. When he rode into Charlestown a little later the news was already general, the bells were ringing without intermission, and before the high, pillared court house the Jefferson Guards were falling into rank. The bells tolled on — insurrection, civil war. Men had thought about those things when they picked up their newspapers after the peaceful industry of the day. The time had come at last. Dr. Starry's encouragements were needless. Beyond the ranks of the militia, other men and boys were forming in line; they, like the Guards, were not uniformed, they carried all odd sorts of weapons — flintlocks, hunting rifles, shotguns — but they were in earnest. At ten o'clock this new company, with officers just elected to their dignity, boarded the train for the Ferry with the equally raw soldiers of the Jefferson Guards. But by the time the train from Charlestown was on its way, telegrams were already in the hands of the President of the United States, the Governor of Virginia, and Major-General George H. Stewart, Commander of the First Light Division, Maryland Volunteers. At three o'clock the conductor of the Baltimore train had received a message from John Brown that he might proceed, but he was suspicious of the bridge until daylight assured him that all was safe. At

the first station where the telegraph was in service he notified the master of transportation at Baltimore of the night's
bloody events, but that official was just as trusting as Secretary Floyd. " Your dispatch is evidently exaggerated and
written under excitement," he replied to Conductor Phelps.
" Why should our trains be stopped by Abolitionists, and
how do you know that they are such and that they number
one hundred or more? " But the president of the railway
was neither so dubious nor trusting; he straightway informed
those important men whose duty it was to put down insurrections, keep the peace, and maintain the union of the land.
When the telegram lay spread out before him the old timor-
ous Buchanan must have felt for a moment as he did when
the tidings of Secession interrupted the pleasure of a
wedding party. " My God! Not in my time, not in my time,"
he murmured.

When the Baltimore train pulled slowly into the bridge
John Brown could have known that the news of his attack
was on its way to the world. By seven o'clock the operator
at Monocracy station undid all the work of Captains Cook
and Tidd in cutting the telegraph lines from the Ferry. At
the trial John Brown pled in mitigation of the charges
against him: " We allowed the conductor to pass his train
over the bridge with all his passengers, I myself crossing the
bridge with him, and assuring all the passengers of their perfect safety." John Brown has been criticised for his excess
of humanity in permitting the train to go on and spread
the news of the capture of the Ferry to the whole country.
The only answer to the criticism is an impolite one: " Why
not? What could be gained by holding the train? " By the
time the Monocracy operator bent over his key the bells of
Charlestown were ringing the Jefferson Guards to their

ranks; and it was these men who before noon sprung the trap.
John Brown's humanity was inexpensive if admirable; the
strategic criticism of it has as little bearing on success or failure as his own plea had on the subject of his guilt or innocence
before the law. His kindness of heart did not add to the
chances against him, for the real chance he took was a failure
of the slaves to rise.

When Cook took his detail and the wagon over to the Maryland side, there was still no doubt that a few more hours
would see the bees swarming. Cook's task now was to hive
them — to arm the slaves and organize them at the farm and
at the neighboring schoolhouse which was to be occupied as
another temporary storage for some of the rifles from the
farm. Mr. Byrne, on horseback early that damp morning,
met the wagon with its nondescript escort. As he drew aside
to let them pass, he heard his name peremptorily called.
The speaker stepped up beside the horse, and Mr. Byrne recognized John Cook, whom he had known in town. " I am
sorry to say that you are my prisoner." Mr. Byrne looked
down at his acquaintance and smiled as if appreciating a
piece of humor. " You are certainly joking." " I am not! "
replied Cook, and Byrne caught sight of the rifle barrel protruding from beneath the fellow's coat. Byrne had no choice
but to return to his house with Leeman, Cook, and the less
courteous Tidd.

On the porch Byrne met his brother and in a hurried whisper gave the substance of all his apprehensions: " Civil war! "
Once inside, the captors took seats without invitation. Cook
began talking, making a " higher law speech," as he called
it, while Byrne walked nervously up and down the room, his
mind busy with thoughts of the future. Involved in his own
fearful reflections, Byrne only caught from Cook's talk a

familiar quotation: " All men are created free and equal." All men are created free and equal — but to Byrne's mind it only meant brother against brother, State against State, civil war. The speech was finally interrupted by the appearance of Byrne's cousin. The cousin was a lady who felt very strongly on the matter of her carpets and her company. She took one look at her relative in his preoccupied pacing about the room and at the three shabby strangers who held their rifles in readiness. " Cowhide those scoundrels out of the house," were her first words. " Why do you suffer them to talk to you? " Like Colonel Washington, she recognized no odds in a few Sharpe's rifles. But the situation was not so simple to Byrne.

Tidd proceeded with the wagon and his negro helpers to the Kennedy farm to get some of the boxes of rifles, while Cook remained in charge of Byrne. As far as further reënforcements of slaves were concerned they had to be satisfied with the other Mr. Byrne's answer: " You must do as I do when I want them — hunt for them." The party took their prisoner with them down the Ferry road. The four-horse team strained before the wagon with its load of long ominous boxes; the axles, swollen by the dampness of the morning, creaked, and retarded the wagon as with an added weight. Before a log schoolhouse they came to a halt. Mr. Currie, the teacher, was informed that his schoolhouse was to be used as a shelter for the long boxes, that these strangers had come to free the slaves, that they would do it at all costs, and that only those men who voluntarily surrendered their slaves would be protected. The boxes were unloaded and piled in the crude schoolhouse. Cook, Tidd, and the negroes remained behind to guard Currie and hive the bees. The puzzled children scattered to their houses.

A hundred yards or so south of the schoolhouse Leeman and his prisoner met William Thompson, who was on the business of delivering the message to Owen that all was well at the Ferry. Thompson came up smiling and extended his hand. "How are you, Byrne?" "Good morning, Mr. Thompson. I'm well, how are you?" Byrne was disposed to put a cheerful face on things, and smiled, and asked about news from the Ferry. "Oh, the people are more frightened than hurt," he said, and passed on. It began to rain. Leeman and Byrne sat by the roadside, huddling together under the prisoner's umbrella. "Our captain is no longer I. Smith," said Leeman, "but is John Brown of Kansas notoriety." Byrne did not pay great heed, for his mind was still occupied with thoughts of the bloody civil war which seemed so imminent. He could not believe that men without powerful numbers would be foolish enough to attack the slave border. So they sat close under the umbrella, Leeman confident and excited now that action had begun, and Byrne trying hard to keep cheerful before his own apprehensions; the rain dripped from the bare branches, thumped the tight fabric of the umbrella, and, far away, drifted like a slow mist down the valley of the confluent rivers.

When Leeman and his prisoner reached the Ferry shortly after nine o'clock they found only a little change in the situation of the early morning. There had been no organized attempt to dislodge the raiders from their several positions at the bridge, the armory, and the rifle works. Kagi, with his exposed and isolated command at the last place, sent back message after message to John Brown pleading that the town be evacuated at once; he did not lack courage but he did lack his chief's assurance that the slaves would soon be pouring down to the armory and rifle works in irresistible

363

numbers. But John Brown was certain that another half
hour, another hour, would give him a force for the offensive
action he contemplated. And John Brown was right; retreat
would mean inevitable ruin. He could only wait and take the
one chance.

Meanwhile breakfast was ordered and served from the
Wager House for the captors and their prisoners, but John
Brown, like Washington and Allstadt, refused to take a bite
for fear of poison. During the lull in fighting after breakfast, John Brown discussed with his more influential prisoners the possibility of a truce which would leave him in undisturbed possession of the armory. A Mr. Brua walked out,
despite the desultory fire from the citizens, and urged them
not to shoot for the sake of the prisoners confined in the
watch-house. But the townspeople completely lacked organization, they were excited, and they wanted very much to dispose of those troublesome fellows at the bridge, armory, and
rifle works. Furthermore, they had now supplemented their
few squirrel rifles and shotguns by a supply of arms stored
in one of the workshops out of high water. By ten o'clock a
steady point-blank fire was being directed on the armory
from houses nearby and various spots of cover on the hillside. The prisoners crouched in the watch house. The separated detachments of John Brown's men could not reply ef-
fectively. They were scattered officers without commands —
but the slaves must come soon. It was noon, and there was
no sign.

From the Maryland end of the bridge there was a sudden
burst of rifle fire. It was not reënforcements — slave or free
— coming at last. It was the Jefferson Guards. They had
crossed to the Maryland bank a mile or so upstream, struck
the road from the Kennedy farm, and marched directly to

INTERIOR OF THE ENGINE HOUSE DURING ATTACK BY MARINES
(From *Frank Leslie's Weekly*, November 5, 1859)

the bridge head. The detachment stationed there, Oliver Brown, Newby, and William Thompson, fell back immediately. The scattered fire from the armory could not stop the businesslike rush of the Jefferson Guards. They reached the bridge mouth and without hesitation occupied the Wager House. Dangerfield Newby, running for the cover of the armory, was shot dead in his tracks by a rifleman hidden in a house at the foot of the hill. The body was left where it had fallen to be mutilated by mob vengeance, and the unhappy slavewoman's " one bright hope " was snuffed out for good and all.

Colonel Gibson and Captain Rowan of the Jefferson Guards had a right to be well pleased with their strategy. The rush from the Maryland side for the bridge had definitely cut off the chief means of escape from the town, and the position in the Wager House separated John Brown and those with him in the armory from any contact with Hazlett and Anderson at the arsenal or Kagi's men at the rifle works. Captain Botts led the second volunteer company of Charlestown to the Shenandoah bridge and Galt House, a saloon which stood on the bank of the Shenandoah itself, and groups under John Avis and Richard Washington occupied several houses between the hill and arsenal, from which they could lay a direct fire into the armory yard. From this point Washington aimed the shot which brought down the first man of the raiders.

With the taking of the bridge it became apparent to all that the party at the armory were on the defensive, and by this time it was equally clear that the number of men actually in the town had been overestimated. John Brown himself realized now that time was an issue; the slaves had not taken the first chance of revolting, and the only hope was now to hold out with some semblance of strength until they saw their opportunity. The protection of night might bring them in. John Brown went into the watch house, which was under the same roof but had no connecting door with the engine house; he surveyed his group of forty odd prisoners and selected the most important as hostages. " I want you, sir," he said, as he indicated each man. He took five around into the engine house and then came back for another lot. " I want you, sir." Eleven men, including Colonel Washington, Byrne, the Allstadts, Brua, and various officials of the armory, were crowded into the back part of the small engine house, while the defenders, less confident now but still hopeful, settled themselves to hold out against the terrifying odds.

John Brown sent William Thompson out with a prisoner to treat for a cessation of firing; the citizens did not hesitate to debate the ethics of the situation and promptly took Thompson and locked him up in a room of the Wager House. But the truce of even a few hours was all important to John Brown; it would not be long until the early autumn darkness, and under its cover the slaves must come. Despite the capture of Thompson, John Brown ordered his son Watson and Stevens to go out with the protection of a prisoner for a parley. Under a white flag the three men stepped into the open. There was a rattle of firing, and both Watson and Stevens fell. Watson, terribly wounded, crawled back to the watch house. Stevens lay still in a gutter with two charges of slugs in his body. It was one of Brown's own prisoners, Mr. Brua, who came out to the wounded man, picked him up, and carried him to the Wager House. Perhaps he was shamed by the dishonor of his fellow townsmen in firing on the white flag, or perhaps it was simple goodness of heart which made him risk his own life to carry the fallen raider to safety; in any case, when the act was done, he turned and walked back to take his place again among the other prisoners in the engine house.

"My men have been shot down like dogs under a flag of truce," John Brown complained to Captain Sinn when that officer held a parley at the engine house in the evening. "Men who take up arms that way can only expect to be shot down like dogs," replied Captain Sinn, who was an honorable and gallant man. That answer rings with an almost savage downrightness now — but it was a savage business. The citizens had already seen two unarmed men shot down like dogs by the strangers. They had no responsible organization, and they were inflamed by the desire for revenge and by liquor. But it is well, for the sake of common human decency, to recall Mr. Brua picking up Stevens from the gutter and then walking back to his place with the prisoners. There is sometimes a puzzling balance in the affairs of men: when Watson crawled across the armory yard did his father remember a certain white flag on the plains of Kansas?

Just after Watson Brown and Stevens went out with their flag of truce Leeman slipped from the upper end of the armory yard and tried to cross the Potomac to safety. There was no hope. Bullets whipped up the water around him. He took cover on an islet in the stream, but a fellow waded out and, when a demand for surrender was unanswered, shot him dead. All afternoon a sporadic fire was kept up at the boy's body where it lay sprawled on the rocks in the river.

But the score was evened. A wealthy slaveholding farmer, George Turner, rode into town with his shotgun to see what all the trouble was about. A bullet from the armory yard struck him in the neck, causing instant death. The kindly old Fontaine Beckham, agent for the railway and mayor of the town, was the next victim. The poor fellow, greatly disturbed by the death of his man, Shephard, crept up on the trestle-work near the station to watch the outlaws who were causing all this violence in the streets of his town. Crouching in the protection of the engine house building, Edwin Coppoc saw a man peering around the corner of the water tank, some thirty yards. " If he keeps on peeking, I'm going to shoot." Coppoc fired, but missed. The prisoners recognized Beckham and shouted in protest, but Coppoc's rifle was raised again. Beckham crumpled up with his head twisted against the timbers of the trestle. George Chambers, the saloonkeeper, laid the body straight on the railway tracks, and the dead man's son-in-law carried it into his house. The terms of Beckham's will provided for the liberation of four slaves; and in such a fashion John Brown's men accomplished something of their purpose.

Chambers and Harry Hunter, Beckham's grandnephew, went directly to the Wager House and into Thompson's room. They levelled their guns at the prisoner. Christine Fouke heroically threw herself before him; she did not want her carpets spoiled by blood. They dragged Thompson out by the throat, paying no heed to his prophetic threat: " Though you take my life eighty million will rise to avenge me, and carry out my purpose of freeing the slaves! " One wonders how much either of those two objects were in the minds of the armies that marched and countermarched for four years across Virginia. But now Chambers and Hunter put their revolvers to Thompson's head and fired; before he fell a dozen balls were buried in him. After the body was thrown through the openwork of the bridge into the shallows of the river it was still a target for the rifles of men who didn't have the courage to show themselves before the engine-house. From some vague access of shame or pity the mob spared the wounded Stevens. Thus Beckham was avenged — not in the fashion, probably, which he himself would have chosen. " I had just seen my loved uncle and best friend I ever had, shot down by those villainous Abolitionists," Harry Hunter declared at the Brown trial," and felt justified in shooting any that I could find; I felt it my duty, and I have no regrets." The killing was not better or worse than the deeds of most mobs. It was very cowardly, as is any mob action. This mob, from one point of view, had more justice on its side than most, and, remembering that extenuating justice, can one call the act an " execution "? John Brown once put his pistol to the head of a defenseless victim and showed his young men how one thing might be done as well as another; that deed, also, has been termed an " execution."

It was the middle of the afternoon when the useful Dr. Starry organized a party under the command of a young man named Irwin for the assault on the rifle works. They opened a brisk fire as soon as they got within range, and at the first volley Kagi and his men fled through the back way, and, climbing out on the Winchester Railway tracks, tried to ford the Shenandoah. On the opposite bank another group of the attackers met and turned them back into the river. The three fugitives attempted to reach a large flat rock in the middle of the shallow Shenandoah. Kagi stumbled and died in the water; he died quietly, without a struggle, rolling slightly in the wash of the stream. Leary was hit. A citizen named Holt waded out to Copeland. Both Copeland's rifle and Holt's gun missed fire because of damp. Holt clubbed the gun and came on. The mulatto saw the hopelessness of his situation, and surrendered. On the bank there were cries of " Lynch him, lynch him ! " When Holt brought in the trembling yellow fellow the people were already knotting their handkerchiefs together as a rope for the hanging. But Dr. Starry was there to push Copeland into a corner of the armory wall, protect him by the body of his horse, and fight off the turbulent crowd. Finally a policeman arrived and took the prisoner away. Leary, mortally hurt, was not disturbed by the mob.

The Jefferson Guards by their rush at the bridge had cut off the one direct way of escape for the outlaws, but their work ended there. Captain Alburtis and his Martinsburg company reached the Ferry about the time of Mayor Beckham's death, and promptly deployed into the armory yard from the rear. It was John Brown's own tactics — close quarters. All of his men were driven into the engine house, with their last path of escape through the armory buildings to the Potomac definitely closed for good and all. Eight of the Martinsburg men were wounded, but their manœuvre finished the work begun by the Jefferson Guards. The only members of the Provisional Army who escaped from the town were Osborn Anderson and Hazlett, whose post in the armory buildings was completely overlooked by the attackers. Anderson, the negro from Canada, once wrote the account of their flight, claiming that they held their places until Colonel Lee's marines executed the final assault. The fellow would have just as worthy a part in the story if he had later told the truth.

Up in the log schoolhouse Cook guarded the arms and his prisoner, the worried Mr. Currie. At least Mr. Currie felt that he was a prisoner and, under the circumstances, did not like to put the matter to test. Now and then they could hear the faint report of a rifle. In the middle of the afternoon the firing became rapid and continuous; sometimes the individual shots would lift and merge into a remote steady sound. Currie could stand it no longer; "Mr. Cook, what does this mean?" "Well," said Cook with an air of confidence, "it simply means this; that those people down there are resisting our men, and we are shooting them down." Currie was very preoccupied and worried; at last Cook let him go home under oath that he would divulge nothing he had seen.

The second wagon load of arms was delivered at the schoolhouse by Tidd and some of the slaves. Cook's confidence had dwindled a little now, and he set off with a negro, to the Ferry to see for himself. Two boys whom he met on the road told him that his companions were hemmed in by the troops, and he despatched the negro to give Tidd the distressing news that the game was up. He himself went on. From a position on the mountainside he could look down on the whole scene. There were the rivers bending together under Loudon and Maryland Heights, with the houses of the town on the neck of land between. There were the bridges, the engine house, the neat lawns and flower plots of the armory, the station hotel, and the shining rails of the tracks which splayed out of the dark mouth of the Potomac bridge and disappeared down the distant valley. It must have looked very small, and unimportant, and complete, laid out at his feet. People below scurried back and forth in the uneven streets of the town, or clustered together at points of cover. And from those points on the long arc swung around the engine house, puffs of smoke, very small and unimportant, burst. The steady sound of the rifles echoed between the hills.

Cook saw a body of men on the High Street from which they could fire directly down on the engine-house. In the hopeless case Cook did the last, equally hopeless service, for his friends. He raised his rifle, hoping to draw the fire of those men on High Street; and Cook was very proud of his fine marksmanship. There was an answering volley from the people, half a mile away, on High Street. A ball cut off a small branch to which he was clinging and tumbled him through the brush and rocks some fifteen feet down the steep slope. He was bruised and lacerated, but unwounded. He had made his gesture.

There was nothing else to be done. Cook climbed down to the lock on the canal, where he learned that all the outlaws but seven were dead. When he stopped at the house of an Irish family on his way back to the schoolhouse to get coffee and food, they told him that John Brown himself had been killed late in the afternoon. He left them and hurried up the road with his news of the disaster. The schoolhouse was deserted and dark, and no one answered his calls in the pine grove across the road. Finally Tidd, Owen Brown, Barclay Coppoc, Meriam, and one of the negroes came down the road and were challenged. Cook gave them the account of the miscarriage of all their prospects; they decided that an attempt at rescue would be madness. The negroes they had armed and stationed in the timber could not be found, and when the fugitives lay down for a little sleep the last slave crept away and returned to his master. The insurrection was over.

John Brown could not see the liberated slaves when they laid down the pikes or guns, which they had so uncomprehendingly and obediently carried about all day, and slunk off homeward through the trees. The possibility of the insurrection was still before him; Cook, Owen, and the others, with hundreds of slaves at their back, at that very moment might be lying on Maryland Heights, waiting to fall on the disorganized militia who filled the town. All afternoon and evening company after company had come in: from Shepherdstown, Virginia, the Shepherdstown Troop and the Hamtramck Guards; from Frederick, Maryland, three companies, the first men to appear in uniform; and from Winchester one militia company. The men were untrained and poorly equipped, and many were drunk. A surprise attack might have accomplished much; at least, it might have won a free way across the bridge with a chance for the old thrust southward with an army of slaves. But there were no slaves. Miles away, sick with fatigue and disappointment, Cook and the others slept fitfully on the bare ground under the pine trees of Maryland Heights.

A man with a white handkerchief tied to an umbrella approached the engine house. It was a summons to surrender, but now John Brown abated his earlier demands only a little.

Capt. John Brown answers:

In consideration of all my men, whether living or dead, or wounded, being seen safely in and delivered up to me at this point with all their arms and ammunition, we will then take our prisoners and cross the Potomac bridge, a little beyond which we will set them at liberty; after which we can negotiate about the Government property as may be best. Also we require the delivery of our horse and harness at the hotel.

JOHN BROWN.

But Colonel Baylor would accept no arrangement whereby the prisoners were to be carried across the river, and John Brown knew that the eleven prisoners meant his salvation. There was a piece of cannon in the town, and the presence of Colonel Washington and the others was all that kept it from being trained on the engine-house. Their presence also served as a very good excuse for certain deficiencies in the militia's performance. In a very few years these same men, with odds against them, would be managing such affairs with more expertness.

There was no more satisfactory result from the parley which Captain Sinn, of the Fredererick militia, held at the engine house. " Men who take up arms that way can only expect to be shot down like dogs," the Captain replied to John Brown's complaint about his own flag of truce. " I knew what I had to go through before I came here," said John Brown; " I weighed the responsibility and will not shrink from it. I had full possession of the town and could have massacred all the people if I had thought proper to do so. I believe that I am entitled to some terms." The reply which Sinn should have made is very simple: " What good would you have gotten from the massacre? " But certainly the prisoners who overheard the colloquy with Sinn felt some gratitude for John Brown's forbearance. One of them, J. E. P. Daingerfield, put it so; ' he had made me a prisoner, but had spared my life and that of other gentlemen in his power; and when his sons were shot down beside him, almost any other man similarly situated would have exacted life for life." But a lawyer described the matter in a more hard-headed way, when he remarked at the trial that what John Brown refrained from doing had as little bearing on the case as the dead languages. And, in a sense, he was right.

Even if Captain Sinn's logic was brutal, his heart was kind. The surgeon of his command was sent to the engine house to do what he could for Watson Brown. He staunched the flow of blood from the fellow's wounds and made him as comfortable as possible. Oliver was apparently hurt beyond any aid, and Stewart Taylor, who had foretold his own end, lay dead on the brick floor near the door where he had been struck. The five surviving men, and their prisoners, watched the surgeon about his futile task. Dr. Taylor finished, gathered his things together, and rose with an air of professional finality from beside Watson. He promised to come again the next morning, and, with a good-night, slipped through the narrow opening between the doors. And so disappeared their last link of decent kindness and humanity with the world outside.

When the doctor slipped through the door, the people behind him knew that his promise to return in the morning would never be fulfilled; they knew that the first light, whether Dr. Taylor wished it so or not, would begin the business of killing and not of healing. Nothing remained but to wait until that time. There was no light; the loopholes which had been knocked in the brick walls showed only as points of slightly less obscurity in the general darkness. The damp brick of the walls and the heavy bullet-shattered doors did not keep out or mitigate the penetrating cold of the autumn night. No one had slept for more than thirty-six hours, and there had been no food since morning. But it would not be much longer now; it was the last vigil.

Sometimes they could hear the noises of people in the streets who were keeping their courage awake by drink and a few random shots and laughter. They did not hear, but they might have guessed, the measured, steady tread of the sentinels of the United States Marines who now picketed the armory yard. Now and then the silence in the engine house would be broken by the slight clatter of a rifle or revolver against the brick floor, by a subdued word or two, or by the groans of the wounded sons. Again and again Oliver begged, in his agony, to be shot. " No, my son, have patience; I think you will get well," his father replied, and when that comfort, believed neither by speaker nor listeners, failed, he said what was left to be said. " If you die, you die in a good cause, fighting for liberty. If you must die, die like a man." For liberty, or whatever else it may have been that brought him to Virginia, Oliver Brown was now dying; in the quiet of the night, before the Marines came with their bayonets, it was over.

John Brown's own thoughts seem to have been running on that strange compulsion which had brought him here to sit in the dark, listening to the groans of his sons, with the heavy sword of Frederick and Washington lying futilely at his side. Twenty-four hours earlier the statement of his reasons and purposes had been very clear. " I want to free all of the negroes. I have possession now of the U. S. armory, and if the citizens interfere, I must only burn the town and have blood." But the idea of freedom for those black people who had failed him was somehow not quite enough now. He cast back for something more personal, more intimate, more powerfully his own to justify him in the extremity. " Gentlemen," he said to the prisoners, " if you knew my past history, you would not blame me for being here. I went to Kansas a peaceable man, and the pro-slavery people from Kentucky and Virginia hunted me down like a wolf. I lost one of my sons there." His words were almost like the reveries of age — the reveries in which old men try vaguely to piece out some chain of cause and effect, of reason and deed, to account for themselves and their place. It was almost an echo of the idea which Morton had so easily quoted to Sanborn: " L'experience demontre, avec toute l'évidence possible, que c'est la société que prépare le crime. . . ." It was as if, for the first time, John Brown was thinking of himself as a mere victim, and not as an active agent who willed the deed and its accomplishment. John Brown looked back later at those hours in the engine house and felt as if the disaster had fallen from some defect in his own will; he felt, simply, that with just a little more effort of faith and will all would have been well for him. Looking back, he could not comprehend that time of indecision and weakness. " It is by my own folly that I have been taken." He gave too harsh a judgment on himself, and the reason for it was the same which always kept him from understanding the real necessity which hurried him along the way to the mountains of Virginia. For a little while in the face of that disaster which he had thought could never come to pass, the faith went out of him, and in its place was only fatalism. "And now," he concluded to his prisoners, " I am here." Near him his sons lay, and at his side lay futilely the sword of Frederick and of Washington. It was the symbol of one revolution which succeeded somehow, and of another revolution which, somehow, did not succeed.

At two o'clock on the morning of October 18, Lieutenant-Colonel Robert E. Lee of the Second United States Cavalry, in charge of the operations at Harper's Ferry under his brevet commission of Colonel, notified his aide, First Lieutenant J. E. B. Stuart, that the assault on the insurrectionists' position would be executed at dawn. A midnight attack would have endangered the prisoners, and for the same reason which prompted this postponement the assault was to be made by bayonet with a small body of picked men. An opportunity for surrender would be given, but no one expected its acceptance. Colonel Lee offered the privilege of the attack to Colonel Shriver of the Maryland militia, who declined for a sound reason. " These men of mine have wives and children at home. I will not expose them to such risks. You are paid for doing this kind of work." Colonel Baylor, the senior Virginia officer, likewise passed by the opportunity for distinction to get a court-martial in the end. Colonel Lee had made his gestures of courtesy; it was now business. " Lieutenant Green," he inquired of that officer of the Marines, " would you wish the honor of taking those men out? " Lieutenant Israel Green was paid for such work; he took off his cap and thanked the Colonel.

It was dawn. Colonel Lee stood on a little rise of ground, within point-blank pistol range of the engine house. He wore ordinary civilian clothes. Lieutenant Israel Green held his twelve Marines in readiness for the expected assault and another twelve, with fixed bayonets, were detailed to support the movement if necessary. Lieutenant Jeb Stuart had orders to approach the engine house and make the final demand for surrender; if this was rejected, it was his duty to step back from the doors and give the signal for Green's Marines to take those men out. Every point of vantage was crowded by people who wanted to see the show. Those men in the engine house took their places and laid their weapons beside them on the floor, ready to hand. There was no shouting, no tumult, now; everywhere was the silence of waiting. The Marines stood erect and businesslike in their files, with their awkward blue cloaks belted about them against the cold.

Under the gaze of the several thousand spectators, Lieutenant Stuart walked up to engine house. John Brown opened the doors about a hand's breadth and blocked the crack with his body while the parley proceeded. In his hand was a cocked carbine. The officer was greatly surprised; " Why, aren't you old Osawatomie Brown of Kansas, whom I once had there as my prisoner? " " Yes," came Brown's answer, " but you did not keep me." Stuart presented the demand for surrender:

Colonel Lee, United States army, commanding the troops sent by the President of the United States to suppress the insur-

rection at this place, demands the surrender of the persons in
the armory buildings.

If they will peaceably surrender themselves and restore the
pillaged property, they shall be kept in safety to await the orders of the President. Colonel Lee represents to them, in all
frankness, that it is impossible for them to escape; that the
armory is surrounded on all sides by troops; and that if he is
compelled to take them by force he cannot answer for their
safety.

R. E. Lee
Colonel Commanding United States Troops."

John Brown would have none of it. Time and again he
made his old request to remove across the river with his
hostages. He gave his proposition in every conceivable form
and with great tact, but the Lieutenant was firm in his reply that Colonel Lee would accept no conditions. Some of the
prisoners begged that Lee should come to talk with Brown,
but Stuart assured them that it was perfectly useless. John
Brown knew what surrender meant — a length of hemp rope.
" No," he said to Stuart, " I prefer to die just here."

Jeb Stuart stepped smartly back from the doors and
waved his cap. Green gave the order instantly, and his men
came on at the double. With them came Green himself, armed
only with a light dress sword, and Major W. W. Russell, who
carried a rattan cane to aid him in the voluntary service of as-
sisting the Lieutenant. No one was hit in the rush, and
the Marines were at the doors trying to beat an opening with
sledge hammers. The stout timbers, though ripped and shattered by rifle balls, still held, for inside they were heavily
bolted, and braced by a fire-engine rolled against them. The
prisoners huddled in the back part, knowing that a few minutes more would bring them freedom. The five outlaws kept
methodically, blindly firing at the swaying doors. They, too,

379

knew that the time had come. Suddenly the battering at the doors ceased. One of the men turned to John Brown: " Captain, I believe I will surrender." " Sir, you can do as you please," was the answer. John Brown himself preferred to die just here; he was perfectly firm and composed, waiting. Byrne and Daingerfield shouted to the attackers: " One man surrenders, one man surrenders!" Their voices were lost in a terrific blow low down on the doors which split and buckled with the shock. The Marines were using a ladder as a battering ram.

There was another shock. A ragged hole burst in the right-hand door. On the instant Lieutenant Green plunged through, his flimsy blade in hand, and, rising, rushed to the rear of the building between the two engines. " This is Osawatomie," Washington calmly said, pointing to Brown. Green leaped at him with a powerful upward thrust of his sword, which seemed to lift Brown from his feet, and let him crumple forward with his head on his knees. But the light blade caught on a belt or bone, and twisted, and Green, seizing it by the middle, brought the hilt down time and time again on the old man's head until he lay still. The first two Marines to follow Green fell at the breach, and then their comrades were in with the bayonets. They caught one fellow, skulking beneath the engine, and pinned another clean to the wall with a single thrust. It was no time to ask questions. Green shouted the order to hold, and the fight was over. It had lasted only some two or three minutes, from the time the door gave under the impact of the ladder.

The bodies of the wounded and the dead were brought out and stretched side by side on the clean lawn of the armory. John Brown lay almost insensible, with his hair tangled and matted with blood from the blows of Green's sword. The digni-

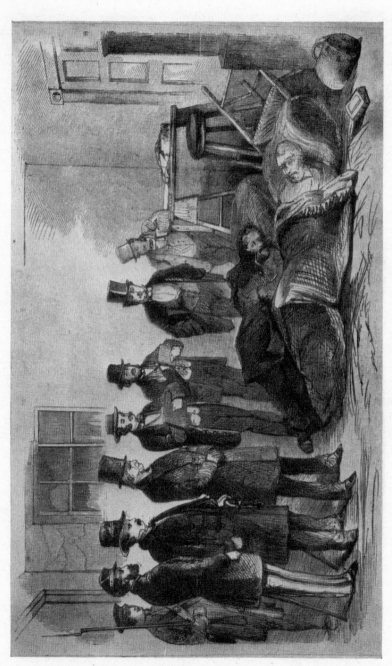

GOV. WISE EXAMINING PRISONERS

(From *Frank Leslie's Weekly*, October 29, 1859)

fied, gentle Colonel Lee, whose business was just this one of spilling blood, gave the captives such consideration as he could, and his Marines held back the crowds of people with whom curiosity had now replaced apprehension. The eleven shaken, hungry prisoners came out from the engine-house, where they had been confined so long. Colonel Washington picked up the sword of Frederick and Washington from the fire-engine on which it had been carelessly dropped and carried it out with him where the bodies lay on the neat grass.

13

THE SOUR APPLE TREE

MR. BROWN," said Congressman Vallandigham, "who sent you here?" " "No man sent me here; it was my own prompting and that of my Maker, or that of the Devil, whichever you please to ascribe it to. I acknowledge no master in human form." Such was the answer which, more than any other, should have instructed the men who stood about John Brown's pallet in the paymaster's office of the armory. Here stood Governor Wise, who had arrived from Richmond a few hours after the final assault and whose duty it now was to discover the nature of this threat against his State. With him were Senator Mason, Colonel Washington, Congressman Vallandigham of Ohio, Congressman Faulkner of Virginia, Lieutenant J. E. B. Stuart, and Andrew Hunter, who within a week or so would be presenting the case of the Commonwealth of Virginia against John Brown. There were the reporters, ready to give the record of this ominous colloquy to the world; and so they put down the names of Mason, and Wise, and Jeb Stuart and Lee without really guessing what history was in those names. In the midst of them all John Brown lay on his miserable pallet; the Governor, looking curiously down at him, was reminded of nothing so much as of a hawk lying on its back with broken wings, talons still curved for fight, and glittering hard eyes fixed on the people who had taken it. By his side was Stevens with hands folded on his powerful chest in that posture which men assume when they feel themselves mortally hurt. Now and then he groaned in pain. But Stevens was to live until, after months of waiting, the gallows had its due.

Colonel Lee was very courteous to his prisoners. Despite the curiosity and excitement of those prominent men about him, Lee made the offer to exclude all visitors if the prisoners so desired. But Brown was " glad to make himself and his motives clearly understood." " How do you justify your acts," inquired Senator Mason. " I think, my friend," said Brown, " you are guilty of a great wrong against God and humanity — I say it without wishing to be offensive — and it would be perfectly right in any one to interfere with you so as to free those you wilfully and wickedly hold in bondage. I do not say this insultingly." " I understand that," said Mason. The prisoner continued : " I think I did right, and that others will do right to interfere with you at any time and all times. I hold that the Golden Rule, ' Do unto others as you would others should do unto you,' applies to all who would help others to gain their liberty." He did not repeat to the Senator what he had once said about the Golden Rule : " better for a whole generation. . . ." Again and again during the long interview he insisted that this, and this alone, had moved him, and that he had expected no reward. " I want you to understand, gentleman," he said, and turned to the reporter of the *Herald*, " — and you may report that — I want you to understand that I respect the rights of the poorest and weakest of colored people, oppressed by the slave system, just as much as I do those of the most wealthy and powerful. That is the idea that has moved me, and that alone. We expect no reward, except the satisfaction of endeavoring to do for those in distress and greatly oppressed, as we would be done by." And when the reporters exercised their privilege and published these things, they looked very well indeed in print; ever since they have looked, in print, just as well. The question is, how would they have looked in blood?

Mr. Vallandigham asked just that question when he said: "Did you expect a general rising of the slaves in case of your success?" John Brown, with death before him, improved his moral position by a falsehood. "No, sir; nor did I wish it. I expected to gather them up from time to time and set them free." "Did you expect to hold possession here till then?" inquired Vallandigham. "Well, probably I had quite a different idea," replied Brown; "I do not know that I ought to reveal my plans." But he did reveal part of his plans when he answered one question: "Brown, suppose you had every nigger in the United States, what would you do with them?" "Set them free," said Brown. "*Your intention was to carry them off and free them?*" "*Not at all*," said Brown. Later he was to deny this, and then to try to whip the denial into consistency with his previous statement, the terms of the Provisional Constitution, and the evidence from his captured papers. Now, as Senator Mason held in his hands a copy of the Constitution, John Brown said, "I wish you would give that paper close attention." There is no need to dwell on the immediate contradictions, which the prisoner believed one remark would obscure; "I do not know that I ought to reveal my plans."

For John Brown's handful of men to hold the Ferry would have required the intervention of the heavenly hosts or a general slave insurrection. To escape from the Ferry at all, prompt action would have been required before the capture of the bridge by the Jefferson Guards, and escape from the Ferry would not have implied final safety. It is true that Cook and Hazlett were taken only because they showed themselves in search of food, but the successful flight of Owen and his companions proved nothing, for general attention was still focussed on the Ferry and they were not pursued with the tenacity or by the numbers which would certainly have been on the trail of the main body the instant it crossed the river. Yet John Brown said: " It is by my own folly that I have been taken. I could easily have saved myself from it had I exercised my own better judgment, rather than yielded to my feelings." " You mean if you had escaped immediately," inquired Senator Mason. " No," said Brown; " I had the means to make myself secure without any escape, but I allowed myself to be surrounded by a force by being too tardy." " Tardy in getting away? " " I should have gone away, but I had thirty-odd prisoners, whose wives and daughters were in tears for their safety, and I felt for them." The subject bore heavily on his mind. Later in the afternoon he said much the same thing to Vallandigham: " I am here a prisoner, because I foolishly allowed myself to be so. You over-rate your strength in supposing I could have been taken if I had not allowed it. I was too tardy after commencing the open attack — in delaying my movements through Monday night, and up to that time I was attacked by the government troops. It was all occasioned by my desire to spare the feelings of my prisoners and their families and the community at large."

John Brown felt that he had been taken because of an excess of humanity, a failure in resolution, a defect in will — in other words, because of his own folly. There are two deductions that might be made from all this. " I had the means

to make myself secure without any escape," said John
Brown. The chief weapon of such an insurrection as he
planned was excitement among the slaves and a peculiar
terror among the people, and he had failed to avail himself
of this weapon. *He himself had not shown the slaves how one
thing might be done as well as another.* If he had stood in
the presence of a few slaves and put his pistol to the head of
their master, those slaves would have been pledged to his
program of violence and involved in it for good and all. Nat
Turner had shown his negroes how, with the consequence of
a bloody insurrection, and John Brown, at Pottawatomie, had
once shown his own young men. But in Virginia he neglected
to throw with his own hand that first small stone to start the
avalanche, and the avalanche had not occurred. He had been
too logical in taking the base of supplies and waiting for
the slaves to come in; he should have begun his program of
terror at one plantation house, and after that it might have
spread by its own momentum. Before dawn there would have
been time to occupy the arsenal. Now, when he realized his
folly and weakness, it was too late. He was candid enough to
call it folly.

" I shall be very attentive to you, sir," John Brown said
to Colonel Washington when he first was brought to the
watch house, " for I may get the worst of it in my first encounter, and if so, your life is worth as much as mine." Washington and the other men in the engine house were, as John
Brown repeatedly called them, simply hostages. In the long
debate at the stone quarry he had told Frederick Douglass
that the capture of these influential citizens would give him
the whip hand of the situation; he would be able to dictate
terms because *their lives would be worth as much as his own
life and the lives of his men.* Now, hostages serve no purpose

unless there is a definite threat against them. When John Brown failed in his first encounter and the time came, he lacked the resolution to make good that earlier threat to Washington, and, by consequence, Colonel Baylor completely ignored the terms offered on Monday evening. " I am here a prisoner and wounded, because I foolishly allowed myself to be so. You over-rate your strength in supposing I could have been taken if I had not allowed it. I was too tardy after commencing the open attack — in delaying my movements through Monday night, and up to that time I was attacked by the government troops. It was all occasioned by my desire to spare the feelings of my prisoners and their families and the community at large." John Brown was merely saying that if he had not foolishly refrained from making use of the hostages he could have escaped at any time up to the arrival of the Marines. He indulged in that self-reproach again and again: " I could easily have saved myself from it had I exercised my own better judgment, rather than yielded to my feelings."

On principle, John Brown had absolutely no scruple against killing in cold blood any plantation master or hostage. " Those men who hold slaves have even forfeited their right to live," John Brown had said to Douglass in their first conversation more than ten years before, and since that time he had learned something more about the business of bloodletting. But in the operations at the Ferry his hand was cramped by other considerations, as well as those of common human feeling. To open the conquest with a midnight massacre in which he himself had a part would have jeopardized that Northern sympathy on which the fulfillment of his plans so much depended; the forms of " Christian warfare " had to be maintained. To escape from the Ferry by force on

Monday, before the arrival of the Jefferson Guards, or by
the threat to the hostages afterward, would have meant
throwing away the last chance for a slave insurrection; it
was the one long chance which John Brown had played and
lost. One cannot know at precisely what hour he realized that
it was lost, but one can understand why he did not avail himself of the last weapon — the threat on the hostages. Was it
worth it? The hope by which his whole existence had been
sustained was gone for good and all. Escape in itself was
failure. Failure was the one thing he had not contemplated
and his devices for escape had been words and nothing more;
he could not have believed that things would reach this
pass. " Your life is worth as much as mine," he said to Washington, but the threat expired on the breath with which it
was spoken. The game was not worth the candle, resolution
was gone with his hope, and instead of faith, faith in God or
the Devil, or in himself, there was only fatalism. " No," he
said, " I prefer to die just here."

When he was brought from the engine-house, when his
wounds were dressed, and when he knew that he was not to die
as he had expected, something of the old spirit came back.
He could not understand himself and how his will and resolution had failed him. Now, as he lay on his pallet, he remembered with something of regret that weapon for escape which
he had failed to employ. " It is by my own folly that I have
been taken." But he had more to say; cut and bruised and
bleeding, he kept something of his old talent for putting
other people in the wrong. " A lenient feeling towards the
citizens led me into a parley with them as to compromise," he
said to a reporter, " and by prevarication on their part I was
delayed until attacked, and then in self-defense was forced to
entrench myself." And again, he declared to the *Herald* re-

porter: " These wounds were inflicted upon me — both sabre cuts on my head and bayonet stabs in the different parts of my body — some minutes after I had ceased fighting and had consented to surrender, for the benefit of others, not for my own." Aside from the falsehood of the statements, they would be unjust even if true; the time for surrender was when Lieutenant Stuart came to the door, and not when the Marines dropped at the breach. But even then John Brown had not surrendered; the refusal was, perhaps, his way of suicide. It is unpleasant to recall John Brown's words, for they rob the scene of something of the worth which his courage had earned and the dignity which was its due.

" I wish to say, furthermore," John Brown had prophesied toward the end of the interview, " that you had better — all you people at the South — prepare yourselves for a settlement of that question that must come up for settlement sooner than you are prepared for it. The sooner you are prepared the better. You may dispose of me very easily; I am nearly disposed of now; but this question is still to be settled — this negro question I mean — the end of that is not yet." And in the evening Governor Wise and his staff sat about a table in the Wager House, trying to do something in preparation for that settlement. Their idea of preparation was to crush what they felt to be a widespread conspiracy behind the present affair. " I have numerous sympathizers throughout the entire North," John Brown had said, but he would confess nothing which might implicate others.

Outside, in the streets of the town, irresponsible crowds of militiamen, who had come to fight and remained to drink, rushed about, laughing, quarreling, and shouting in the darkness. For an hour they had listened to the Governor's speech making; they liked being called " Sons of Virginia," but an hour was a long time. And now the Governor, likewise weary of his oratorical efforts, sat in the hotel with those important men who were his companions. Around the floor lay members of the "Richmond Greys," trying to make themselves as comfortable as possible on the hard planks. Guttering tallow candles inadequately lighted the scene — the sprawling forms of the militiamen, the excited faces of the central group, and the pile of papers on the table. John Brown need have confessed nothing. Those papers, taken in the old carpetbag at Kennedy farm, told the whole story.

Governor Wise read them aloud by the light of the candles. There were the Provisional Constitution, several hundred letters, newspaper clippings, and a roll of maps of the Southern States with census reports of black and white population attached. In the afternoon their prisoner denied that he had either intention or desire for a general slave insurrection — a statement which would simply divert the attention of his hearers and the larger audience beyond from the unspeakable consequences of insurrection to the moral issue. Sometimes he was more frank: " if I could conquer Virginia, the balance of the Southern States would nearly conquer themselves, there being such a large number of slaves in them." Conquer — *conquer* was the word; and conquest is not accomplished by slave stampedes or guerilla jay-hawking.

The men who sat about the table were not deceived in this, but they were deceived in their belief that John Brown would never have undertaken his business without a powerful and well-organized conspiracy behind him. The Provisional Constitution and the portentous roll of maps told the story of the conquest, and the letters told that of the conspiracy. These men could not be blamed for failing to realize what an ineffectual lot of conspirators had once sat before Gerrit Smith's fire, or how little those conspirators understood the designs of their agent. They did not realize that, in a sense, John Brown was the conspiracy. When Emerson, Lydia Child, Garrison, Wendell Phillips, Henry Ward Beecher, Sanborn, and the hundreds of less able, if not less honest, demagogues had said what they had to say and made the gallows glorious like the cross, a large number of equally honest men and demagogues in the South felt that they were faced, not by a conspiracy, but by a nation. These people in the South should have understood that most of the people in the North who listened to the " higher law " sermons went home, promptly forgot that the gallows was glorious like the cross, and were content to mind their own business and vote, in the process of minding that business, for a high tariff. But the people in the South failed to understand, made their own speeches, and retained their touching faith in the laborious justice of the law. When in the end this simple faith was blasted, they marched off to fight against the hand of God, leaving their wives and daughters in the care of those same slaves who were to have managed John Brown's conquest. It is a complicated picture.

John Brown was himself the conspiracy; " I acknowledge no master in human form," he said. If Wise and his friends did not realize this, and scented higher game, they still gave John Brown his due, and, on some points, a little more than his due. " He has coolness, daring, persistence, the stoic faith and patience, and a firmness of will and purpose unconquerable. He is the farthest possible removed from the ordinary ruffian, fanatic, or madman. Certainly, it was the best planned and best executed conspiracy that ever failed." Such was Vallandigham's verdict, and Governor Wise, when back at his capital, had much the same thing to say. " He is

a bundle of the best nerves I ever saw cut and thrust and
bleeding and in bonds. He is a man of clear head, of courage,
fortitude, and simple ingenuousness. He is cool, collected,
and indomitable, and it is but just to him to say that he was
humane to his prisoners as attested to me by Colonel Washington and Mr. Mills, and he inspired me with great trust in
his integrity as a man of truth. He is a fanatic, vain and
garrulous, but firm, truthful, and intelligent." On one point
the Governor gave Brown a little less than his due; he called
him a man of " simple ingenuousness." Possibly the Governor recalled a bit of dialogue between Brown and one of
the bystanders. " Do you consider this a religous movement? " " It is, in my opinion, the greatest service a man can
render to God." " Do you consider yourself an instrument in
the hands of Providence? " " I do," replied John Brown. The
Governor, most likely, considered that ingenuous. In any
case John Brown also gave an instructive definition of Providence: " No man sent me here; it was my own prompting and
that of my Maker, or that of the Devil, whichever you please
to ascribe it to."

On Wednesday morning, October 19, John Brown and
Stevens were placed in a wagon and driven to the railway
station under a strong guard of Marines to protect them
against the possibility of a merciful lynching. Emperor
Green and Coppoc walked between the files of soldiers, while
the following crowd became more and more excited. But when
they reached the waiting train and the shouts of " Lynch
them, lynch them! " rose, the Governor was there to call
back, " Oh, it would be cowardly to do so now! " The train
drew out of the station, along the river for a way, and then
from sight. The sound of the engine diminished into silence,
and the crowd at the station turned back to its business, its

talk, and its impressive funerals for the citizens who had fallen. The Sheriff of Jefferson County and the United States Marshal for the Western District of Virginia committed their four prisoners to the jail at Charlestown to await trial.

When an indictment is found against a person for a felony, in a court wherein he may be tried, the accused, if in custody, shall, unless good cause be shown for a continuance, be arraigned and tried in the same term.

Under this clause in the Virginia Statutes an immediate trial of the Harper's Ferry outlaws was required, for in Charlestown the Grand Jury was then sitting and Judge Richard Parker had opened the semi-annual term of the Circuit Court on October 20. There was no apparent reason why the prisoners should not be brought to justice as soon as possible, for the evidence was clear, the law demanded immediate trial, and the State of Virginia recognized no advantage in submitting the case to the Federal courts. The Federal Government was directly involved by the attack on the arsenal and indirectly by the whole nature of the conspiracy, but Virginia was insisting on a primary principle in retaining jurisdiction. In the case of John Brown himself there was little hesitation; in that of his companions more debate occurred, for the temptation was strong to embody in fact a subsidiary principle concerning the slave problem by turning Stevens over to the Federal Government for prosecution. There was only one difficulty in such a proceeding; none of the murders except that of Private Quinn occurred on Government property, and since Stevens had been wounded many hours before the Marine assault, some doubt existed as to his conviction in a Federal court. Over against this could be balanced the great advantage the Federal court possessed in

being able to summon "the greater villains" who resided
beyond the jurisdiction of the State of Virginia; and meanwhile some of these villains had made haste to reside beyond
the jurisdiction of the United States. But less than two weeks
after the execution of John Brown this political use for
Stevens was rendered unnecessary by the appointment of a
Senate Committee to investigate "the late invasion and seizure of public property at Harper's Ferry. "With the National Government on the track of the "higher and wickeder
game" Virginia was ready to dispose of Stevens as she had
disposed of his master.

The immediate trial and the wounds of two of the prisoners
provided an unexpected capital for the "liberal" newspapers
in the North. At first the Republican press hurried to repudiate John Brown and all of his works, for it was felt that this
sort of thing might prove disastrous in the Presidential contest of the next year, but it was not long before editors and
politicians alike recognized an opportunity in the situation.
When the time came, however, there was still no place in the
Republican Party for Abolitionist sentiment; John Brown
was denounced in the same terms which applied to Border
Ruffians from Missouri and Secessionists from South Carolina. The Chicago Convention which nominated Abraham
Lincoln in 1860 unanimously resolved that the attempt of
John Brown was criminal, and it would be a little too unkind
to assume that the motives behind this were those of expediency and nothing more. But in the autumn of 1859 the
"liberal" press, not having the hopeful political stake of the
Republican Party organs, abhorred and deplored; it abhorred the means John Brown had employed, but deplored
the conditions which made it necessary; it deplored the mis-
guided effort in a holy cause, but abhorred the barbarous

conduct of Virginia in suppressing that effort. Garrison wrote in the *Liberator:*

In recording the expressions of sympathy and admiration which are so widely felt for John Brown, whose doom is so swiftly approaching, we desire to say — once for all — that, judging him by the code of Bunker Hill, we think he is as deserving of highwrought eulogy as any who ever wielded sword or battle-axe in the cause of liberty; but we do not and cannot approve any indulgence of the war spirit.

And Lydia Child wrote a touching letter to Governor Wise concerning the prisoner. " He needs a mother and sister to dress his wounds, and speak soothingly to him. Will you allow me to perform that mission of humanity? " Of course it did not matter to Mrs. Child that John Brown received professional medical attention in Virginia; she had a good heart and was not interested in facts. In the course of an involved correspondence, the woman finally got a woman's direct answer from Mrs. Mason: " We endeavor *to do our duty in that state of life it has pleased God to place us.*" This was a social philosophy and a theology which Mrs. Child and some others could not possibly have understood.

John Brown was tried immediately and before his wounds healed. Most of the people who expressed their horror at such inhumanity did not know the Virginia law or that those wounds were at the worst never serious, but if they had known, it would probably not have mattered. No one can say what they expected Virginia to do; conviction, within a week or a year, was certain, and only the madhouse remained as an alternative to the gallows. But the madhouse was the last thing which the admirers wanted for their hero, for the madhouse, to say the least, would reflect no credit on their own judgment of heroism. But references to the wounded old man on his cot of pain made good copy for newspapers and grounded well in speeches, and, as usual, the more judicial or apathetic majority of editors and orators did not make as much noise as the chosen ten of their brethren who broke the pitchers and blew the rams horns. Meanwhile the Virginians wanted to quiet the excitement and get justice done as soon as possible. Andrew Hunter, the special prosecutor, wrote to the Governor: " The Judge is for observing all the judicial decencies; so am I, but at double quick time." On October 25, one week after his capture, John Brown and his men were arraigned before the Examining Court at Charlestown.

In the open place where the Jefferson Guards had fallen into rank only a week before, the curious crowds now pressed and jostled. Cannon were trained on the court house with an equal threat against any men who had thoughts of rescue or lynching. The files of militia marked a short avenue from the jail to the high, pillared court house, and between the files the prisoners walked to their examination. The cuts and bruises from Lieutenant Green's sword were still distinctly visible on John Brown's head, but he carried himself with something of the old vigor. Stevens appeared terribly weak from his wounds and could move only with the help of an attendant. With these two walked Coppoc, Copeland, and Emperor Green. Inside the dingy court room the men who would pass on the indictments waited with the stale tobacco smoke, the stale breath of the place, the worn chairs, and all the judicial decencies. When the prisoners entered there was no demonstration.

Every man present knew that all of this was perfunctory show and that no hope existed; the evidence and the law could be clearly read by anyone. There were the witnesses, the sworn statements to fact which everyone knew already, and the several indictments which everyone knew could only be found true and binding. They asked John Brown whether he had counsel, and he rose to answer not that question but another: " Virginians, I did not ask for any quarter at the time I was taken. I did not ask to have my life spared. The Governor of the State of Virginia tendered me his assurance that I should have a fair trial; but, under no circumstances whatever will I be able to have a fair trial. If you seek my blood, you can have it at any moment, without this mockery of a trial. I have had no counsel; I have not been able to advise with anyone. I know nothing about the feelings of my fellow prisoners, and am utterly unable to attend in any way to my own defence. My memory don't serve me; my health is insufficient, although improving. There are mitigating circumstances that I would urge in our favor, if a fair trial is to be allowed us: but if we are to be forced with a mere form — a trial for execution — you might spare yourselves that trouble. I am ready for my fate. I do not ask a trial. I beg for no mockery of a trial — no insult — nothing but that which conscience gives, or cowardice would drive you to practice. I ask again to be excused from the mockery of a trial. I do not even know what the special design of this examination is. I do not know what is to be the benefit of it to the Commonwealth. I have now little further to ask, other than that I may not be foolishly insulted only as cowardly barbarians insult those who fall into their power." The Court heard him out with deference. After all, John Brown had earned the right to have his say, and they could understand why, after the collapse, he preferred a sudden end to a dwindling through repetitive testimonies, briefs, pleas, sentences, and all the judicial decencies. The trial, of course, was a mockery, not because it was unfair, but because the evidence was too sure. The mitigating circumstances had as little relevance as the dead languages. But the Court respected the courage in that defiance.

The justice of the peace who presided at the examination assigned Mr. C. J. Faulkner and Mr. Lawson Botts to the defendant as counsel. The former was released on the plea that he had been active at the Ferry during the trouble, and Mr. Thomas Green took his place. John Brown stated that he had written for Northern lawyers, but that he could not recall their names at the moment. He neither definitely recognized nor rejected the counsel appointed, but Stevens accepted without protest. Mr. Green and Mr. Botts were able lawyers, and they were honestly prepared to do all possible in their graceless position. Early in the afternoon the Court of Examination reported its findings, and Judge Parker presented the case to the Grand Jury.

At noon on the next day the Grand Jury brought in a true bill on all three of the counts charged: treason to the Commonwealth, conspiring with the slaves to commit treason, and murder. The prisoners were ordered to appear in court to plead to the indictments, but Captain Avis, the jailer, returned the news that John Brown refused to stir. They brought him in on a cot; Stevens already lay on his mattress on the floor of the court room. Most of the time John Brown rested with his eyes closed and the counterpane drawn close up to his chin, as if all this talk and argument of the Court were nothing to him. Only once he rose and made an active protest against the progress of the trial: "I do not intend to detain the Court, but barely wish to say, as I have been promised a fair trial, that I am not now in circumstances that enable me to attend a trial, owing to the state of my health. I have a severe wound in the back, or rather in one

MRS. BROWN ESCORTED TO HER HUSBAND IN JAIL

kidney, which enfeebles me very much. But I am doing well, and I only ask for a very short delay on my trial, and I think I may be able to listen to it; and I merely ask this, that as the saying is ' the devil may have his dues,' no more. I wish to say further that my hearing is impaired and rendered indistinct in consequence of wounds I have about my head. I cannot hear distinctly at all; I could not hear what the Court has said this morning. I would be glad to hear what is said on my trial, and am now doing better than I could expect to be under the circumstances. A very short delay would be all I would ask. I do not presume to ask more than a very short delay, so that I may in some degree recover, and be able at least to listen to my trial, and hear what questions are asked of the citizens, and what their answers are. If that could be allowed me, I should be very much obliged." It would not matter — a week or a year.

Judge Parker ordered the arraignment to proceed and the prisoners to plead before he considered the appeal for delay. John Brown stood and two bailiffs held Stevens up in accordance with the dignity of the Court. The indictments were read: treason, conspiracy, and murder. The prisoners entered a plea of not guilty. The appeal for a stay of the trial was denied after the testimony of the jail physician that John Brown was perfectly able to stand trial and that neither his hearing nor mind was impaired by the injuries. By the election of the prosecution John Brown's case was the first to be considered, since the five defendants had chosen independent trials. Before the adjournment for the day the jury was selected, after eight members had been challenged by the defense. Messrs. Green and Botts made no effort to secure a transfer of the trial to another less excited county, though such a motion for change of venue might have been sus-

tained. Messrs. Green and Botts, no doubt, were as hopeless
as they were conscientious.

With the opening of the Court on Thursday, October 27,
the real contest began. There was Judge Parker — a rather
small man of severe dignity in bearing and mildness in manner. He sat on the case with a rigorous impartiality, firmness, and an eminent honesty, which could be questioned by
no one who possessed any knowledge of the proceedings. Andrew Hunter carried the burden of this prosecution which
he realized was historic. There had been no misjudgment in
his appointment; distinguished in his presence, handsome of
face, grave and possessed in speech, and learned in the law,
he was an impeccable choice for the place and duty. If he
pressed the case implacably on every point, he never exhibited the least asperity; if he was confident of the end, his
confidence was without insolence; and if it appeared his duty
to hang John Brown as the criminal and the conspirator, he
retained a respect for certain qualities of the man. The
eminent Mr. Vorhees, who later opposed him as Cook's attorney, admitted that Hunter was more than an able adversary, and that his ability was without a " single tone of
malevolence or exasperation." While Hunter debated every
detail of the trial, the regular attorney for the Commonwealth
sometimes nodded in his chair, sleeping off his whisky.
" When Harding began to speak, if you shut your eyes and
listened, for the first few minutes you would think Patrick
Henry had returned to earth; after that he dwindled away
into ineptitudes." With all his oratory and his whisky Harding was simply a nuisance to his distinguished colleague.
Against these prosecutors Green and Botts fought hard but
to no purpose. The uncouth but impressive Green rose before
the jury and presented the mitigating circumstances for his

client with a jumbled, almost illiterate speech and wild, angular gestures, but while he stood on his legs everyone in the packed court room felt some strange doubt of the conviction. The Northern newspaper men were amused by his " whar " and " thar," but they recognized his power. And meanwhile Botts sat hunched in his chair, acutely following the debate, and ready to leap out like an uncoiled spring at the least flaw in the argument of the prosecution. John Brown lay still on the cot, with the counterpane pulled up to his chin, and with his eyes, which Governor Wise had once thought like a hawk's eyes, now closed.

Green and Botts possessed one powerful defense for their case. When the proceedings opened on Thursday morning they had in their hands a telegram from Akron, Ohio, testifying that insanity was heriditary in the Brown family. John Brown absolutely refused to avail himself of the defense. It would have meant a repudiation of himself, and in comparison to such a thing the danger of the noose was inconsequential; it would have meant that he himself was nothing, and all his life, since the youthful period of doubt when he felt a " steady, strong desire to die," had been spent in a ruthless, passionate attempt to prove to the world that he, John Brown, was something. In refusing the plea he was simply risking his life once more to establish that desire for which he had already risked his life so many times before. Now, in the middle of the trial, he did not see the next step so clearly and had not quite discovered the final set of terms for the demands of his nature, but he knew, beyond the shadow of a doubt, that he could not take the excuse of insanity. " I will add, if the Court will allow me, that I look upon it as a miserable artifice and pretext of those who ought to take a different course in regard to me, if they took any at all, and I view it with contempt more than otherwise. As I remarked to Mr. Green, insane persons, so far as my experience goes, have but little ability to judge of their own sanity; and if I am insane, of course I should think I know more than all the rest of the world. But I do not think so. I am perfectly unconscious of insanity, and I reject, so far as I am capable, and attempt to interfere in my behalf on that score." The issue was to arise again and again, but for John Brown that first statement settled it once and for all.

With the plea of insanity eliminated, Green and Botts could only declare their belief in the nobility of John Brown's intentions and indicate some of the atrocities which he might have, but had not, committed. Aside from certain technical moves the whole effort of the defense was dependent on these arguments. John Brown prepared an outline for his counsel:

We gave to numerous prisoners perfect liberty.
Get all their names.
We allowed numerous other prisoners to visit their families, to quiet their fears.
Get all their names.
We allowed the conductor to pass his train over the bridge with all his passengers, I myself crossing the bridge with him, and assuring all the passengers of their perfect safety.
Get that conductor's name, and the names of the passengers, so far as may be.
We treated all our prisoners with the utmost kindness and humanity.
Get all their names, so far as may be.
Our orders from the first and throughout, were, that no unarmed persons should be injured, under any circumstances whatever.
Prove that by ALL the prisoners.
We committed no destruction or waste of property.
Prove that.

In following this program the defense was at first embarrassed by lack of funds, for the considerable sum taken from John Brown at the time of his capture was not immediately restored to him. Certain witnesses summoned by the defense failed to appear, but the frank and generous testimony of the important men who were confined in the engine house established every point in question. And among others, there was Captain Sinn, who had said, " Men who take up arms that way must expect to be shot down like dogs "; now he was offering his testimony for John Brown, " so that Northern men would have no opportunity to say that Southern men were unwilling to appear as witnesses on behalf of one whose principles they abhorred." But Northern men, of course, said that and much more, forgetting that the facts of John Brown's outline had nothing whatever to do with the other facts of Beckham or Hayward or Private Quinn, or of the slave insurrection and the Provisional Constitution. On December 2, the day of John Brown's execution, Abraham Lincoln made one of the few rational and dispassionate estimates of the matter: " Old John Brown has been executed for treason against a State. We cannot object, even though he agreed with us in thinking slavery wrong. That cannot excuse violence, bloodshed, and treason. It could avail him nothing that he might think himself right."

On Friday morning a slight young man, who did not even look his twenty-one years, appeared in Judge Parker's court room and was introduced as George H. Hoyt, a member of the Massachusetts bar. He requested to be made an assistant counsel for John Brown, and Judge Parker, overruling Hunter's demand that the visitor prove his position under the Massachusetts bar, admitted Hoyt to the case. " A beardless boy came in last night as Brown's counsel," Hunter

wrote to Wise; " I think he is a spy." And the prosecutor was
quite right. On the very day that the news of the raid reached
Boston, John Le Barnes engaged Hoyt to go South and
investigate the circumstances with an aim of rescue; the
cover for the mission was Hoyt's extreme youth and his
ostensible duty as a legal defender. Hunter made one guess
beyond Le Barnes and immediately penetrated the whole
scheme, but he was helpless before the Judge's scrupulous
concern.

Despite Hunter's efforts and the slight resentment of
Green and Botts, Hoyt took his place beside the cot of the
defendant, and the trial proceeded. The papers from the
old carpetbag were passed to John Brown as occasion
arose, and he identified them, one after the other, without
protest. Washington, Ball, Allstadt, and the other witnesses
rehearsed the details of the story which everyone already
knew so well. John Brown maintained his composure as the
case was wound up: treason, insurrection, murder. Only
when Harry Hunter took the stand and in answer to his
father's questions described the killing of William Thompson, did John Brown stir and cry out for details. " I felt it
my duty," said the young Hunter, " and I have no regrets."
The man on the cot groaned, but throughout the court room
there was no other sound of sympathy or horror; some of the
people who heard the formal cold account remembered that
they had seen their own friends shot down, without question
or mercy, in the streets of Harper's Ferry. In the afternoon
the prosecution rested.

Green and Botts summoned their witnesses to prove the
two points of the defense: the nobility of John Brown's motives and the humanity of his behavior while in possession of
the town. The second had been freely admitted by the

previous witnesses, and the first had even less bearing in a court of law. Several names were called without answer. In great perturbation John Brown rose to his feet and addressed the Judge.

" May it please the Court; I discover that notwithstanding the assurances I have received of a fair trial, nothing like a fair trial is to be given me, as it would seem. I gave the names, as soon as I could get them, of the persons I wished to have called as witnesses, and was assured that they would be subpoenaed. I wrote down a memorandum to that effect, saying where those parties were; but it appears that they have not been subpoenaed as far as I can learn; and now I ask, if I am to have anything at all deserving the name and shadow of a fair trial, that this proceeding be deferred until tomorrow morning; for I have no counsel, as I before stated, in whom I feel that I can rely, but I am in hopes counsel may arrive who will attend to seeing that I get the witnesses who are necessary for my defense. I am myself unable to attend to it. I have given all the attention I possibly could to it, but am unable to see or know about them, and can't even find out their names; and I have nobody to do any errands, for my money was all taken when I was sacked and stabbed, and I have not a dime. I had two hundred and fifty or sixty dollars in gold and silver taken from my pocket, and now I have no possible means of getting anybody to do my errands for me, and I have not had all the witnesses subpoenaed. They are not within reach, and are not here. I ask at least until tomorrow morning to have something done, if anything is designed; if not, I am ready for anything that may come up."

Hoyt was immediately on his feet with a request for postponement; Judge Tilden of Ohio was expected that night and

he himself was not sufficiently acquainted with the Virginia
law to proceed with the case alone. In view of the prisoner's
open charge of bad faith, the Virginia lawyers were released
from further service, and the Court was adjourned, in accordance with Hoyt's request, until the following morning.
Most of that night the light burned in Mr. Bott's office,
where he sat with the young Massachusetts lawyer, going
over the indictment, the law, and his own notes. The praise
given by the New York *Herald* was not undeserved: " His
counsel, Messrs. Botts and Green, had certainly performed
the ungrateful task imposed upon them by the Court in an
able, faithful and conscientious manner; and only the evening before Brown had told Mr. Botts that he was doing
for him even more than he had promised." There is no evidence that Messrs. Botts and Green remembered with rancor
the accusations brought against them by the excited, almost
petulant, old man who rose up from the cot when the witnesses did not respond to their names. It would not have been
very hard to forgive a little injustice or petulance or ingratitude on the part of that old man who retained in the midst
of his defeat so much of his dignity, his confidence, and his
vocabulary even now when he did not see the way clearly
through the wreckage of his disaster; it was easier, probably,
to forgive now than later when the way appeared clear and
the dignity, the confidence, and the vocabulary were surer.
And so the light burned on in the office until Hoyt fell asleep
from exhaustion and Botts pushed back his papers and went
home.

When the Court resumed the session on Saturday morning
at ten o'clock Judge Tilden had not arrived, but in his place
were two other eminent Northern lawyers; they were Hiram
Griswold of Cleveland and Samuel Chilton of Washington.

Their first step was to request a stay of some few hours, because of the confused condition of the case, but Judge Parker was obdurate on this point; in the matter of counsel John Brown had made his bed, and now he could lie on it. The defense then attempted to gain the same end by insisting that the State adopt one count of the indictment and exclude the other two, but again the Judge decided with adequate legal justification against their motion. Although this last legal effort for delay failed, John Brown endeavored to supplement it in his own fashion; after the recess he sent word from the jail that he was too sick to appear. Hunter was not to be denied and immediately ordered the prison physician to examine the defendant. Dr. Mason made the examination and promptly reported that John Brown was malingering, and so he was brought into the court room on his cot to hear the summing up of the trial. Hunter and Harding attempted to push the business to its end that day, but finally Judge Parker called the special prosecutor up and suggested that to avoid all further cavil at the proceedings the Court should be adjourned until Monday. And when the delay was secure, John Brown, like the biblical invalid, was perfectly able to get up from his bed and walk.

Monday saw the end of the argument. Chilton and Griswold, thwarted in their technical devices, fell back on the more ethical pleas. The prosecution had established its charges: the question of residence and treason on the argument that John Brown occupied Harper's Ferry with the intention of remaining on the ground, the question of murder, and the question of insurrection. " True, he occupied a farm four or five miles off in Maryland, but not for the legitimate purpose of establishing his domicile there," Hunter had argued; " no, for the nefarious and hellish purpose of rallying forces into this Commonwealth, and establishing himself at Harper's Ferry, as the starting point for a new government. Whatever it was, whether tragical, or farcical and ridiculous, as Brown's counsel had presented it, his conduct showed, if his declarations were insufficient, that it was not alone for the purpose of carrying off slaves that he came there. His ' Provisional Government ' was a real thing and no debating society, as his counsel would have us believe; and in holding office under it and exercising its functions, he was clearly guilty of treason. As to conspiring with slaves and rebels, the law says the prisoners are equally guilty, whether insurrection is made or not. Advice may be given by action as well as words. When you put pikes in the hands of slaves, and have their master captive, that is advice to the slaves to rebel, and is punishable with death." Early in the afternoon the case was in the hands of the jury.

Shortly after two o'clock the jurymen filed gravely back into their places. The crowd that packed the court room and corridors, and spread out into the street, seemed to gather upon itself in greater expectancy. The people outside strained to see over the heads of their neighbors and catch some sign; those nearer the doorways could distinguish the faint inconsequential murmur of voices within. " Is the prisoner at the bar, John Brown, guilty or not guilty," the clerk was demanding. " Guilty," the foreman responded. " Guilty of treason, and conspiring and advising with slaves and others to rebel, and of murder in the first degree," continued the clerk's official question. " Aye," said the foreman. In the court room, the corridors, and the porch and street there was no sound of approval or satisfaction, only a slight rustle as the tension relaxed and people realized that it was over. Inside, John Brown seemed to mechanically straighten the counterpane of his pallet and then stretched himself out upon it.

The counsel for the defense entered a motion for an arrest of judgment, and the court adjourned, the lawyers being too exhausted to proceed with the argument on this point. Much remained to be done before the session closed, for Copeland, Coppoc, Green, and Stevens were ready for trial, and Cook had been brought in from the Pennsylvania hills on Friday. When John Brown lay down in his cell after the verdict, the jury for the trial of Edwin Coppoc was sworn in. On the next day Judge Parker heard the debate on the motion for arrest of judgment, but refrained from rendering his decision. That night he prepared his complete opinion, intending to give it the following morning.

But when Judge Parker appeared in the court room on November 2, at the customary early hour, the jurymen for the trial of Coppoc were in their seats. Since the jury of criminal cases in Virginia was held to be judges of law as well as triers of fact, and since the same motion for arrest of judgment might be made by Coppoc's counsel, Judge Parker reserved his opinion for fear of prejudicing the mind of the jury on this matter. Late in the day, when a verdict of guilty had been rendered on Coppoc, the Judge overruled the motion for arrest, and prepared to pronounce the sentence.

John Brown sat motionless beside his counsel, resting his head on his right hand and gazing fixedly at the Judge. The clerk asked the perfunctory question; did the prisoner have anything to say why sentence should not be passed on him. John Brown got slowly to his feet, put his hands on the table before him, and leaned slightly forward over it, as he had once gripped the chair-back and leaned over it when he prayed with his family and workmen in the house at Richmond. He spoke with hesitation; his words came confused and uneasy to his lips.

" I have, may it please the court, a few words to say. In the first place, I deny everything but what I have all along admitted: of a design on my part to free slaves. I intended certainly to have made a clean thing of that matter, as I did last winter, when I went into Missouri and there took slaves without the snapping of a gun on either side, moving them through the country, and finally leaving them in Canada. I designed to have done the same thing again on a larger scale. That was all I intended. I never did intend murder, or treason, or the destruction of property, or to excite or incite slaves to rebellion, or to make insurrection.

" I have another objection, and that is that it is unjust that I should suffer such a penalty. Had I interfered in the manner which I admit, and which I admit has been fairly proved — for I admire the truthfulness and candor of the greater portion of the witnesses who have testified in this case — and I so interfered in behalf of the rich, the powerful, the intelligent, the so-called great, or in behalf of any of their friends, either father, mother, brother, sister, wife or children, or any of that class, and suffered and sacrificed what I have in this interference, it would have been all right. Every man in this Court would have deemed it an act worthy of reward rather than punishment.

" This Court acknowledges, too, as I suppose, the validity of the law of God. I see a book kissed, which I suppose to be the Bible, or at least the New Testament, which teaches me that all things whatsoever I would that men should do to me, I should do even so to them. It teaches me further, to remember them that are in bonds, as bound with them. I endeavored

410

JOHN BROWN RIDING TO HIS EXECUTION

(From *Frank Leslie's Weekly*, December 17, 1859)

to act up to that instruction. I say I am yet too young to understand that God is any respecter of persons. I believe that to have interfered as I have done, as I have always freely admitted I have done, in behalf of His despised poor, I did no wrong, but right. Now, if it is deemed necessary that I should forfeit my life for the furtherance of the ends of justice, and mingle my blood further with the blood of my children and with the blood of millions in this slave country whose rights are disregarded by wicked, cruel, and unjust enactments, I say, let it be done.

" Let me say one word further. I feel entirely satisfied with the treatment I have received on my trial. Considering all the circumstances, it has been more generous than I expected. But I feel no consciousness of guilt. I have stated from the first what was my intention, and what was not. I never had any design against the liberty of any person, nor any disposition to commit treason or incite slaves to rebel or make any general insurrection. I never encouraged any man to do so, but always discouraged any idea of that kind.

" Let me say, also, in regard to the statements made by some of those who were connected with me, I hear it has been stated by some of them that I have induced them to join me. But the contrary is true. I do not say this to injure them, but as regretting their weakness. Not one but joined me of his own accord, and the greater part at their own expense. A number of them I never saw, and never had a word of conversation with, till the day they came to me, and that was for the purpose I have stated.

" Now, I have done."

In the remorseless formula of the law Judge Parker pronounced the sentence of death by hanging. The date for the public execution was fixed on December 2, one month from the day of sentence. Now, as when the verdict of guilty was rendered, there was no sound from the spectators, either of approbation at the sentence itself or protest at the delay of execution. One man clapped his hands and was immediately ordered into custody; people assured a visiting attorney from the North that this underbred culprit was not a citizen of the region. By the order of the Judge the spectators remained in their seats until John Brown had been led away to his cell, and then they rose and quietly departed.

The prisoner had received his sentence of death and had made his last deathless oration. Unhappily, every reference to fact in that oration was a lie. John Brown claimed that his only intention was to run off slaves as he had in Missouri, that he had no design on the liberty of any person or any disposition to incite insurrection, and that he made no effort to induce his men to follow him to Virginia. His own previous testimony contradicted the first declaration, his taking of hostages and arming of slaves the second, and the unwillingness of the older members of his gang to leave Kansas together with his various efforts at recruiting confuted the third. Meriam was almost the only member of his Virginia party to whom his statements would strictly apply. Some weeks later Governor Wise unkindly pointed out to John Brown the major discrepancy between the statements concerning his intention for the slaves. The next day John Brown conferred with Andrew Hunter and did what he could to juggle the delicate matter; he prepared a formal note for the prosecutor.

Dear Sir:
I have just had my attention called to a seeming confliction between the statement I at first made to Governor Wise and that which I made at the time I received my sentence, regard-

ing my intentions respecting the slaves we took *about the Ferry.*
There need be no such confliction, and a few words of explanation will, I think, be quite sufficient. I had given Governor Wise
a *full and particular* account of that, and when called in court
to say whether I had anything further to urge, I was taken
wholly by surprise, as I did not expect my sentence before the
others. In the hurry of the moment, I forgot much that I had
before *intended to say,* and did *not* consider the full bearing of
what *I then said.* I intended to convey this idea, that it was my
object to place the slaves in a condition to defend their liberties,
if they would, *without any bloodshed, but not* that I intended *to
run them out of the slave States.* I was not aware of any such
apparent confliction until my attention *was called* to it, and I do
not suppose that a man in *my then circumstances* should be
superhuman in respect to the *exact purport* of every word he
might utter. What I said to Governor Wise was spoken with all
the deliberation I was master of, *and was intended for truth;*
and what I said in court was *equally intended for truth,* but
required a more full explanation *than I then gave.* Please make
such use of this as you think calculated to correct any *wrong*
impressions I may have given.

Very respectfully yours,

JOHN BROWN

John Brown declared that his object was to put the slaves
in a condition to defend themselves, "*without bloodshed,*"
and not to run them out the slave States. If he ever for a
moment believed that anything of the kind could be accomplished without bloodshed he was little better than an im-
becile; and John Brown was no such fool. If he sincerely contemplated no violence, why did he bring pikes, revolvers, and
Sharpe's rifles, and why did he occupy an arsenal? If he intended to place the slaves in a "condition to defend their
liberties," what was that but the inciting of slaves to rebel,
which he denied in so many words in the speech at the time
of sentence? For justification now he fell back on such casuistry as this in regard to his "intentions" and on the plea of

self-defense. " I only fight those who fight me," he said. It was all so thin that it should not have deceived a child, but it deceived a generation. At the funeral services for Abraham Lincoln, Emerson compared John Brown's speech of November 2, with the Gettysburg oration of the dead President. " His speech at Gettysburg will not easily be surpassed by words on any recorded occasion. This and one other American speech, that of John Brown to the court that tried him, and a part of Kossuth's speech at Birmingham, can only be compared with each other, and with no fourth." Perhaps Emerson was right on the matter of rhetoric; and matters of fact, the questions of truth or falsehood, were often perfectly inconsequential to the sage of Concord. The sage of Concord so gracefully transcended such things.

John Brown excused the " apparent confliction " between his various statements by claiming a lack of preparation and the distress of his circumstances; what he said was " intended for truth." Whether it was truth or not it was intended to be believed, and John Brown always found it very easy to believe anything he himself said. He was interested in putting his case before the world in the most favorable light possible, and he did not recognize the least scruple as to how he accomplished it. He himself was convinced. The intricate business of preparation for the conquest, the full confidence of success, the disappointments and the heart-breaking, desperate consummation seemed very remote to him now; those things had fallen away and he did not think clearly about them if he thought much about them at all. He had played the rôle of a conqueror for a time, and out of the collapse of that he now conceived a new rôle for himself. " I am worth now infinitely more to die than to live," he said. He played this new rôle with the same earnestness, the same confidence of right, the same absolute conviction which he had shown in each of the varying rôles of the past. This rôle fitted his genius as no other ever had, and circumstances were completely with him for the first time in a life of defeats. During that month in prison he appeared more calm, more perfectly possessed, and more dignified than ever before, as if he had tapped some profound secret source of satisfaction. He recognized the situation as inevitable and necessary, for all of this, he said again and again, had been determined before the world began. His will and God's will were one, and that astounding egotism had discovered the last and absolute terms of its expression. He had rejected the world and gained it in that rejection. He was somebody, and his name was in the big print of all the newspapers.

Even in the South there was a considerable sentiment against making John Brown worth something by his death. People believed it to be a dangerous business to make a martyr, when it would be just as easy to treat the same man as a convict or a lunatic. " If old John Brown is executed, there will be thousands to dip their handkerchiefs in his blood; relics of the martyr will be paraded throughout the North." Among the countless letters which daily reached the desk of Governor Wise, demanding the safety of John Brown by threats, arguments, and appeals to humanity, there were many which insisted on just this point; the execution would make a martyr and inflame rather than compose the National difficulties. Of course, those men who did not want the National difficulties composed did want to see the martyrdom. Henry Ward Beecher, who had already done a good deal in his time to keep difficulties from being composed, said before the trial was over: " Let no man pray that Brown be spared. Let Virginia make him a martyr. Now, he has only blundered. His soul was noble; his work miserable. But a cord and a gibbet would redeem all that, and round up Brown's failure with a heroic success."

But in both the North and South a great many of the more rational and responsible public men feared the consequences of making a martyr to order. The Northern members of this faction did not raise the legal question; few people, except the " higher law men," the enthusiasts, and the uninformed, doubted the fairness of the trial and the eminent justice of the verdict. Indeed, John A. Andrew, the war Governor of Massachusetts, referred to the trial as a " judicial outrage," but let it be hoped that the able lawyer, Mr. Andrew, was simply among the uninformed. Another able Northern lawyer, Mr. Vorhees, who was present at the Brown trial and defended Cook, expressed an opinion slightly differing from the opinion of the uninformed Mr. Andrew: " With perfect calmness, forbearing patience and undisturbed adherence to the law, as known and decided throughout generations, that court arises upon my mind with increased and increasing claims to the respect and veneration of the American people and of the world." But men who admitted this felt that strict justice should be sacrificed to public policy. Amos Lawrence, who had given John Brown money for Kansas and had helped pay for the North Elba farm, but who now had outlived any sympathy with John Brown and his kind, wrote to the Virginia Governor, advising the release of John Brown to preclude an inconvenient martyrdom. " From his blood would spring an army of martyrs," Lawrence said, " all eager to die in the cause of human liberty." An entirely different sort of man, Fernando Wood, the mayor of New York, urged the same thing to Wise: " Your proceedings and conduct thus

far in the matter of the conspiracy at Harper's Ferry meets
with general approval, and elicits commendation from your
enemies. The firmness and moderation which has characterized your course cannot be too highly applauded and *today*
you stand higher than any other man in the Union. Now, my
friend, dare you do a bold thing and temper ' justice with
Mercy? ' Have you nerve enough to send Brown to the State
Prison instead of hanging him? Brown is looked upon here
as the mere crazy or foolhardy emissary of other men. Circumstances create a sympathy for him even with the most
ultra friends of the South."

Governor Wise could not help but be aware of his own
fitness as a presidential candidate for 1860, and, being
human, he probably relished the applause retailed in the
letter. But the impulsive and pugnacious Governor was not
to be moved by whatever political threat lay behind Wood's
underscored " *today*." To pardon John Brown, he said, " I
have received petitions, prayers, threats, from almost every
free State in the Union. From honest patriotic men like yourself, many of them, I am warned that hanging will make him
a Martyr. Ah! — Will it? — Why? — The obvious answer
to that question shows me above anything the necessity for
hanging him. You ask: — ' Have you nerve enough to send
Brown to States Prison for life instead of hanging him? '
Yes, if I didn't think he ought to be hung and that I would
be inexcusable for mitigating his punishment. I could do it
without flinching, without a quiver of a muscle against a
universal clamor for his life."

Although in a case of treason the Governor could only
make recommendation to the Legislature, the letters continued to pour in to Hunter and Wise with their outrageous
threats of secretly mustered armies, their appeals, their

abuse, and their arguments. Some of the letters were laid aside, marked " Contemptible nonsense," and some marked " Consider," but none of them much influenced the Governor's decision; in fact, their effect on the executive's stubborn and belligerent nature was, if anything, contrary to the intentions which prompted them. He wrote to Hunter: " I wish you to understand, confidentially, that I will not reprieve or pardon one man *now* after the letters I have rec'd from the North." And so Wise mustered his troops to insure protection in case any of the wild threats of his letters were true, and to prepare, whether those threats were true or not, for the graver threat of the future. No doubt the majority in Virginia and the South was behind him; the hope there of accomplishing anything by " policy " had dwindled from year to year, and the attack on the Ferry made many sincere Unionists in the South reconsider their position. If such a thing was not only condoned but applauded in the North, if the press and pulpit talked about the gallows and the cross, these men had to admit their error and say with considerable regret that the Union they had worked for could not be saved.

At his trial John Brown completely rejected the plea of insanity, but the issue did not die there. Now, along with the other demands for clemency, came further evidence tending to prove that John Brown was irresponsible. As a supplement to the information contained in the telegram from Ohio, George Hoyt secured nineteen affidavits from citizens of the region about Akron and Hudson, and presented this material to Governor Wise. The affidavits recorded nine cases of insanity in the immediate family of John Brown on his mother's side, and six cases among first cousins. To this could be added the two instances among his own children, whose mother, however, had died insane. Those relatives back in Ohio now wanted to save their kinsman even if it meant exposing a family infirmity and losing a martyr to the cause which claimed their sympathy. " Oh, that we had known the amazing infatuation which was urging you on to certain destruction before it was too late! " wrote one of them. " We should have felt bound to have laid hold upon and retained you by violence, if nothing short would have availed. You will not allow us to interpose the plea of insanity in your behalf; you insist that you were never more sane in your life, — and indeed, there was so much ' method in your madness,' that such a plea would be of no avail."

Governor Wise had already received evidence similar to the last affidavits from Hoyt, and had prepared an order for the examination of John by a Dr. Stribling, the superintendent of the Lunatic Asylum at Staunton, Virginia. That order was retracted, and no examination was ever made; by the time the last affidavits were presented, the Court of Appeals had passed on the sentence and the last legal method for proposing this question was definitely eliminated. Governor Wise had given considerable attention to John Brown, and his own convictions were so decided that the services of Dr. Stribling seemed superfluous. " I know that he was sane," the Governor said, " and remarkably sane, if quick and clear perception, if assumed rational premises and consecutive reasoning from them, if cautious tact in avoiding disclosures and in covering conclusions and inferences, if memory and conception and practical common sense, and if composure and self-possession are evidence of a sound state of mind. He was more sane than his prompters and promoters, and concealed well the secret which made him seem to do an act of mad impulse, by leaving him without his backers at Harper's

Ferry; but he did not conceal his contempt for the cowardice which did not back him better than with a plea of insanity, which he spurned to put in at his trial at Charlestown."

It is regrettable that Dr. Stribling did not perform the examination, but on the other hand, the Governor's testimony means something. The evidence of sanity in the case of John Brown must necessarily depend on the estimates made by laymen, such as Wise, and the great weight of this evidence is on the side of sanity. Most of the opinions of insanity were expressed after the Virginia episode and by people who did not understand completely either the methods of organizing the conspiracy or the motives which prompted it. They called Brown a " monomaniac on the subject of slavery," when slavery was merely an incident and an opportunity in his career. " I may be very insane," John Brown wrote from his cell; " and I am so, if insane at all. But if that be so, insanity is like a very pleasant dream to me." In his defeat he had won the very thing for which he had always been fighting.

Undoubtedly, it would be possible to construct an argument for paranoia from certain facts: the matter of heredity; the " steady strong desire to die " in the earlier years of his life; his talent for putting other people in the wrong by adopting the part of an abused and deceived victim; and his egotism, his conviction of being an instrument of Providence, and his delusions of grandeur. But there is other material which does not fall so neatly into the argument. Certainly John Brown was not normal — whatever that may mean. His egotism, his enormous force of will, his power of endurance, his deliberate cruelties, his deliberate charities, his intolerance, his merciless ambition, and the element of religious fanaticism which worked regularly as a device of self-justification — all these things made up an intensity of nature which appeared, beyond doubt, as abnormal. The issue of responsibility remains, and, pragmatically, it is not begging the question to say that John Brown was as responsible for his actions as are the general run of criminals who have suffered similar penalties; that is another problem.

Wise said that John Brown was more sane than his prompters and promoters; certainly he was more intelligent and stronger. If he were insane it is a grave criticism of Sanborn and the other conspirators, and they must assume a horrible weight of responsibility for the whole affair. Sanborn's belief in divinely confirmed missions, especially in his own and John Brown's missions, his absolute certainty that he was right, his irrationality, and his peculiar romanticism give some color to the charge made by Governor Wise; the difference is that Sanborn lacked John Brown's courage and strength, and that difference made the sum total of his other qualities equivalent simply to a habit of rhetoric and a sort of snobbery. If Sanborn had acted out his professions he also might have been called a fanatic. Parker and Higginson were at the same time more rational, more courageous, more intelligent, and stronger than Sanborn, and they were never so well pleased with themselves. As for poor old Gerrit Smith, he went to a lunatic asylum on November 7, 1859.

The first news of the hopeless fighting at Harper's Ferry made the Northern conspirators realize that they had never counted the cost of the business. They had been, under the spell of John Brown's own conviction, so sure of success and of all the important and comfortable consequences of success. They had heard, as they so conscientiously wished, from their agent by action, and now the reflection on their detached position as experimenters did not give as much solace

as in the old days, for the savage realities, which the newspapers retailed, appeared vastly different from whatever
glorious end they had once expected. On the very day after
the Marines stormed the engine house, Frederick Douglass
left for Canada and only a little later sailed for England,
where Edwin Morton also fled. Sanborn sought the advice of
John A. Andrew, who believed that the Northern accomplices might be secretly arrested, and so Sanborn promptly
followed Douglass' example, to try, as he put it, a change
of air for his old complaint. On the day when the trial opened
at Charlestown, Howe and Stearns were likewise on the road
out of the country. In the hospitable house at Peterboro old
Gerrit Smith read the newspapers and saw stark ruin before
him as a prisoner accused of treason to his country. From
the hallucinations of shock and fear he took refuge in the
merciful oblivion of insanity. At Worcester, Higginson remained firm in the general panic. " Naturally," he said of
John Brown, " my first feeling was one of remorse, that the
men who had given him money and arms should not actually
have been by his side "; but the other conspirators had no
such feeling, for, like Sanborn, they had received no clear
and certain call. Only Parker remained as consistent as
Higginson. From Italy, where he had gone to die, he wrote
when the news of John Brown's sentence came; " while reading the accounts of the affair at Harper's Ferry, and of the
sayings of certain men at Boston, whom you and I know only
too well, I could not help wishing I was at home again *to use
what poor remnant of power is left to me in defense of the
True and the Right*." He restated the " natural right " of
the slave to kill his master and affirmed the natural duty
of the freeman to aid the slave in just such a manner. Parker
might not be a fighting man like his brother clergyman

Higginson, who was to command a negro regiment in the Civil War, but Parker, nevertheless, was not the sort of person to try a change of air for his chronic complaint. He would have held his ground, like Higginson, in defense of what he felt to be the Truth and the Right.

Not all of the repudiations of John Brown remained tacit, for, in the middle of November, Howe issued a statement which, in view of Howe's connection with John Brown, deserves the harshest judgments it has received. " That event was unforeseen and unexpected by me," he wrote of the outbreak at Harper's Ferry; " nor does all my previous knowledge of John Brown enable me to reconcile it with his characteristic prudence and his reluctance to shed blood, or excite servile insurrection. It is still, to me, a mystery and a marvel." Howe managed to discover a tardy justification for his falsehoods and repudiation on the grounds that if John Brown were treated as an individual and not as an agent or ally of others he would stand a better chance of legal or illegal escape. Sanborn, who was rather good himself at this sort of *ex post facto* reasoning, did not find much wrong with Howe's behavior, but Higginson retorted with savage directness; " Is there no such thing as *honor* among confederates? " And Howe was deeply grieved.

When Gerrit Smith came out of the seclusion of the Utica Asylum for the Insane after a stay of less than two months, he settled down seriously to the business of proving that in so far as he was concerned there had never been a conspiracy. Denial followed denial. He owned a great regard and personal esteem for the valorous Captain Brown, and at various times had pressed little monetary tokens of that esteem upon him, but as for any funds being contributed to a wicked scheme of violence — Ah, no! In fact, there had never, never, been any conspiracy. He, Gerrit Smith, was a victim of calumny. And after the Civil War he took action for libel against the Chicago *Tribune* for pointing out the convenience of his fit of insanity. For all those years he muttered and brooded and pulled his beard, wasting ink and breath in futile denials and futile rhetorical tributes to the personal nobility of Captain Brown and his own esteem therefor. " We cannot give him up to die alone," one of the conspirators had said as they walked the snow-covered fields two years before, and the speaker was this same old man of big heart, little courage, and less wit.

Sanborn's first trip to Canada was of short duration, but in February when the Senate voted his arrest after he refused to go to Washington to testify, he again moved North. In April he was arrested in his house at Concord, only to be relieved by a posse of his fellow townsmen and a decision of the Court. Stearns and Howe finally appeared before the Mason Committee, expressed their esteem for John Brown as a man, and made tactful denials of everything except vague knowledge of a plan to " relieve slaves by force." " I should have disapproved of it if I had known of it," Mr. Stearns said of the attack; " but I have since changed my opinion; I believe John Brown to be the representative man of this century, as Washington was of the last — the Harper's Ferry affair, and the capacity shown by the Italians for self-government, the great events of this age." The witnesses congratulated themselves on their impregnable moral position, for the questions of the Mason Committee were so awkwardly phrased that these men of conscience could, as Sanborn complacently put it, " without literal falsehood, answer as they did." The politicians, it would seem, were not as competent in causistry as the men of conscience.

Simultaneously with the first efforts of the conspirators to save themselves, plots were arranged to save John Brown. Andrew Hunter was absolutely right in his surmise about Hoyt, who immediately on his arrival in Charlestown interviewed the prisoner to get his opinion of a rescue. That night, October 28, Hoyt wrote to Le Barnes that John Brown " postively refused his consent to any such plan." Besides the prisoner's refusal to countenance an attempt at rescue, there were terrible practical odds against such a thing, as the spy pointed out two days later when he had more thoroughly investigated the situation. " *There is no chance* of his ultimate escape; there is nothing but the most unmitigated failure, & the saddest consequences which it is possible to conjure, to ensue upon an attempt at *rescue*. The country all around is guarded by armed patrols & a large body of troops are constantly under arms. If you hear anything about such an attempt, for Heaven's sake do not *fail to restrain the enterprise*."

But Hoyt's sound advice did not discourage the plans for a rescue. Higginson, Le Barnes, Hinton, and the rest seem to have felt that John Brown's personal objections could be overcome if they could hit on a feasible method. Stearns wrote to Kansas to enlist the services of the redoubtable horse thief, Jennison, who, unhappily, showed no enthusiasm for such a project; the kind and gentlemanly Montgomery and Silas Soulé, who in the spring were actually to reconnoiter in Charlestown for the rescue of Stevens and Hazlett, were likewise much too busy at home. About the time that sentence was passed, Lysander Spooner, of Boston, decided that it would be a good idea to kidnap Governor Wise, take him to sea on a fast tug, and hold him for the release of John Brown. Le Barnes, Higginson, Wendell Phillips, and various other Abolitionists were involved, but they did not agree among themselves as to the best method of procedure; Le Barnes wanted a safe agreement with " professionals " to turn the trick, while Phillips favored enthusiastic amateurs. They found a reliable man and a tug that could outsteam by several knots the gunboat stationed off Richmond, but the capital required amounted to some $10,000 or $15,000. This sum was more than the conspirators could promptly put their hands on, and in consequence the kidnapping scheme, so happily in line with the best maritime traditions of New England, was abandoned in favor of a surprise attack on Charlestown. It was reported that large numbers of men were arming in Ohio under the command of John Brown Jr. and German radicals in New York promised a substantial body of recruits. The plan was simple: — a day or two before the execution or even on that day, the rescuers, heavily armed and carrying " Orsini bombs " and grenades according to Howe's suggestion, were to make a dash on the town, seize the prisoners, and escape on the horses of the militia cavalry. As in the kidnapping project, the matter of money was imperative, for the rescuers demanded $100 each, and a guarantee that the families of all casualties would be provided for. And when Hoyt brought the news from the West that there were no men arming under John Brown Jr. the object was abandoned. Sanborn wrote to Higginson; " So I suppose we must give up all hope of saving our old friend." Perhaps some of them had come to feel with Howe that, after all, John Brown was more valuable dead.

Throughout all this preparation John Brown was perfectly firm in his decision to refuse an escape. Higginson thought that he saw an argument in the tears of Mary Day

Brown, and so made a trip to North Elba to persuade her to visit Charlestown. On the day of sentence they left North Elba. Brown was informed of the matter and telegraphed that his wife should positively be stopped; the message reached her at Baltimore as she was about to leave for Virginia. The letter which John Brown wrote Higginson on the subject indicated that he suspected the ulterior motive in the visit: " If my wife were to come here just now it would *only tend* to distract *her mind* TEN FOLD; and would only add to my affliction; and *can not possibly* do me *any good*. It will also use up the scanty means she has to supply Bread & cheap but comfortable clothing, fuel, &c for herself & children through *the winter*. . . . I lack *for nothing* & was feeling quite cheerful before I heard she talked of *coming on* — I ask her to *compose her mind* & remain *quiet* till the last of *this month;* out of pity to me. I can certainly judge better in the matter than *any one* ELSE." His mind was definitely made up, and Mary Day Brown had to delay the last interview with her husband until the day before execution, when his assent or refusal to be rescued meant less than nothing.

When Samuel Pomeroy of Kansas was admitted to the cell he asked; " You remember the rescue of John Doy. Do you want your friends to attempt it? " And John Brown made the answer which he had made so many times to this question: " I am worth now infinitely more to die than to live." As Hoyt had said, he knew that the attempt at rescue would be a miserable fiasco in the face of the troops assembled in the town; the jail might be broken but the prisoners would never get away with their lives. And even if the escape were miraculously accomplished he could not confront the consequences — a nine days' wonder and then an empty dwindling into old age with the consciousness of failure.

That failure was the one thing he could not stand; it would be a renunciation of himself. He agreed with Henry Ward Beecher, but for reasons vastly different from those of the eminent divine. He had played to the limit of his endurance and power for a tremendous stake — for a conquest — and with that defeated nothing remained for him in the world of men and practical affairs; that failure seemed very far behind him now, and he realized that a gibbet and cord would retrieve it all. "Christ, the great captain of liberty as well as salvation, and who began his mission, as foretold of him, by proclaiming it, saw fit to take from me a sword of steel after I had carried it for a time; but he has put another in my hand ('the sword of the Spirit'). . . ."

Long ago in the few nondescript books of history which pieced out the ground rules of arithmetic in his education, John Brown had learned of a world outside of the frontier town, he had learned to dramatize himself, and he had learned the meaning of ambition. That tall, sedate, and dignified young man, with the imperious eye and the coarse hair brushed back neatly on his unusually small head, had been very sure that he was right in all matters and very sure of his own worth. And so he beat his brothers, read his Bible, believed himself set apart from the vain and petty life about him, and, because he did not yet see how to escape that life, felt a steady, strong desire to die. He wanted desperately, as Milton Lusk put it, to be head of the heap, and doubted, not his worth, but his opportunities. From the time when inflamed eyes stopped his ambition of becoming a minister — that usual career of the more intelligent and ambitious frontier youth — until the time when he rode a murdered man's horse out of the Pottawatomie valley, every effort had ended in some unpredictable failure. Superb energy, honesty and fraud, chicanery, charity, thrift, endurance, cruelty, conviction, murder, and prayer — they all had failed, only to leave him surer than before that he was right and that his plans were " right in themselves." And after each collapse he opened his Bible on his knees and read; " then shalt thou delight thyself in the Lord; and I will make thee to ride upon the high places of the earth; and I will feed thee with the heritage of Jacob thy father: for the mouth of the Lord hath spoken it." There was the law and the promise.

Now, after the last bloody collapse, he sat in his cell and spread open the cheap well-worn pocket Bible. He found his vindication there as he had always found vindication, and again it clearly pointed out his way to him. " I am just as content to die for God's eternal truth and for suffering humanity on the scaffold as in any other way," he wrote to his younger children; " and I do not say this from any disposition to ' brave it out.' " To George Adams he wrote: " I am wonderfully ' strengthened from on high.' May I use that strength in ' showing His strength unto this generation,' and His power to every one that is to come! " " So far as I am concerned, I ' count it all joy,' " was the message to his brother Jeremiah; " ' I have fought the good fight,' and have, as I trust, ' finished my course.' "

But it was not in John Brown's nature, even in these moments, to neglect the more vulgar profits which might be salvaged from his distress; after all, he owed something to his wife and he was confident, now as always, that the world owed him a round sum. " I have been *whiped* as the saying is," he wrote to his wife; " but am sure I can recover all the lost capital occasioned by that disaster; by only hanging a few moments by the neck; & I feel quite determined to make the utmost possible out of a defeat. I am dayly & hourly

429

striving to gather up what little I may from the wreck."
Most of the many letters which left the Charlestown cell contained a tactful and dignified reference to the financial obligation of society to the Brown family; years of assiduous
practice had given John Brown an impeccable technique in
such solicitations and that talent now had full scope. Before
he died he had the satisfaction of knowing that an estate,
as well as a reputation, had been retrieved from his ruin.

All of that last month letters of sympathy, and some of
reproach, came to him, and he sat in the cell, with his open
Bible, and filled page after page with the cramped old man's
script. The letters went out to his family, to the conspirators,
to a kindly Quaker lady, to old Mr. Vaill who had been his
teacher in Connecticut, to his kinsman, Dr. Humphrey,
who regretted that he had not been restrained in his " amazing infatuation," to the impressionable Mrs. Stearns, and
to many others who were known to him only by their present
sympathy. His letters, so dignified, so restrained, so humble
and convincing, built up the outlines of the new conception
of himself — the rôle of the martyr and the Samson now,
and not that of the conqueror. Sitting in the room of Frederick Douglass' house he had once spent day after day,
writing letters in that tight, almost illiterate hand, to build
up the conspiracy for the conquest, and the new letters from
the jail cell organized another conspiracy to retrieve all that
had been lost in the failure of the first. More than once as
Sheriff Campbell read those letters in his duty as censor he
wiped tears from his eyes before he folded the sheets and
passed them on to do their work. " If they hang John
Brown," even Lawrence could remark, " Virginia will be a
free State sooner than they expect. He has played his part
grandly, though the plot of the play is a poor one."

The work was well done. That much was clear when the body was taken down, put in the common pine coffin, and started on the long journey back to North Elba. The retinue of mourners moved over the mountain roads by which John Brown had first brought his family into that harsh country. On December 7 they buried him at the foot of the huge boulder which was to be his monument. A negro family of the neighborhood sang as the body was lowered into the winter earth. Back in the unfinished, draughty house Wendell Phillips had spoken the funeral address in his most expansive style. "History will date Virginia Emancipation from Harper's Ferry," he said. "True, the slave is still there. So, when the tempest uproots a pine on your hills, it looks green for months — a year or two. Still, it is timber, not a tree. John Brown has loosened the roots of the slave system; it only breathes, — it does not live, — hereafter."

In various cities throughout the North — Boston, Cleveland, New York, Philadelphia, Albany, — meetings were held. Garrison, Wendell Phillips, John A. Andrew, Emerson, and all the rest said what they had to say. Garrison, in the heat of the moment, commited himself; "as a peace man — an 'ultra' peace man — I am prepared to say: 'Success to every slave insurrection at the South, and in every slave country.' " " Marvellous old man! " said Phillips; he said that and a great deal more. John A. Andrew said: "whether the enterprise of John Brown and his associates in Virginia was wise or foolish, right or wrong; I only know that, whether the enterprise itself was the one or the other, John Brown himself is right." And Emerson, whose talent in such matters surpassed that of all his contemporaries, had already said; " the new saint awaiting his martyrdom, and who, if he shall suffer, will make the gallows glorious like the cross."

In some of the same cities where such things were said — in Boston, in New York — other meetings were held to protest against this sort of agitation which might rip the Union to its center. Eminent men presided and pled for sanity, for respect of law, for the Union. Speakers pointed out certain things about the Kansas career of John Brown — horse stealing and butchery. But John Brown had denied those things, and so Phillips and the others denied them; John Brown was many, many miles away, from Pottawatomie on the fatal night, and besides, John Brown was a mild man who did not like bloodshed. And because the Civil War was fought, and because there was an Emancipation Proclamation some years after the war began, the things said by eminent men in the protest meetings and in the newspapers were forgotten and the things said in the meetings of commemoration lived on. The tardy war measure of the Emancipation Proclamation, which came when the North had almost forgotten what it was fighting for or decided that it was not worth fighting for, defined John Brown and enshrined all the fine things said by Emerson and the rest. Lincoln, Seward, Stephen Douglas, Eli Thayer, Lawrence, Edward Everett, and Wilson expressed their feelings in vain. The argument in the North between these two general factions was, after all, not about John Brown; it was about two different methods of dealing with slavery and about the relative place of slavery in the National difficulties. John Brown was a cipher, a symbol, in this argument, which had so little concern one way or the other with what sort of a fellow he really was. The argument had been going on for a long time.

Now while John Brown wrote his letters and waited for the

time to pass, the gaudy militia paraded the streets of Charlestown, learning to keep in step and carry their muskets smartly
in preparation, as Hunter prophetically said, for coming
events. There were rumors even now of invasion; alarms
would be given, the troops would fall into rank, and the
cavalry would clatter out of town on some wild-goose chase.
Night after night mysterious fires from burning barns or
haystacks lighted up the sky, making the perturbed citizens
believe that the rescue attack had come at last. The fires were
never explained; perhaps the slaves did set them, as was
generally believed. But long before the day of execution the
people and the militia had grown skeptical about alarms, and
remained perfectly calm when some blood-curdling story was
brought in or when Colonel Lucius Davis had the bugles
sounded merely to test the alacrity of his men.

Many visitors were admitted to the cell to talk with John
Brown and have a look at the old man who was causing all
this excitement. The militiamen came in curious squads of
ten or fifteen, Henry Clay Pate came with his hurt pride,
Governor Wise and his politicians came to put their questions, strangers from the North came to confront the hostile
stare of the townspeople and express their sympathy for the
martyr, and ministers of the region came to pray with the condemned man and help him to salvation. The prisoner remained dignified and impressive, and most of the visitors left
his cell with a strange respect for his veracity and courage;
and John Brown's courage was worthy of any man's respect.
To the ministers John Brown was very direct; he " would
not insult God by bowing down in prayer with any one who
had the blood of slaves on his skirts." He wrote to a sympathizer in the North: " There are no ministers of Christ here.
These ministers who profess to be Christian, and hold slaves

or advocate slavery, I cannot abide them. My knees will not
bend in prayer with them, while their hands are stained with
the blood of souls."

John Brown found nothing but kindness at the hands of
his jailer, Captain Avis, who had been one of the leaders
against him at Harper's Ferry. The prison guards, the
sheriff, and various citizens likewise showed him marks of
consideration and generosity which he freely admitted in the
letters of his last month. " I am in charge of a jailer *like* the
one who took charge of ' Paul & Silas,' " he wrote to his
family during the trial; " & you may rest assured that both
kind hearts & kind faces are more or less about me; whilst
thousands are thirsting for my blood." On November 29,
John Brown inscribed his pocket Bible to a certain citizen of
Charlestown who had dressed his wounds. " There is no commentary in the world so good, in order to a right understanding of this blessed book, as an honest, childlike, and
teachable spirit." He marked those passages which, he said,
had most influenced his life. More than twenty years later, a
Virginia, or rather a West Virginia, clergyman, wrote to an
English author concerning those marked passages: " The
very copy of the Bible owned and used by him in jail here, lies
before me. Its passages touching ' oppression,' etc., are heavily and frequently pencilled, but no *pencil mark distin-
guishes or emphasizes a single passage that is distinctly
Christian.* He was *religious,* but not *Christian;* religion was
the crutch on which his fanaticism walked." The point, it
seems, must be granted to the Reverend Abner C. Hopkins.

But that Bible which gave vindication to crime, a crutch to
fanaticism, and consolation in suffering, was also a confes-
sional. During that time, while he waited for death, John
Brown denied again and again any complicity in the Pot-

JOHN BROWN ASCENDING SCAFFOLD
(From *Frank Leslie's Weekly*, December 10, 1859)

tawatomie massacre; the truth, he knew, would alienate the sympathy of hundreds of people to whom he was already the " new saint," and so he was taking his chances on meeting his God with the equivocation and lie still on his lips. But before that moment he marked a passage in *Exodus*, perhaps with the feeling of somehow washing his hands of the old blood-guilt: " And it came to pass in those days, when Moses was grown up, that he went out unto his brethren, and looked on their burdens: and he saw an Egyptian smiting an Hebrew, one of his brethren. And he looked this way and that way, and when he saw that there was no man, he smote the Egyptian, and hid him in the sand. And he went out the second day, and, behold, two men of the Hebrews strove together: and he said to him that did the wrong, Wherefore smitest thou thy fellow? And he said, Who made thee a prince and a judge over us? thinkest thou to kill me, as thou killedst the Egyptian? And Moses feared, and said, Surely the thing is known." That whole pitiful affair must then have risen to his mind with great clarity — the savage dogs leaping out of the shadow, the pleading women, the hacked bodies by the roadside and in the water of the stream, the thud of hoofs on the spring earth. Among his letters was one which purported to be from Mahala Doyle: " My son John Doyle whose life I beged of you is now grown up and is very desirous to be at Charlestown on the day of your execution, would certainly be there if his means would permit it that he might adjust the rope around your neck if Gov. Wise would permit it." In such a fashion her letter concluded.

On November 30, John Brown wrote the last letter to his family.

I am waiting the hour of my public *murder* with great composure of mind, & cheerfulness: feeling the strongest assurance

that in no other possible way could I be used to so much advance
the cause of God; & of humanity: and nothing that either I or
all my family have sacrifised or suffered: *will be lost*. The reflection that a *wise & merciful, as well as just & Holy God:* rules
not only the affairs of *this world;* but of all worlds; is a rock to
set our feet upon; under all circumstances: *even* those more
severely *trying ones:* into which our own follies; & rongs have
placed us. I have now no doubt but that our seeming *disaster:*
will ultimately result in the most *glorious success.* So my dear
shattered & broken family be of good cheer; & believe & trust in
God; *"with all your heart & with all your soul";* for ' *he* doeth
All thinks well." Do not feel ashamed on my acount; nor *for
one moment* despair of the cause; or grow *weary of well doing.*
I bless God; I never felt stronger confidence in the certain and
near approach of a *bright Morning;* & a *glorious day;* than I
have felt; & do now feel; since my confinement here. I am endeavoring to " return " like a " poor Prodigal " *as I am,* to my
Father: against whom I have *always* sined: *in the hope;* that he
may kindly, & forgivingly "meet me: though *a verry great
way off."*

And he urged them to study the Bible with a childlike, honest,
and teachable spirit, to learn by experience as soon as might
be whether it was of divine origin or not, to love the stranger
still, to be faithful unto death, and to " *Owe no man anything* but to love one another." This was his final admonition: " John Brown writes to his children to abhor with *un-
diing hatred,* also: that ' sum of all vilainies '; Slavery."

The next day Mary Day Brown sat beside a captain of
militia in the carriage when it took the Charlestown road
from the Ferry. Nine cavalrymen rode as a silent escort. Toward the end of the short winter afternoon she reached
Charlestown, and began the deferred interview with her
husband. For the most part their talk ran upon practical
matters dealing with what he had gathered from the wreck,
with the education of the younger children whom John

Brown wished to be "matter of fact women," and with the family economy. He showed her the will which Andrew Hunter had drawn for him and which, after these many years, assigned fifty dollars to the New England Woolen Mills. A lifetime of suffering had disciplined Mary Day Brown to endurance, and in this last grief it did not fail her. When the evening came and John Brown begged that she be allowed, in the face of the Governor's strict orders, to remain with him for the night, it was he who lost self-control and broke into a rage of protest. But this quickly passed, and they parted in great composure. Mary Day Brown drove back through the darkness to await the body which Governor Wise had decided should be delivered to her and not to the surgeons, and John Brown turned again to his letters of farewell. After a while, he slept.

On December 2, Longfellow made an entry in his diary: "This will be a great day in our history; the date of a new Revolution, — quite as much needed as the old one. Even now as I write, they are leading old John Brown to execution in Virginia for attempting to rescue slaves! This is sowing the wind to reap the whirlwind, which will come soon." Early that morning the prisoner was awake and reading his Bible. He wrote a last note of some three or four lines to his wife, enclosing a codicil to his will and the epitaphs of his dead sons and himself which he wished chiseled on the old tombstone of his grandfather John. The guard came and escorted him to say good-bye to Stevens and the others, whose time had not yet come. He had no word for Hazlett, whose presence at the Ferry was not yet legally established and who still held some faint hope of escape on that ground. To Cook, whose harmless confession he considered treachery, John Brown gave no blessing but a reproach: "You have made false state-

ments, — that I sent you to Harper's Ferry." For a moment
Cook dropped his head and said nothing; one cannot debate
with a friend on the way to his death. At length he replied;
" Captain Brown, you and I remember differently." That
was all. As John Brown left the jail he handed a piece of
paper to one of the attendants:

Charlestown, Va, 2nd, December, 1859.
I John Brown am now quite *certain* that the crimes of this
guilty land: will never be purged *away;* but with Blood. I had
as I now think: vainly flattered myself that without *very much*
bloodshed; it might be done.

They led him out to the porch of the jail. A common wagon
with a team of white horses waited in the roadway; before it
three companies of infantry held their regular files. Farther
on he could see company after company swinging into forma-
tion. " I had no idea that Governor Wise considered my execution so important," he said, as if he did not know that for
weeks the town had been full of troops. He climbed into the
wagon and seated himself on the coffin. The escort received
the order of march, and the driver spoke to his horses.

On a low rounded knoll stood the scaffold, and around it
the fifteen hundred troops were massed in a great hollow
square. Cannon were trained on the scaffold. From the ranks
of one of the companies the son of Governor Wise watched
his father's decision being fulfilled, and in Company " F " of
Richmond another militiaman held his musket and waited.
The militiaman was John Wilkes Booth. Behind the scaffold could be seen the red and grey uniforms of the Virginia
Military Institute cadets, and at their head stood a bearded,
preoccupied man, who would be known before long as " Stonewall " Jackson. He had prayed that John Brown might be
spared, and now, in the fulfillment of his duty, he witnessed

EXECUTION OF JOHN BROWN

(Charlestown, Virginia, December 17, 1859)

the rejection of his prayer. A clear noon sun shone on the varied uniforms of the militia and on the broken fields and woods which stretched away to the misty Blue Ridge, at whose base the long curve of the Shenandoah swept down to the Ferry. The wagon drew into the square of troops on the high field. " This is a beautiful country," said John Brown. " I never had the pleasure of seeing it before."

He mounted the scaffold before his attendants and the officials, and stood there for a moment in his loose-fitting old clothes and carpet slippers, while the others followed him. Lifting his loosely bound hands he took off his hat and dropped it to the rough planking of the floor; the hood was lowered and the rope adjusted to his neck. " I can't see, gentlemen; you must lead me." They placed him on the drop and all was ready. In silence the troops of the escort deployed back to their prearranged stations. The sheriff asked John Brown if he wished a private signal just before the end. " It does not matter to me," he answered in an unnaturally composed, deliberate voice, " if only they would not keep me waiting so long." At last the manœuvre was concluded. The sheriff's hatchet flashed in its downward stroke to release the trap. The rope spun through, jerked heavily with the weight below, and vibrated for a moment. Over the entire field — the cluster of officials, the officers sitting their horses, the steady ranks of militia — there was no sound. Distinctly, calmly, impersonally, came the voice of Colonel Preston; " So perish all such enemies of Virginia! All such enemies of the Union! All such foes of the human race! "

BIBLIOGRAPHICAL NOTE

A Matter of Opinions

A SHORT while after the butchery on Pottawatomie Creek, the " Union-splitter " and hopeful revolution-maker, James Redpath, came to the secret camp by the fallen oak, where John Brown curtly replied to this inquisitive guest: " I shall, as captain, communicate whatever is proper about the conduct and intentions of this company." In his *Public Life of Captain John Brown,* which appeared in 1860, the " Union-splitter " continued his chosen profession and communicated precisely what was proper concerning the public life and private character of his hero. Among a number of other things which his delicate sense of propriety forbade him to communicate was John Brown's complicity in the Pottawatomie massacre. The Civil War, which confounded so many problems and clarified so few, followed close on the heels of Redpath's book to supplement the confusion which he had already contributed to this particular problem of John Brown's life.

The faithful Sanborn, who had listened in vain " for a clear and certain call " to go to Harper's Ferry and get shot or hanged, rendered a far more valuable service to his master, when he published, in 1885, *The Life and Letters of John Brown.* By this time James Townsley had made his confession concerning Pottawatomie and thus rendered futile the denials and studied silences of John Brown's surviving sons and confederates. When Sanborn recovered from the considerable shock of the confession, he, like the sons and confederates, began a program of elaborate and often contradictory rationalizations. Indeed, nothing else was to be expected from the Brown family, and nothing else was to be expected from Sanborn, for a renunciation of John Brown would have been almost equivalent to a renunciation of himself. And so he prepared, one after the other, his instructive *mémoires justificatives*.

Charles Robinson was of stouter stuff; when he learned the truth, or rather a part of the truth, he was honest enough to eat a good many of his own fine words about the value of John Brown's public services. But Robinson's estimate was political in its emphasis and dealt primarily with the matter of " public services "; to him John Brown was simply an unscrupulous " Union-splitter " who was willing to cut any throat, innocent or guilty, for the good reason of precipitating civil war. Robinson did not further investigate the trail of purpose which led through the valley of Pottawatomie to the Charlestown gibbet, and Sanborn by a process of suppression, distortion, metaphysics, and rhetoric did what he could to completely obscure all tracks. To Sanborn, Hinton, and the rest of the old guard, Governor Charles Robinson was a heretic, traitor, and worse. But there were a few other heretics: among them was Eli Thayer himself.

With professions of impartiality and the methods of scholarship, Oswald Garrison Villard presented his impressive work to the world. *John Brown: A Biography Fifty Years After*, made all other books on the subject which had appeared before 1910, seem as mere trifling with the matter. It offered a great mass of new material, disposed of many legends, and settled a number of debated points for good and all. " But to Salmon Brown and Henry Thompson," Mr. Villard remarks in his preface, " is due the writer's ability to record for the first time the exact facts as to the happenings on the Pottawatomie, and the author is also particularly indebted to Jason Brown, Miss Sarah Brown, Mrs. Annie Brown Adams, and Mrs. John Brown,

Jr." Thus Mr. Villard states his authorities, not only for the "exact facts as to the happenings on the Pottawatomie," but also for a good many other exact facts. Unhappily, some people have felt that the Brown boys and such decidedly interested witnesses and actors are not the proper authorities for a disinterested estimate. In some matters Mr. Villard's reasoning runs somewhat like that of another biographer, R. J. Hinton, who wrote: " Brown told me he was not a participator in the Pottawatomie homicide. John Brown was incapable of uttering a falsehood." By way of example it may be pointed out that Mr. Villard discredits Townsley's testimony on the basis of a confusion of the name of Watson Brown, who was at North Elba in May, 1856, with that of one of the other sons who walked into the Pottawatomie valley and rode out. But this particular error is as nothing when weighed against the self-interest, contradictions, and proven dishonesty involved in the various statements of Mr. Villard's chosen authorities for some points. An invaluable service has been performed in presenting these statements, but they should be judged only in the complete context of all available evidence; the *murderers themselves* are on the stand. It is safer, for instance, to believe Townsley's testimony that John Brown began the bloody business by shooting old Doyle than it is to believe John Brown's own statement that he killed no man except, perhaps, in fair fight, or to believe Salmon's equivocations concerning this particular affair. The same principle holds true in the general consideration of evidence.

After Townsley let the cat out of the bag, the sons substituted evasions and justification for their previous denials, and they succeeded so well that the public attention, as one more downright critic once indicated, has been directed to the murders and not to the motives which prompted them. Mr. Villard has a great deal to say about the murders, which, of course, he does not attempt to justify, but he has very little to say about the theft of murdered men's horses, which, one feels sure, he would not attempt to justify. But he has described in considerable detail John Brown's later and more ambitious ventures in raiding and rustling through Kansas and has explained them as unselfishness put on a war basis. The question, however, is something like this: what did John Brown intend to do with the cattle and other profits which were snatched from him by the untimely battle of Ossawatomie? Were they to go back to Free State settlers from whom, we are told, they had been first stolen by pro-slavery people? Even the Covenant made no professions of such extravagant philanthropy.

Concerning the question of motive behind Pottawatomie, Mr. Villard makes a remark which would sum up equally well his attitude toward the complete history of the desperate and unscrupulous career in Kansas: " And always it must not be forgotten that his motives were wholly unselfish, and that his aims were none other than the freeing of a race." This attitude is but a projection of the treatment of John Brown's earlier business life, which, in the end, is quite as instructive as the episodes of throat-cutting and cattle-lifting. Mr. Villard has prepared an important, detailed account of John Brown's business affairs, and deduces from that record of embezzlement, fraud, speculation, and self-righteousness that he was an ingenuous, honest man who simply made a few mistakes because he owned a poor head for business. In other words, it might be concluded — not too facetiously — that it took five murders to shock Mr. Villard into admitting that John Brown had no " true respect for the laws."

Probably the most interesting aspect of *A Biography Fifty Years After* is the author's treatment of the Virginia climax. His premise is that John Brown contemplated nothing more than a series of slave stampedes somewhat like the program laid down in Hugh Forbes' " Well Matured Plan." In such case the Harper's Ferry attack was only a badly planned and badly executed "raid," and the Provisional Government was, as the defense at Charlestown maintained, a harmless debating society. But John Brown knew well enough that a "raid" without insurrection would be a flash in the pan, just as he knew that an insurrection, unaccompanied by a general sectional crisis, would end in failure. In the light of his convictions and intentions the movements at Harper's Ferry were satisfactorily executed. He did not err in a small way, but in his larger estimate of the national political situation and in his estimate of the attitude of the slaves. If he had not made the first error he would never have contrived the Provisional Government and planned the conquest; if he had not made the second he would have begun the conquest differently by showing the slaves "how one thing might be done as well as another."

Mr. Villard's treatment of John Brown's Kansas life and his intentions in Virginia has been subjected to an analysis of remorseless ingenuity by Hill Peebles Wilson in *John Brown: Soldier of Fortune.* If Mr. Villard is by far the ablest and most scrupulous spokesman of the defense, Mr. Wilson is the most acrimonious, the most downright, and the soundest prosecutor. Like his predecessor, Governor Robinson, Mr. Wilson found himself betrayed by his erstwhile hero, and his *Critique* owes much to the Governor's work on the subject. But contrary to Robinson's estimate he discredits the political interests as a motive and considers Abolitionism as a mere pretext which John Brown used to cover his brigandage in Kansas and exploited to organize his last great speculation of the conquest of the South. He defines John Brown as a figure who "will rank among adventurers as Napoleon ranks among marshals; as Captain Kidd among pirates; and as Jonathan Wild among thieves."

In a reaction from the "complex character" discussed by Mr. Villard and the others, Mr. Wilson has proceeded to the contrary extreme of brutal simplicity and self-explanatory consistency in the picture of John Brown. This has apparently led the writer to overlook certain aspects of the problem. For instance, he dates John Brown's intention to meddle directly with slavery in 1857, holding that the idea of the conquest first took shape then; but Frederick Douglass' connections with Brown, the *Ramshorn* journalism, and the Gileadites give a certain amount of evidence to the contrary which cannot be easily put aside.

This attempt on the part of Mr. Wilson to establish as legalistic and formal consistency obscures a more essential consistency in John Brown's character as well as certain matters of fact. John Brown is interpreted as an absolutely self-conscious hypocrite — the sort of man who would be more admirable than John Brown from one point of view and less effective from any point of view. In other words, Mr. Wilson neglects, just as does Mr. Villard, one of the most significant keys to John Brown's career and character; his elaborate psychological mechanism for justification which appeared regularly in terms of the thing which friends called Puritanism and enemies called fanaticism. For instance, Mr. Wilson accounts for John Brown's attitude toward his trial, the projects of escape, and the execution on the basis of a profound disillusionment; he still exploited his situation in order to provide for his family, but, after playing to the extreme limit of his resources and losing, he himself had no further interest in life. This is a dramatic and perhaps a plausible interpretation, but somehow it does not lie quite true with the rest of the story.

If that last month in prison can be fully understood then John Brown is understood, for though he now wielded the "sword of the Spirit" he was still the same man who shot the fine sheepdog, embezzled the money of the Woolen Mills, slaughtered and stole in Kansas, organized the Provisional Government, and said to Colonel Washington, "your life is worth as much as mine." But that last month can only be understood in terms of the many earlier years of struggle, brooding, vicissitude, and prayer. Such an understanding is the final aim of this book.

Any reader interested in John Brown's career is indebted to Mr. Villard for the indispensable service of preparing a comprehensive bibliography. *John Brown: A Biography Fifty Years After* was published in 1910 and by consequence there are certain additions. It is hoped that the following list will provide some modest supplementary items to that work already so thoroughly done. Otherwise, this list is simply intended as a guide to the more important materials and is intended neither as a complete bibliography of the subject nor as a complete statement of the sources for the present book.

Books Dealing Only with John Brown

PATE, HENRY CLAY. *John Brown as Viewed by H. Clay Pate.* New York: the Author. 1859.

REDPATH, JAMES. *The Public Life of Captain John Brown.* Boston: Thayer and Eldridge. 1860.

WEBB, RICHARD D. *Life and Letters of Captain John Brown.* London: Smith Elder & Co. 1861.

SANFORD, F. B. *Memoirs of John Brown,* written for the Rev. Samuel Orcutt's History of Torrington, Conn. — with Memorial Verses, by William Ellery Channing. Concord, Massachusetts. 1878.

BROWN, G. W. *Reminiscences of Old John Brown.* Rockford, Ill. Abraham E. Smith. 1880.

SANBORN, F. B. *The Life and Letters of John Brown.* Boston: Roberts Bros. 1885.

VON HOLST, HERMANN. *John Brown.* Edited by F. P. Stearns. Boston: Cupples and Hurd. 1889.

WILLIAMS, EDWARD W. *The Views and Meditations of John Brown.* Washington: the Author. 1893.

JOHN BROWN

HINTON RICHARD J. *John Brown and His Men.* With some
Account of the Roads they Travelled to Reach Harper's
Ferry. New York: Funk & Wagnalls. 1894.

CHAMBERLIN, JOSEPH EDGAR. *John Brown.* Boston: Small,
Maynard & Co. 1899.

CONNELLEY, WILLIAM ELSEY. *John Brown.* Topeka, Kansas:
Crane & Co. 1900.

NEWTON, JOHN. *Captain John Brown of Harper's Ferry.*
London: T. Fisher Unwin. 1902.

AVEY, ELIJAH. *The Capture and Execution of John Brown.*
A Tale of Martyrdom. Elgin, Ill.: the Author.

WINKLEY, J. W. *John Brown the Hero.* Boston: James K.
West Co. 1905.

HILL, FREDERICK TREVOR. *Decisive Battles of the Law.* New
York: Harper and Brothers. 1906.

DU BOIS, W. E. B. *John Brown.* Philadelphia: George W. Jacobs
& Co. 1909.

VILLARD, OSWALD GARRISON. *John Brown,* 1800-1859. A
Biography Fifty Years After. Boston and New York:
Houghton Mifflin Co. 1910.

WILSON, HILL PEEBLES. *John Brown: Soldier of Fortune.* A
Critique. Lawrence, Kansas: the Author. 1913.

BRADFORD, GAMALIEL. *Damaged Souls.* Boston and New York:
Houghton Mifflin Co. 1923.

Books Related to John Brown

ANDERSON, OSBORN P. *A Voice from Harper's Ferry.* Boston:
the Author. 1861.

ANDREAS, A. T. *History of the State of Kansas.* Chicago. 1883.

Anti-Abolition Tract, No. 3. "The Abolition Conspiracy to
Destroy the Union." New York: Van Evrie, Horton & Co.
1863.

Anti-Slavery History of the John Brown Year, being the

BIBLIOGRAPHICAL NOTE

Twenty-Seventh Annual Report of the American Anti-Slavery Society. New York: American Anti-Slavery Society. 1861.

Anti-Slavery Tract, No. 7, New Series. " Testimonies of Capt. John Brown at Harper's Ferry." New York: American Anti-Slavery Society. 1860.

ATCHISON, D. R., RUSSELL, WILLIAM H., ANDERSON, JOS. C., BOONE, A. G., STRINGFELLOW, B. F., BUFORD, J. " The Voice of Kansas. Let the South Respond." *De Bow's Commercial Review.* August, 1856.

BAILEY, JUDGE L. D. " Border Ruffian Troubles in Kansas." Some Newspaper Articles written for the *Garden City Sentinel* and *Kansas Cultivator.* Edited by Charles R. Green. Lyndon, Kansas. 1899.

BANCROFT, FREDERICK. *Life of William H. Seward.* New York: Harper and Brothers. 1900.

BARKER, JOSEPH. *Slavery and Civil War, or the Harper's Ferry Insurrection.* With a Review of Discourses on the Subject by Rev. W. H. Furness, Hon. J. R. Giddings, and Wendell Phillips, Esqre., Philadelphia.

BLACKMAR, F. W. *The Life of Charles Robinson, the First State Governor of Kansas.* Topeka: Crane & Co. 1902.

BOTTS, J. M. *The Great Rebellion.* New York: Harper & Brothers. 1866.

BRADFORD, SARAH H. *Harriet Tubman, the Moses of Her People.* New York: J. J. Little & Co. 1901.

BRANDT, ISAAC. *History of John Brown.* Des Moines: Watters-Talbott Printing Co. 1895.

BREWERTON, G. D. *The War in Kansas.* New York: Derby and Jackson. 1856.

BROWN, G. W. *False Claims of Kansas Historians Truthfully Corrected.* Rockford, Ill.: the Author. 1902.

Brown, Capt. John, the Life, Trial, and Conviction of. New York: Robert M. DeWitt. 1859.

JOHN BROWN

BROWN, SPENCER KELLOGG. *His Life in Kansas and his Death as a Spy, 1842–1863, as disclosed in his diary.* Edited by George Gardner Smith. New York: D. Appleton & Co. 1903.

BRYANT, WILLIAM CULLEN and GAY, SYDNEY HOWARD. *A Popular History of the United States.* New York: Charles Scribner's Sons. 1883.

BURGESS, JOHN WILLIAM. *Civil War and the Constitution, 1859–1865.* New York: Charles Scribner's Sons. 1901.

BURGESS, JOHN WILLIAM. *The Middle Period, 1817–1858.* New York: Charles Scribner's Sons. 1897.

CHADWICK, F. E. *Causes of the Civil War.* New York and London: Harper and Brothers. 1906.

CHADWICK, J. W. *Theodore Parker, Preacher and Reformer.* Boston: Houghton Mifflin Co. 1900.

CHANNING, EDWARD. *A History of the United States,* Vol. VI. New York: Macmillan Co. 1925.

CHESTNUT, C. W. *Frederick Douglass.* Boston: Beacon Biographies. 1899.

CHILD, LYDIA MARIA. *Letters.* Boston: Houghton Mifflin Co. 1883.

CONNELLEY, WILLIAM ELSEY. *An Appeal to the Record.* Topeka, Kansas: the Author.

CONNELLEY, WILLIAM ELSEY. *James Henry Lane.* Topeka, Kansas: Crane & Co. 1899.

CONWAY, MONCURE D. *Autobiography, Memories and Experiences.* Boston: Houghton Mifflin Co. 1904.

Cook, John E., Confessions of, Brother-in-Law of Governor A. P. Willard, of Indiana, Published for the Benefit of Samuel C. Young, a Non-Slave-holder, who is Permanently Disabled by a Wound Received in Defense of Southern Institutions. Charlestown: D. Smith Fichelberger. 1859.

Bibliographical Note

CURTIS, GEORGE TICHNOR. *Life of James Buchanan.* New York: 1883.

DABNEY, R. L., D.D. *Life and Campaign of Lieutenant-General Thomas J. Jackson.* New York: Blelock and Co. 1866.

DAVIS, JEFFERSON. *Rise and Fall of the Confederate Government.* New York: D. Appleton & Co. 1881.

DAVIS, MRS. VARINA JEFFERSON. *Jefferson Davis, Ex-President of the Confederate States:* A Memoir. New York: 1890.

DODD, W. E. *The Cotton Kingdom.*

DODD, W. E. *Jefferson Davis.* Philadelphia: 1907.

DODD, W. E. *Statesmen of the Old South.* New York: Macmillan Co. 1921.

Douglass, Frederick, Life and Times. Hartford: Park Publishing Co. 1882.

Doy, John, of Lawrence, Kansas, Narrative of. New York: Thomas Halman. 1860.

ELSON, WILLIAM HENRY. *History of the United States of America.* New York: Macmillan Co. 1904.

Fanaticism and Its Results: Facts versus *Fancies.* By a Southerner. Baltimore: Joseph Robinson. 1860.

FOWLER, WILLIAM C. *The Sectional Controversy.* New York. 1862.

FROTHINGHAM, O. B. *Theodore Parker: a Biography.* Boston: J. R. Osgood & Co. 1874.

FROTHINGHAM, O. B. *Gerrit Smith.* New York: G. P. Putnam's Sons. 1878.

GARRISON, F. J. and W. P. *William Lloyd Garrison: the Story of His Life told by His Children.* New York: Century Company. 1885–1889.

GIHON, JOHN H. *Geary and Kansas.* Philadelphia: J. H. C. Whiting. 1857.

GLADSTONE, THOMAS H. *Kansas: or Squatter Life and Border Warfare in the Far West.* London: G. Routledge & Co. 1857.

GREELEY, HORACE. *The American Conflict.* Hartford: O. D. Case & Co. 1866.

GREELEY, HORACE. *Recollections of a Busy Life.* New York. 1868.

GRIMKE, A. H. *William Lloyd Garrison the Abolitionist.* New York. 1891.

GRINNEL, J. B. *Men and Events of Forty Years.* Boston: D. Lathrop Company. 1891.

GUE, B. F. *History of Iowa.* New York: Century History Co. 1903.

HART, ALBERT BUSHNELL. *Salmon P. Chase.* Boston: Houghton Mifflin Co. 1899.

HELPER, HINTON, ROWAN. *The Impending Crisis of the South: How to Meet it.* New York: A. B. Burdick. 1860.

HENDERSON, G. F. R. *Stonewall Jackson.* London: Longmans. 1898.

HIGGINSON, THOMAS WENTWORTH. *Cheerful Yesterdays.* Boston: Houghton Mifflin Co. 1898.

HIGGINSON, THOMAS WENTWORTH. *Contemporaries.* Boston: Houghton Mifflin Co. 1899.

HINTON, RICHARD J. *Rebel Invasion of Missouri and Kansas.* Chicago: Church and Goodman. 1865.

HOLLAND, FREDERICK MAY. *Frederick Douglass, the Colored Orator.* New York: Funk and Wagnalls. 1891.

HOLLIS, CHRISTOPHER. *The American Heresy.*

HOLLOWAY, J. N. *History of Kansas.* LaFayette, Ind.: James Emmons & Co. 1868.

HOVENDEN, THOMAS. *Last Moments of John Brown.* Painted by Thomas Hovenden, M.A., 1884. Etched by Thomas Hovenden, M.A., 1885. (Sketch of the subject of the painting, and opinions of the press concerning the painting.) Philadelphia: G. Gebbie. 1885.

Howard Report. "Report of the Special Committee appointed to Investigate the Troubles in Kansas." 34th Congress,

1st Session. Report No. 200. Washington: Cornelius Wendell. 1856.

HOWE, JULIA WARD. *Reminiscences.* Boston: Houghton Mifflin Co. 1899.

Howe, Samuel Gridley, Letters and Journal. Edited by his daughter, Laura E. Richards. Boston: Dana Estes & Co. 1908–1909.

HUGUES, THOMAS. *A Sketch of the History of the United States,* by J. M. Ludlow, to which is added " The Struggle for Kansas," by Thomas Hughes. London: Macmillan & Co. 1862.

HUME, J. F. *The Abolitionists.* New York: G. P. Putnam's Sons. 1905.

HUNT, GAILLARD. *John C. Calhoun.* Philadelphia. 1908.

Insurrection at Harper's Ferry, and a Faithful History of Know Nothingism and Black Republicanism and Their Proposed Union under the Irrepressible Conflict Doctrine of Seward and His Allies, North and South. Baltimore. 1859.

JACKSON, MARY ANNA. *Life and Letters of Thomas J. Jackson.* By his wife. New York: Harper and Brothers. 1892.

Jackson, Stonewall, Memoirs of. By his widow, Mary Anna Jackson. Louisville: The Prentice Press. 1895.

JONES, WILLIAM. *General Robert E. Lee — Soldier and Man, Life and Letters of,* New York: Neale Publishing Co. 1906.

" Kansas — Report of Commissioners of Kansas Territory." Printed in *Reports of Committees of House of Representatives,* 36th Congress, 2d Session. Part 1, Vols. 2 and 3. March 2, 1861. Washington. 1861.

Kansas State Historical Society Publications and Collections. Ten vols.

" Kansas." *U. S. Biographical Dictionary, Kansas Volume.* Chicago and Kansas City: S. Lewis & Co. 1879.

John Brown

Lane, Samuel A. *Fifty Years and Over of Akron and Summit County*. Akron: Beacon Job Department. 1892.

Lawrence, Amos A., Life of. By his son, William Lawrence. Boston: Houghton Mifflin Co. 1888.

Lee, General Robert E.; Recollections and Letters of. By his son, Captain Robert E. Lee. New York: Doubleday, Page & Co. 1904.

Leech, Rev. Samuel Vanderlip. *The Raid of John Brown at Harper's Ferry as I Saw It*. Washington: Published by the Author. 1909.

Lincoln, Abraham, Speeches of. L. E. Chittenden, compiler. New York: Dodd Mead & Co. 1895.

Longfellow, Henry Wadsworth, Life of. Edited by Samuel Longfellow. Boston: Houghton, Mifflin & Co. 1891.

Longfellow, Samuel, Memoir and Letters of. Edited by Joseph May. Boston: Houghton Mifflin Co. 1894.

Lothrop, T. K. *William H. Seward*. Boston: Houghton Mifflin Co. 1895.

Martyn, Carlos. *Wendell Phillips, the Agitator*. New York: Funk and Wagnalls. 1890. *Mason Report*. "Report of the Select Committee of the Senate appointed to inquire into the late invasion and seizure of the public property at Harper's Ferry." Rep. Com. No. 278, 36th Congress, 1st Session.

May, Samuel J. *Some Recollections of our Anti-Slavery Conflict*. Boston: Fields, Osgood & Co. 1869.

McClellan, H. B. *Life and Campaigns of J. E. B. Stuart*. Boston: Houghton Mifflin Co. 1885.

McDougall, G. M. *Fugitive Slaves*. Boston: Ginn & Co. 1898.

Merriam, George S. *The Negro and the Nation*. New York: Henry Holt & Co. 1906.

Mott, James and Lucretia, Life and Letters of. Edited by Anna Davis Hallowell. Boston: Houghton Mifflin Co. 1884.

Morison, S. E. *The Oxford History of the United States*.

BIBLIOGRAPHICAL NOTE

London: Humphrey Milford. Oxford University Press. 1927.

NICOLAY, JOHN G. and JOHN HAY. *Abraham Lincoln*. New York: The Century Co. 1890.

NICOLAY, J. G. *Outbreak of the Rebellion*. New York: Charles Scribner's Sons. 1881.

Ohio, History of Portage County. Chicago: Warner, Beers & Co. 1885.

Ohio, History of Summit County. Chicago: Baskin & Battey. 1881.

ORCUTT, REV. SAMUEL. *History of Torrington, Connecticut*. Albany: S. Munsell. 1878.

PEARSON, HENRY GREENLEAF. *The Life of John A. Andrew*. Boston: Houghton Mifflin Co. 1904.

PHILLIPS, WENDELL. *Speeches, Lectures and Letters*. Boston: James Redpath. 1863.

PHILLIPS, WENDELL. *Speeches, Lectures and Letters*. Second Series. Lee and Shepard. 1891.

PHILLIPS, WILLIAM A. *The Conquest of Kansas by Missouri and Her Allies*. Boston: Phillips, Sampson & Co. 1856

PIERCE, EDWARD L. *Correspondence of Charles Sumner. Memoirs and Letters of*. Boston: 1877.

POLLARD, E. A. *Life of Jefferson Davis*. Philadelphia: 1891.

REALF, RICHARD. *Richard Realf's Free-State Poems*. Edited by Col. Richard J. Hinton. Topeka: Crane & Co. 1900.

REALF, RICHARD. *Poems — with a Memoir by Richard J. Hinton*. New York: Funk and Wagnalls Co. 1898.

REDPATH, JAMES. *Echoes of Harper's Ferry*. Boston: Thayer & Eldridge. 1860.

REID, WHITELAW. *A Memorial of Horace Greeley*. New York: 1873.

RHODES, JAMES FORD. *History of the United States*. New York: Macmillan Co. 1904.

ROBINSON, CHARLES. *The Kansas Convict*. Lawrence, Kansas: Journal Publishing Co. 1898.

ROBINSON, SARA T. L. *Kansas: Its Interior and Exterior Life*. Boston: Crosby, Nichols & Co. 1856.

ROBLEY, T. F. *History of Bourbon County, Kansas, to the Close of 1865*. Fort Scott, Kansas: Published by the Author. 1894.

ROOSEVELT, THEODORE. *Life of Thomas Hart Benton*. Boston: 1887.

ROPES, HANNAH ANDERSON. *Six Months in Kansas, by a Lady*. Boston: John P. Jewett & Co. 1856.

SANBORN, F. B. *The Philanthropist, Dr. S. G. Howe*. New York: Funk & Wagnalls. 1891.

SANBORN, F. B. *Recollections of Seventy Years*. Boston: Richard G. Badger. 1909.

SEWARD, WILLIAM H. *His Works*. Edited by George E. Baker. Boston: Houghton Mifflin Co. 1884.

SIEBERT, W. H. *The Underground Railroad*. New York: Macmillan Co. 1898.

SMITH, GOLDWIN. *The Moral Crusader: a Biographical Essay on William Lloyd Garrison*. New York. 1892.

SMITH, H. A. *One Hundred Famous Americans*. New York: George Routledge & Sons. 1886.

SMITH, T. C. *Parties and Slavery — 1850–'59*. Harper and Brothers. 1906.

SPEER, JOHN. *Life of Gen. James H. Lane*. Garden City, Kansas: John Speer, Printer. 1897.

SPRING, LEVERETT W. *Kansas, the Prelude to the War for the Union*. Boston: Houghton Mifflin Co. 1885.

STEARNS, FRANK PRESTON. *The Life and Public Services of George Luther Stearns*. Philadelphia: J. B. Lippincott Co. 1907.

STILL, WILLIAM. *Underground Railroad*. Philadelphia: Porter. 1872.

BIBLIOGRAPHICAL NOTE

THAYER, ELI. *A History of the Kansas Crusade.* New York: Harper and Brothers. 1889.

Three Years on the Kansas Border, by a Clergyman. New York and Auburn: Miller, Orton & Mulligan. 1856.

Trials; Remarkable Trials of all Countries, with the Evidence and Speeches of Counsel. New York: S. S. Peloubet & Co. 1882.

TURNER, FREDERICK JACKSON. *The Frontier in American History.* New York: Henry Holt & Co. 1920.

VALLANDIGHAM, CLEMENT LAIRD. *Speeches, Arguments, Addresses and Letters.* New York: J. Walter & Co. 1864.

VILLARD, OSWALD GARRISON. *William Lloyd Garrison.*

VICTOR, ORVILLE JAMES. *History of American Conspiracies.* New York: James D. Torrey. 1863.

Virginia State Papers. Address of the Hon. C. G. Memminger, Special Commissioner from the State of South Carolina, before the Assembled Authorities of the State of Virginia. Doc. No. LVII.

Virginia State Papers. Calendar of Virginia State Papers, Vol. II.

Virginia State Papers. Court of Appeals of Virginia. " Commonwealth *vs.* Brown." Richmond. 1859.

Virginia State Papers. Document No. 1. Appendix to Message 1. Documents Relative to the Harper's Ferry Invasion. Richmond.

War of the Rebellion. Official Records of the Union and Confederate Armies.

War, Sec. of. Official Report for 1856. Exec. Doc. No. 1, 34th Congress, 3d Session, House of Representatives.

WARDEN, R. B. *Voter's Version of the Life and Character of Stephen A. Douglas.* Columbus, O. 1860.

WASHINGTON, B. T. *Frederick Douglass.* Philadelphia and London: G. W. Jacobs Co. 1907.

JOHN BROWN

WIGHAM, ELIZA. *The Anti-Slavery Cause in America and Its Martyrs.* London. 1863.

WILDER, D. W. *The Annals of Kansas.* Topeka, Kansas: George W. Martin. 1875.

WILLIAMS, GEORGE W. *History of the Negro Race in America from 1690–1880.* New York: G. Putnam's Sons. 1883.

WILSON, H. *History of the Rise and Fall of the Slave Power in America.* Boston and New York: Houghton Mifflin Co. Cambridge: The Riverside Press. 1872.

WILSON, HENRY. " State of Affairs in Kansas." Speech of Henry Wilson in the Senate, February 18, 1856. Washington: Republican Association of the District of Columbia. 1856.

WISE, BARTON H. *Henry A. Wise of Virginia.* New York: Macmillan Co. 1899.

WISE, HENRY A. *Seven Decades of the Union.* Philadelphia: J. B. Lippincott & Co. 1872.

WISE, JOHN S. *The End of an Era.* Boston: Houghton Mifflin Co. 1899.

ZITTLE, CAPT. JOHN H. *A Correct History of the John Brown Invasion.* Edited and published by his widow. Hagerstown, Maryland. 1905.

Articles

ALLABEN, A. E. " John Brown as a Popular Hero." *Magazine of Western History.* November, 1893.

APPLETON, W. S. " John Brown and the Destruction of Slavery." *Massachusetts Historical Society Proceedings.* Series II. Vol. 14. 1901.

BACON, LEONARD WOOLSEY. " John Brown." (Review of Sanborn's *Life and Letters of John Brown.*) *New Englander and Yale Review.* April, 1886.

BOTELER, A. R. " Recollections of the John Brown Raid, with comment by F. B. Sanborn." *Century.* July, 1883.

Bibliographical Note

Bowman, George E. "Peter Browne's Children." *The Mayflower Descendant*. January, 1902.

Bowman, George E. "The Settlement of Peter Browne's Estate." *The Mayflower Descendant*. January, 1903.

Brown, John. Letters: Found in the Virginia State Library in 1901. *Virginia Magazine of History and Biography*. Vols. IX–XI. 1901–1903.

Brown, Justin, Newton. "Lovejoy's Influence on John Brown." *The Magazine of History*. September–October, 1916.

"Brown, Owen. A Letter." *Atlantic Monthly*. July, 1874.

Caskie, George E. "Trial of John Brown." *American Law Review*. May–June, 1910.

Cooke, G. W. "Brown and Garrison." *American*. Vol. II. October, 1885–April, 1886.

Cotterell, George. "Sanborn's Life and Letters of John Brown. Brown's Character Estimated." *The Academy*, London. February, 1886.

Daingerfield, John E. P. "John Brown at Harper's Ferry." *Century*, June, 1885.

Dana, Richard Henry, Jr. "How We Met John Brown." *Atlantic Monthly*. July, 1871.

Day, W. G. "John Brown's Invasion of Virginia." *Southern Magazine*. October, 1873.

Featherstonhaugh, Thomas. "Bibliography of John Brown." Baltimore: the Friedenwald Company. 1897. Reprint from Publications of the Southern History Association. July, 1897.

Featherstonhaugh, Thomas. "John Brown's Men — with a supplementary Bibliography of John Brown." Harrisburg, Pa.: Harrisburg Publishing Company. 1899. Reprint from Publications of Southern History Association. October, 1899.

JOHN BROWN

FLEMING, WALTER L. "The Buford Expedition to Kansas." *American Historical Review*. October, 1900.

GREEN, ISRAEL. "The Capture of John Brown." *North American Review*. December, 1885.

GRIFFIS, REV. WILLIAM ELIOT. "Refutation of Several Romances about the Execution of John Brown." *Southern Historical Society Papers*, Vol. 13. Richmond. 1885.

GUE, B. F. "John Brown and His Iowa Friends." *Midland Monthly*. February and March, 1897.

HARRIS, RANSOM LANGDON. "John Brown and His Followers in Iowa." *Midland Monthly*. October, 1894.

HINTON, RICHARD J. "John Brown and His Men." *Frank Leslie's Popular Magazine*. 1889.

HINTON, RICHARD J. "Old John Brown and the Men of Harper's Ferry." *Time*. London. July, 1890.

HUHNER, LEON. "Some Jewish Associates of John Brown." *Magazine of History*. September and October, 1908.

HUNTER, ANDREW. "John Brown's Raid." *New Orleans Times-Democrat*. September 5, 1887.

JENKS, LELAND H. "The John Brown Myth." *American Mercury*. March, 1924.

KEELER, RALPH. "Owen Brown's Escape from Harper's Ferry." *Atlantic Monthly*. March, 1874.

KIMBALL, GEORGE. "Origin of the John Brown Song." *New England Magazine*. New Series, Vol. I. December, 1889.

LEECH, REV. S. V. "The Raid of John Brown into Virginia." *The Athenæum of West Virginia University*. April 14, 1900.

LEWIS, WALTER. "Life of Capt. John Brown." *The Academy*. London. February 20, 1886.

MORSE, J. T. JR. "Review of F. B. Sanborn's Life and Letters of John Brown." *Atlantic Monthly*. February, 1886.

NORTON, C. E. "Review of Redpath's 'Public Life of Captain John Brown.'" *Atlantic Monthly*. March, 1860.

BIBLIOGRAPHICAL NOTE

PARKER, JUDGE RICHARD. "John Brown's Trial." *St. Louis Globe-Democrat.* April 8, 1888.

PHILLIPS, WILLIAM A. "Three Interviews with John Brown." *Atlantic Monthly.* December, 1879.

"Robinson's 'The Kansas Conflict.' " Reviewed in *The Nation*, June 30, 1892.

ROSENGARTEN, J. G. "John Brown's Raid."*Atlantic Monthly.* June, 1865.

SANBORN, F. B. "John Brown in Massachusetts." *Atlantic Monthly.* April, 1872.

SANBORN, F. B. "John Brown and His Friends." *Atlantic Monthly.* July, 1872.

SANBORN, F. B. "The Virginia Campaign of John Brown." *Atlantic Monthly.* December, 1875.

SANBORN, F. B. "A Concord Notebook." *The Critic.* October, 1895.

SANBORN, F. B. *New Hampshire Biography and Autobiography.* Concord, New Hampshire. July, 1905.

SANBORN, F. B. "Gerrit Smith and John Brown." *The Critic.* October, 1905.

SANBORN, F. B. "The Real John Brown." *Sunday Magazine.* July 29, 1906.

SANBORN, F. B. "The Early History of Kansas, 1854–1861." *Proceedings of Massachusetts Historical Society.* February, 1907.

"Sanborn's Life and Letters of John Brown." Reviewed in *The Nation*, October 15, 1885; in *The Dial*, October, 1885; in the (London) *Academy, February* 20, 1886; in the *Atlantic Monthly*, February, 1886.

SHACKLETON, ROBERT, JR. "What Support did John Brown Rely Upon? " *Magazine of American History.* April, 1893.

SPRING, LEVERETT W. "John Brown at Dutch Henry's Crossing." *Lippincott's.* January, 1883.

461

JOHN BROWN

SPRING, LEVERETT W. " Catching Old John Brown." *Overland Monthly*. June, 1883.

SPRING, LEVERETT W. "John Brown and the Destruction of Slavery." *Proceedings of the Massachusetts Historical Society*. March, 1900.

STEARNS, FRANK P. "John Brown and his Eastern Friends." *New England Magazine*, July, 1910.

UTTER, DAVID N. "John Brown of Ossawattomie." *North American Review*. November, 1883.

VILLARD, OSWALD GARRISON. "How Patrick Higgins Met John Brown." *Harper's Weekly*. June 26, 1909.

WASHINGTON, B. C. "The Trial of John Brown." *The Green Bag*. April, 1899.

WRIGHT, GENERAL MARCUS J. "The trial and Execution of John Brown." *Papers of the American Historical Association*. October, 1890.

WRIGHT, GENERAL MARCUS J. "The Trial of John Brown, Its Impartiality and Decorum Vindicated." *Southern Historical Society Papers*, Vol. 16.

INDEX

Index

INDEX

INDEX

INDEX

ROBERT PENN WARREN (1905–1989) was born in Guthrie, Kentucky. After graduation from Vanderbilt University and graduate study at the University of California and at Yale, he attended Oxford University as a Rhodes scholar. He taught at Louisiana State University, where he was a founder and editor of *The Southern Review*. He also taught at Southwestern College, Vanderbilt, Minnesota and Yale. *John Brown: The Making of a Martyr* was Robert Penn Warren's first work, published in 1929. *Night Rider* (1939), his first novel, was followed by *At Heaven's Gate* (1948) and *All the King's Men* (1946), which won the Pulitzer Prize. Other novels include *World Enough and Time* (1950), *Band of Angels* (1955), and *A Place to Come to* (1977). He also published a collection of short stories, *The Circus in the Attic*, and many critical studies and textbooks. A winner of numerous distinguished literary awards, he published several collections of his poetry, and was named the first Poet Laureate of the United States.

C. VANN WOODWARD, Sterling Professor Emeritus of History at Yale University, is one of the pre-eminent historians of the South. His books include *The Old World's New World* (1992), *The Future of the Past*, (1989), *Thinking Back: The Perils of Writing History* (1986), *American Counterpoint: Slavery and Racism in the North-South Dialogue* (1971), *The Burden of Southern History* (1960), *The Strange Career of Jim Crow* (1955), *Origins of the New South* (1951) and *Reunion and Reaction: The Compromise of 1877 and the End of Reconstruction* (1951). From his home in Hamden, Connecticut, he continues to write and maintains his numerous scholarly activities.